The Muslim World in
Modern South Asia

The Muslim World in Modern South Asia

POWER, AUTHORITY, KNOWLEDGE

Francis Robinson

The Muslim World in Modern South Asia: Power, Authority, Knowledge by Francis Robinson was first published by Permanent Black D-28 Oxford Apts, 11 IP Extension, Delhi 110092 INDIA, for the territory of SOUTH ASIA.

Not for sale in South Asia

Published by State University of New York Press, Albany

© 2020 Francis Robinson

All rights reserved

No part of this book may be used or reproduced in any manner whatsoever without written permission. No part of this book may be stored in a retrieval system or transmitted in any form or by any means including electronic, electrostatic, magnetic tape, mechanical, photocopying, recording, or otherwise without the prior permission in writing of the publisher.

For information, contact State University of New York Press, Albany, NY
www.sunypress.edu

Library of Congress Cataloging-in-Publication Data

Names: Robinson, Francis, author
Title: The Muslim world in modern South Asia : power, authority, knowledge / Francis Robinson, author.
Description: Albany : State University of New York Press, [2020] | Includes bibliographical references and index.
Identifiers: ISBN 9781438483016 (hardcover) | ISBN 9781438483030 (e-book) | ISBN 9781438483023 (paperback)
Further information is available at the Library of Congress.

10 9 8 7 6 5 4 3 2 1

To

the late Ram Advani

bookseller extraordinary

who made it a pleasure to work
in Lucknow over forty years

Contents

	Acknowledgments	ix
	Transliteration	xiii
	Glossary	xv
	Introduction	1
1	The Islamic World in the Age of Western Dominance	23
2	Global History from an Islamic Angle	60
3	Education in the Muslim World to the End of the Eighteenth Century	85
4	On How Since 1800 Islamic Societies Have Been Built from Below	131
5	Crisis of Authority: Crisis of Islam?	152
6	Strategies of Authority in Muslim South Asia in the Nineteenth and Twentieth Centuries	180
7	Islamic Reform and Modernities in South Asia	204
8	Iranian Influences on South Asia	233
9	South Asia and West Asia from the Delhi Sultanate to the Present: Security, Resources and Influence	257
10	The Memory of Power, Muslim 'Political Importance' and the Muslim League	280

11	The Modern State: Citizenship, Multiculturalism and Globalisation	300
12	What Ralph Russell Meant and Means to Me	320
13	Love on the Roof	329
14	Hunting the Tiger	336
15	The Garden of the Eight Paradises	339
16	Uses for Grass	346
17	The Muslim Commander Bond	354
18	Aromatherapy	358
19	Love of Mahal	361
20	Cosmopolis of a Shared Worldview	366
21	In Reverse	372
22	Women, Leadership, and Mosques: Changes in Contemporary Islamic Authority	380
	Index	385

Acknowledgments

The chapters in this book were first published in the following books, journals and magazines:

'The Islamic World in the Age of Western Dominance', Francis Robinson (ed.), *Islam in the Age of Western Dominance*, vol. 5, *New Cambridge History of Islam* (Cambridge: Cambridge University Press, 2010), pp. 1–21.

'Global History from an Islamic Angle', James Belich, John Darwin, Margaret Frenz, and Chris Wickham (eds), *The Prospect of Global History* (Oxford: Oxford University Press, 2016), pp. 127–45.

'Education in the Muslim World to the End of the Eighteenth Century', Robert Irwin (ed.), *Islamic Cultures and Societies to the End of the Eighteenth Century*, vol. 4, *New Cambridge History of Islam* (Cambridge: Cambridge University Press, 2010), pp. 497–531.

'Crisis of Authority: Crisis of Islam?', in *Journal of the Royal Asiatic Society*, 3rd series, 19, 3 (July 2009), pp. 339–54.

'Strategies of Authority in Muslim South Asia in the Nineteenth and Twentieth Centuries', *Modern Asian Studies*, 47, 1 (2013), pp. 1–21, and subsequently in Usha Sanyal, David Gilmartin, and Sandria B. Freitag (eds), *Muslim Voices: Community and the Self in South Asia* (New Delhi: Yoda Press, 2014), pp. 16–36.

'Islamic Reform and Modernities in South Asia', *Modern Asian Studies*, 42, 2/3 (2008), pp. 259–81, and subsequently in Filippo and Caroline Osella (eds), *Islamic Reform in South Asia* (Delhi: Cambridge University Press, 2013), pp. 26–50.

'Iranian Influences on South Asia', *Journal of the Iran Society*, vol. 2, no. 12 (September 2013), pp. 7–27.

'South Asia and West Asia from the Delhi Sultanate to the Present: Security, Resources and Influence', in Working Papers: Symposium on the Academic Chairs of His Majesty Sultan Qaboos bin Said and Their Contribution to the Development of Human Knowledge, 1–3 November 2010, Sultan Qaboos University (Muscat: Ministry of Higher Education, n.d.), pp. 74–86.

'Memory of Power, Muslim "Political Importance" and the Muslim League', R. Ahmad (ed.), Papers Presented at the Three-Day International Conference on the All-India Muslim League (1906–1947), 18–20 December 2006, Islamabad (Islamabad: National Centre for Historical Research), vol. 2, pp. 157–75.

'The Modern State: Citizenship, Multiculturalism and Globalization', Hassan Bashir and Phillip W. Gray (eds), *Deconstructing Global Citizenship: Political, Cultural, and Ethnic Perspectives* (Lanham: Lexington Books, 2015), pp. 1–16.

'What Ralph Russell Meant and Means to Me', *Annual of Urdu Studies*, 24 (2009), pp. 242–48.

'Love on the Roof', *Times Literary Supplement*, 29 August 2008, p. 10.

'Hunting the Tiger', *Times Literary Supplement*, 18 January 2013, p. 11.

'Uses for Grass', *Times Literary Supplement*, 2 November 2007, pp. 7–8.

'The Muslim Commander Bond', *Times Literary Supplement*, 1 January 2010, pp. 24–5.

'Aromatherapy', *Times Literary Supplement*, 5 April 2013, p. 13.

'Love of Mahal', *Times Literary Supplement*, 14 May 2010, p. 9.

'In Reverse', *Times Literary Supplement*, 22 January 2010, pp. 7–8.

'The Garden of the Eight Paradises', *Journal of the Royal Asiatic Society*, 3rd series, vol. 18, part I, January 2008, pp. 89–92.

'Women, Leadership, and Mosques', *Journal of the Royal Asiatic Society*, 3rd series, vol. 23, part I, January 2013, pp. 142–4.

'Cosmopolis of a Shared World View', *The Book Review*, vol. XXXIX, no. 10 (October 2015), pp. 19–20.

Transliteration

For consistency the conventions of *Encyclopaedia of Islam*, 3rd edition, have been imposed on all texts, outside quotation marks. No macrons or underdots are inserted although the ain and hamza have been. Italics have been used only when strictly necessary.

Glossary

adab	the rules of conduct, the Muslim idea of a harmonious life.
Akhbārīs	the school of Shi'a jurisprudence which rejects the methods of the Usulis and demands close adherence to the meaning of the akhbar, the hadith.
'ālim	learned man; singular of 'ulama'.
Dār al-iftā	an office for delivering fatwas.
Dār al-'ulūm	a place of advanced religious learning, superior to a madrasa.
dawla	earthly prosperity.
dīn	religion in its broadest sense.
'Eīd un-Nabī	the Prophet's festival, his birthday.
firmān	an edict delivered by the Mughals or the Ottomans.
ḥadīth	tradition, the sayings and doings of the Prophet based on the authority of a chain of transmitters.
ḥajj	the pilgrimage to Mecca.
ḥājjī	one who has made the pilgrimage to Mecca.
ḥakīm	a practitioner of Greco-Islamic medicine; *see* Unani.

ḥawza	a circle of Islamic scholars, or place of Islamic studies, especially amongst the Shi'a.
ijāza	permission to transmit knowledge, e.g. hadith.
'ilm	knowledge, plural 'ulum, of the texts in the madrasa curriculum.
inshā	draughtsmanship, as practised by a bureaucrat.
iṣlāḥ	reform.
jāhilīyya	ignorance of the message of God, a charge often made against secular governments in the modern world.
jihād	legitimate war waged against non-Muslims by a mujahid, pl. mujahidin; personal struggle against one's baser instincts.
Kayasth	Hindu caste found in the north of South Asia.
kufr	unbelief, the practices of a non-Muslim.
Khalīfa	one who has received Khilafat from a Sufi pir.
Khatri	a predominantly Hindu caste found in the north of South Asia.
Khilāfat	the successorship to the Prophet Muhammad as the leader of the Muslim community; also the successorship to a Sufi pir giving permission to make disciples.
khums	the tax of one-fifth of moveable property paid by Shi'as to the public treasury each year.
madrasa	a school for 'ulama'.

maktūbat	the collected letters of Sufi shaykhs or scholars.
malfūzat	the recorded sayings and doings of a Sufi saint, usually by his disciples.
ma'qūlāt	the rational sciences in the madrasa curriculum.
marsiyā	a largely Shi'a genre of poetry in which the glories and sufferings of Husayn and the other Imams are evoked.
maslak	a system of religious belief and worship.
mathnawī	a poem in rhyming couplets, the classic example being the mathnawi of Jalal al-Din Rumi.
mawlānā	'Our Lord', a title given to a person respected for religious learning.
mawlawī	title given to a learned man.
mawlid	the anniversary of the Prophet's birth, 12 Rabi al-Awwal.
Mohurram	the first month of the Islamic year, in which the martyrdom of Imam Husayn is remembered.
muḥalla	neighbourhood within a city.
mujaddid	renewer, title given to a major religious reformer.
mujāhidīn	those waging jihad, a legitimate war against non-Muslims.
mullā	Muslim functionary, member of the 'ulama', title of respect for a Muslim scholar.
mujtahid	an 'alim recognised as competent to give independent opinions on the shari'a.

mushāʿira	a poetic symposium.
naʿt	verse in praise of the Prophet Muhammad.
Niẓām-i Muṣṭāfā	the Prophet's system.
pesantren	the private Islamic boarding schools of Java.
pīr	a Sufi master able to lead his disciples on the mystical path.
qāḍī	a judge who administers the shariʿa.
Qurʾān	*lit.* recitation; the Word of God transmitted to Muhammad by the angel Gabriel.
sabhā	an association or organisation.
shahr-i āshob	poetry of the ruined city; poetry remembering past greatness.
sharīʿa	Islamic law.
shijra	a form of genealogical tree which might be given by a Sufi pir as he made a person a disciple. This would show how spiritual knowledge had passed down from Muhammad and ʿAli through the founder of his order and down to his pir.
shirk	idolatry; paganism.
silsila	*lit.* 'chain', referring to Sufis linked by common spiritual descent from a founder.
sīra	the biography of the Prophet Muhammad.
Ṣūfī	an exponent of tasawwuf, Islamic mysticism.
Sunna	the example of the Prophet Muhammad, one of the sources of the faith, together with the Qurʾan and hadith.
sūra	a chapter of the Qurʾan.
tadhkirah	a collective biography.

tajdid	the work of religious renewal which might be undertaken by a mujaddid.
Tanzimat	'Reorganisation'. The term used to describe the period 1839–76 in Ottoman history and its reforms which culminated in the first Ottoman constitution in 1876.
taqlīd	imitation, unquestioning acceptance of the achievement of Islamic scholarship as it has been handed down, the opposite of ijtihad.
taṣawwuf	Islamic mysticism.
tawḥīd	the unity of God.
taʿzia khāna	the place in a home or an imambara where the effigy of the tomb of Imam Husayn is kept.
Tibb	the system of Greco-Islamic medicine practised by a hakim.
ʿulamāʾ	religious scholars.
ʿulūm-i ʿaqlīyya	the rational sciences; *see* maʿqulat.
ʿulūm-i naqlīyya	the transmitted sciences; *see* manqulat.
Ūnānī	Greek, hence Unani Tibb, Greco-Islamic medicine.
Uṣūlīs	The school of Shiʿa law which accepts forms of intellectual and analogical reasoning as legitimate methods of jurisprudence.
waḥdat al-shuhūd	the 'unity of appearance'; phenomenological monism contrasted with *waḥdat al-wujūd*, the 'unity of being', ontological monism. The former emphasises the transcendence of God and the latter the immanence of God.
waḥdat al-wujūd	see *waḥdat al-shuhūd*.

Introduction

THE ESSAYS IN THIS volume were written over the past ten years. Nine started out as public lectures and one as a funeral oration. Two were contributions to the *New Cambridge History of Islam* while the remainder were reviews for the *Times Literary Supplement* and academic journals. Naturally, they bear the stamp of Western concerns over this period. There has been the awareness amongst scholars, but not nearly enough in Western government or the general public, that the past two centuries have been a period of Western dominance in the Muslim world. Moreover, this dominance has clashed for much of the period with manifestations of the Islamic revival, a process of renewal and reform which has been, and still is, productive of new ideas and new organisations. Amongst the more striking examples of the latter have been the tens of thousands of madrasas which have sprung up throughout the Muslim world – supported for the most part by the donations of the faithful – steadily fashioning the infrastructure of an Islamic society from below. This has been an extraordinary manifestation of the desire in Muslim societies at large that both the materials of revelation and the skills to make them socially useful should continue to inform their world. Sufi orders, too, have continued to shape the hearts of men and women so that they serve God's purposes in the modern world. Alongside these institutions, long engaged in the transmission of knowledge, there have also flourished a host of modern Muslim organisations, increasingly embracing women as well as men.

It was out of these modern organisations, for the most part, that movements of resistance to the West emerged, notable amongst them al-Qaʻida and the Islamic State in Syria (ISIS or Daesh). Great cities of the world – Madrid, Paris, New York, London, Brussels, Birmingham – have all been attacked by Muslim terrorists. Fears have grown in many countries about the radicalisation of young Muslims. Some, indeed, did travel to Afghanistan/Pakistan and to Syria in order to participate in jihad. Whereas research in Islamic matters in the twentieth century appeared to have little political salience, apart from a flurry of interest around the Iranian revolution, research in the twenty-first century has taken place in the context of strong government and societal concern for explanations of why some Muslims seemed to hate the West.

The essays in this book have not been written with the direct aim of answering this question. But several do respond to this question in general terms by reminding us of the dominance of the West in the Muslim world over the past two centuries, by showing how this has created the opportunity for the key structures of an Islamic society to be rebuilt from below, and by explaining the nature of the shock delivered to the authority of Muslim civilisation by Western power.

There was a further aspect of context to the writing of these essays; it was the concerns of Western scholarship. One which has been prominent is the issue of 'modernity'. We no longer, thank heaven, following Weber, Talcott Parsons and the theorists of mid-twentieth-century USA, see all societies modernising along the same Western pattern. Modernity takes shape in different ways in different societies and so some have come to talk of 'modernities'. This said, there is an enduring concern about the relationship between Islamic reform and modernities. I think of Islamic reform's assault on the authority of the past, its assault on forms of magic (although not all manifestations of reform disapprove of all forms of magic), its emphasis on personal responsibility in faith, and its emphasis that belief should be revealed in social action. These ideas are to be found at work in Islamist movements such as the Muslim Brotherhood and the Jamaʻati-Islam through to reformed 'ulama' groups such as the Deobandis, and various women's movements that carry forward the reforming process. A second academic concern has been that of authority. European dominance threatened every aspect of Muslim civilisation. In recent decades scholars have become increasingly aware of the depth of the challenge the West presented and the creativity demonstrated by Muslims, whether theologians, men of letters, Unani hakims or musicians, in striving to sustain the authority of their practices in the context not just of the European presence but of the increasing competition with each other stimulated by that presence. A third academic concern has been assessing the significance of the rise of the modern state, processes of globalisation and their impact on traditions of cosmopolitanism and multiculturalism. One of the features of the twentieth century is the way in which the emergence of the modern nation-state from former empires, especially after World Wars I and II, led to the destruction of cosmopolitan spaces and traditions as well as massive movements of refugees. Subsequently, processes of globalisation have resulted in major migrations of people from the developing to the developed world in search of better standards of life. Incorporating these people, many of them Muslims, into their largely Christian societies, has become a matter of urgent concern. Should local values dominate, or should concessions be made to multiculturalism? The noise of the discourse is constantly to be heard. For some Western societies it is the most important issue of the day.

 A further aspect of my context is the group of postgraduate research students who have been working with me over the period. In the British system this can be quite an intense relationship as the student is not normally advised by a committee, as in the USA, but by a single supervisor, who may or may not be assisted by an adviser. I generally learn much from my postgraduate research students; indeed, in the years 1997 to 2004 when I was a full-time administrator, they kept me alive academically. The mark of my association with at least some of these students can be seen in some of the essays in this book; I just hope that they in their turn benefited from me.

During the period 2008 to 2012 my Royal Holloway post was divided 50:50 with the University of Oxford, courtesy of the Oxford Centre for Islamic Studies, where I was the Sultan of Oman Fellow. The meant, among other things, that I taught a course for the excellent M.Phil. in South Asian Studies and supervised Oxford postgraduate research students. Five completed their D.Phil.s with me, and one of them was Yaqoob Bangash whom I inherited from the Beit Professor, Judith Brown. He worked on the integration of the princely states in Pakistan, a subject which had suffered from sixty years of neglect.[1] Uther Charlton-Stevens was a second scholar whom I inherited from Judith Brown. His thesis has brought about a substantial advance in our understandings of Anglo-Indians and their politics in the triumphant phase of Indian nationalism.[2] Nikhil Puri, who was more social scientist than historian, produced a remarkable analysis of the different types of madrasa in Bangladesh and West Bengal and their struggles with each other and the state for social control.[3] Tahrat Shahid, who was also more of a social scientist than a historian and came from a World Bank background, explored the problems of reforming family laws in favour of women in Bangladesh.[4] My final D.Phil. student was Megan Robb, who worked on the *Madinah* newspaper of Bijnor in British India's United Provinces. Both the newspaper and the place had fascinated me for a long time; the *Madinah* was one of the most widely respected Muslim papers in the first half of the twentieth century, and Bijnor was a qasbah in which Hindus dominated the municipal board in the early twentieth century and Muslim separatist ideas flourished.[5]

Two Oxford students whose Master's theses I supervised came to do their Ph.D. theses with me at Royal Holloway. The first was Layli Uddin, who turned her M.Phil. thesis on Mawlana Bhashani into a major study of the political mobilisation of peasants and lower-class urban workers in East Pakistan in the years from the

1930s to the 1970s.⁶ The second was Eve Tignol who explored in depth a theme which has long fascinated me. I have tackled it briefly in the essay 'Memory of Power, Muslim "Political Importance" and the Muslim League' in this volume. Eve's exploration covered poetry, particularly in the *shahr-e ashob* style, reaching back to the eighteenth century but also moving forward into the 1930s, and taking in cities as sites of memory along the way.⁷

Other postgraduate research students who worked with me at Royal Holloway were: Sumaira Noreen, who studied the development of the secondary education system with reference to Pakistan before and after independence;⁸ Tommaso Bobbio, who through studying the impact of urban planning in the city of Ahmedabad, brought a new dimension to our understanding of the causes of communal rioting;⁹ and Shuja Mahesar, who studied the impact of the green revolution in the Khairpur region of the Lower Indus valley and brought home to me the dramatic changes which flowed from this event.¹⁰ Six other postgraduate research students are currently working with me: Neha Vermani on Mughal food practices; Fakhar Bilal on how Deobandi madrasas came to be established in Pakistan; Ismail Mathari Porkundil on the problems of innovation in Indian madrasas in the twentieth century; Amna Khan on the seventeenth-century saint Sultan Bahu of Jhang, and the reception of his teachings down to the present; Kirsten Seymour on Sufi resistance to the tide of Islamic reform in the North West Frontier region of Pakistan; and Sudipto Mitra on the role of middlemen in the recruitment of indentured labour in the nineteenth century.

Two further scholars deserve mention as part of the context within which I have worked. First, Daniel Morgan, whose Oxford M.Phil. thesis on Shah Wali Allah I supervised. He then went on to the University of Chicago to continue his work on Wali Allah with Muzaffar Alam. This meant that when I went as a visiting professor to Chicago in 2016 he was able to support me as a research assistant and as a friend. The second is Ali Usman Qasmi, who came to Royal Holloway as a Newton International Postgraduate

Fellow. He used his Newton award to excellent effect, funding two conferences, one with Justin Jones of Oxford on the Shi'a in South Asia; and the second with Megan Robb on Indian Muslims who had opposed the Muslim League. Substantial publications were the outcome of both these events.[11] At the same time 'Ali Usman completed two important monographs, one on the Ahl al-Qur'an and a second on the Ahmadiyya in Pakistan.[12]

One's research students provide an important context but so too do one's major projects of the moment. For half of the period covered by these essays I was doing the research for and writing my biography of Mawlana Jamal Miyan of Farangi Mahall.[13] It meant that I was much engaged with the educational and devotional world of Farangi Mahall, with the campaign for Pakistan, with the sharif class of the UP who drove that campaign and subsequently came to play a major role in running the new state. These were men whose ancestors had come from outside India to rule it. They often held high-ranking positions under the British and, after Independence, held similar positions either in Pakistan or international organisations. As I worked on Jamal Miyan's papers in Karachi, I would often meet their descendants in the Sind Club.

So much for aspect of general context. Let me now turn to the specific contexts of each essay. The first four essays all, one way or another, look at the Islamic world as a whole. Two were among those I contributed to the *New Cambridge History of Islam*, a project led with much wisdom by Michael Cook and with notable drive by the distinguished Cambridge University Press editor, Marigold Acland. Chapter 1 here is my introduction to the volume which I edited, *The Islamic World in the Age of Western Dominance*. It sets out the two great processes which have shaped the Muslim world over the past two hundred years. The first was the onset of Western power from around 1800, involving processes of brutal invasion right up to the twenty-first century, structural changes brought about by integration into the capitalist system, the emergence of the modern nation-state and equally the emergence of new elites educated in Western rather than Islamic knowledge.

The second great process was the Islamic revival, which began as a process of renewal in Islam before the West arrived and then came to interact vigorously with it. At the heart of the revival was a shift in piety from an other-worldly Islam of contemplation to a this-worldly Islam of action on earth to achieve salvation. Arguably it was the greatest change to take place in Islamic piety for one thousand years. The essay traces the movement's connectedness and its spread throughout the Islamic world. It notes its two great products: Islamic modernism which has tried to build bridges between Islamic understandings and Western knowledge, and Islamism which has tried to capture the modern state for the purposes of particular Islamic understandings. Several themes are noted along the way: the relative decline of 'ulama' and Sufis as transmitters of Islamic knowledge and the rise of laymen and women; the growing prominence of women as transmitters and interpreters of Islam; the increasing shift in the leadership of the Muslim world to the East of the Hindu Kush; and the growth of a significant Muslim presence in the West. Just as this essay was deemed an appropriate introduction to the Cambridge volume on the Muslim world since 1800, so it is also appropriate to this collection of essays.

Chapter 2, 'Global History from an Islamic Angle', was written for a conference in September 2012 titled 'New Directions in Global History', which I believe was to mark the foundation of the Oxford Centre for Global History. The aim of the piece, as the title suggests, was to demonstrate that global history did not necessarily need to be seen from a Western angle. Indeed, from the eighth century CE the Islamic world developed a 'world system' which preceded Immanuel Wallerstein's Western world system. This was the main driving force of human affairs. Moreover, although it came to be overrun by Western power, that Islamic world system continued to expand within its frame. The chapter goes on to consider particular phenomena of global reach and significance which flow from research on Muslim societies: the tales of storytellers which cross vast regions of the world; understandings of astrology and astronomy which have been widely shared; and particular commodities the impact of whose production and consumption has been of global significance. The chapter concludes by addressing the 'Protestant Turn' in religious piety, experienced throughout Muslim societies in the nineteenth and twentieth centuries, but also experienced in other leading world faiths. It raises the issue of the relationship of such religious change to 'modernities'.

Chapter 3, 'Education in the Muslim World to the End of the Eighteenth Century', was written for *Islamic Cultures and Societies to the End of the Eighteenth Century,* the volume of the *New Cambridge History of Islam* edited by Robert Irwin. It was a wonderful opportunity to build on my research on the 'ulama' of Farangi Mahall[14] and consider education from the classical era to *c.* 1800, taking in spiritual education, children's education, slave education, popular education and women's education along the way. The essay was to explain how, on its own terms, the Islamic system of education was remarkably successful both in reproducing itself and in developing creative responses to the challenges of Europe. But ultimately, because at its heart its purpose was conservationist, it failed to master the challenge of Europe.

Chapter 4, 'On How Since 1800 Islamic Societies Have Been Built from Below', flows logically from Chapter 3 in that it explains the way in which the transmitters of Islam, in particular 'ulama' and their madrasas, have played the central role in sustaining the Islamic dimension of Muslim societies over the past two hundred years. It shows how from the nineteenth century the spread of Western power and ideas led to the ending of state-supported Islamic education both in societies ruled by Muslims as well as in those ruled by the West. It then demonstrates how Muslim societies themselves replaced one hundred-fold what the state no longer provided, paying for the institutions themselves. In most societies sustaining the Islamic dimension was the work of the 'ulama' but in some, for instance Turkey, it was the work of the Sufi orders. The content of this chapter was delivered as a public lecture in the Divinity School in Chicago in March 2016 as one of the requirements of my post as visiting professor. Some of those present were unhappy with my emphasis on the role of faith in rebuilding Islamic societies from below. For them the financing of nearly a hundred thousand madrasas in South Asia was largely a function of Saudi and Gulf money. While I am willing to acknowledge that foreign money had a role to play in places, it would be a mistake, as Arshad Alam has shown, not to acknowledge the role of people's faith.[15]

Chapter 5, 'Crisis of Authority: Crisis of Islam?', and Chapter 6, 'Strategies of Authority in Muslim South Asia', address the issue of authority in Islamic civilisation which had been so grievously challenged by the dominance of the West. Chapter 5 was a lecture which I was asked to give at Royal Holloway (it took place in March 2008) as part of a celebration of the CBE to which I was appointed in 2006 for 'contributions to Higher Education and the History of Islam'. Part of me thought that it was a bit rough that I should have to do more work to celebrate my achievement, but the realist reminded me that I was fortunate that there were people interested in what I had to say. The lecture argued that Western dominance had led to a loss of authority in Muslim civilisation in general and in the religious sphere in particular. It showed how the old systems of establishing authoritative religious knowledge had begun to weaken, how religious authority had started to fragment as new interpreters emerged, as lay interpreters came forward to challenge the 'ulama', and as the individual human conscience came to be given an increasingly important role in establishing correct action.

Chapter 6, 'Strategies of Authority in Muslim South Asia', explores the issue of authority amongst South Asian Muslims from the nineteenth century and widens the field to consider Unani medicine and literature as well as religion. It was given a few months later in September 2009 as a keynote address at 'Muslim Voices: Traditions and Contexts', a conference in honour of my much-valued colleague, Barbara Metcalf, at Ann Arbor, University of Michigan. Starting from the position that authority is always a work in progress, the lecture examined the strategies of the 'ulama', writers and Unani hakims in sustaining their authority and noted that all rejected the Persianate Mughal past and embraced instead Arab models, the Prophetic model, and in various ways British models and British authority. The lecture also noted the irony that just at the time Muslims were letting go of Mughal models of authority the British were coming to adopt them. The lecture also contained a running discussion of the revolutionary shift towards rooting authority in society at large and the techniques to do so.

Chapter 7, 'Islamic Reform and Modernities in South Asia', had its initial form as a paper written for a conference held by Filippo and Caroline Osella on Islamic Reform in South Asia in the summer of 2006. It gave me an opportunity to round off, at least for the moment, my thinking on the subject which had been developing over the previous twenty years – for the stages in the process see the first endnote to the paper. Around this time, I also made the acquaintance again of S.N. Eisenstadt, whom I had got to know at the University of Washington, Seattle, in 1986. Eisenstadt was very supportive of the direction of my thinking, which was hardly surprising given his *The Protestant Ethic and Modernization* (New York, 1974). My argument was, as Eisenstadt had argued in the case of Protestantism, that key aspects of Islamic reform – its strong combination of 'this worldliness and transcendentalism', its strong emphasis on 'individual activism and responsibility' and 'the direct relationship of the individual to the sacred and the sacred tradition' – gave it transformative potential. Of course, Islamic reform was operating in many different contexts and, in these contexts, it was an important, and on occasion the most important, element in fashioning forms of Muslim modernity.

Two further essays consider the long-term relationship between West Asia and South Asia. Chapter 8, 'Iranian Influences on

South Asia', is on the rise and decline of Iranian influences in South Asia. It was first delivered as a lecture to the Iran Society in London in 2012, but there was a pleasing cyclical completion in doing so as the lecture drew on a lecture on a similar theme which I had given in September 1977 at the British Institute of Persian Studies in Tehran. The lecture shows how with the establishment of Mughal rule in South Asia from the sixteenth century Persian influences became consolidated: South Asian courts became an Eldorado for ambitious Iranians; the Emperor Akbar made Persian the language of government of his empire; and in religious matters, the rational subjects which had been brought to a peak in Iran came to rival the revealed subjects in the madrasa curriculum. Iranian poetry became a dominant presence in Sufi practice. Arguably Persian influences reached their peak in the eighteenth century after the decline of Mughal power. Almost all the successor states retained Persian as the language of government, including the East India Company; South Asia remained a destination for ambitious Iranians, and several Shi'a dynasties were established, becoming potent patrons of things Iranian. All this was brought to an end in the nineteenth century when the British became the hegemonic power and changed the language of government to English at the higher level and the vernacular at the local level. The second challenge to Iranian influences was the rise of Islamic reform with its aims to replace Persianate elements in ritual and learning with Arab elements. The latter half of the twentieth century saw Iranian influences increasingly confined to the Shi'as (no small community, numbering about 60 million in 2000) and the achievements of the region's industrial magnates of Iranian descent – the Tatas, Wadias, Godrejs and Ispahanis.

Chapter 9, 'South Asia and West Asia from the Delhi Sultanate to the Present', offers an overview of the changing relationship between South Asia and West Asia from the twelfth century to the present. It demonstrates how down to 1800, South Asia was invaded by the powerful armies of West and Central Asia and the many influences they brought with them. From 1800 all changed. South Asia increasingly became a transmitter of ideas and of power to the West Asian region. Particularly dramatic was the role of South Asia as a base from which the British projected power into West Asia in World Wars I and II. Important too in the second half of the century was the role of the Gulf region, broadly construed, to the South Asian economy. Of course, South Asian cultural influences from the poet Iqbal to the Islamic thinker Mawdudi through to Bollywood have been notably strong in recent decades. West Asia has been emerging as India's extended neighbourhood, an important part of her great power status and the place in which, China permitting, it will be most fully expressed.

This essay began as a lecture which was to inaugurate the Indian Foreign-Ministry-funded Centre for West Asian Studies at the University of Calcutta. The lecture hall was full. But I was very surprised when I had finished speaking to be met with almost total silence. Someone behind me leaned over and said, 'You mustn't mind. They won't have understood a word you have said.' He meant the students who made up the audience. There is nothing like the workings of language policy in higher education to put a visiting speaker in his place! Eventually, there were some questions from retired Indian Foreign Service people in the audience. The lecture itself had a second outing as a contribution to a conference celebrating the fortieth anniversary of the accession of Sultan Qaboos of Oman in 2010.

Chapter 10, 'The Memory of Power, Muslim "Political Importance" and the Muslim League', was given as a lecture at a fascinating occasion of which I was very pleased to be part. It was the celebration by the government of Pervez Musharraf of the December 1906 founding of the All-India Muslim League in Dacca. So, academics came together with some notably sharp-shouldered politicians to celebrate the League's centenary in December 2006 in Islamabad. I was pleased to see that the authorities had invited former members of the Muslim League from Bangladesh, and gave them great courtesy. President Musharraf's speech was delivered in a Durbar Hall that reminded me of the Chihil Sutun in Isfahan. The speech was memorable for its Churchillian style – I wondered if Musharraf practised by listening to tapes of Churchill's speeches – and the occasion was striking for the fact that only one of the many women in the audience wore any form of head covering.

During the conference and surrounding events one man caught my eye for his style and courtesy and the way in which others acknowledged him. This was Gohar Ayub, the son of former President Ayub Khan, a man who had been at the centre of affairs for forty years. As it happened, he chaired the session in which I gave my paper. I noted his concentration as I spoke and was delighted the following day to receive from him a small gift and letter of appreciation. He clearly warmed to a talk which emphasised the memory of power and Muslim 'political importance' as a motivating force behind the elites who led the Muslim League. The chapter demonstrates that these ideas were instinct in the Aligarh movement. They were set out most explicitly in the memorial to the Muslim deputation to the Viceroy in 1906 and were frequently repeated in addresses to All-India Muslim League sessions down to 1947. This idea, moreover, was accepted by many British who regarded Muslims, whom wrongly they imagined to be a unified community, as an important group that they needed to keep on their side. As I noted above, my former research student, Eve Tignol, has greatly expanded our understanding of the memory of power and its significance for South Asian Muslims in the last century of British rule.

Chapter 11, 'The Modern State: Citizenship, Multiculturalism and Globalisation', was delivered as a plenary address to a conference on 'Deconstructing Global Citizenship' staged by the branch of Texas A&M University in Qatar. I addressed the themes of the modern state, citizenship, multiculturalism and globalisation from a historical perspective. Focusing in particular on the Muslim world, the chapter is about the cosmopolitan worlds that existed before the rise of the nation-state and shows how these were destroyed by the rise of the modern nation-state after World War I. It then explores how processes of globalisation in the last third of the twentieth century increasingly undermined the nation-state. At the same time, the increased movement of peoples across the world was forcing nation-states to consider how they might embrace diversity. Multiculturalism became the watchword of the moment, raising the issue of whether or not particular cultural practices should be permitted to trump human rights. Indeed, more generally since the Nuremberg trials of 1945–46 the idea has emerged that individuals have a duty to humanity that is greater than their obligations to their colleagues and the commands of their nation-states. This consideration has come increasingly to lie behind ideas of humanitarian intervention in nation-states.

****

I now turn to the short essay and reviews. Of the latter, chapters 13, 14, 16, 17, 18, 19 and 21 were all written for the *Times Literary Supplement*. I have retained the titles given them by the *Supplement*. Chapter 20 was written for the Indian journal *The Book Review*; I have retained their title. Chapters 15 and 21 were written for the *Journal of the Royal Asiatic Society*; their titles I have supplied.

Chapter 12, the short essay, was the oration I gave at the funeral of Ralph Russell in the autumn of 2008. For nearly fifty years Russell had been the leading scholar of Urdu in the UK. He had created a much-loved Urdu course and also retired early from the School of Oriental and African Studies to devote his energies to teaching Urdu to the community at large, and in particular to train those who might themselves become teachers of the language. At the same time, he produced a series of major works on Urdu poets and poetry. These had a great impact on me, enabling me to make contact with north Indian Muslim sensibilities more effectively than my limited language skills permitted me to do. It was wholly characteristic of this generous and humane man that after my review of his *Ghalib: Life and Letters* appeared in *Modern Asian Studies*, he phoned me to thank me. No one else has done that. Again, he thanked me with a handwritten note for my contribution to his festschrift. No one else has done that.

Chapters 13 and 14 are both reviews of wonderful translations. The first is Dick Davis' translation of Fakhr al-Din Gorgani's *Vis and Ramin* composed for the Seljuk governor of Isfahan, *c.* 1050. Davis quite rightly describes it as 'one of the most extraordinary and fascinating love narratives produced anywhere in the medieval world, Islamic or Christian'. It is sensual, erotic and dramatic with great set pieces, placed at intervals in the poem, like arias in an opera, which expose the inner lives of the characters and stretch emotions to the limit. Davis has done a great service in resurrecting this too-little-known work. Chapter 14 reviews another work rescued from obscurity. It is the late Aditya Behl's translation of the Sufi master, Shaykh Qutban Suhrawardi's *The Magic Doe*, composed in 1503 as an introduction to mystic practice for disciples at the Sharqi court of Jawnpur in what is now Uttar Pradesh. Like Gurgani's *Vis and Ramin* it was designed for oral performance in groups. It could be read as a straightforward love story in which a prince falls in love with Mirigawati, a doe-woman, but must pass through a series of ordeals before he can consummate his love. Or alternatively it could be read as a Sufi text, a journey in search of love in which the seeker goes through stages, experiences the tension between earthly and heavenly love, and does not achieve his objective until he has succeeded in annihilating his self. Behl's teacher, Wendy Doniger of the University of Chicago, made sure that his translation of this Sufi romance from Hindawi, or old Hindi, was published. In both cases Dick Davis and Davis/Behl reminded me of what wonderful literature there is to be discovered in Asian languages.

One of the greatest works of Asian literature is, of course, the *Baburnama*, the memoirs of Zahir al-Din Muhammad Babur, who founded the Mughal Empire. Chapters 15 and 16 both address this great work in one way or another. In Chapter 15, 'Garden of Eight Paradises', I review Stephen Dale's *The Garden of the Eight Paradises: Babur and the Culture of Empire in Central Asia, Afghanistan and India (1483–1530)* which is arguably the greatest work of Timurid history written over the past fifty years. Of course, the *Baburnama* has an important part to play and Dale places it most skilfully in its Timurid context. The great achievement, however, is Dale's use of Babur's poetry in Chughtay Turki and Persian to get access to the individual and his emotional states. Dale learned Chughtay Turki especially to be able to do this. Dale quite rightly presses on us E.M. Forster's suggestion that late-Timurid Samarqand should be compared with Renaissance Florence, and Babur with Lorenzo de Medici. 'Uses for Grass', Chapter 16, reviews Dilip Hiro's abridgement of the *Baburnama* for Penguin Classics, which reduces it from 300,000 words to 100,000. Unfortunately, he chose Beveridge's early twentieth-century translation as his base rather than Wheeler Thackston's excellent recent one. His introduction makes no mention of Dale's great biography and there is no bibliography. This really was an opportunity missed.

The storyteller has been, until recently, a major feature of the Muslim world. One of the major stories told from West Asia through to Southeast Asia was that of Amir Hamza, the Prophet Muhammad's uncle. The Mughal emperor, Akbar, liked it so much that he would himself recite it in the harem, and would also have it told in camp for which purposes he commissioned 1,400 paintings on cotton backed with paper which were to be shown as the story was related. Chapter 17, 'The Muslim Commander Bond', is a review of Musharraf Farooqi's translation into English of Abdullah Bilgrami's abridgement of Ghalib Lakhnawi's original text. It needed abridging; the classic edition is of 46 volumes each of 1000 pages. The text of the abridged version is itself 948 pages. But the length should not deter the reader. The stories rattle along as Hamza defeats many enemies, converts many to Islam, loves many women (while continuing to honour his first love Mehr-Nigar), enjoys much ribaldry and gets the better of the demons and fairies of the enchanted world. It is not difficult to imagine how these tales, united to the skills of the storyteller, would have held their listeners spellbound as they became caught up in a world of magical realism. The *TLS* editor used my description of Hamza as 'Muslim Commander Bond' as the title for the review and indeed he was. But I would have been just as happy if he had used Farooqi's reference to the storytellers as 'sweet-lipped historians' or 'nimble scribes of fancy' as a title.

Chapters 18 and 19 take us to the courts of early-modern India. 'Aromatherapy' focuses on the use of scent in the culture of the great cities of the early-modern Deccan – Bijapur, Golconda and Hyderabad. One prime area was the garden, which was a place of pleasure where poetry and picnics might be consumed and men and women enjoy each other's company. Gardens were made to delight the senses: trees were planted to create vistas, flowers placed to delight the eye, water was managed to please both eye and ear, and scented plants were positioned to perfume the air both by day and by night. 'Scent is the food of the soul', declared a tradition of the Prophet, 'and the soul is the vehicle of the faculties of man.' But the role of scent was not restricted to gardens; it was also used to furnish a space, to establish a mood. We learn that there were nine ways of perfuming a bedroom with individual bouquets and the author draws on Persian and Urdu poetry written in Bijapur and Golconda to illustrate that scented gardens in these early-modern Muslim worlds acted both as context and metaphor.

Chapter 19, 'Love of Mahal', takes us to the court of the Mughal Emperor, Shah Jahan, in the first half of the seventeenth century. We are introduced to the bloody succession struggles which both preceded his reign and ended it. His great love of women is not ignored, in particular that for his second wife, Mumtaz Mahal, who was to bear him fifteen children in eighteen years. Nor is his passion for architecture, in which he introduced the high Mughal style with its plentiful use of white marble, ignored. Indeed, he brought this passion to its peak in his construction of the Taj Mahal, which celebrated his other great passion, Mumtaz Mahal. Rightly, the book I review here gives particular emphasis to the role of women and to the extent of the correspondence between the Mughals and the Safawids in neighbouring Iran. This is the first biography of Shah Jahan since Saksena's work of 1932. It is most certainly handsomely produced but does not say much that is new. For this we need to go to: Munis Faruqi's *The Princes of the Mughal Empire, 1504–1719* (Cambridge: Cambridge University Press, 2012) who throws new light on the functions of the succession struggles; Rajeev Kinra's *Writing Self, Writing Empire: Chandar Bhan Brahman and the Cultural World of the Indo-Persian State Secretary* (Berkeley: University of California Press, 2015) who takes us into the world of Shah Jahan's chief minister; and Ruby Lal's *Empress: The Astonishing Reign of Nur Jahan* (New York: W.W. Norton and Co., 2018) who takes Mughal biography to a new level as she examines the life of the woman who competed with Shah Jahan to control the succession to Jahangir.

Recently scholars have begun to take much more seriously the connections of South Asian Muslims in the world outside the subcontinent. Chapter 20, 'Cosmopolis of a Shared Worldview', reviews a book which is very much part of this tendency. Its author is concerned to show how networks of primarily Indian Muslims grew in the nineteenth century in the spaces which lay between the British and Ottoman empires, and also to a lesser extent the Russian empire. Important underpinnings of these networks were shared positions on Islamic reform, improvements in communications brought about by the British, and print. These helped to fashion a shared world of ideas and feelings which linked India to Mecca, Cairo, Istanbul, and further afield. Seema Alavi's *Muslim Cosmopolitanism in an Age of Empire* supports her case by introducing us to five men who illustrate the working of her Muslim cosmopolis. We meet: Sayyid Fadl who, after leading anti-British activity in Malabar, came with Ottoman support to have a network of connections which stretched from Acheh in Sumatra through Arabia to North Africa; Mawlana Rahmat Allah Kayranawi, who fled India after the Mutiny uprising and established the Madrasa Sawlatiyya in Mecca, which became a centre both for reform and for Indian Muslims; Hajji Imdad Allah, who also fled to Mecca after the Mutiny uprising, teaching many Indian students and giving spiritual guidance to many in India by letter; Nawab Siddiq Hasan Khan of Bhopal, one of the founders of the Ahl-i Hadith movement, whose eighty books promoting his reforming ideas were published throughout West Asia making him a major intellectual presence throughout Alavi's Muslim cosmopolis; and Mawlwi Jafar Thanesri whose vision of his land was framed by the British legal and administrative framework, but he was able to use his Islamic identity to range more widely. Alavi makes an important point about how in the nineteenth century Indo-Muslim horizons were spreading well beyond India, a process which continued throughout the twentieth century.

An occupational hazard of reviewing any book which deals with Israel is an assault from the country's 'attack dogs' who seem constantly to patrol Western publications to make sure that the view of the past that is presented is acceptable from their point of view. 'In Reverse' was my review of Eugene Rogan's excellent *The Arabs: A History*, which importantly enabled Arab voices to be heard. It admitted that they had been badly treated by the imperial powers and also that they had made mistakes. Rogan set out to produce as balanced a presentation of matters Arab/Israeli as possible. To emphasise his even-handedness I noted how he balanced the unprovoked attack by Jewish forces on the Arab village of Dayr Yasin on 9 April 1948 against a Palestinian attack on a Jewish medical convoy in Jerusalem. This immediately brought an assault from the attack dogs. The figure of 250 villagers killed at Dayr Yasin, which I had quoted from Rogan, was wrong; the numbers were much less, even Palestinian sources said so. I had to publish a retraction. This said, one did wonder about the delicate feelings expressed over the precise numbers of Arabs killed at Dayr Yasin, a well-known *cause célèbre*. It was just a couple of paragraphs away from the bloody details of Israel's 'Cast Lead' operation in Gaza in 2008–9, which did $1.4bn worth of damage, killed 1300 Palestinians and wounded 5100. Against this carnage just 13 Israelis died and 8 were wounded.

'Women, Leadership and Mosques', the final chapter, arose from a conference on women's religious authority in Islam organised by Hilary Kalmbach and Masooda Bano at Oxford in 2009. In pre-modern times there had always been some women who engaged in the transmission of knowledge, in particular Hadith. Bano and Kalmbach, aware of the growing numbers of women's madrasas and of women's religious leadership, even of men, aimed to discover where matters stood now. The twenty essays in the book answer three main questions: (1) How is space created for the exercise of women's religious authority and what are the relative roles of male invitation, state intervention and women's initiative in achieving this? (2) How have women used these opportunities to consolidate their positions as religious authorities? (3) What has been the impact of female authority on Muslim women themselves? The answers to these questions demonstrated that women's religious leadership was already a major fact in the Muslim world; that the world of scholarship needed to take it much more seriously than it had done; and that the Bano/Kalmbach collection of essays should be a starting point in doing so. In fact, they had opened up a whole new subject, centred around one likely to be of the first importance in the development of the Islamic world in the twenty-first century.

This book addresses a series of themes central to Islamic societies over the past 200 years: the impact of Western dominance; the crises of civilisational authority following from this dominance; the role of traditional education both in making Muslim societies and then in remaking them in an era of Western dominance; the relationship between Islamic reform and forms of Muslim modernity; and the relationship between the rise of the modern state, the decline of cosmopolitanism, the growth of globalisation and the challenge of multiculturalism; the shift of leadership in the Muslim world to the lands east of the Hindu Kush; the rise of women as transmitters and interpreters of knowledge, and therefore sources of Islamic authority; and the significance of the memory of power, a memory which had a very specific resonance in British India, but one which has not completely disappeared from the Muslim world at large. The twenty-first century will see these themes elaborated; the process will be fascinating.

FRANCIS ROBINSON
Royal Holloway, University of London
April 2019

Notes

1. Yaqoob's thesis was published as *A Princely Affair: The Accession and Integration of the Princely States of Pakistan, 1947–55* (Karachi: Oxford University Press, 2015).
2. Uther's thesis was published as *Anglo-Indians and Minority Politics in South Asia: Race, Boundary Making and Communal Nationalism* (London: Routledge, Royal Asiatic Society Books, 2018).
3. Nikhil's D.Phil. thesis was: 'Minds of the Madrasa: Islamic Seminaries, the State and Contest for Social Control in West Bengal and Bangladesh' (Oxford, 2015).
4. Tahrat's D.Phil. thesis was: 'Imagining Lines? "Islam", "Secularism" and the Politics of Family Laws in Bangladesh: The Politics of Religion and its Impact on Women's Rights in Bangladesh' (Oxford, 2016).
5. Megan's thesis is entitled: 'Print and the Urdu Public: Muslims, Newspapers, and Urban Life, 1900–1947.'
6. Layli's Ph.D. thesis was entitled: 'In the Land of Eternal Eid: Maulana Bhashani and the Political Mobilisation of Peasants and Lower-Class Urban Workers in East Pakistan, *c.* 1930s–1971' (London, 2015).
7. Eve's Ph.D. thesis was entitled: 'The Muslims of Northern India and the Trauma of the Loss of Power, *c.* 1857–1930s' (London, 2016)
8. Sumaira's Ph.D. thesis was entitled: 'Dynamics of Secondary Education Organisation in Pakistan: An Historical Perspective from 1947–1970' (London, 2014).

9. Tommaso's Ph.D. thesis has been published as a book: *Urbanization, Citizenship and Conflict in India* (London: Routledge, Royal Asiatic Society Books, 2015).
10. Shuja's Ph.D. thesis was entitled: 'Economic and Social Change in Khairpur (Pakistan) 1947–1980' (London, 2012).
11. The outcome of the Shi'a conference was published in Justin Jones and Ali Usman Qasmi (eds), *The Shi'a in Modern South Asia: Religion, History and Politics* (Delhi: Cambridge University Press, 2015). The outcome of the 'Muslims against the Muslim League' conference was published in Ali Usman Qasmi and Megan Eaton Robb (eds), *Muslims against the Muslim League: Critiques of the Idea of Pakistan* (Delhi: Cambridge University Press, 2017).
12. These were: *Questioning the Authority of the Past: The Ahl al-Qur'an Movements in the Punjab* (Karachi: Oxford University Press, 2012) and *The Ahmadis and the Politics of Religious Exclusion in Pakistan* (London: Anthem Press, 2014).
13. This has now been published under the title: *Jamal Mian: The Life of Maulana Jamaluddin Abdul Wahab of Farangi Mahall, 1919–2012* (Karachi: Oxford University Press, 2017).
14. Francis Robinson, *The 'Ulama' of Farangi Mahall and Islamic Culture in South Asia* (Delhi: Permanent Black, 2001).
15. See the excellent chapter on fundraising for the Madrasa Ashrafiya, Mubarakpur, Azamgarh district, U.P., in Arshad Alam, *Inside a Madrasa: Knowledge, Power and Islamic Identity in India* (New Delhi: Routledge, 2011), pp. 111–32. All donations came from private citizens. The madrasa certainly benefited from the oil boom, but the donors were Mubarakpuris working in Saudi Arabia and the Gulf. The research of my student, Fakhar Bilal, on Khayr al-Madaris in Multan also reveals the large quantity of donations from private citizens, in this case swelled by the impact of the Green Revolution.

1

The Islamic World in the Age of Western Dominance

MUSLIM SOCIETIES SINCE 1800 have been influenced by two developments of the first importance. First, the Islamic world system, which from its emergence had walked hand in hand with power, came to be dominated by forces from the West. This domination, moreover, was not just one of conquest and rule; there came with it economic, social, intellectual and political forces of great transformative power. Second, every Muslim society came to be animated by movements of Islamic revival and reform. These movements took different shapes according to the circumstances of the societies in which they flourished. By the end of the twentieth century the programmes of these movements were distinctive features in the lives of most societies and the defining features of some. From the outset it should be clear that the roots of religious reform lie deep in the pre-modern history of Muslim societies, that aspects of the movement were already manifest in the eighteenth century and that their prime purpose was inner renewal. However, the period of Western dominance gave urgency and extra purpose to these movements. From context to context there were different interplays between Western power and manifestations of Islamic revival. As time went by Western understandings of Muslim societies came increasingly to be coloured by their experience of the revival. In the same way movements of revival were both shaped by the contact with the West and energised by their resistance to it.

The onset of Western power in Muslim lands was swift and often brutal. The symbolic beginning was Napoleon's invasion of Egypt in June 1798. In fact, Muslim power had been on the retreat from at least 12 September 1683, when the Ottoman forces besieging Vienna had been ordered to retreat, never to return. Since then there had been a slow erosion of power on the margins of their world: the Dutch had gained a substantial foothold in island South East Asia, the British in India, the Russians in the Crimea, the Habsburgs in the Balkans. But this was the moment when Europe asserted itself in the central Islamic lands for the first time since the Crusades, and did so with armies bearing the banners of reason, nationalism and state power.

Within three years the British and the Ottomans had driven the French away. But this did not in any way impair the rapid movement of European power into Muslim lands. In 1800 the Dutch government took over from its East India Company in island South East Asia and spread its authority throughout the archipelago until the process was completed by the end of the Acheh War in 1908. In India, in 1799, the British defeated the last major independent Muslim power in Mysore. By 1818, once they had the descendants of the Mughal emperors as virtual prisoners in Delhi, they were acknowledged as the paramount power in the subcontinent. By 1858, after sacking the old Mughal capital in the suppression of the Mutiny uprising, they ruled all India, either directly or indirectly.

The strategic demands of British India meant further British expansion into Muslim lands. The Afghans, fortunate in their terrain, their warlike habits, and their position as a buffer between British India and tsarist Russia, succeeded in preserving their freedom. In the Gulf, however, British influence steadily grew, as it did in southern Iran and along Arabia's southern shore. The completion of the Suez Canal in 1869 and European competition for power led to British domination of the Nile Valley. In 1882, they occupied Egypt, which led in 1898 to the establishment of a condominium with the Egyptians over the Sudan, in which the British held effective authority. On the western shores of the Indian Ocean they shared out the considerable possessions of the sultans of Zanzibar with Germany and Italy. On the eastern shores, they had from the 1870s begun to assert their hegemony over the sultans of the Malay states.

At the same time tsarist Russia spread southwards and eastwards to absorb its Muslim neighbours. At the beginning of the nineteenth century Russia pressed forward in the Caucasus, conquering the Iranian territory of northern Azerbayjan. By 1864, after a bloody struggle for Daghistan, the whole region was occupied. In Central Asia, the lands of the Kazakhs were secured by 1854, the Khanate of Khokand by 1873, the lands of the Turkomans by 1885 and those of the Tajiks by 1895; protectorates were established over the ancient khanates of Khiva and Bukhara. After the Russian Revolution these became Soviet republics.

The French advance into North and West Africa was no less dramatic, and was accompanied in some areas, as the Russian one had been, by a great influx of European settlers. In 1830 they invaded Algeria; in 1881 they declared Tunisia a protectorate and in 1912 Morocco. The first two were the main focus of French settlement. By 1912 they had also expanded from Senegal eastwards across the savannah lands to the borders of the Anglo-Egyptian Sudan, subduing a string of Muslim states, several of which owed their origins to the Muslim revival. Only the British, who drew the sultanate of Sokoto into their main West African colony of Nigeria, also ruled large numbers of Muslims in the region. Other European powers picked up what crumbs they could; in 1912, for instance, Spain asserted a protectorate over the northern tip of Morocco, and Italy conquered Libya. By the outbreak of the First World War all the Muslims of Africa, except those in Ethiopia, were under European rule.

The Ottoman Empire was not exempt from the surging tide of European power. Through the nineteenth century European powers steadily put more and more pressure on the empire's Balkan territories as they annexed a piece of land here and competed for influence there. The outcome was that the Christian peoples of the Balkans – Greeks, Serbians, Romanians, Bulgarians, supported by one European power or another – threw off Ottoman rule and brought the sizeable Muslim populations of the region beneath their sway. By the First World War only the rump of Rumelia remained of the empire's European territories. The war itself saw the Arab peoples of the empire also fall under European rule as the British, with Arab help, drove Ottoman forces in the Fertile Crescent back into Anatolia, and divided the spoils with their French allies. By 1920 the Ottomans, whose subjects were now mainly Turks, were fighting to hold on to their Anatolian heartland, which the Europeans proposed to dismember, seizing chunks for themselves and creating a Greek Christian province in the west and an Armenian Christian state in the east.

In a mere 120 years or so almost all the Muslim peoples of the world had fallen under European rule.[1] Only the Muslims of Afghanistan, the Yemen and central Arabia could pretend to real independence; those of Iran had one qualified by the division of their country into Russian and British spheres of influence. Great cities – Damascus, Baghdad, Cairo, Samarqand, Delhi – all redolent of the changing phases of Muslim glory and achievement, were now subject to European authority. Muslim peoples were in the hands of their European masters. But worse was to come. In 1924 the caliphate was abolished: not an act of European power, but of Mustafa Kemal, as he sought to bring a secular focus and new strength to the fledgling Turkish Republic. In one sense this meant little; the office of caliph had long been divorced of any real sense of power and leadership of the Muslim community. But, in another sense it symbolised much; its demise meant the breaking of a link that reached back to the time of the Prophet Muhammad and which spoke of how successful, until recently, the community had been.

The period from the post-First World War settlement to the 1960s saw most Muslim societies achieve freedom from European rule. First, the two peoples whose freedom was threatened by the designs of European imperialism, the Turks and the Iranians, succeeded in asserting their independence. The Ottomans under the remarkable leadership of Mustafa Kemal drove all foreign armies out of Anatolia and established a modern Turkish nation-state. In Iran the Cossack Brigade officer Rida Shah Pahlawi followed in his wake, enabling Iran to loosen the bonds of imperial control fashioned in the Anglo-Persian agreement of 1919. The limitations of his achievement, however, were demonstrated when in the Second World War both Britain and Russia were able to reassert their interests in the country. The two decades following this war saw the bulk of Muslim peoples gain their independence. In 1947, this was the fortune of one quarter of the world's Muslims when, amidst appalling slaughter of Muslims by Hindus and Sikhs, and of Hindus and Sikhs by Muslims, British India achieved independence as the sovereign states of India and Pakistan. In 1949 Indonesia emerged from Dutch rule and by 1971, after Pakistan split into Pakistan and Bangladesh, it had become the world's most populous Muslim state. In 1957 the Malay states followed suit from British rule, becoming Malaysia in 1963. Between 1946 and 1958 it was the turn of Egypt, Libya, the Sudan and the Arab states of West Asia, which colonial power interacting with local forces had forged from the former Ottoman territories. Only the peoples of Palestine, Christians of course as well as Muslims, failed to share in the new world of infant nation-states, as Zionist settlers, whose ambition to found a homeland had been endorsed by the Balfour Declaration of 1917, forced the creation of a Jewish state in 1948. In the late 1950s and 1960s the Muslim peoples of North, West and East Africa gained their freedom, along with those of the southern Arabian shore and the Gulf. This left the Muslim peoples under Soviet rule as the last remaining group of significant numbers without their freedom. This they gained in the early 1990s.

Freedom from European rule, however, did not bring freedom from Western power. As they gained their freedom, many Muslim states, particularly in the central Islamic lands, found themselves entangled in the Cold War rivalries of the great powers. Turkey, Iran and Pakistan became part of what was known as the 'northern tier' of defence against the expansionism of the Soviet Union. Pakistan's generals in 1958 would keep Washington closely informed of their intention to launch a coup.[2] Arab socialist republics, on the other hand – Egypt, Syria and Iraq – allied themselves with the Soviet Union; for a time, it seemed the better way of asserting their independence and gaining some extra strength in confronting Israel. There were significant interventions, or attempted interventions, in the affairs of Muslim societies: the Anglo-American overthrow of Musaddiq's regime in Iran in 1953, which arguably held back the growth of democracy for decades; the inglorious Anglo-French invasion of Egypt in 1956 to secure the canal zone, which was the last 'hurrah' of the old European imperial powers; in 1958 the USA sent troops to the Lebanon and the British to Jordan with the aim of stemming the onward march of Arab nationalism; in 1979 the Soviet Union invaded Afghanistan, leading to resistance organised by the USA, Saudi Arabia and Pakistan, among others, which had a considerable impact on Muslim lives from Central Asia, through Afghanistan and Pakistan to Kashmir; from 1982 there was the substantial support which the USA, the USSR and France, in particular, gave to Iraq in its eight-year war with Iran; in 1983 and 1984 there was the intervention of the USA in the Lebanon which was supposed to hold back the advance of Syrian, and therefore also Soviet, influence.

From the 1990s the USA was the hegemonic power in the Muslim world. Russia imposed its will in its backyard, most notably and with brutal force on the Chechens of the Caucasus. Elsewhere the 'new world order' was decreed by the USA. It forced the Indonesians out of their rule of Christian East Timor. Very belatedly, although here British foot-dragging bears a heavy responsibility, the USA delivered aid to assist the Muslim Bosnians in resisting ethnic cleansing by the Christian Serbs.[3] With greater speed it used massive force to relieve the Kosovan Muslims from Serbian oppression. Various states stood up to the hegemonic ambitions of the USA, among them Libya, the Sudan, Syria and Iran; indeed, the continuing capacity of the Islamic Republic of Iran to resist American pressure has demonstrated the greater strength of the revolutionary regime in the face of outside forces as compared with the Qajar and Pahlawi regimes that preceded it. All have been warned; they have been designated 'states of concern'. In two cases, one an organisation, the other a state, active opposition to the hegemonic will led to awesome displays of American power. From the early 1990s Osama bin Laden's al-Qa'ida al-Sulbah ('the Solid Base') organisation had conducted a series of assaults on symbols of American power, which culminated on 11 September 2001 in the attacks on the World Trade Center in New York and the Pentagon in Washington. In the autumn of 2001 the USA responded by destroying the Taliban regime in Afghanistan, which sheltered bin Laden. In 1990 Saddam Husayn of Iraq invaded Kuwait. The immediate response was the destruction of Saddam's invading force by Western armies in the first Gulf War, the establishment of a major American military presence in Kuwait and Saudi Arabia, action throughout the 1990s to contain Iraq, which led, when those containment measures appeared to be weakening, to an Anglo-American invasion of the country in the spring of 2003 and to the destruction of its Ba'thist regime. A Muslim of historical bent might reflect that, some 205 years after the French entered Cairo, the West was playing the same old game in Baghdad, forcing its way into a major capital city of the Muslim world and claiming that it was bringing freedom and enlightenment to the people.

Nothing has more constantly reminded Muslims of the power of outside forces in their lives than the existence and the policies of the state of Israel. They know that the process of Zionist settlement in Palestine would not have been successful without British support, however qualified. They know that the emergence from the mid-1950s of Israel as a major power in West Asia would not have been possible without the unstinting material and political support of the West. They know that Israelis have only been able to achieve their colonial settlement of Arab lands seized in the war of 1967, and in breach of international law, because of American support. They know, too, that Israel has treated Palestinians with scant justice and much brutal force – though no more brutal than that deployed by many Muslim regimes – with the assurance of American support. For many Muslims the injustices meted out to the Palestinians symbolise both the injustices many experience in their own lives and their own impotence in the face of overwhelming power. In the twenty-first century Muslims know that the power of the West to intervene in their world in pursuit of its ends is greater than ever it was in the nineteenth.

The growing power of the West in the Muslim world meant much more than the capacity to dictate the boundaries of states or the lifespans of regimes. It transformed many of the structures of Muslim societies, as it has those of societies throughout the globe. The economies of Muslim societies came to be integrated into a global economy, driven by the industrial revolutions of the West, with their continuous processes of scientific and technological innovation. Whether it was in the plantations of South East Asia, the cotton fields of Egypt or the oilfields of the Middle East, whole new worlds of production and exchange were created which overshadowed those of peasant husbandry, handicraft production and the bazaar – undermining the communal solidarities they had bred and the Islamic institutions which had rested upon them for centuries. No new physical presence signalled the changes taking place more dramatically than the new Western-style cities, which more often than not grew up alongside the old ones, and which brought a new world of broad streets, glass-fronted shops, public clocks for the precise regulation of time and suburban hinterlands of slums, flats and villas.

Forms of the modern state were introduced either during the period of colonial rule or as part of an attempt to keep the Europeans out by threatened Muslim regimes. Powered by ever-growing bureaucracies, such states were increasingly concerned to reach down to individual citizens, direct them towards their purposes, and make them focus their first loyalty upon the state. Such states were likely to be intolerant of tribal and other competing sources of allegiance. Their relationship with the 'ulama', and others concerned to focus Muslim energies on godly ends, was likely to be more strained than previously in Islamic history. Western knowledge, which seemed to be a key source of Western power, increasingly came to be used in Muslim societies. It was needed to run the modern economy and modern state; it was particularly needed to enable Muslim societies to strive to keep up with the West and to be strong enough to look after themselves in an age of Western domination. Inevitably, the great traditions of madrasa learning came to be pushed to one side, as also the attitudes that pervaded the madrasa. No longer was the search for knowledge primarily a process of trying to discover and preserve all that one could learn from an age of past perfection. Now the emphasis was on innovation, the discovery of new ideas, new facts, new processes and the testing of all old knowledge in the light of new understandings.

New elites formed to run the new economic and political structures: bankers, traders, commercial farmers, industrial workers, bureaucrats, soldiers, politicians, intellectuals, journalists. All embraced the new knowledge to the extent that they needed it. Some were educated in the languages of Europe: English, French, Dutch, German, Russian. Many became divorced from their heritage of learning, and sought to understand it primarily through Western sources. Even those who did come to lead the cultural resistance to the West often drew on its wisdom to make their case. Thus, the thought of Muhammad Iqbal, poet-philosopher of the Pakistan movement, owed much to that of Nietzsche, Bergson and Renan, and that of 'Ali Shari'ati, who prepared the Western-educated young for the Iranian revolution, to Sartre, Fanon and Massignon. This was the case, moreover, even for the founding fathers of Islamism for whom the preservation of Islamic cultural authenticity meant so much. Sayyid Qutb, the leader of the second stage in the development of Egypt's Muslim Brotherhood (*Ikwan al-Muslimin*), was profoundly influenced by the French fascist thinker and Nobel Prize-winning biologist Alexis Carrel; Mawlana Mawdudi, the creator of the subcontinent's Jama'at-i Islam, was deeply read in Western thought from Plato, through Darwin and Marx, to George Bernard Shaw.

Through these new elites, as well as through the education systems of the colonial states and their successors, ideas derived from the European Enlightenment came increasingly to circulate in Muslim societies. There was a growth in the scientific mentality and the idea that knowledge should be tested against the advances of scientific discovery, a process which was likely to disenchant the world and threaten the supremacy which could be claimed for God. There were the outcomes of the Enlightenment political achievements of the American and French revolutions with their emphasis on the rights of man, the political freedom of individuals and the sovereignty of the people as the source of state power. In the twentieth century there was the considerable influence of socialist thought among secular elites, attracted by its critique of Western capitalism, its apparently 'progressive' nature and its proposal of a secular communitarian ethic instead of the Islamic one. For much of the twentieth century Muslim elites drew on aspects of these ideas as they strove to free themselves from Western dominance. On achieving independence command economies were often adopted to limit the economic impact of the West.

Crucial to the spread of knowledge of Europe, indeed of all forms of knowledge in Muslim societies, was the sustained adoption from the nineteenth century of print. Muslims had known about the printing-press for 300 years, but its adoption had been resisted for a range of reasons, among them a shrewd understanding of its potential impact on the authority of religious and political leadership. From the nineteenth century, however, Muslim elites began to use the press with vigour. Muslim states saw its potential for building up state power; other Muslims saw its potential in supporting either their struggle for power within society or the campaigns to overthrow colonial rule. Lithographic printing became a major new activity for the artisans of towns and cities, and printed matter – books in particular – an important new trade for the Muslim world. The growth of the newspaper industry was extremely important. In part this was because it created a new public space in which ideas could be transmitted and discussed, but in part too, and especially after the introduction of the telegraph in the second half of the century, because it increasingly integrated Muslims into a global world of shared news and information – though not, of course, of shared perception. From the mid-nineteenth century, the press led the expansion of the horizon of Muslim minds. If, at first, they were focused on the doings of their courts or governments, by the early twentieth century they readily embraced the Muslim world, and after the First World War were developing a global reach from Japan and China through Europe to the Americas.[4]

From the second half of the twentieth century, and particularly from the 1970s, the pressures of Western capitalism and Western culture became increasingly intense. The increase in pressure was initiated from within the Islamic world. The major oil-price rise of 1973, which was engineered through OPEC (Organisation of Oil Exporting Countries), brought much new wealth to the Muslim oil-producing countries, at least some of which spread more widely through the Muslim world as the oil-producing economies sought labour and bought influence. Growing numbers of Muslims engaged with Western consumerism. The big change, however, came with the Thatcher/Reagan market revolution in the West, which cut public spending, privatised nationalised industries, freed financial services and deregulated foreign-exchange markets. This 'capitalist revival', as it has been called, transformed the conditions for economic success so that they no longer lay in manufacturing production but in the financing and marketing of goods and services. This process was boosted first of all by the collapse of the Soviet bloc and the removal of both an alternative economic model and a restraint on Western capitalism. It was also boosted by the way in which the major Western powers used the institutions of global economic governance such as the International Monetary Fund, the World Trade Organisation, and the World Bank to impose their vision of good practice on the weaker economies of the world. Indebtedness made Muslim economies, along with other weaker ones, susceptible to being restructured on Western terms. Towards the end of the twentieth century Muslim societies were increasingly facing the choice of either liberating their economies, with the huge risks of economic, social and political instability that such action would involve, or of falling further and further behind the economic development of much of the rest of the world.[5]

In the case of Western ideas and culture, in particular its consumerist culture, influences were pouring into Muslim societies. Increased trade, travel and tourism played a role in this, but of major importance were the internet and satellite television. The former provides access to an extraordinary panoply of representations of humanity and human interests in institutional and individual form, while at the same time enabling Muslims to interact with the world of Muslim ideas and organisations as never before. The latter was bound to have an attraction in environments in which the media were often exposed to state control and censorship. Nevertheless, the satellite channels were dominated by news gathered by Western news corporations and edited to suit Western agendas and by entertainment in large part generated in the West and projecting individualism, consumerism, sanitised violence and female liberation. Muslim states, however repressive, have had difficulty in restricting access. Individual Muslims have been enabled to interact with the West as never before.

Western domination set Muslim societies major challenges. At first, they did not seem to demand a fundamental transformation of the way in which Muslims thought and lived. Indeed, in the early stages of colonial rule European men often adapted themselves to the societies to which they had come, learning the languages, using local systems of law and marrying local women. But as Western power grew, the fundamental nature of its challenges became clearer. There was the challenge of defeat. How was it that the community, which the Qur'an described as the 'greatest nation raised up for mankind' and which had been throughout its history an expanding and dominant force, had come to be subjected to the power of the West? There were the challenges posed by Western science and philosophy to God, His relationship to nature and to man, and to the life hereafter. There were the challenges from capitalism and Enlightenment values to aspects of the organisation of Muslim society on which the Qur'an had ruled precisely. European capitalism challenged the Qur'anic prohibition on taking interest; the new European commitment to the rights of man challenged the Qur'anic acceptance of slavery; while the new European belief in the equality of all human souls challenged the inferior position that the Qur'an seemed to have designated for women.[6]

The greatest challenge, however, came at the level of the state. The modern state seemed to be the prime source of Western strength. It was aspects of this state that Muslims introduced to make themselves strong enough to keep the Europeans out and which Europeans introduced to exploit the resources of their colonies. The key feature of the modern state was its increasing control of all available material and human resources and compensating involvement of the people, in one way or another, as legitimisers of these purposes. This raised the question: was it possible to continue to fashion a Muslim society if all activities and institutions, educational, legal and political, were devoted to state purposes rather than God's purposes? Was it possible to remain a Muslim society when controlled by state structures that were concerned to fashion the strongest aspirations of the people in terms of their relationship with the state rather than with God? A major theme of Islamic history in the nineteenth and twentieth centuries is the attempt by Muslim peoples to answer these questions, as they sought to acquire the power to resist the West. This said, by the latter part of the twentieth century the role of the modern state had given rise to a somewhat ironical reflection. On the one hand, its capacity to protect Muslim societies from the economic and cultural forces of globalisation was subject to an increasingly intense and successful siege. On the other hand, many such states were increasingly being hollowed out from within by the developing organisations of Islamic revivalism.

The challenges of the West were often met in Muslim societies with great creativity. But they also gave rise to feelings ranging from nostalgia at the loss of past glory and mortification at present Western power through to resentment swelling to rage at Western bullying, injustice and aggression. Nostalgia was the theme of one of the greatest works of nineteenth-century Indian literature, the *Musaddas*, or elegy, of Altaf Husayn Hali. This great set-piece poem on the rise and decline of Islam and its causes came to be used as the anthem of India's Muslim separatist movement, leaving audiences in tears:

> When Autumn has set in over the garden,
> > why speak of the springtime of flowers?
> When shadows of adversity hang over the present,
> > why harp on the pomp and glory of the past?
> Yea, these are things to forget:
> > but how can you with the dawn forget the scene of the night before?
> The assembly has just dispersed;
> the smoke is still rising from the burnt candle.
> The footprints on the sands of India still say:
> A graceful caravan passed this way.[7]

The Islamic World in the Age of Western Dominance   37

Mortification came with the realisation of European power. 'So, it went on until all had passed leaving our hearts consumed with fire for what we had seen of their overwhelming power and mastery,' declared the secretary to the Moroccan envoy to France after watching a review of French troops in 1846. 'In comparison with the weakness of Islam . . . how confident they are, how impressive their state of readiness, how competent they are in matters of state, how firm their laws, how capable in war.'[8]

But, as Western power enveloped the Muslim world, there was growing protest. 'The British and the European nations do not consider Asians and Africans as human beings, and thus deny them human rights,' declared Husayn Ahmad Madani, principal of the great Indian reformist school of Deoband, in his autobiography written after his internment in Malta during the First World War. 'The British are the worst enemies of Islam and the Muslims on earth.'[9] The position of Muhammad Iqbal, who accepted a knighthood from the British, was not so very different:

> Against Europe I protest,
> And the attraction of the West.
> Woe for Europe and her charm,
> Swift to capture and disarm!
> Europe's hordes with flame and fire
> Desolate the world entire.[10]

The rejection of Europe, or by now the West in general, both as a destructive force and as a false model of progress, was a theme of many of the leading ideologues who prepared the way for the Iranian revolution. 'Come friends', said 'Ali Shari'ati in the 1960s, echoing his muse Fanon, 'let us abandon Europe; let us cease this nauseating apish imitation of Europe. Let us leave behind this Europe that always speaks of humanity, but destroys human beings wherever it finds them.'[11] As the United States replaced Europe in the demonology of the Muslim world, it became the focus of resentment. Ayat Allah Khumayni's howl of rage, when in 1964 the Iranian parliament granted American citizens extra-territorial rights in Iran in exchange for a $200 million loan, spoke for all Muslims who had felt powerless in the face of bullying from the West from the bombardment of Alexandria in 1882 to the continuing plight of the Palestinians since 1948: 'They have reduced the Iranian people to a level lower than that of an American dog.'[12]

Such feelings were no less strongly held in the Arab world, where as Arabs came to feel the weight of Western colonialism, the Crusades were a key reference point. The myth of Saladin as the great leader of resistance to the West and his victory over the Crusaders at Hattin was a central theme of the Palestinian struggle under the British mandate. Indeed, the Israeli state came to be seen as the modern version of the Latin kingdom of Jerusalem, which was established by what Sayyid Qutb called 'the Crusader spirit which runs in the blood of all Westerners'.[13] A similar image was conjured up in Arab and Muslim minds when Osama bin Laden on 20 February 1998 proclaimed the formation of a 'world front for Jihad against Jews and Crusaders':

> The ruling to kill Americans and their allies – civilians and military – is an individual duty for every Muslim . . . to liberate the al-Aqsa Mosque [in Jerusalem] and the Holy Mosque [in Mecca] from their grip, and in order for their armies to move out of all the lands of Islam, defeated and unable to threaten any Muslim.[14]

The long tradition of Muslim resentment and protest at Western power (and its results) in Muslim lands is unsurprising, but it is a response that has been too often overlooked.

If the growing domination of the West was one context for Muslim societies in the nineteenth and twentieth centuries, the second was the Islamic revival. Throughout the period, to a greater or lesser extent, Muslim societies were animated by the revival from West and North Africa, through the central Islamic lands to China and South East Asia. The revival took many different forms, depending on specific social, economic and political circumstances, and as time went on came increasingly to influence Muslim responses to the West.

At the heart of the Islamic revival was a shift in the balance of Muslim piety from an other-worldly to a this-worldly Islam. This meant a devaluing of a faith of contemplation of God's mysteries and of belief in His will to intercede for man on earth, and a valuing instead of a faith in which Muslims were increasingly aware that it was they, and only they, who could act to create a just society on earth. Throughout the history of Muslim societies there had been tension between other-worldly and this-worldly piety. The Prophet and his companions had promulgated a this-worldly activist socio-political ethic, but as the Muslim community expanded to embrace Christian and other mystical traditions, and as Muslims came to reflect on the Qur'an and the religious practice of the Prophet, an other-worldly or Sufi strand developed in their piety. The tensions this might involve were exemplified in the life of that great medieval thinker al-Ghazali, as he tells us in his autobiography, *al-Munqidh min al-Dalal (The Deliverance from Error)*, of how he first served this world and then the other world, but finally realised that his duty as a Muslim lay in this-worldly action.

From the fourteenth century Muslim piety increasingly came to be dominated by an other-worldly emphasis. The dominant influence in this move was the thought of the great Spanish Sufi Ibn 'Arabi, whose doctrine of *wahdat al-wujud*, the unity of being, played an enormously important role in accommodating a myriad local religious practices within an Islamic umbrella as Islam expanded to embrace societies from West Africa to South East Asia. Moved, more often than not, by political decay and corruption in their worlds, the 'ulama' and Sufis, and later on, the lay folk who led the movements of Muslim revival, were concerned to renew the faith of their societies by removing all practices that compromised the sovereignty of God and His guidance for mankind, and by promoting the requirement to act on earth to achieve salvation. The revivalist world was one that stressed the Muslim's personal responsibility to act for the good of the community.

Associated with the shift in piety was a set of processes which worked to shape the new activist Muslim. There was an attack on all ideas of intercession for man with God at, for instance, saints' shrines, which at its extreme meant opposition to any form of structure over a grave. There was for some – though not all – revivalists an attack on the great legacy of medieval Islamic scholarship so that believers might turn afresh to the Qur'an and hadith (tradition, the reported sayings and doings of the Prophet). This was in part so that believers might return to God's guidance to chart an effective course in challenging times, but in part too so that they might focus on the dynamic example of the early community. Increasingly, the example of the Prophet was given new emphasis as a model for Muslim lives, as evinced by the organisations that took his name, for instance, the Tariqa-yi Muhammadi (The Brotherhood of Muhammad) of early nineteenth-century India, and the numbers of biographies of him that came to be written. Some of the new emphasis on the Prophet was as a replacement for Sufi saints as the focus of warm and intensely human devotion, but the prime reason was his role as the model of the ultimate man of action.

This new emphasis on the responsibility of each Muslim to help fashion a Muslim society was accompanied by developments which assisted Muslims in doing so. The leaders of the Islamic revival realised that an Islamically educated community was their best defence against both Western power and cultural domination as well as Muslim rulers who wished to impose it upon them. Forms of Islamic education, usually operating outside the framework of the state, have been promulgated, such as the *pesantren* of Java, the madrasas of South Asia, the educational networks of the followers of Badi'al-Zaman Nursi in Turkey and the preaching tours of the Tablighi Jama'at (Preaching Society). The printing press was adopted.

Right in the forefront were reformist 'ulama' who, although they worried about their distancing from the transmission of knowledge, nevertheless saw the potential of print for creating an Islamically informed constituency in society. For most leaders of the Islamic revival print has been a crucial means of communication. Further stages in the democratisation of Islamic knowledge came with the translation of the Qur'an, hadith and other major Islamic texts into the languages of Muslim peoples. For the first time many Muslims were able to read and understand these texts. This development has been accompanied by the adoption of other forms of media technology and mass communication – radio, television, film, audio and video cassettes and recently the internet. This democratisation of Islamic knowledge has been largely empowering of Muslim individuals, organisations and communities. It has made the will of ever larger numbers of Muslims a fact in the life of Muslim societies. It has helped to make a growing reality of the new concept of caliphate – the caliphate of man. The idea of man as God's vice-regent on earth seems first to have been promulgated in the modern era by Muhammad'Abduh; it was enthusiastically adopted by Muhammad Iqbal, and has been the watchword of Islamic thinkers from Mawdudi in South Asia to al-Banna and Qutb in Egypt through to Shari'ati and Mutahhari in Iran. The shift in the balance of piety from an other-worldly to a this-worldly focus is, arguably, the most important development in Muslim piety of the past thousand years.

The expansion of this-worldly piety, and the activism it demands, has released a great surge of energy through Muslim societies. From time to time, manifestations of this revivalist spirit have clashed with forces from the West, giving rise in Western understandings of an Islam both fanatical and implacably opposed to it. But, in truth, the Islamic revival has always been primarily about inner religious renewal. It is a process that bears many similarities to the Protestant reformation in Christianity: the attack on intercession, the emphasis on personal responsibility, the emphasis on literacy and the study of the sources, the role of print, the empowering of individual believers. Indeed, some leaders of the revival drew specific comparisons. Jamal al-Din al-Afghani was explicit in his admiration for the determination of the European Protestants to ignore their priests and to make up their own minds after studying the sources; not surprisingly, he cast himself as the Muslim Luther. 'We are today', declared Muhammad Iqbal in his lectures on the reconstruction of religious thought in Islam, 'passing through a period similar to that of the Protestant revolution in Europe.'[15]

The roots of the Islamic revival were established well before any serious Western presence in the Muslim world. There was a long scholarly preparation. One key figure was the fourteenth-century Hanbali scholar of Damascus Ibn Taymiyya, whose critique of Ibn'Arabi and of other-worldly Islam has been an inspiration to supporters of the revival right down to the present. Among manifestations of the preparation was the reaction led by the scholar 'Abd al-Haqq and the Naqshbandi Sufi Ahmad Sirhindi in the early seventeenth-century to the compromises that Mughal rulers made with Hindus, and Indian Muslims with Hinduism; there was the great debate in the court of Acheh in the mid-seventeenth century over the interpretation of Ibn'Arabi's thought, which attracted the attention of leading scholars at Medina; there was the work of 'Abd al-Ghani of Nablus (1641–1731), prolific scholar and Naqshbandi Sufi, in revitalising theology and reforming Sufism; there was the similar work in India of Shah Wali Allah (1702–62), scholar of hadith and Naqshbandi Sufi. One important development in spreading reforming thought was the expansion of the Naqshbandi Sufi order deriving from Ahmad Sirhindi and bearing his purified Sufi message – if somewhat diluted – from India to Mecca, Damascus, Istanbul, Kurdistan and the Balkans. Another development was the work of Mustafa al-Bakri (d. 1749), the chief pupil of 'Abd al-Ghani of Nablus, in reviving the Khalwati Sufi order, which gained great influence at al-Azhar in Cairo, becoming both the main framework for reformist ideas in Egypt and a major vehicle for their transmission to much of Africa. Particularly important in spreading reforming thought was a leading group of teachers of hadith at Medina. Major figures in the group were Ibrahim al-Kurani, who settled the great debate at Acheh, and Muhammad Hayat al-Sindhi. Their pupils included many leading reformers: 'Abd al-Ra'uf of Singkel, Shah Wali Allah of Delhi, Mustafa al-Bakri of Damascus, Muhammad Ibn 'Abd al-Wahhab (1703–92) and Shaykh Muhammad Samman (1717–75). A good number of the pupils of the Medina school also overlapped with those of the Mizjaji family of the Yemen, including several of the above, as well as Muhammad Murtada al-Zabdi (d. 1791), an Indian pupil of Shah Wali Allah, who became a great figure in eighteenth-century Cairo, and Ma Mingxin (d. 1781), who was to spread the 'New Sect' teaching among the Chinese Naqshbandiyya. In the eighteenth century the lifeblood of reform flowed readily along the connections of 'ulama' and Sufis through much of the Muslim world.

For much of the nineteenth and twentieth centuries, the major vehicle of the revival was what has come to be known technically as 'reformism'. It was a movement of 'ulama' and reformed Sufis which aimed for the most part to hold the central messages of reform within the great tradition of scholarship handed down from the past, although for some that tradition might be pared down to the bare essentials of Qur'an and hadith on which they would use their independent reasoning power.

Throughout the period Arabia was a major source of reforming ideas and influence. Central to this was the movement of Muhammad ibn 'Abd al-Wahhab, which from 1744 gained political backing from its alliance with the Sa'udi family of the Najd. Twice this alliance gained overall power in Arabia. The first Sa'udi–Wahhabi empire, which did great damage to the holy shrines of Iraq and the Hijaz, was destroyed by the armies of Muhammad 'Ali's Egypt. The second, which was established with the foundation of the Sa'udi kingdom in the 1920s, has existed down to the present. Throughout the period it has been an engine of Islamic reform;

the term Wahhabi in many areas of the Muslim world came to denote a particular reforming style and zeal. When in the second half of the twentieth century oil brought great wealth to the Saudi–Wahhabi regime, it was able, often with political as well as religious purposes in view, to put considerable resources behind its preferred movements of reform.

From the early nineteenth century the influence of these events in Arabia was felt elsewhere in the Muslim world. In South East Asia, for instance, it exacerbated the tensions between those who supported strict Islamic interpretations and those who wished to accommodate their religious practice to the local milieu. In the Minangkabau region of Sumatra there was the so-called Padri movement, notably active from 1803 to 1837, in which a Wahhabi-style reform movement endeavoured to impose its will upon the people. In Java there was the reformist campaign led by Dipanegara from 1825 to 1830 which, in the context of a Europeanising aristocracy and the misery that European rule had brought to the countryside, aimed to purify Islam and improve the conditions of the people. Although there are no certain connections between this movement and the mainstream of reform, the basis existed in the enduring links of Javan trade and scholarship to Arabia. Then from 1873 to 1910 there was the great jihad in the north Sumatran province of Acheh against Dutch rule, which had resonances that reach down to the twenty-first century. If the last movement was a war of resistance which was strengthened by reform and support from without, the former were movements of inner renewal which came to collide with the colonial power. In the twentieth century much of the reformist spirit came to be channelled through the reformist Muhammadiyya (often mistakenly seen to be modernist). Founded in 1912, it both internalised reform by fostering the human conscience as the arbiter of rightly guided behaviour and externalised it by action in society, establishing schools, orphanages and hospitals. Related organisations were devoted to preaching. Down to the late twentieth century it was a continuing source of reforming vigour.

South Asia saw similar developments. The first half of the nineteenth century saw two notable movements. There was that of Sayyid Ahmad of Rai Bareli which drew for the most part on reforming ideas passed down through the Naqshbandi Sufi lines descended from Sirhindi, but was also stimulated by reformist influences from Mecca. Calling themselves the Tariqa-yi Muhammadi, they fled British-controlled India to establish their own Islamic society on the North-West Frontier. Sayyid Ahmad was killed in 1831 but his followers were to spread his message down to the First World War. The second movement was that of the Faraidi in Bengal which, beginning in 1821, was profoundly influenced by reformist ideas brought back by Hajji Shari'at Allah after more than twenty years in Arabia. Initially a movement for purification, after the Hajji's death it became an underground brotherhood opposed to the British. As in South East Asia the reformist current eventually came to be expressed in a form of 'Protestant' Islam in which the individual human conscience was fashioned as the guardian of individual Islamic behaviour and thus the guarantor, in the absence of Muslim power, of the existence of an Islamic society. At the heart of this movement was the Deoband madrasa, founded in 1867. One hundred years later it claimed over eight thousand madrasas worldwide founded in its image. Reformism found South Asia particularly fertile soil, being expressed through several movements, among them the Tablighi Jama'at, or Preaching Society, which is acknowledged by many as the most widely followed movement in the Islamic world. From the 1970s the numbers of Deobandi madrasas in Pakistan began to increase rapidly; those in the North-West Frontier Province came to form the base from which the Taliban militias emerged to take power in Afghanistan.

In much of the rest of Asia reformist thought was carried by members of the Naqshbandi Sufi order. Some of the drive came from India from the westward expansion of Sirhindi's ideas. Particularly important was Mawlana Khalid Baghdadi (1776–1827) who, after studying in Delhi at the feet of Sirhindi's successors, carried his teachings into West Asia. This said, activity also stemmed from other branches of the order in the Caucasus, Central Asia and China.

In the Caucasus two striking movements of reform came into conflict with expanding Russian power. In the first, Imam Mansur preached a pure reformed Naqshbandi message in Daghistan from 1785 to his death in 1794. And in the second Imam Shamil from 1834 continued Mansur's work in Daghistan, resisting mighty Russian invasions for over thirty years, and remaining to this day an inspiration to the continuing resistance of the neighbouring Chechen people. In Kazan in the Volga Basin there was significant activity led by Baha al-Din Waisi (1821–93), leading to passive resistance against the Russian regime. In Anatolia the Kurd Sa'id Badi' al-Zaman Nursi sustained the spirit of Naqshbandi reform in the hostile environment of Atatürk's Turkish republic. In Central Asia, however, the homeland of the Naqshbandis, activity was limited to a three-day holy war against the Russians in Andijan.

China, on the other hand, saw remarkable Naqshbandi-led activity. In east Turkistan there were six Naqshbandi-led uprisings against Manchu rule, the last of which led to the regime of one Ya'qub Beg from 1867 to 1877. Although it is not possible certainly to associate these uprisings with the reformist spirit, we should note that Ya'qub Beg imposed a strict Islamic regime. Elsewhere in China, however, there is striking evidence of Naqshbandi reformist influence. There is the opposition of the 'New Sect' Naqshbandis to the 'Old Sect', which supported forms of acculturation to the Chinese environment in religious practice. In 1781 this broke into open conflict around the great Chinese Muslim centre of Lanzhou. In the nineteenth century New Sect militancy grew as more reforming influences entered the region from West and South Asia, and led to two great rebellions. The first ravaged Gansu and Shaanxi from 1862 to 1877, during which time its leader, Ma Hua-long, tried to establish a Muslim state. The second raged across Yunnan from 1856 to 1873, its leader Du Wenxiu succeeding in creating a Muslim state in half the province. The first leader of the Yunnan rebellion was Ma Texin who, like so many in the reforming tradition, was the first scholar to translate the Qur'an into his native language.

In Africa the role of the Naqshbandiyya as the carriers of reformist ideas was taken by the Khalwatiyya and the Idrisiyya and their offshoots. The former, we have noted, was an old order given new life by Mustafa al-Bakri; the latter was a new order founded by the Moroccan, Ahmad ibn Idris (1760–1837), who settled in Mecca and taught a Sufi way with a Wahhabi-like programme. In the nineteenth century reformist movements inspired by these sources surged across Africa.

One significant branch of the Khalwatiyya was the Tijaniyya, founded by the Algerian Ahmad al-Tijani (1737–1815), who had been taught by Mahmud al-Kurdi, a leading pupil of al-Bakri. His order spread to Algeria and Morocco, to the Nilotic and Central Sudan, and especially to West Africa. At the heart of its success in the last region was Hajji 'Umar Taal (1794–1864), a Fulani from Futa Toro in Senegal. On pilgrimage in the 1820s he adopted reformist teachings after spending three years in Medina as the pupil of a Tijani shaykh. Returning to West Africa he created a theocratic empire, which stretched from the bend in the Niger to Upper Senegal, and which survived until in 1893 it was conquered by the French. The second significant branch was the Sammaniyya, which was founded by Shaykh Muhammad Samman and spread in the Nilotic Sudan, Eritrea and southwest Ethiopia. This spiritual tradition led to one remarkable manifestation of revival and reform, the Sudanese Mahdiyya. The movement was led by Muhammad Ahmad (1840–85) who, under instruction from two Sammaniyya shaykhs, became a strict follower of the shari'a, eventually banning Sufism. Declaring himself in 1881 to be the expected Mahdi, he waged war against the Turko-Egyptian regime which was hated for its innovations, and founded in 1885 a theocratic Mahdist state. In 1898 this was readily overcome by the British as they advanced up the Nile, but its example has remained an inspiration in the politics of the Sudan down to the present.

The Idrisiyya also produced two significant branches, both of which stemmed from men who had failed in the competition to succeed Ahmad ibn Idris as shaykh in Mecca. The first was Muhammad 'Ali al-Sanusi (1787–1859), who established himself in the 1850s in Jaghbub in the Libyan desert and preached a pure reforming message. Unlike many of his fellow reformers, he set out to create his theocratically organised society by peaceful means, establishing Sufi lodges as cells of reformed Islamic culture. In the latter half of the nineteenth century these spread along the Sahara trade routes until they reached from Cyrenaica to Timbuktu and the kingdom of the Waday. Of course, they collided with the advancing French and Italians, but survived to become the basis of Libyan resistance to foreign domination. The second man was Ibrahim al-Rashid, whose nephew and pupil, Muhammad ibn Salih, founded the Salihiyya, based in Mecca, whose most notable product was Muhammad 'Abd Allah Hasan (1864–1920). From 1895 Hasan led a major reforming movement in British Somaliland which for twenty years involved a holy war against lax Sufis, the Ethiopians and the British. He died undefeated and remains a symbol of Somali resistance against oppression.

Not all African movements received their stimulus from pulses of reform in the Islamic world at large. In West Africa, the work of Hajji 'Umar Taal apart perhaps, the main reformist drive was locally generated. The leaders were the Fulani from Senegal who intermarried with Berber tribes drifting south across the Sahara. From the fifteenth century they had slowly moved eastwards, where they came to mix uneasily with semi-Islamised and pagan communities from the Senegambia to Bornu. They drew on long traditions of Saharan Islamic scholarship and mysticism. The most important leader, 'Uthman dan Fodio (1754–1817), never travelled to Cairo or Mecca, was rooted in the Saharan traditions of scholarship and, unlike many reformers who wished to escape the medieval legacies of Islam, drew on the full range of classical and post-classical scholarship from al-Ghazali to al-Suyuti. In his world, unlike West or South Asia, the full classical tradition remained a dynamic inspiration. 'Uthman's jihad, which was launched in 1804, followed a century or more of Fulani jihads as they travelled eastwards. It led to the formation of the sultanate of Sokoto in the Hausa lands which grew by the mid-nineteenth century to embrace Adamawa in the south-east, Nupe in the south and Ilorin to the south-west. The work of reform explains the vigour of Islam in the West African hinterland as colonial powers expanded into it in the nineteenth century and the prominent role it has come to play in many states in the twentieth century, not least among them the great state of Nigeria.

It is axiomatic that the spirit of revival and reform was expressed differently in different social, economic, cultural and political environments. We have noted how in areas where state power was strong it might be expressed through educational movements and peaceful proselytisation, while in areas where state power was weak or non-existent it might be expressed through warfare leading to state creation. But, as Western power came in the late nineteenth and twentieth centuries to embrace Muslim societies ever more tightly and its threat to Islam as a faith and a way of life came to be understood more clearly, the basic programme of reform – returning to the Qur'an and hadith and purifying Sufi practice – was not enough to meet the threat.

One response of the reforming spirit to this heightened awareness of the Western threat was Islamic modernism. This was typically the response of Muslim ruling elites who were concerned to face up to the realities of Western scientific advance and Western dominance. At one level such modernists wanted Muslims to master Western science and technology, which they perceived to be the source of Western strength. Thus, they pioneered educational developments, often outside the control of the 'ulama', to bring about this change. But at the deepest level they wished to review

Islamic knowledge as a whole, including its founding pillars of the Qur'an and hadith, in the light of Western learning. They were determined that there should be harmony between Western science and Islamic understanding. Among the leading modernists were Sayyid Ahmad Khan of India, Namik Kemal of the Ottoman Empire, Muhammad 'Abduh of Egypt, Jamal al-Din al-Afghani and the Tatars, Shihab al-Din al-Marjani, Jar Allah Bigi and Isma'il Bey Gasprinskii. Some came from reformist backgrounds, but all knew that the reformism of the 'ulama' was inadequate to meet the challenges of the times. For a time, some modernists were attracted to pan-Islamic responses to the West, but after the First World War they began to focus their attention on the nation-state. For the great Indian modernist Muhammad Iqbal, this was to be a state built on Islamic principles – a Pakistan. Arguably, in its constitution and legislation such as the Muslim Family Laws Ordinance (1961), Pakistan in its first two decades was a laboratory of Islamic modernism.

The movement for revival and reform in its modernist garb was too rarefied an Islamic understanding to achieve acceptance in Muslim societies beyond a narrow elite. Moreover, it carried with it the danger for many of endorsing Islam and Islamic institutions as central features of national life and identity. The elites of most societies adopted secular national identities for their peoples based on history, ethnicity, language or the state structure they controlled. Islam and its institutions were given a subordinate role to play, and in some cases virtually no role to play at all. Such was the thinking of Atatürk and Rida Shah Pahlawi and their followers as they built the modern Turkish and Iranian states. So too was the thinking of the great nationalist movements that struggled against colonial power: the Wafd in Egypt, the Ba'th in Syria and Iraq, Sukarno's nationalists in Indonesia, Ben Bella's Front de Libération Nationale in Algeria. After independence, secular philosophies – nationalist, liberal, socialist – became even more prominent among Muslim elites. Moreover, such ideas informed their use of state power; as Islam was driven more and more into private space, secular values were given fuller rein in public space, national rather than Islamic values informed education and women were required increasingly to serve the purposes of the state rather than those of family or God's law.

The second response of the reforming spirit was a range of movements which fall under the general term Islamism. For Islamists 'ulama'-led reform was inadequate because it failed to address issues of Western power and dominance, the modernists were inadequate because they permitted Islam to be judged by Western knowledge, and the nationalists were a disaster, in part because they sidelined Islam, permitting secular values to rule in their societies, and in part because their policies simply failed to meet either the material aspirations or the psychological needs of their people. The founders of Islamism, Hasan al-Banna, who created the Muslim Brotherhood of Egypt and the Arab world in 1928, and Sayyid Abul A'la Mawdudi, who created the Jama'at-i Islami of the South Asian world in 1941, were typical of the movement's leadership in subsequent decades. The former, a schoolteacher, and the latter, a journalist, both came from reforming backgrounds, but had been educated outside the old madrasa system of the 'ulama' and were well-acquainted with Western learning. Islamists started from the principle that all human life must be subordinated to the guidance sent by God to human beings; as Mawdudi said, the shari'a offers a complete scheme of life 'where nothing is superfluous and nothing wanting'. It followed that whereas most Islamist movements have been concerned to continue reformist traditions of fashioning an Islamic society from within by bringing about changes in individual and community behaviour, they have also been concerned to influence the workings of the state, if not seize power within it. Thus, they would assert the shari'a in their societies, bring about the Islamisation of knowledge and economics, promote 'Islamic' values and standards of behaviour, and curb or overthrow elites who seemed to prefer the values of the West to the Islamic system, or nizam, they wished to promote. Throughout the Muslim world from the 1950s to the 1970s Islamist organisations sprang up, more often than not providing much-needed basic services – schools, hospitals and clinics – but also welfare associations, youth clubs and political and paramilitary organisations. The leadership tended to be highly educated in Western disciplines – doctors, engineers, university teachers; support came from those often excluded from the workings of power – the growing middle and lower-middle classes which underpinned the modern state and modern economy, students, and the vast numbers who in these years moved from the countryside to the cities of the Muslim world.

From the 1970s the challenge of Islamist movements in the politics of Muslim societies became increasingly evident. In Turkey Necmettin Erbakan, leader of the Islamist National Salvation Party, became deputy prime minister. In Pakistan, General Ziya'al-Haqq led the implementation of an Islamic system after the design of Mawlana Mawdudi. In Egypt, President Anwar Sadat found himself under increasing pressure from Islamist forces, pressure which was greatly increased after his peace with Israel in 1977, leading to his assassination by a splinter group of the Muslim Brotherhood in 1981. Iran, moreover, saw one of the great revolutions of the twentieth century, akin to the Russian or the Chinese, when in 1979 Islamists joined forces with 'ulama' under the leadership of Ayat Allah Khumayni in overthrowing the Pahlawi regime, with its secular orientation and Western alliances. This first full-scale Islamist regime, although placed in the special Shi'i environment of Iran, has been an inspiration to Islamist movements as well as a laboratory in which it has been possible to observe the experimental top-down creation of a modern Islamic state and society. In the following decades Islamist movements played a major role in the political discourses of all Muslim societies, and not least those that emerged in the 1990s after the dissolution of the Soviet empire. Some, noting that after the Iranian revolution Islamists have had limited further success, have talked of the failure of political Islam.[16] But such a judgement tends to ignore the shifts of political discourse in an Islamist direction in many societies where their parties are present, and arguably the globalisation of Islam.[17]

For most of their existence Islamist movements focused primarily on their own societies. International connections might be made through Cairo, Mecca, London, Paris, or through transnational support for campaigns of resistance against external oppression: for instance, those of the Hizb Allah against the Israeli presence in the Lebanon; of the Kashmiris against India's presence; and the jihad against the Soviet occupation of Afghanistan. After their success in driving the Russians from Afghanistan in 1989, two leaders of the mujahidin, 'Abd Allah 'Azam, a Palestinian, and Osama bin Laden, a Saudi citizen, considered how they might refocus the organisation and the forces they had created. They noted that Islamists were unlikely to achieve their objectives in individual Muslim societies because of the support which the USA and its allies gave to the elites in power; to bring change in their own countries they must internationalise their activities and target the USA and its allies. Thus al-Qa'ida emerged to create a worldwide strategic framework of Islamist political and military organisations. From the early 1990s it launched a series of attacks on Western interests, of which the most audacious was the air assault on New York and Washington on 11 September 2001. The increasing global dominance of the West had led some Muslims to organise globally to resist it.

Thus, two great processes have dominated the history of the Muslim world in the nineteenth and twentieth centuries: the growth of Islamic revivalism and the growth of Western power. The origins of the former were rooted deep in the centuries before 1800; its messages were carried along the connections of 'ulama' and Sufis which reveal the workings of the Islamic world system that preceded that of the West. As time went on the Islamic revival came increasingly to interact with the West, in part being shaped by it and in its turn shaping Western perceptions of the Muslim world. In this context the major theme of my approach to the writing of Islamic history is to see its central subject as the relationship between the transmitters and interpreters of the central messages of Islam – 'ulama', Sufis and, increasingly, lay folk – and the wielders of political power in their societies. From the beginning of the Islamic revival these transmitters have been concerned to renew the faith of their societies, often spreading Islamic knowledge through the population as never before. As time has passed, and as they have come to sense the power of the modern state to shape society as a whole, some have sought to impose their will upon it.

Alongside the grand narrative of the interactions between the transmitters and the wielders of power, there is a series of sub-themes. One has been the relative decline of Sufis and 'ulama' as transmitters of Islam and the rise of lay folk, supported by new social formations. Sufis have suffered: the Islamic revival has targeted many of their practices; the cult of the Prophet has grown to displace that of local saints; secular education has cast an Enlightenment chill over mystical beliefs; and Muslims have become increasingly divorced from the great heritage of medieval learning that enriched the higher Sufi understanding. Nevertheless, wherever there has been oppression, as in Soviet Russia, Sufi orders have been at the heart of the resistance. 'Ulama' have fared less badly. Print and, subsequently, electronic communication have robbed them of their exclusive hold over Islamic knowledge and its interpretation, while the secular systems of education and law usually adopted by modern Muslim states have pushed them towards the margins of society. Indeed, Muslim elites in the twentieth century tended to see them as symbols of Muslim backwardness. 'Ulama', however, have been rather more flexible than their opponents have given them credit for. In some societies, as in South and South East Asia, they have provided significant levels of education outside the framework of the state, in others, as in the Shi'i communities of Iran, Iraq and the Lebanon, they have taken the leading role in resisting oppression. Moreover, wherever they are in the Muslim world, they represent the link to the Islamic religious tradition and to the skills needed to interpret it. But, for all that may be said about the continuing vitality of traditional Islamic scholarship, the major development of the twentieth century has been the emergence of Islamic thinkers and leaders from outside the ranks of the 'ulama': Iqbal and Mawdudi in India and Pakistan; al-Banna and Sayyid Qutb in Egypt; Hassan al-Turabi, a lawyer from the Sudan; Rashid al-Ghannushi, a teacher from Tunisia; Mahdi Bazargan, an engineer from Iran; and Harun Nasution, an intellectual from Indonesia. The Islamist project has been in the main a lay project, driven forward by the aspirations of a rising bourgeoisie.

A second sub-theme has been the growing prominence of women in the political discourse and public lives of Muslim societies. Movements of Islamic revival could make women a major target of their attention. In societies where public space was increasingly occupied by Western or secular values, it was women who, by upholding an Islamic rule for themselves and their households, became key pillars of Islamic civilisation. Such was the grave responsibility bestowed upon them by Islamic reformism in India. Indeed, through much of the Muslim world women have been made to bear the brunt of the cultural revolutions foisted upon them by their menfolk, such as the attacks on the veil by secular dictators such as Atatürk and Rida Shah Pahlawi, or the forcing of women back into veiling, as happened in the Iranian revolution and under the Taliban regime in Afghanistan. Nevertheless, there is much evidence to suggest that the increasingly large-scale presence of veiled women in the public spaces of Muslim towns and cities from the 1980s in part reflects patriarchal preference and a desire for cultural authenticity but in part too the major role women were coming to play in the modern state and economy. It is worth noting that, while fourteen centuries of Muslim history see just two short-lived female rulers of major Muslim states, Shajar al-Durr in thirteenth-century Egypt and Sultana Radiyya in thirteenth-century Delhi, the years since the 1980s have seen four: Khaleda Zia in Bangladesh, Benazir Bhutto in Pakistan, Tansu Çiller in Turkey and Sukarnoputri Megawati in Indonesia.

Through Islamic history, the leadership of the Muslim world in ideas, in wealth, and in power has shifted from region to region. For much of the period from 1800 the Ottoman Empire was the Muslim great power, and arguably some of that mantle fell upon republican Turkey as the state that seemed to have absorbed more of the Western lessons of progress than most. In the latter part of the twentieth century the Iranian revolution, in the context of the general rise of Islamism, saw the Turkish model go out of fashion. The Iranian experiment, which horrified some Muslims but excited many with its defiance of the West and its assertion of a distinctively Islamic model of progress, was the first time for some centuries that Iran had had a leading role in Muslim affairs, and the first time in the history of the Muslim community that its Shi'i branch had set such a striking example for others to follow.

At a more fundamental level, the period saw a general shift in the centre of gravity of the Muslim world. For the first time, more Muslims came to live East of the Hindu Kush than to the West. The Indian subcontinent, which in the early modern period had begun to transmit ideas to the rest of the Muslim world, now through its interactions with the British Empire became a significant exporter of ideas, such as those of Iqbal and Mawdudi, and organisations such as that of the Tablighi Jama'at. In the latter part of the twentieth century, the shift in economic dynamism to South East and East Asia brought new weight to the Malaysian and Indonesian presence in the Islamic world, and in the latter particular significance to the Islamic leadership given to democratic development.

It is one of the ironies of the period that at a time when the West has come to dominate the Muslim world, Muslims have at last achieved what they failed to win in many centuries of attempted conquest: a significant presence in the West, outside Spain. At the beginning of the twenty-first century these communities number around 10 million in Europe and 6 million in North America, with much smaller but also significant communities in Latin America and Australasia. By and large these communities have migrated for economic reasons, but many have fled political upheaval, from Pakistan and Palestine in the mid-twentieth century to Chechnya and Kosovo at the end. For the first time, from a Western point of view, engaging with Muslim communities has not just been an aspect of foreign policy but of domestic policy. For Muslims there have been the perennial problems of integration and assimilation, of how to be both a Muslim and a citizen of a Western society. In the process Western societies and their Muslim communities have learned much from each other, sometimes fruitfully, at other times less so.

The West, after overwhelming the Islamic world system and exposing Muslim societies to an increasingly intense interaction, left it as a world of nation-states. This was a world of many different voices: different national voices, different voices within nations, different voices within movements. It most certainly did not speak as one. Nevertheless, there has continued to be a level at which Muslims identify as Muslims, at which they know, as God told them, that they are 'the best community raised up for mankind'. If for Muslim believers this community is a living fact, for those who are Muslims primarily by culture, a shared history and sense of brotherhood still lingers. This sense of community, which is supported by powerful strands running through Islamic history, law and rites, was manifest in Muslim responses to the steady loss of Muslim power in the world, and not least in the extraordinary response of Indian Muslims to the destruction of Ottoman power in general and the caliphate in particular. It was also manifest in the many attempts from the 1880s to build pan-Islamic organisations, which achieved realisation of a kind through Saudi intervention in the 1960s and the creation of the World Muslim League and the Islamic Conference organisation. The sense of the brotherhood of all Muslims at the level of the ordinary Muslim has been much nourished by the development of global media. The fate of Palestine, Bosnia and other places where Muslims have suffered have been matters of urgent concern. During the last quarter of the twentieth century more and more young Muslims have travelled to take up arms in far-away places to defend their fellow Muslims. This sense of brotherhood is one strand which holds together the al-Qaʿida organisation. At the beginning of the twenty-first century the community loyalties of Muslims throughout the world remains a fact that still carries political potential.

The interactions of Muslim societies with the West in this period reveal no clash of civilisations. They have shaped each other and their perceptions of each other. Moreover, Muslims have had as many different responses to the West as have Westerners to the world of Islam. Study of the many ways in which Muslims, the heirs to a great civilisation, have striven to draw on its resources to meet the massive challenges of the nineteenth and twentieth centuries and be true to themselves, is the best way to reduce any sense of clash. Muslim tenacity in respecting the roots of their civilisation, and at times their creativity in finding solutions to the challenges of modernity, are examples from which all can learn and all should respect.

Notes

1. While the master narrative is one of Western advance, in areas beyond Western control Muslim communities were coming to feel the weight of alien rule, for instance, the Uyghurs of China's Xinjiang and the Muslims of Buddhist Thailand.
2. Ayesha Jalal, *The State of Martial Rule: The Origins of Pakistan's Political Economy of Defence* (Cambridge: Cambridge University Press, 1990), p. 275.
3. Brendan Simms, *Unfinest Hour: Britain and the Destruction of Bosnia* (London: Allen Lane, 2001).
4. Francis Robinson, 'Islam and the Impact of Print in South Asia', *Islam and Muslim History in South Asia* (Delhi: Oxford University Press, 2000), pp. 66–104.

5. Simon W. Murden, *Islam, the Middle East, and the New Global Hegemony* (Boulder, Colorado: Lynne Rienner Publishers, 2002).
6. W.G. Clarence-Smith, *Islam and the Abolition of Slavery* (Oxford: Oxford University Press, 2006).
7. Gail Minault, trans., in G. Minault, 'Urdu Political Poetry during the Khilafat Movement', *Modern Asian Studies*, 8, 4, 1974, pp. 459–71. N.B.: The attribution in Minault's article is not quite correct; the excerpt is from Hali's *Shikwa*. I am grateful to Eve Tignol for pointing this out.
8. S.G. Miller (trans. and ed.), *Disorienting Encounters: Travels of a Moroccan Scholar in France in 1845–1846: The Voyage of Muhammad as-Saffar* (Berkeley: University of California Press, 1991), pp. 193–4.
9. H.A. Madani, *Safarnamah-i Malta* (Deoband, 1920), quoted in R. Malik, 'Mawlana Husayn Ahmad Madani and Jamiyat 'Ulama-i Hind 1920–1957: Status of Islam and Muslims in India', Ph.D. thesis, University of Toronto (1995), pp. 44–5.
10. A.J. Arberry (trans.), *Persian Psalms (Zabur-i Ajam) . . . from the Persian of the late Sir Muhammad Iqbal* (Karachi, 1968), p. 76.
11. Quoted in Hamid Algar's introduction to H. Algar (trans.), *On the Sociology of Islam: Lectures by Ali Shari'ati* (Berkeley: Mizan Press, 1979), p. 23.
12. 'The Granting of Capitulatory Rights to the U.S.', Ayat Allah Khumayni's speech of 27 October 1964, in Hamid Algar (trans. and annot.), *Islam and Revolution: The Writings and Declarations of Imam Khomeini* (Berkeley: Mizan Press, 1981), p. 182.
13. Quoted in C. Hillenbrand, *The Crusades: Islamic Perspectives* (Edinburgh: Edinburgh University Press, 1999), p. 602.
14. Quoted in Y. Bodansky, *Bin Laden: The Man Who Declared War on America* (Roseville, CA: Prima Lifestyles, 1999), pp. 226–7.
15. Muhammad Iqbal, *The Reconstruction of Religious Thought in Islam* (Lahore: Sh. Muhammad Ashraf, 1975), p. 163; for the shift to this-worldly piety, see Francis Robinson, 'Other-Worldly and This-Worldly Islam and the Islamic Revival', *Journal of the Royal Asiatic Society*, 3rd series, 14, 1, April 2004, pp. 47–58.
16. Olivier Roy, *The Failure of Political Islam* (Cambridge, MA: Harvard University Press, 1995).
17. Olivier Roy, *Globalized Islam: The Search for a New Ummah* (New York: Columbia University Press, 2004).

2

Global History from an Islamic Angle

THIS SUBJECT IS APPROACHED from the following background: an upbringing in the 1960s 'Expansion of Europe' tradition in Cambridge; a period in the 1970s spent with the late Freda Harcourt in developing a subject called 'World History since 1900' in the University of London;[1] a research life with a particular focus on the lives of learned and holy men and religious change in South Asia;[2] and a writing life which has, from time to time, reached beyond South Asia to embrace the Muslim world as a whole.[3] That remarkable Chicago historian, Marshall Hodgson, who died in 1968, has been a source of inspiration, as he has been to many others. He set out to write a world history but by the time he died had only succeeded in covering, incompletely, the Muslim world. There is much to be learned from his attitude of respect for his subject of study, manifest for instance in his notorious fastidiousness in the use of nomenclature. His history was published in 1974 under the title *The Venture of Islam: Conscience and History in a World Civilisation*.[4]

From this background, this essay will address first the expansion of the Muslim world from the eighth to the eighteenth century as a global phenomenon and then its continuing expansion in the age of Western domination. This will be followed by comment on some specific phenomena of global reach and significance which flow from research on Muslim societies: the tales of storytellers which cross vast regions of the world; understandings of astrology and astronomy which have been widely shared; and of particular commodities whose production and consumption have had an impact on the whole world. We will conclude by addressing the 'Protestant turn' in religious piety, experienced throughout Muslim societies in the nineteenth and twentieth centuries, but also experienced in other leading world faiths. Often its expression is entangled with modernities. Out of a discussion of these various themes some signposts to future directions in global history should emerge.

The Muslim World and Global History

Some may be reluctant to treat civilisations as worthy units of study for the global historian. This may flow from a desire to focus attention away from the expansion of the Western world-system, which absorbed a great deal of scholarly energy in the second half of the twentieth century. It may also flow from a desire to escape from the essentialism implicit in Samuel Huntington's *Clash of Civilisations*.[5] This said, there are things to be gained from studying the Muslim world system, which preceded the Western one, parts of which continue to operate beneath the sway of Western dominance.

The expansion of the Muslim world was a major global phenomenon. Muslims emerged from Arabia in the mid-seventh century to defeat the Byzantine empire and overwhelm the Sassanian empire within a decade of the death of the Prophet in 632 CE. This was followed by a further one hundred years of rapid expansion so that by 750 CE Muslims ruled from North Africa and Spain through to the Talus river in Central Asia and the Indus basin in South Asia. In the process they made the cities of West Asia buzzing *entrepôts* of goods, new technologies and new ideas from lands covering the Mediterranean basin, the Indian Ocean rim through to China. From the thirteenth century the Muslim world continued to expand into West Africa, South and Southeast Asia, preparing the way for the position today when more Muslims live East of the Hindu Kush than to the West. The Mongol invasions were initially a disaster, but were turned to advantage by the conversion of the Il Khans to Islam and the further expansion of the Muslim world into Central Asia. Up to the seventeenth century Muslim society was the most expansive in the Afro-Asian region and the most influential. It occupied the 'geographical pivot of history', as expounded by Halford Mackinder in his 'heartland thesis'.[6] China and Japan in the northeast, and Europe in the northwest, were on the periphery. China certainly exported important innovations such as paper and gunpowder, but also received a host of influences from the Muslim world, in particular through the Mongol Yuan dynasty, ranging from cartography and astronomy and medicine to a host of new crops. Europe, once Muslim civilisation had absorbed its Hellenic gifts, was in its turn the receiver of influences from the Muslim world, which it still struggles to recognise in full. Such was the respect for Islamic learning as late as the second half of the seventeenth century that the Royal Society has several shelves of books in Arabic collected in the first ten years of its existence. Early fellows of the Society, like Robert Boyle and Christopher Wren, made a point of learning Arabic. By this time the Muslim world, although still dominated by its three gunpowder empires – the Ottoman, Safawid and Mughal – no longer seemed to have overwhelming power in its possession. Nevertheless, given its many centuries of dominance across the Afro-Asian world, and its influence on lands beyond, it must surely continue to be a subject for global historical study.

One outstanding fact about the Muslim world was its connectedness. Over the past fifty years we have learned much about this; it has created a thirst for learning more. One aspect of this connectedness was the way the Muslim world was linked by trade, in particular the long-distance trade across land and sea; the shipping trade-routes around the Indian Ocean rim which linked East

Africa and Arabia to Iran, India, Southeast Asia and China; the caravan trade-routes across land – the Silk Route linking China to the cities of Central and West Asia, the routes across the Sahara from Cairo to the cities of trade and scholarship of North and West Africa. Symbolic of the connectedness of the medieval Muslim world was the way in which the Moroccan traveller, Ibn Battuta, was able to spend twenty-four years in the fourteenth century travelling amongst Muslim communities from West Africa to China. The widespread use of Arabic eased his passage; the widespread use of Islamic law enabled him from time to time to gain a post as a qadi.

A much more powerful dimension of the connectedness of the Muslim world was the way in which it was linked by the teacher–pupil relationships of the 'ulama' (learned men) and the master–disciple relationships of Sufis (holy men). 'Ulama' and Sufis were the men, although a surprising number of women were also involved, who studied the central messages of Islam, the Qur'an and Hadith, and the wide range of skills needed to make them socially useful as law. Their relations with wielders of political power on the one hand, and society at large on the other, are the central threads of Islamic history.

A key requirement for such religious specialists was that they should travel in search of knowledge. And they travelled widely. The twelfth-century Sufi, Ibn 'Arabi, for instance, travelled from his birthplace Murcia in Spain to the great Islamic cities of Spain and North Africa, to Cairo, Jerusalem and Mecca, and then to Baghdad, Damascus and the leading cities of Anatolia. As the Sufi or 'alim travelled – Sufi and 'alim were usually just two sides of one individual – they strove to sit at the feet of the leading religious specialists of their time. In the case of 'ulama' they learned books from leaders in their field, and collected the ijazas, or licences to teach, which gave them authority over these books, at the same time telling the scholar how this authoritative knowledge had been passed down from the original author of the book, through many teachers of the book, to him. Crudely, more ijazas meant more authority. In bolstering the authority of a particular intellectual tradition, or town, or family there grew up the tradition of writing tabaqats or tadhkirahs, collective biographies, which would show both how knowledge had been passed down through time and how it had been sought from across the Islamic world. For us they reveal the networks of teacher–pupil/master–disciple relationships which formed the arteries and veins of the Islamic world along which the life-giving blood of knowledge travelled.[7] They show us too, as Evrim Binbas has taught us to see, how such a fifteenth-century network might underpin what he terms a 'Republic of Letters' in Central and West Asia in which scholars wrote to each other from Cairo, Istanbul, Damascus, Isfahan and Samarqand.[8] They show us, too, how a scholar might rely on the advice of a former teacher. So, from seventeenth-century Sumatra 'Abd al-Ra'uf of Singkel wrote to his old teacher Ibrahim al-Kurani in Medina to get a dispute about the interpretation of the ideas of Ibn al-'Arabi resolved.[9]

We can see these networks of 'ulama' and Sufis at work most vividly as they form the channels along which reforming ideas travel throughout the Muslim world in the seventeenth and eighteenth centuries. So, in the eighteenth century, the Chinese Muslim reformer, Ma Mingxin, studied with the Mizjaji family of 'ulama' in the Yemen and then took reforming ideas back home, leading to major risings against Ching rule in Western China.[10] So the brilliant Indian, Murtada al-Zabdi, studied with the great Indian reformer, Shah Wali Allah, before travelling to the Yemen and then to Cairo where, from his own records, we know that he was the 'go-to man' for West African scholars visiting the city – the links between Zabdi and African reforming movements have still to be studied.[11] So, too, we can trace the influence of the assault of the Naqshbandi Sufi master, Shaykh Ahmad Sirhindi, on the eclectic religious practices of the Mughal emperors, Akbar and Jahangir. This reforming impulse, summarised in Sirhindi's *Maktubat* (collected letters) travelled along the connections of the Naqshbandi

Sufi order into, amongst other regions, Anatolia where it helped to inspire the early twentieth-century Sufi, Badi'al-Zaman Sa'id Nursi's alternative vision for Turkish development from that of Ataturk.[12] It is this vision which helped underpin the Kayseri phenomenon, the industrialisation from below of Anatolia from the 1960s. It is this vision, too, which lies behind the AKP, the moderate Islamist party which currently rules Turkey.[13] Azyumardi Azra's *The Origins of Islamic Reformism in Southeast Asia: Networks of Malay-Indonesian and Middle Eastern 'Ulama in the Seventeenth and Eighteenth Centuries* is a major step forward in charting the connections between reform and connectedness.[14] But there is still much work to be done to understand the Islam-wide reach of Muslim networks on the eve of the era of European dominance.

The question remains, what did Western power, which swept over the Muslim world from 1800, and which has continued to dominate it in one form or another ever since, do for spread of the Muslim world and its connectedness? One outcome was a continuing process of Islamisation; the dynamics of Western Christian rule did much, for instance, to deepen the Islamic presence in Indonesia and in East and West Africa. A second outcome was a further expansion of Muslim peoples so that they came to have a truly global reach: Muslim sects such as the Ahmadiyya and the Nizari Isma'ilis took advantage of the British Empire to spread under its umbrella.[15] Muslims from the old Muslim world seized the economic opportunities offered by the West to establish themselves in Western Europe, North and South America, the Caribbean, South Africa and Australia.[16] The old forms of connectedness continued, not least as 'ulama' and Sufis came to represent their societies against their elites, who had been co-opted by the West. Sufis came to have notable international followings: the disciples of Baba Farid of Pakistan's Pak Pattan in Malaysia, of Bombay's Ghulam Muhammad in South Africa, of Hazrat Shah 'Zindapir' from Pakistan's northwest frontier in the English midlands, and of Lucknow's Bahr al-'Ulum in California.[17] The teacher–pupil relationship underpinned the spread of the reformist activism of India's Deoband throughout Pakistan, but particularly to the troubled lands to the west where in the northwest it informed the early development of the Taliban and in Iranian Baluchistan where it began to provide intellectual leadership to Muslims from Central Asia.[18] The teacher–pupil relationship also underpinned the growing activism of the Shi'a of West Asia; it is not possible to understand Lebanon's Hizb Allah without also learning of its leadership's teacher–pupil connections to the great hawzas of an-Najaf and Qum.[19] Connections such as these usually escaped British imperial administrators, as they may escape intelligence services today.

New forms of connectedness have come to mingle with and overlay the old ones. Transnational Islamist organisations have emerged. I think of the Muslim Brotherhood and the Jama'at-i Islami which currently challenge Western elites for power in West Asian and South Asian states. I think of the Tablighi Jama'at, or preaching society, which is said to be the most widespread Muslim organisation in the world. There are many other Muslim NGOs of which the most notable are the International Institute of Islamic Thought based at Herndon in Virginia and the Fethullah Gulen educational movement which, inspired at one remove by the teachings of Badi'al-Zaman Sa'id Nursi, is based in over fifty countries. Beyond this there are state-based organisations such as the Sa'udi-funded World Muslim League and the Islamic Conference Organisation.

Modern connectivity, however, no longer rests just with person-to-person contact or on institutional bases, it also exists in the media. This has grown from the development of the press in the nineteenth century, which helped Muslims to begin to conceive of their community of believers in pan-Islamic terms as a civilisation, to the emergence of wireless, television and the internet in the second half of the twentieth century, which have greatly enhanced the civilisation-consciousness, the umma-consciousness, of the ordinary Muslim. Osama bin Laden was brilliantly successful in using these tools to reach out to the ordinary Muslim and to help turn the community of believers into a community of conscience.[20] There is real value in studying the connectedness of the Muslim world and the systems which support it, not just for the modern intelligence services but also for the global historian, who wishes to understand how this remarkable civilisation has spread and held together over the past 1400 years.

At this point there is one issue which needs to be addressed. Some might see a danger in paying especial attention to religious knowledge and its transmitters in the working of Muslim societies as leading towards the Orientalist trap of essentialism. However, to ignore the role of 'ulama' and Sufis, and their connectedness across the Muslim world, would be to turn away from a real understanding of how that world, and its constituent Muslim societies, works. Providing there is awareness of the dangers and no temptation to explain all developments in Muslim societies in terms of Islam, there should be no problem. Indeed, the religiously based systems of connectedness in the Muslim world are an important global story.

Shared Worlds of Knowledge and Experience

Let us turn to those potential global history subjects which flow from research on the Muslim world: storytelling, astrology and astronomy, and the impact of commodities.

The World of Storytelling

The world of storytelling, and widely shared stories and fables, is a possible line of enquiry for the global historian. The modern technologies of print, wireless, television, film and electronic social networks have existed for the briefest of moments. For most of human time imaginations have been stretched, and senses been alternately delighted and terrified, by the art of the storyteller. This art, though a dying one in its face-to-face form, continues to the present day as a profession in the teahouses of Morocco, or for instance, in the coffee houses of Iran and amongst the Wayang puppeteers of Java. As a private art it continues amongst families across the world; its undimmed capacity to delight children reminding us of its power through time.

There is a world of shared stories which reaches out from West Asia into Europe and North Africa, and also into South and Southeast Asia. It may well reach more widely; of this we need to know more. Two of the apparent starting points for stories are the Old Testament and the Epic of Gilgamesh which share themes, amongst them the Garden of Eden and Noah's Flood. But the Epic's influence ranges more widely than this. Martin West has demonstrated its considerable influence on Greek epic down to Homer.[21] Its influence on both the Hindu and the Muslim world of South Asia can be found in the presence of Khwaja Khidr, who is usually depicted as an old man dressed in green and standing on a swimming fish.[22] There are great Muslim epics whose origin and influences stretch across the region. There is the extraordinary Persian romance, *Vis and Ramin*, composed for the eleventh-century Seljuk court in Isfahan, whose origin reaches back to the Pahlawi Parthian past and whose influence is thought to have spread through the Seljuk court in Damascus, and contact with Crusaders, to become the basis of the European story of Tristan and Isolde.[23] There is the mystical romance, *Mirigawati* or the 'Magic Doe', composed by the Sufi Qutban Suhrawardi in 1503 for the Sharqi Sultan of Jawnpur in what is now India's eastern Uttar Pradesh. In a story designed both for courtly delight and for the training of young mystics, the Sufi learns how through the conquest of desire to annihilate the self. In the process we have reflections of Homer's *Odyssey* and the tale of Sinbad the Sailor.[24] Then there is the epic of the Prophet's uncle, *Amir Hamza*, so beloved of the Mughal emperor Akbar. This has had a life which probably began in the seventh century CE and runs down to the present. It has been cherished cross the Indian Ocean region and in its nineteenth-century Calcutta-published version carries references ranging from the Sassanian court at Ctesiphon through to East India Company soldiers.[25] Arguably the peak of the Islamic story-telling tradition exists in the *One Thousand and One Nights*, which first came to light in full manuscript form in thirteenth-century Syria. In this collection we see how the Arabs drew on the storytelling traditions of the land and peoples they conquered – Greeks, Romans, Copts, Jews, Berbers, Persians. This has been an extraordinary source of folktales and stimulus to the imagination both for the West and the East. Indeed, the West has raided it for stories to be told in all media as hungrily as the Arabs raided the resources of their subject peoples.[26] Christopher Shackle has shown the remarkable impact of just one story, that of *Sayf al-Muluk*, as it travelled through a range of cultures in South Asia.[27]

It is possible that the global significance of folk literature was lost sight of once it came to be captured for nationalist purposes from the nineteenth century onwards. But there is much more to be learned from its connectivity across the Eurasian region, and indeed beyond that region. If in doubt, consider the impact of just one book, Martin West's *The East Face of Helicon: West Asiatic Elements in Greek Myth and Poetry* (1997). Before he published this book it was perhaps still possible to consider the classical literature of Greece and Rome as a world unto itself. Now the young classicist wonders whether it might not be wise to learn an Oriental language or two.

Astrology

Astrology is a second area of shared knowledge and experience worthy of the attention of the global historian. There has been considerable reluctance until recently to consider its significance for understanding aspects of Muslim societies up to the nineteenth century. In this respect Muslim societies are little different from human societies at large. From the beginning of time humans have sought to find meaning in the heavens, and for much of this time there has been the belief that there is a connection between movements in the heavens and human affairs.

This search for meaning in the heavens was worldwide, present no less in the Mayan civilisation of Central America and the Andean of South America than in the worlds of Babylon, India and China. In Greek hands it gained a form of scientific basis as it became linked to advances in mathematics, in particular the work of Ptolemy of Alexandria (fl.13–70 CE) whose *Almagest* gave a mathematical account of the movement of the heavenly bodies. It remained orthodoxy until Copernicus. The Graeco-Roman achievement in the field was inherited by the Muslim world which brought more scientific underpinning through the work of its observatories, the use of the astrolabe and the development of Zij tables. From here it travelled, along with those other elements of classical learning which Muslims had either preserved or developed, into late medieval Europe where it was to penetrate deeply into the intellectual and political life of the Renaissance.[28]

Astrology always had its enemies. Cicero rejected it on the common sense grounds that inheritance and upbringing must influence a person's life more than the subtle and invisible forces from the stars.[29] Leading Christian and Muslim thinkers, for instance St Augustine and al-Ghazali, rejected it as a pagan or secular philosophy.[30] Nevertheless its influence remained powerful until the Copernican revolution began to be felt from the seventeenth-century onwards. Since then, while continuing to exist, indeed flourish in Islamic lands and further east, in Europe it was increasingly the resort of the irrational and the charlatan until gaining a mild reprieve at the hands of Jungian psychology. This said, it has attracted political elites: the German High Command in World War Two and Nancy Reagan after the failed assassination of her husband, while Indira Gandhi's devotion to astrology did not save her from being assassinated. In the UK popular astrology has a continuing existence in the horoscope features of the red top press and *Old Moore's Almanack*, which still sells up to half a million copies a year.[31]

To all of this one might say – so what! Why does it make it worthy of study by the global historian? Frankly, anything which has helped shape human understanding, or misunderstanding, across the globe and for millennia, demands our attention. I was extremely resistant to it until others showed how it might explain the decoration of a royal tomb or the design of a major Sufi shrine complex.[32] In recent years scholars sensitive to astrology have taught us how to interpret Timurid political thought and, most particularly, have placed aspects of the first one hundred years of Mughal rule in South Asia in a completely new light.[33] Astrology is not only a lost world of understanding but also one in which Christian and Muslim shared a similar cosmological understanding as Serge Gruzinski has so charmingly shown recently in his exposition of the language in which a Christian in late-sixteenth-century Mexico thought about the Ottoman Empire and a Turk in early-seventeenth-century Istanbul thought about the Americas.[34] There is serious heuristic value in an understanding of astrology. An openness to it should be part of the armoury of any global historian wishing to reach back beyond the contemporary era.

Commodities of Global Impact

Environment, climate, diseases and pandemics are well-established subjects for the global historian. But there are other factors which have global reach and impact and are therefore worthy subjects too. Consider commodities – which have had a considerable impact on the societies in which they have been produced, and a considerable impact across the world as they have been consumed. Their production and consumption may well raise ethical issues. Cotton, sugar, tobacco, coffee, opium and oil may cause wars, make men rich, bring ill-health and death. On occasion not only have they changed individual lives, they have also shaped and continue to shape individual societies. Thinking in terms of global impact another six commodities might have been considered – tea, alcohol, wool, gold, coal and copper. Doubtless, there are other candidates. The first six are addressed here because they have had an impact on Muslim societies that continues.

Let us consider cotton in greater detail for a moment. The first evidence of the growing and processing of cotton stems occurs in c. 3000 BCE in China, India and the Americas. At the beginning of the Christian era there was a notable cotton trade between India and the Arab lands. The Muslim conquest of Spain helped to bring cotton production into Europe. By the sixteenth century cotton cloth was highly sought after in European markets. From the seventeenth century the development of Britain's trading empire made cotton a commodity of global importance. Britain first stimulated Indian production to provide cotton goods for the European and North American markets and then destroyed it as production of cotton goods was transferred from the handloom weavers of India to the machines of Britain. In the nineteenth century India became primarily a producer of raw cotton. Such was the centrality of cotton to the relationship between Britain and India that Mahatma Gandhi made the production of hand-spun cotton cloth, khadi, and the wearing of clothes made of it, the symbol of Indian nationalist resistance to the British. The twentieth century saw the destruction of the British cotton industry and the transfer of mass textile manufacture to developing economies. Thus, the manufacture of cotton goods has come to contribute to new industrial revolutions across the world, many new opportunities for exploitation, and environmental devastation such as the draining of the Aral Sea by the wanton demands of Uzbekistan's cotton monoculture.

This thumbnail sketch suggests why the global historian might take cotton seriously. Turning to a more specific Islamic angle,

Richard Bulliet's recent Yarshater lectures at Harvard offer a striking demonstration of the impact of cotton on the early Islamic world. The Prophet Muhammad was opposed to luxurious apparel so a distinct preference for cotton clothing, as opposed to silk, developed amongst Muslims. In the years after the seventh-century Arab conquest of Iran this led to the establishment of cotton cultivation in the Iranian plateau; the transition of the Iranians from being primarily Zoroastrian to being primarily Muslim can in part be measured by the spread of cotton cultivation. For the ninth and tenth century Bulliet talks of a 'cotton boom' during which Iran was transformed from a territory of landed estates and autarchic villages to one of towns, trade and a rich cultural life. Then, there came the 'big chill', a hundred years of climate change, which hit Iran's cotton industry severely and brought a rapid decline in prosperity. The cultivated classes – rich merchants, poets, administrators and historians – left the plateau to seek their fortunes in Muslim courts from Anatolia to Bengal. They took with them their language, Persian, and their high levels of skill in government.[35]

Like cotton, sugar has also changed the face of human history. From its early mass production in places like Tawahin as-Sukka in the eleventh-century Jordan Valley, it was to influence the formation of colonies, the development of slavery, and the composition of peoples. From the eighteenth century it has had a substantial impact on diet particularly in the West. In consequence it keeps tens of thousands of dentists in business. Today the average human being consumes 24 kg of sugar a year. In richer societies it is recognised to be a growing general health hazard.[36]

Coffee emerged from Sufi khanqahs (monasteries) in fifteenth-century Yemen to become the top agricultural export of twelve countries today and the world's seventh largest legal agricultural export by value. It has been prohibited in Muslim societies from time to time but it is also the first drink one might offer a guest in contemporary Arabia. Through much of the world it helps to sustain sociability. There is no agreement as to whether its health effects are positive or negative.[37]

Tobacco, as we know, is acknowledged to be a major health hazard, the direct cause of at least five million deaths a year and a contributing factor to many others. Tobacco first entered the wider world from the Americas in the early seventeenth century; it was not accepted without challenge in either the Muslim or the Western world.[38] The cultivation of tobacco is harmful to the environment in which it is produced. It also tends to make profits for large corporations rather than the small producer. Its adoption by different classes and by different genders across the world over the past two hundred years can be seen as a marker of social, economic and cultural change. Today, consumption is falling in the Western world while it rapidly increases in the developing world.[39]

The cultivation of opium poppies for anaesthetic and occasionally ritual purposes goes back at least to Neolithic times. Only in the nineteenth century was it overtaken for medical purposes by morphine and its derivative forms. Mughal emperors drank opium compounds for pleasure; they used the drink in concentrated form to execute princes without shedding blood. During the seventeenth century smoking opium with tobacco became a recreation in China. Chinese consumption led to a massive expansion of opium production in India and its trade to China, as has been so wonderfully imagined in two recent novels by Amitav Ghosh.[40] Opium thus became the cause of wars between Britain and China. In its refined form as heroin it has been entangled with wars in its three main centres of production – Mexico, Southeast Asia's 'Golden Triangle' and Afghanistan/Pakistan. Arguably heroin production in the last region has always been a greater threat to the West than the Taliban and al-Qa'ida.[41]

Nothing matches the production and consumption of oil and oil products for their impact on the Islamic world in particular and the world in general. Oil has dictated, and still dictates, the drawing of territorial boundaries; it fosters lopsided economic development; it tends to favour dictatorships over democracy; it leads to invasions and declarations of war. But for the entanglement of oil and oil products with the workings of all world economies, we would not be consuming this carbon resource to a level that threatens the very existence of the earth as a human habitation. Oil is the greatest of the commodities that command our attention. But all six commodities that we have considered have had an impact on human history in their production and consumption which make them worthy of the attention of the global historian.

The 'Protestant Turn'

Let us consider a process of change widely experienced by humankind as it has moved into the modern era. This is the 'Protestant turn' in human piety. That 'turn' in Muslim religious piety has long been a source of fascination. Its origins lie deep in the Islamic past in the tensions between revelation and the magical practices of mysticism. These came to a head in the eighteenth century in the teaching of Muhammad ibn 'Abd al-Wahhab in Arabia and Shah Wali Allah in India. The new 'Protestant' understandings of Islam derived from these teachings spread throughout the Muslim world in the nineteenth and twentieth centuries as it became subject to Western power. Key features of this 'Protestant' turn were: a new focussing of the believer's attention on the Qur'an and Hadith; translation of these texts from Arabic into the languages of the Muslim world so that there could be meaningful engagement with them; attacks on all forms of magic, in particular the idea that there could be intercession for man on earth; and a stronger emphasis than before on the horrors of the Day of Judgement. The aim was to fashion, in a world where Muslims no longer held political power, the individual human conscience as the basis of a Muslim society. Each individual was to become an active force in creating a Muslim society; belief now meant a this-worldly piety of social action. From the nineteenth century to the present these elements can be seen at work in Muslim societies from Indonesia to Morocco.

Several significant outcomes flow from these moves towards a 'Protestant' piety. The new emphasis on conscience and personal responsibility led to changes in Muslim senses of the self which Charles Taylor, arguing from a European Christian perspective, has taught us to associate with modernity. There is self-instrumentality, the idea of the individual human being, male and female, as the active, creative, agent on earth. This was an idea prominent in the life and ideas of men such as Sayyid Ahmad Khan, founder of South Asia's Islamic modernist thought, and Muhammad Ilyas, founder of the Tablighi Jama'at, the Preaching Society. It was no less alive in those most influential Muslim thinkers of the twentieth century, Muhammad Iqbal of British India and 'Ali Shari'ati of Iran. With the idea of man as the active agent on earth there also came the idea of action as a form of self-affirmation. Man affirms and indeed empowers himself by increasingly fulfilling his human potential. Inevitably this leads to tension between human desire for personal fulfilment and society's concern that human desire should be kept focused on godly ends.[42]

The affirmation of the self leads to the affirmation of the ordinary things of the self which Taylor terms 'one of the most powerful ideas in modern civilisation', a process which can be seen most wonderfully and most humanly in the changing ways in which Muslims have come to write the life of the Prophet. The final theme in the new Muslim self is the growth of self-consciousness and the reflective habit. A willed Islam had to be a self-conscious one. It opened up an internal landscape where the battle of the pious for the good would take place.[43]

Alongside these new senses of the self, Islamic reform and its 'Protestant' turn undermined the old system of religious authority and opened the way to self-interpretation of the scriptures. Up to this point, as we have noted, religious authority rested with religious specialists, to whom knowledge had been passed down person-to-person through time and who monopolised interpretation. They transmitted knowledge to society more widely by their example, their edicts and their sermons. Reform with its insistence on personal engagement with scripture, with its translation of scripture into vernacular languages, with its strong support for adopting print, and its fashioning of the individual human conscience, began to change all this. Reform encouraged literacy, as did colonial governments to a lesser extent. Independent Muslim states in the second half of the twentieth century came to invest in literacy to the extent that in Southeast Asia it is in the high nineties among school-leaving cohorts. Over the past thirty years this has been followed in much of the Muslim world by a move towards mass higher education. These developments have largely destroyed the old forms of religious authority and opened the way to widespread self-interpretation. A brother- and sisterhood of all believers has begun to emerge. A major feature of the modern Muslim world is the scripture reading group in particular for women. No one now knows, it is frequently said, who speaks for Islam.[44]

A striking feature of the 'Protestant' turn is the way in which it has been carried forward in Muslim societies by rising social formations. Indeed, I would argue that this process in the twentieth century has represented a reform of Muslim society from below, some might even say a re-Islamisation. The context of this has been the presence of Western power with two key outcomes: the co-option of the elites of Muslim societies to serve Western political, economic and cultural purposes; and revolutionary economic and social change within Muslim societies with the formation of industrial, commercial, administrative and professional classes. 'Ulama' groups such as the Deobandis in India and the Muhammadiyya in Indonesia, Islamist parties such as the Muslim Brotherhood throughout the Arab world and the Jama'ati Islami throughout South Asia have found support in these social formations. As time has gone on they have tended to get the better of socialist and nationalist alternatives espoused by the elites. These 'ulama' and Islamist groups, with their support in the middle- and lower-middle social strata, are those challenging for power today, as they have done with success in Turkey and Indonesia, and as they are doing with rather less success amid the complexities of the Arab world. It is helpful to compare their rise with the outcomes of the industrial transformation of Britain in the eighteenth and nineteenth centuries; the emergence of new social groups, the association of these groups with nonconformity and Methodism, which came in part at least to be transferred politically into the politics of the Liberal and Labour parties.

You will gather from this that I am likely to see useful comparison between the European reformation and that currently taking place in the Muslim world. Certainly, Muhammad Iqbal saw things thus: 'We are today,' he declared in his *Reconstruction of Religious Thought in Islam*, 'passing through a period similar to that of the Protestant revolution in Europe . . .'[45] We should make this comparison in spite of the explicit disapproval of Marshall Hodgson.[46] This said, we do now know so much more of what has been happening than he did some fifty years or so ago. However, manifestations of the 'Protestant' turn do not end here. In the nineteenth and twentieth centuries we can see a similar shift towards a faith of personal responsibility and this-worldly action in the other great religions of South Asia. The Singh Sabhas of the Sikhs in the late nineteenth century drew on the example of this-worldly action of the early Gurus to make sure that all Sikhs had the knowledge and understanding to resist Christian and Hindu missionary activity.[47] Angarika Dharmapala's 'Protestant Buddhism' pioneered a new piety in which lay folk had access to religious texts, engaged in a faith of salvation, and expressed this new private internalised piety in a life of this-worldly asceticism.[48] A similar 'Protestant' turn can be seen in the shift in the focus of nineteenth-century Hinduism from social structure to the individual human being. There was a new emphasis on personal dharma and individual realisation. Individual Hindus had to take personal responsibility for their religion and culture, which no longer meant renunciation, but social involvement and social action.[49] In all these faiths, as well as Islam, it is possible to make a connection between their 'protestant' turn, their new this-worldliness and their pursuit of political power – even on occasion their use of violence.

This widespread 'Protestant' turn in the nineteenth century raises issues of origin and meaning. In the case of Islam, it derived from tensions long present in the faith which came to interact with the contexts of economic, social and ideological change presented by British India. Similar deep-rooted change exists in the case of Sikhism. In those of Hinduism and Buddhism, on the other hand, there do seem to have been specific and formative interactions with Protestant Christian missionaries which, along with the context of British India, helped fashion the new piety.

All these 'Protestant' manifestations of piety represent some of the modernities of India's religions. In the case of the 'protestant' piety represented by reform throughout the Muslim world, it is now a commonplace of scholarship to regard it as a profoundly modern , being both fashioned by modernity as it also strives to shape it, protesting against the outcomes of enlightenment rationalism. It seeks to assert a moral community – transcendent and with moral absolutes – in order to confront the uncertainties and relativism of our time. In an excellent recent work Roxanne Euben has shown how much Western social theorists from Hannah Arendt to Charles Taylor have to share with the leading theorists of Islamism, Sayyid Qutb and Mawlana Mawdudi.[50]

The 'Protestant' turn in human piety, which began just under five hundred years ago, and which has gained considerable pace over the past two hundred years, as it has mingled with worldwide economic and social change, is a great global development – a global event – one worthy of the serious attention of the global historian.

****

These areas have come to mind in addressing future directions in global history from an Islamic angle: the role of Muslim power and Islamic civilisation itself as a factor in global history; the continuing significance of the connectedness of the Muslim world in supporting its role in global history; the shared worlds of stories and storytelling and astrology and astronomy; the impact of the production and consumption of major commodities; and the significance of the 'Protestant' turn in major world religions. There are other global issues worthy of exploration from an Islamic angle: the great move against hierarchy and patriarchy and towards equality for all human beings, surely one of the great global movements of recent times; and the issue of establishing authority (religious or civilisational) in conditions of imperialism – a problem which has beset the Muslim world over the past two hundred years and which may afflict all societies in a globalising era. There are other subjects: global history from an Islamic angle is rich in possibilities.

Notes

1. Freda Harcourt and Francis Robinson, *Twentieth-Century World History: A Select Bibliography* (London: Croom Helm, 1979).
2. A typical product of this interest is: Francis Robinson, *The 'Ulama' of Farangi Mahall and Islamic Culture in South Asia* (Delhi: Permanent Black, 2001).
3. See Francis Robinson, *Atlas of the Islamic World since 1500* (Oxford: Phaidon, 1982), and Francis Robinson, ed., *The Cambridge Illustrated History of the Islamic World* (Cambridge: Cambridge University Press, 1996).
4. Marshall G.S. Hodgson, *The Venture of Islam: Conscience and History in a World Civilisation*, 3 vols (Chicago: University of Chicago Press, 1974).
5. S.P. Huntington, *The Clash of Civilisations and the Remaking of World Order* (New York: Simon and Schuster, 1996).
6. Halford Mackinder, 'The Geographical Pivot of History', *The Geographical Journal*, 1904, 23, pp. 421–37.
7. For the role of these relationships in the making of Muslim societies, see Francis Robinson, 'Knowledge, its Transmission and the Making

of Muslim Societies' in Francis Robinson, ed., *Cambridge Illustrated History of the Islamic World* (Cambridge: Cambridge University Press, 1996), pp. 208–49.

8. I.E. Binbas, 'Sharaf al-Din 'Ali Yazdi (ca 770s–858/ca. 1370s–1454): Prophecy, Politics and Historiography in Late Medieval Islamic Historiography' (Ph.D. Diss.: The University of Chicago, 2009), pp. 76–107.

9. A.H. Johns, 'Friends in Grace: Ibrahim al-Kurani and Abd al-Ra'uf al-Singkili', in S. Udin ed., *Spectrum: Essays Presented to Sutan Takdir Alisjahbana* (Jakarta: Dian Rakyat, 1978).

10. John O. Voll, 'Linking Groups in the Networks of Eighteenth-Century Revivalist Scholars: The Mizjaji Family in Yemen', in Nehemia Levtzion and John O. Voll, eds, *Eighteenth-Century Renewal and Reform in Islam* (Syracuse NY: Syracuse University Press, 1987), pp. 69–92.

11. *Ibid.,* and Stefan Reichmuth, 'Murtada al-Zabidi (1732–91) and the Africans: Islamic Discourse and Scholarly Networks in the Late Eighteenth Century', in Scott S. Reese (ed.), *The Transmission of Learning in Islamic Africa* (Leiden: Brill, 2004), pp. 121–53.

12. In the midst of a spiritual crisis in the years after the defeat of the Ottoman Empire in World War One, Sirhindi's *Maktubat* showed him that his one true guide was the Qur'an. Sukran Vahide, Ibrahim M. Abu-Rabi' ed, *Islam in Modern Turkey: An Intellectual Biography of Bediuzzaman Said Nursi* (Albany: State University of New York Press, 2005), pp. 165–7.

13. ESI, 'Islamic Calvinists: Change and Conservatism in Central Anatolia', Berlin/Istanbul, 19 September 2005, www.esiweb.org; M. Hakan Yavuz, *Islamic Political Identity in Turkey* (NewYork: Oxford University Press, 2003).

14. Azyumardi Azra, *The Origins of Islamic Reformism in Southeast Asia: Networks of Malay-Indonesian and Middle East 'Ulama' in the Seventeenth and Eighteenth Centuries* (Crows Nest NSU: Allen & Unwin, 2004).

15. Francis Robinson, 'The British Empire and the Muslim World', in Judith Brown and Wm. Roger Louis, eds, *The Oxford History of the British Empire: Volume IV, The Twentieth Century* (Oxford: Oxford University Press, 1999), pp. 398–420.

16. Humayun Ansari, 'Islam in the West', in Francis Robinson, ed., *The Islamic World in the Age of Western Dominance*; M. Cook ed., *New Cambridge History of Islam* (Cambridge: Cambridge University Press, 2010), vol. 5, pp. 686–716.

17. Robert Rozehnal, *Islamic Sufism Unbound: Politics and Piety in Twenty-First Century Pakistan* (Houndmills, Basingstoke: Palgrave Macmillan, 2007), pp. 134–6ff.; Nile Green, *Bombay Islam: The Religious Economy of the West Indian Ocean 1840–1915* (Cambridge: Cambridge University Press, 2011), pp. 208–34; Pnina Werbner, *Pilgrims of Love: The Anthropology of a Global Sufi Cult* (London: C. Hurst & Co, 2003), pp. 30–60.
18. Stephane A. Dudoignon, *Voyage au pays des Baloutches (Iran oriental, an XVIII–XXI siècle-de la Republique Islamique)* (Paris: Editions Cartouche, 2009); Sana Haroon, 'The Rise of Deobandi Islam in the North-West Frontier Province and its Implication in Colonial India and Pakistan 1914–1996', *Journal of the Royal Asiatic Society* 18, 1, January 2008, pp. 47–70.
19. See Nicholas Noe, ed., *Voice of Hezbollah: The Statements of Sayyed Hassan Nasrallah* (London & New York: Verso, 2007), especially the introduction by Nicholas Blanford.
20. For an overall argument about modern connectedness, see Francis Robinson, 'The Islamic World from World System to Religious International', in Abigail Green and Vincent Viane (eds), *Religious Internationals in the Modern World: Globalization and Faith Communities since 1750* (Houndmills, Basingstoke: Palgrave Macmillan, 2012), pp. 111–35.
21. M.L. West, *The East Face of Helicon: West Asiatic Elements in Greek Poetry and Myth* (Oxford: Clarendon Press, 1997).
22. 'Al-Khadir', C.E. Bosworth *et al.* (eds), *The Encyclopaedia of Islam*, 2nd ed., vol. IV (Leiden: Brill, 1978), pp. 902–5.
23. Fakhraddin Gorgani, Dick Davis (trans. and intro.), *Vis & Ramin* (Washington DC: Mage Publishers, 2007), pp. viii–xl.
24. Wendy Doniger (ed.), *The Magic Doe: Qutban Suhravardi's Mirigavati, A New Translation by Aditya Behl* (New York: Oxford University Press, 2012), especially Behl's Introduction, pp. 9–38.
25. Musharraf Ali Farooqi (trans.), and Hamid Dabashi (intro.), Ghalib Lakhnavi and Abdullah Bilgrami, *The Adventures of Amir Hamza: Lord of the Auspicious Planetary Conjunction* (New York: Modern Library, 2007).
26. Robert Irwin, *The Arabian Nights: A Companion* (London: Allen Lane, 1994).
27. Christopher Shackle, 'The Story of Sayf al-Muluk in South Asia', *Journal of the Royal Asiatic Society,* Series 3, 17, 2, 2007, pp. 115–29.

28. Peter Whitfield, *Astrology, a History* (London: The British Library, 2001), pp. 9–187.
29. Ibid., p. 69.
30. Ibid., pp. 81–2, 94.
31. Ibid., pp. 188–202.
32. For instance, for an explanation of the light symbolism on Humayun's tomb in Delhi, see Glenn D. Lowry, 'Humayun's Tomb: Form, Function and Meaning in Early Mughal Architecture', *Muqarnas*, 4, 1987, pp. 133–48; and for the astrological basis for the design of the shrine at Uchch, Pakistan, see Hasan Ali Khan, 'Shia-Ismaili Motifs in the Sufi Architecture of the Indus Valley AD 1200–1500' (Ph.D. Diss., School of Oriental and African Studies, University of London, 2009).
33. See, for instance, A. Azfar Moin, *The Millennial Sovereign: Sacred Kingship and Sainthood in Islam* (New York: Columbia University Press, 2012)
34. Serge Gruzinski, *What Time is it There? America and Islam at the Dawn of Modern Times* (London: Polity Press, 2010).
35. Richard W. Bulliet, *Cotton, Climate, and Camels in Early Islamic Iran: A Moment in World History* (New York: Columbia University Press, 2009).
36. Graham Chandler, 'Sugar Please', *Saudi Aramco World*, 83, 4, July/August 2012, pp. 36–43; Jelle Bruinsma, ed., *World Agriculture Towards 2015/2030: An FAO Perspective* (London: Earthscan Publications, 2003), p. 119.
37. Ralph S. Hattox, *Coffee and Coffeehouses: The Origins of a Social Beverage in the Medieval Near East* (Seattle: University of Washington Press, 1985); Bennett Alan Weinberg and Bonnie K. Bealer, *The World of Caffeine: The Science and Culture of the World's Most Popular Drug* (London: Routledge, 2002), pp. 267–316.
38. Such was the debate on the acceptability of smoking in the Ottoman Empire that the great scholar of Damascus, 'Abd al-Ghani Nabulusi, felt impelled in 1681 to write a long treatise on the subject to say that although he did not like the practice it was perfectly legal. Samer Akkach, *Letters of a Sufi Scholar: The Correspondence of 'Abd al-Ghani al-Nabulusi (1641–1731)*, pp. 105–8.
39. Eric Burns, *The Smoke of the Gods: A Social History of Tobacco* (Philadelphia: Temple University Press, 2007).
40. Amitav Ghosh, *Sea of Poppies* (London: John Murray, 2008); *River of Smoke: A Novel* (London: Penguin Group, 2011).

41. P-A. Chouvy, *Opium: Uncovering the Politics of the Poppy* (Cambridge Mass: Harvard University Press, 2010).
42. Francis Robinson, 'Religious Change and the Self in Muslim South Asia since 1800', in Francis Robinson, *Islam and Muslim History in South Asia* (Delhi: Oxford University Press, 2000), pp. 105–21.
43. Ibid.
44. Francis Robinson, 'Crisis of Authority: Crisis of Islam?' *Journal of the Royal Asiatic Society*, 3rd series, 19, 3, pp. 339–54.
45. Muhammad Iqbal, *The Reconstruction of Religious Thought in Islam* (Lahore: Sh. Muhammad Ashraf, 1975), p. 163.
46. Marshall G.S. Hodgson, *Rethinking World History: Essays on Europe, Islam, and World History*, edited by Edmund Burke III (Cambridge: Cambridge University Press, 1993).
47. T.N. Madan, *Secularism and Fundamentalism in India: Modern Myths and Locked Minds* (Delhi: Oxford University Press, 1997), p. 187.
48. T. Brekke, *Makers of Modern Indian Religion in the Late Nineteenth Century* (Oxford: Clarendon Press, 2002), pp. 63–115.
49. Ibid., pp. 13–62; Madan, *Secularism*, pp. 203–32.
50. Francis Robinson, 'Islamic Reform and Modernities in South Asia', *Modern Asian Studies*, 42, 2/3, 2008, pp. 259–81.

3

Education in the Muslim World to the End of the Eighteenth Century

THE ENGLISH TERM 'knowledge', Franz Rosenthal reminds us, does not fully convey the 'factual and emotional' weight of the Arabic 'ilm. '*Ilm*, he continues, 'is one of those concepts which have dominated Islam and given Muslim civilisation its distinctive shape and complexion'.[1] The central role of knowledge, of course, flows from the importance of making Islamic civilisation's greatest treasures, the Qur'an and Hadith, live and work in each day, each year and each generation of Muslim life. There is no part of Muslim life, Rosenthal continues, 'that remained untouched by the all-pervasive attitude toward 'knowledge' something of supreme value for the Muslim being. *'Ilm* is Islam even if the theologians have been hesitant to accept the technical correctness of this equation.[2] Without knowledge there could be no salvation.

It was for this reason that the famous treatise on teaching and learning by the thirteenth-century scholar al-Zarnuji made the pursuit of learning a requirement for all Muslims, male and female.[3] They were to seek knowledge, moreover, as the oft-repeated tradition stated 'even if it be in China'.[4] This was, furthermore, an activity that should consume them from the cradle to the grave, so al-Zarnuji (d. 602/1223) tells the story of Muhammad ibn al-Hasan (d. 179/795), who appeared to a believer in a dream to say that he had been so absorbed in thinking about the manumission of slaves that he had not noticed his own death.[5] Such was the emphasis on learning that traditions exalting the superiority of learning over prayer, or the ink of the scholar over the blood of the martyr, were frequently quoted. The impact of learning, as well as the esteem in which it was held, was so emphatic that the thirteenth-century Baghdadi scholar 'Abd al-Latif (d. 620/1231) in his advice to students declared:

> Know that learning leaves a trail and a scent proclaiming its possessor: a ray of light and brightness shining on him, pointing him out, like the musk merchant whose location cannot be hidden, nor his wares unknown.[6]

This said, it was understood that a Muslim's learning should be in accordance with his status in the world. Every believer should know the requirements of the five pillars of Islam. Beyond this, believers should know enough to conduct their occupations and professions lawfully in the sight of God.[7] Nevertheless, there was a predilection to place a high value on achievement in learning, and unsurprisingly the learned gave it the highest value. Man, declared Ibn Khaldun (d. 808/1406), 'reaches perfection of his form through knowledge'.[8]

By the same token Muslim societies accorded scholars great honour. They were, after all, the guardians in their time, and the transmitters to future generations, of the central messages that helped to mould Muslim societies. They were often referred to as the 'heirs to the Prophets'. 'Kings are the rulers of people', went one oft-quoted tradition, 'but scholars are the rulers of kings'.[9] In their role as teachers – and there were few scholars who did not teach – students were to esteem and venerate them as they were their own fathers:

> In venerating the teacher [among other things it is necessary to avoid] walking in front of him or sitting in his place. Also, one should not begin speaking in his presence without his permission, and then

one should not speak to any great extent before him. One should not ask him any [question] when he is weary. One should observe the correct time . . . In short one should seek his approval, avoid his resentment, and obey his commands in those things which are not sinful in the eyes of God.[10]

This respect for the teacher as the transmitter of the central messages of Islam was typical of Muslim societies down to the twentieth century.

With this respect went an expectation of the highest standards of behaviour. In his *Ihya*, al-Ghazali (d. 505/111) sets out 'the signs of the learned man of the hereafter'; he focuses on the next world rather than this; he practises what he preaches; he fosters piety; he avoids luxury in food and dress; he shuns the powerful; he is deliberate and careful in giving his opinion; he is sincere, humble, avoids innovation and so on.[11] But scholars, being no more than human, found it difficult to sustain these high ideals. There was a constant stream of criticism of those who fell short of the ideal. Al-Ghazali himself was deeply critical of the scholars of his day, who, out of self-interest, placed their weight behind government decrees, or who, as 'prattling wearers of flowing robes', became obsessed by the minutiae of law at the cost of the true meaning of the Qur'an.[12] Indeed, al-Ghazali's life itself, as depicted in his autobiography *al-Munqidh min al-dalal* (The Deliverance from Error), formed a journey in which he came to realise the worthlessness of worldly advancement as compared with growth in spiritual understanding.[13] Shaykh Sa'di Shirazi's (d. 691/1292) *Gulistan*, which was used in schools wherever Persian was spoken from Istanbul to Bengal, and from Central Asia to East Africa, reveals a sharp nose for the hypocrisy of the learned, whether it was the teacher who did not practise what he taught, or the notorious qadi of Hamadhan who was found stupefied with drink, in bed with a boy.[14] Such was the sartorial splendour of the 'ulama' in Mamluk Egypt, in particular their wearing of outsize turbans, that the streetplayers of Cairo would perform a satire called 'The Manner of the Judge' in which the scholarly interpreters of the shari'a were lampooned, parading in outsize turbans, sleeves and long scarves.[15]

The Fields of Knowledge

Throughout the middle period of Islamic history knowledge tended to be divided into two broad fields: the 'ulum naqliyya, the transmitted or traditional sciences, all of which owed their existence to God's revelation to man through Muhammad, and the 'ulum 'aqliyya, the rational sciences, all of which were derived from man's capacity to think and in which he was guided by his human perceptions. These might equally be referred to as Greek, foreign or ancient sciences. This was how Khwarizmi (fl. 364–77/975–87) divided knowledge in the fourth/tenth century.[16] It is how Ibn Khaldun described it in the eighth/fourteenth century.[17] It was, moreover, the classic division of knowledge in the academic curricula developed under the Ottomans, Safawids and Mughals.[18] In these curricula the subjects associated with adab, the literary arts, were more often than not made supportive of the traditional sciences.[19] Nevertheless, in the fourth/tenth century Ibn al-Nadim (d. 389/995) and in the fifth/eleventh Ibn Butlan (d. 485/1066) identified the literary arts as a separate field; and so, for expository purposes, shall we.[20]

In his *Muqaddima*, Ibn Khaldun lists the subjects that make up his two main fields of knowledge. In the traditional sciences the first, of course, was the Qur'an; the seven established ways of reading it; and the forms of Qur'an commentary (tafsir). The second related to Hadith, the systems for establishing sound transmission and the great collections of traditions, of which al-Bukhari's *Sahih* held the highest rank. This was followed by jurisprudence (fiqh), the classification of the laws of God, as derived from the Qur'an and the traditions, including especial attention to the laws of inheritance. There followed the principles of jurisprudence (usul al-fiqh), the disciplines by which jurists and scholars reached decisions on matters of law plus the forms of disputation that lay at the core of legal studies. Speculative theology (kalam) was also included, in spite of the dangers to orthodoxy it might represent, because the skills the discipline developed were crucial to defending articles of faith and to refuting the claims of innovators.[21] The final major subject in the field was Sufism (tasawwuf), the approach of which 'is based upon constant application to divine worship, complete devotion to God, aversion to false splendour of the world, abstinence from the pleasure, property, and position to which the great mass aspires, and retirement from the world into solitude for divine worship'.[22] This had been the very particular experience of al-Ghazali. It was also the personal achievement of al-Ghazali to bring orthodoxy and Sufism into close enough contact for the two sides to respect each other's positions, for the most part, in word and deed. This said, by Ibn Khaldun's time the emergence of the wujudi doctrines of Ibn al-'Arabi and the increasing manifestation of ecstatic practices was causing discomfort amongst jurists and muftis (experts in Islamic law who deliver legal opinions, fatawa).[23] It was a discomfort felt throughout the middle period of Islamic history, and much more so in recent times.

The rational sciences, according to Ibn Khaldun, were four in number. They were derived from the Greek works, the translation of which into Arabic began during the caliphate of Harun al-Rashid (r. 170–93/786–809) and continued to the end of the tenth century, and the impact of which produced a major intellectual awakening. The first was logic (mantiq), which protected 'the mind from error in the process of evolving unknown facts'.[24] Aristotle was the man who had systematised the subject and made it the first philosophical discipline. It was for this reason that he was called 'the First Teacher', and his book on logic 'The Text'.[25] Major commentaries and abridgements were written by al-Farabi (d. 339/950), Ibn Sina (d. 428/1037) and Ibn Rushd (d. 595/1196). The second area was physics (al-tabi'yyat), the elements perceived by the senses, minerals, plants and animals, plus the movements of the heavens. Two subsets of this subject were medicine, where Galen was the leading Greek authority and Ibn Khaldun acknowledged a host of Muslim physicians of 'surpassing skill'; and agriculture, which involved the cultivation and growth of plants through irrigation, proper treatment, improvement of the soil and so on.[26] Metaphysics ('ilm al-ilahiyyat) was the third major division, with all the dangers of uncontrolled philosophical speculation that went with it. Ibn Khaldun was clear about where its boundaries should be drawn: 'When the Lawgiver (Muhammad) guides us towards some perception, we must prefer that (perception) to our own perception.'[27] The fourth area was the mathematical sciences (ta'alim), which included geometry, arithmetic, astronomy and music – the theory of tones and their definition by numbers. A series of further subdivisions were recognised – for instance, the craft of calculation, algebra, business, arithmetic, the arithmetic of inheritance laws, spherical figures, conic sections, and mechanics, surveying, optics and astronomical tables.[28]

Scholars in the middle Islamic period differed over precisely what subjects constituted what has been termed adab humanism.[29] We shall follow the analysis of the leading scholar of this subject. Grammar was the most important part of adab studies. It was central to everything a scholar did in Arabic, from poetry through to the writing of formal documents and the making of speeches. But it was more than this; it was essential to maintaining the purity of the language of the Qur'an, and of understanding it and interpreting it.[30] Of course there were many maxims. 'Grammatical speech is the beauty of the lowly', went one, 'and solecism the blemish on the great'.[31] Poetry, with prose in close attendance, was the 'premier art of adab, as grammar is its premier instrument'.[32] It was the field of adab, moreover, in which literary production was more prolific than in almost all others combined. In a society in which capacity to fashion beautiful words was a central means of praise and persuasion no less than the command of a large stock of verse, and the capacity to deploy it in conversation to telling effect was the mark of a cultivated man. 'Poetry', declared Abu'l-'Abbas al-Nashi' (d. 293/906), 'is the bond of words, the rich ransom of humanism, the retaining wall of eloquence, the locus of skill, the range of the soul, the illustration of rhetoric'.[33] Eloquence, Makdisi tells us, was the most essential part of Arab humanism, 'the kernel and apex' of adab studies.[34] The spur, of course, was the Qur'an, which Muslims knew they could not emulate but which, nevertheless, made eloquence highly prized throughout the Muslim world. 'Learn how to speak eloquently', the caliph al-Ma'mun's prime minister told his son, 'for it is through speech that man is superior to all other animals; and the more skilful you are in speaking, the more worthy you are of humanity'.[35] There was the idea, moreover, that eloquence was less about decorative language than about the effective match of language and meaning. 'Eloquence', declared a tenth-century poet, 'consists in words reaching their meaning before travelling too long.'[36] Allied to eloquence was oratory, which might embrace all subjects and all occasions in Muslim public life, but which was always classically deployed in the khutba, or sermon, in Friday/congregational prayers. 'A good part of the affairs of religion', declared the eleventh-century scholar Abu Hilal al-'Askari (d. after 400/1009), 'fall to the lot of oratory: for oratory is that part of ritual prayer which is the pillar of religion and feast days, Fridays and the gatherings of the Faithful.'[37]

Yet another form of adab in which eloquence had its place was the art of letter writing. This was an essential tool of government and diplomacy no less than the means by which personal relationships were sustained across distances. Manuals of good practice were produced, and the many collections of model letters have been an important source for historians down to the present. History as akhbar-history, literary history, as opposed to ta'rikh, chronologically dated history, was a further dimension of adab, which reaches towards the historical novel and forms of biography.[38] Finally, there was the moral philosophy of adab, which was 'an eclectic combination of foreign and Islamic traditions'. These might embrace Persian moral thought and Greek philosophical ethics as well as the Qur'an and the sunna (the example of the Prophet Muhammad).[39] Moral philosophy became a particular feature of wa'z, the academic sermon, which might be given by an independent scholar in a range of contexts from mosque or madrasa through to his own home. In the eleventh and twelfth centuries wa'z became an important vehicle for the assertion of traditionalist understandings against those of the rationalists.[40]

The relationship between the traditional sciences and the other two is worthy of comment. The relationship with the rational sciences was never particularly smooth. Some scholars were always suspicious of an intellectual tradition whose sources lay outside Islamic history – which was not unreasonable, as few could forget the attempt of the rationalists in the third/ninth century to impose their understanding of revelation of the traditionalists. Endowments, moreover, establishing madrasas tended to exclude the teaching of rational subjects as inimical to Islam, although madrasa libraries might still contain their books.[41] On occasion hostility might go much further, as for instance, when the Ayyubid sultan al-Malik al-Kamil (r. 615–35/1218–38), forbade the 'ulama' of Damascus from teaching or studying any subject but the traditional sciences; students of the rational sciences were expelled.[42] This was an extreme action but evidence of the tension between the fields of knowledge frequently cropped up. It lay behind the great rivalry in Timur's court in Samarqand between Sa'ad al-Din Taftazani (d. 792/1389), who favoured the traditional sciences, and Sayyid Sharif al-Jurjani (d. 816/1413), who favoured the rational sciences.[43] In Timur's time it is generally thought that Jurjani had the upper hand, but the patronage of Timur's successor, Shah Rukh, in establishing a madrasa at Herat a few years later shifted the advantage back to Taftazani's position.[44] This tension also lay behind the debate at the end of the fifteenth century between Muhammad al-Maghili (d. 909/1503 or 910/1504) and al-Suyuti over the study of logic.[45] This said, teachers might give courses in both fields, while student patterns of learning often included subjects from the two fields as well.[46] As time went on the areas in which the rational sciences flourished most vigorously were Timurid Central Asia, Shi'ite Iran and Mughal northern India.

The relationship between the traditional sciences and adab studies was less fraught. A strong link between the two was sustained by the centrality, to the traditional sciences, of knowledge of Arabic and how to use it well. 'Whoever seeks to learn hadith without knowing grammar', went one tradition, 'is like a jackass whose feedbag has no oats.'[47] A second strong link was that the Qur'an itself was the foundation and inspiration of many adab disciplines. This is not to suggest, however, that the relationship was completely harmonious. The masters of hadith were not welcome among the humanists. 'Here come the bores', declared one poetry teacher as students of hadith joined his teaching circle.[48] Nevertheless, we can conclude with Makdisi that 'the ideal education was to master both worlds of learning, to be a scholar and a humanist, to combine the critical scholarship of the 'alim [religious scholar] and the urbane elegance and refinement, zarf, of the old humanist adib.'[49]

The Transmission of Knowledge

The transmission of knowledge was not, for the most part, a matter of formal institutional arrangements. It was an informal and intensely personal process between teacher and pupil – thus, when Muslims talked of the bringing of learning to a particular region, or its revival, they talked of the impact of individual scholars, as Ibn Khaldun did about the return of serious learning to northwest Africa in the thirteenth century;[50] as the Kano Chronicle described the impact of al-Maghili on the city at the end of the fifteenth century,[51] and the Muslims of Madras in 1941 described the impact of Bahr al-'Ulum Farangi Mahalli (d. 1225/1810) on southern India at the end of the eighteenth.[52] Because the personal relationship was so important, it made the student's choice of teacher critical. He was urged to take time over the business and consider very carefully the man's learning, piety and age.[53] The personal element, moreover, was underlined by the great biographical dictionaries which recorded with whom a student studies and what he studied, but little if anything about where he studied. The quality of an education 'was judged', Berkey tells us, 'not on *loci* but on *personae*.[54]

The personal nature of the transmission of knowledge was emphasised by the halqa, or study circle, in which teaching took place, and the etiquette that governed its proceedings. Such circles might operate in a variety of environments, as the teacher found convenient: in a mosque, private house, shop or madrasa; or perhaps under a tree or on a river bank. The teacher decided who was to be admitted to the circle, when it would meet, as well as the sequence of subjects and the methods of instruction. Teaching began and ended with prayers. The teacher would sit on a cushion or a chair with his back to a wall or a pillar, and his students would sit cross-legged in a semi-circle before him. As the student improved in his studies he was invited to sit closer to the teacher; thus biographies might state of an able student that the teacher 'brought the student close to him'.[55] Biographical dictionaries used the term suhba, 'companionship' or 'discipleship', to describe the relationship between the teacher and his closest students. Derived from the days of the Prophet and his Companions, it implied, as Ephrat tells us, 'an extremely close personal and intellectual relationship between teacher and student, one fostered over the course of many years'.[56] The world of 'ilm from the Maghrib to South East Asia was held together by tens of thousands of such relationships.

The personal nature of the teacher–student relationship was further expressed in the precise method of transmitting knowledge. Oral, person-to-person transmission was greatly preferred to private study. 'The Qur'an', declared Ibn Khaldun in discussing the art of teaching, 'has been the basis of instruction, the foundation of all habits that may be acquired later on.'[57] The Qur'an, the recitation, was realised and received as divine, by being read out aloud. It was always transmitted orally. It was thus that the Prophet had transmitted the message he received, it was as an aid to memory and oral transmission. Learning the Qur'an was the first task of young Muslim boys and girls, and in this context again it was orally transmitted. The usual method was that each day the teacher would dictate some verses, which the students would write on their slates, or have written for them, and they spent the rest of the day learning them. Those who were able to recite them successfully the next day, in addition to what had been recently transmitted, would have fresh verses dictated to them.

Oral transmission in the early Islamic centuries had a similar role to play in the publication of a book. Its writing down, like that of the Qur'an, was merely an aid to oral publication. The author would dictate his first draft either from memory or from his own notes; the copyist would then read it back to him. Publication would then take place through the copyist reading the text to the author in public, usually in a mosque. During the process the author might make additions and emendations, and several readings might be required before it was given his authorisation. This was known as his ijaza, which meant 'to make lawful'. Thus, the author gave permission for the work 'to be transmitted from him'. Further copies had real authority only when they had been read back to the author and approved.[58]

A teacher would transmit one of the great texts of Islamic education in a similar way. He would dictate the book to his students, who might write it down, but almost certainly would commit it to memory – in time such pedagogical texts came to be written in rhyme to help the memory. Subsequently there might be an explanation of the text, depending on its nature. The completion of the study of the book would involve a recitation of the text with an explanation. If this was done to the teacher's satisfaction, the student would be given an ijaza, a licence to transmit that text, which has been well described by Berkey as 'a personal authority' over the text.[59] On that ijaza would be the names of all those who had transmitted the text, going back to the original author. The pupil was left in no doubt that he was now the trustee of knowledge transmitted from person to person from the past.

It might be asked why person-to-person transmission of knowledge, involving recitation out aloud, should persist in a society where scholars were highly proficient in reading and writing, paper was plentiful and book production a major activity. The problem was that there was scepticism about the written word, the understandable scepticism of an oral society, in which an individual might be in the most literal sense bahr al-'ulum, an ocean of knowledge. 'Language', declares Ibn Khaldun, 'is merely the interpretation of ideas that are in the mind.' Oral expression was crucial to extracting the meaning from the language. The study of books and written materials placed a veil between representation and meaning; it 'separates handwriting and the form of letters found in writing from the spoken words found in the imagination.'[60] To understand words properly the student had to read them out aloud. As the Qur'an gained full realisation only in being recited out aloud, so too did the academic book only give of its full meaning to the student by being read, or recited, aloud. Truth, it was felt, was more likely to be transmitted in speech than in writing. The halqa could be a very noisy affair.

The emphasis on person-to-person transmission had at least two important consequences for the Muslim world. One was that most scholars travelled widely so that they could receive knowledge in person. The custom had begun with the early collection of hadith. It was vigorously continued by later scholars, spurred by a real desire for truth but not unaware of the increase in authority that such journeys might bring. Of course, the search for knowledge came in time to be combined with that for academic position. So 'Abd al-Latif moved from Baghdad to Mosul, from place to place in Anatolia, to Cairo twice, to Damascus twice, to Jerusalem twice and to Aleppo twice. The Spanish scholar-mystic Ibn al-'Arabi (d. 638/2140) travelled from Murcia to Seville, Tunis, Fez, Cordoba, Almeria, to Tunis again, twice each to Cairo, Jerusalem, Mecca and Baghdad, and to Mosul, Malatya, Sivas, Konya and Damascus. So too, the remarkable writer of pedagogical texts, Sayyid Sharif al-Jurjani, travelled from Taju by the Caspian to Herat, Karaman, Alexandria, Constantinople, Shiraz and to Samarqand, where he was to become a great figure at Timur's court. When a scholar could not get knowledge from an author in person, he strove to get it from a scholar whose isnad, or chain of transmission from the original author, was thought to be the most reliable.

The second consequence of person-to-person transmission, which flowed from the first, was that the Muslim world came to be covered by networks of teacher–student connections. From the eleventh century Baghdad found itself at the centre of such a network.[61] From the fifteenth century Timbuktu in West Africa was also such a centre.[62] Cairo was always a great centre, a role exemplified in the fifteenth century by the endowment deeds of several of its large madrasas which enabled students to visit their families all over the world.[63] An ijaza given by the Egyptian polymath al-Sakhawi (d. 902/1497) to Ibn al-Hishi (b. 848/1444) in Mecca is equally revealing of a truly cosmopolitan world of scholarship.[64] It is thus that we can begin to see how 'ilm, and its person-to-person transmission across the Muslim world, was one of the key links that held this world together.

The deeply personal nature of this person-to-person transmission is brought home by the wording, and perhaps the underlying humour, of the following ijaza bestowed by 'Izz al-Din ibn Jama'a (d. 819/1416):

> The student mentioned herein presented before me also in a good, precise, orderly, masterful, and excellent manner, a presentation of one whose memorisation is perfect, whose pronunciation is adorned

by excellent performance, and whose fortune has been bestowed abundantly by the spring of divine concern. He raced through the text like a fleet courser in a lion-infested plain . . . I hereby permit him to transmit from me the above-mentioned book, all that is permitted for me to transmit, and all that may be transmitted from me, of my own writings and those of others, in poetry and prose, in the transmitted, rational, and traditional sciences, according to the conditions recognised by the specialists in transmission.[65]

Among the aids to learning – and this went for all fields of knowledge – were memory, disputation and notetaking. Memory, as the support merely of the transmission of knowledge, was the attribute of the ordinary scholar. Above this level, for the humanist and scholastic, it was the support for creativity and understanding, and finally at the forefront of knowledge it might be the basis of ijtihad, producing one's own ideas.[66] The biographical dictionaries are full of stories, doubtless some exaggerated, of prodigious feats of memory, of whole libraries restored from memory after a fire.[67] Moreover, men literally dipped into the memory of great scholars. 'When we needed knowledge', one wrote, 'we ladled from his ocean what was not to be had in books.'[68] The transmission of knowledge was only really valued from those who produced it from memory.[69] In consequence the educational guides spoke of those things that helped memory: for instance, working early in the morning; avoiding heavy foods, and places where one might be distracted, and those things that hindered it, for instance, 'eating fresh coriander, acid apples and beholding a man crucified.'[70] For all its centrality memorisation was not an end in itself. Real learning also meant understanding, being able to use critically the materials memorised and apply them to academic problems. 'Memorizing two words is better than hearing two pages', went one aphorism, 'but understanding two words is better than memorizing two pages.'[71]

Forms of instructive conversation (mudhakara), and the notebook (daftar) were further aids to memory. At one level such conversations might involve students drilling or quizzing each other after a lesson. At another level this conversation might develop into a munazara, or formal disputation, over a point of grammar perhaps, or drawing on verse to debate a particular theme. At the apex of education, for a scholar about to emerge as a professor of law, mastery of disputation was the final stage. Great debates had all the thrills, in performance and in recollection, of boxing matches.[72] Taking notes was crucial to prompt the memory and help preserve undistorted what had been transmitted. Scholars jealously guarded their notebooks: al-Ghazali told a robber that he could take everything but his notebooks. 'My boon companion is my cat', declared the adab scholar Ibn Faris (d. 395/1005), 'my notebook, the intimate of my soul.'[73]

The enormous emphasis on person-to-person transmission of knowledge should not lead us to think that self-teaching did not take place. It tended not to happen in the traditional sciences, where issues of authority were crucial and where teachers and students were often supported by institutional stipends and scholarships. But in the rational sciences and in adab studies self-teaching was not uncommon. This is evident from the numbers of books written specifically for the autodidact – for instance, Khwarizmi's *Miftah al-'ulum* (Keys to the Sciences), which covered all the main fields of knowledge, or Ibn Hindu's (d. 410/1019) *Miftah al-tibb* (The Key to Medicine). Some scholars admitted to teaching themselves, so Ibn Sina (d. 428/1037) taught himself medicine as a teenager and Fakhr al-din Razi (d. 606/1209) taught himself the rational sciences while holding a position in a college of law. This said, the enduring preference was, whatever the subject, that the student should learn from a teacher. 'I command you not to learn your sciences from books unaided', 'Abd al-Latif of Baghdad advised his students, 'even though you may trust your ability to understand.'[74]

The ijaza the student received after successfully completing the learning of a book at the feet of his teacher was a potent symbol of authority. As we have noted, it gave the student authority over a text – over part of the knowledge that helped to shape Islamic civilisation. In a specific social environment it was a symbol of the authority he derived from a close bond to a more senior scholar. It also enabled him to access some of the authority of those mentioned in the ijaza's isnad, back to the original author of the book. It was also a form of authority that existed outside, and often opposed to, political power. Arguably in its supreme form it was not a licence to transmit knowledge but the ijazat al-tadris wa'l-ifta', the authorisation to teach law and issue legal opinions, that Makdisi has argued was the origin of the European *licentia docendi*.[75] The force of the ijaza, in whatever form, as a source of authority was evident in medieval Muslim society. So, the great Egyptian scholar Ibn Suyuti refused to transmit books in a sphere in which he was an acknowledged expert because he had taught himself and therefore could not do so on the authority of a teacher.[76] Scholars went to great lengths to compile collective biographies indicating the authority that scholars in a family, a school of law or a place had gathered through their ijazas. And so, too, in the ultimate accolade the prestige of the practice was underlined in its abuse as ijazas came to be given without learning the text, or to children who were too young to understand what was going on, or they were just requested by letter.[77]

Madrasas and Education

The informality and non-institutional nature of the transmission of knowledge raises the issue of the purpose and function of the madrasa, the foundation classically associated with Islamic secondary/higher education. The term itself was derived from the second form of the verb darrasa, which, used without a complement, means 'to teach law', giving rise to the term dars, a lecture on law, and mudarris, a professor of law: a madrasa was a school or college in which law was the main subject.[78] From the tenth century purpose-built madrasas began to be founded. In time they came to embrace a growing range of provision: stipends for staff; scholarships for students; cells for teachers and students; a residence, perhaps for the founder's family; a mosque; and a mausoleum where the founder's family might be buried. These foundations began in Khurasan and from the eleventh century spread westward. In 1067, the Saljuq vizier Nizam al-Mulk (d. 485/1092) founded his famed Nizamiyya madrasa in Baghdad, where al-Ghazali was to hold a professorship. Down to the end of the twelfth century this was followed by the founding of a further twenty-three madrasas.[79] By the 1090s the institution reached Damascus, which had fifty-three madrasas by 1261, and in Cairo by the fifteenth century, there were more than seventy-three. The first madrasa was founded in Mecca in 1175, in Delhi in the early thirteenth century, and in Tunis in 1252.[80] By this time, as Berkey suggests, the madrasa 'had become perhaps the most characteristic institution of the medieval Near Eastern urban landscape'.[81]

The evolution of the madrasa did not stop at this point. Indeed, from the thirteenth through to the fifteenth centuries, madrasa foundations came to be just part of what has been termed an 'educational-charitable complex'. One of the first of these was completed in 1267–8 by Muhammad Juwayni (d. 681/1283), the vizier of the Ilkhan Hulegu. Built in Yazd, it comprised a mosque, a madrasa, a hospital, a pharmacy and a madhouse; it was established as one institution by its founding endowment.[82] This form, which might also embrace a library, a Sufi convent, an orphanage, an observatory and a hostel for travellers, spread across Iraq and Iran, reaching a peak in Timurid Khurasan and Transoxania. Notable examples were that of Ulugh Beg (r. 851–3/1447–9) in Samarqand, which it is said had 10,000 registered students, 500 of them in mathematics,[83] and that of vizier Mir 'Ali Shir Nawa'i (d. 906/1500), the Ikhlasiyya in Herat, which embraced a wide range of functions and, according to Khwandamir (d. 940/1534 or 943/1537), fed 1,000 people a day.[84] The idea of the educational-charitable complex also spread to Mamluk Syria and Egypt. Ten years after the inauguration of Juwayni's complex in Yazd, the tomb of the Mamluk sultan Baybars al-Malik al-Zahir (r. 658–76/1260–77) was transformed in this fashion. Over fifty years later this was followed by the largest such development in Cairo, the mausoleum complex of Sultan al-Nasir al-Hasan (r. 748–52/1347–51), which had provision for among other things 120 Qur'an readers and 506 students.[85] Such was the fashion for these complexes that earlier foundations began to transform themselves in their image.[86]

There was a view that the spread of madrasas was designed to fashion the ideological forces that made the eleventh-century 'Sunni revival' which ended a period of Shi'ite dominance in Iran and Egypt. This view was substantially undermined by George Makdisi, who argued instead that the spread of madrasas was part of a process of institutionalising the teaching of law. He saw madrasas 'as having an organised and differentiated student body, a specialised curriculum, a professoriate certified to teach, and an institutional educational goal – the certification of teachers and jurists'.[87] More recent research – based admittedly on one city, Damascus, but borne out by research elsewhere – suggests that there is little support for this argument: students had no collective sense of belonging to a group; they did not follow a particular curriculum in law, but put together their own programmes of study; they did not receive ijazas from their madrasas, but from their teachers; indeed, madrasas seemed to have had no formal corporate existence.[88]

Madrasas were founded by sultans, administrators, soldiers, scholars and judges; they were also founded by the wives of such men. The law of waqf, which controlled the transfer of property for charitable purposes, enabled the founder to make whatever provisions he or she wished providing they did not contravene the tenets of Islam. Awareness of the social and political context in which madrasas came to be founded, plus a study of waqfiyyas, or founding documents, has enabled a more nuanced understanding of the reasons for their spread to emerge. In the context of Mamluk Cairo, for instance, the building by sultans of great fortress-like madrasas was part of the politics of display and commemoration. Such foundations were also a way for the elite, who were not associated with learning, to annex the prestige of scholarship; and if a mausoleum was part of the foundation there was the added bonus of the material remains of the founder and his/her descendants being surrounded by the pursuit of knowledge, by worship. Such foundations also enabled great families to provide posts for all kinds of retainers in their urban milieu. We should not, however, discount genuine pious purpose – which were matters of no small concern, for instance, to Cairo's Mamluks.[89] This said, there was a powerful material incentive to found madrasas: the process of endowment enabled the rich to hand on some of their wealth to their descendants. Once the charitable purposes of a waqf had been met, it was legitimate for the remaining resources to go to the descendants of the founder in whichever way had been stipulated.[90] Equally it was possible for the controllership of the endowment to be held by a family member – in one case in Mamluk Cairo the controllership was worth more than three times the professorship of law.[91] Education, moreover, was not necessarily a high priority; in one madrasa foundation preachers, Qur'an readers, porters and cleaners had priority over teachers and students in payment; in another there was no mention of teachers and students at all.[92]

This does not mean that the spread of madrasas was insignificant in the development of Muslim education. Whereas it did not lead to the formalisation of educational processes which has been ascribed to it, it did enhance the great informal work of transmitting knowledge. The madrasa was yet another forum in which person-to-person transmission of knowledge might take place. Furthermore, the generous provision of stipends and scholarships, for whatever purpose, greatly enhanced education, at the same time helping to contribute to the professionalisation of the 'ulama' in general, and the study of the traditional sciences in particular. Arguably these developments contributed to the homogenisation of religious life,[93] shaping a Sunni identity[94] and what has been interpreted as a 'Sunni re-centring'.[95]

The Spread of Education Beyond the Central Islamic Lands

The pattern for transmitting knowledge with the emphasis on person-to-person transmission and the involvement on occasion of madrasas, which had developed in Iran, Iraq and Egypt, spread through the rest of the Muslim world. One area of shared influences, though not exclusively so, was Mongol and post-Mongol Central Asia and Iran, plus the Ottoman and Mughal empires. A feature was the flourishing of the rational sciences in, for instance, circles round Nasir al-Din Tusi (d. 672/1274) at Maragha, Sayyid Sharif al-Jurjani in Samarqand, Ulugh Beg in Samarqand and Jalal al-Din Dawwani (d. 908/1502) in Shiraz. The rational sciences became more welcome in madrasas, with a consequent impact on theology and religious thought in general. Timurid patronage made Samarqand and Herat into great teaching centres. It was in Samarqand that Sayyid Sharif al-Jurjani and Sa'ad al-Din Taftazani wrote their many renowned commentaries, for instance, al-Jurjani's *Mawaqif* and Taftazani's *Mukhtasar*, which became the staple of teaching from Istanbul to Calcutta down to the twentieth century.[96]

The Ottoman Empire was the only part of the Islamic world to develop a rigidly hierarchical madrasa system. In the empire's early years scholars travelled to Cairo or Damascus to complete their education; they had, moreover, a particular admiration for the scholarly and literary achievements of Timurid Samarqand and Herat. By the late sixteenth century the Ottomans had established their full hierarchy of madrasas. At the bottom there were the 'exterior' madrasas which dealt with preparatory work in Arabic, the rational sciences and adab studies. These had three grades according to the salary of the teachers. Next there were the 'interior' madrasas which taught the traditional sciences. These too were graded. At the top of the system were the semaniye madrasas which Mehmed II (r. 848–50/1444–6 and 855–86/1451–81) and

Sulayman the Magnificent (r. 926–74/1520–66) established in their mosque complexes.[97] Strict control was exercised over the progress of both students and teachers through the hierarchy; students were not permitted to progress from one grade to the next until they had satisfactorily completed all that was required of the grade. Students and teachers progressed out of the madrasas into jobs in the judiciary, bureaucracy and noble households.[98] This was an imperial system in which the curriculum and appointments were controlled by the sultan and which retained this form until the nineteenth century. Nevertheless, the personal nature of the transmission of knowledge remained; it was normally only by the grant of an ijaza from his teacher that a student could progress from grade to grade.[99] As elsewhere, adab studies were also pursued beyond the madrasa; in the case of one distinguished Ottoman bureaucrat, in the tavern and the salon.[100] The rational sciences flourished in the early Ottoman centuries, especially under Mehmed II, and this was reflected in a good balance in the curriculum between them and the traditional sciences.[101] But from the late sixteenth century they came under increasing pressure, their fate being symbolised by the destruction of Taqi al-Din's (d. 993/1585) observatory in Galata in 1580.[102]

The Mughal Empire saw a rather different development in education. There was, for instance, a complete absence of hierarchy or system. Education was a matter for individual teachers; formal madrasas were a rarity. The rational sciences, moreover, came to play a larger role in scholarship than elsewhere in the Sunni world. Key to this was the translation of much of the scholarship in the field from Central Asia and Iran into northern India. One important moment was the arrival of Fadl Allah Shirazi (d. 997/1589) at the court of the emperor Akbar (r. 963–1014/1556–1605). He introduced the works in the field of Jalal al-Din Dawwani, Ghiyath al-Din Mansur Shirazi (d. 949/1542) and Mirza Jan Shirazi, which led to the subsequent study of Mir Baqir Damad (d. 1040/1631 or 1041/1632) and his brilliant pupil Sadr al-Din

Shirazi (d. 1050/1640). The next two centuries saw extraordinary developments in the field, in particular among scholars from the qasbahs of Awadh.[103] The murder of one of the key figures in the movement, Qutb al-Din Sihalwi, in 1691, led to the formalisation of these developments in teaching. The Mughal emperor Awrangzib (r. 1068–1118/1658–1707), responded to the murder by granting the sequestered property of a European merchant in Lucknow, Farangi Mahall, to his four sons. One son, Mulla Nizam al-Din (d. 1161/1748) formulated the *Dars-i Nizami*, a course which in Farangi Mahalli hands made ample room for the advances in the rational sciences in Central Asia, Iran and Awadh, and which introduced a new style of teaching, focusing on the most difficult books. The Farangi Mahallis and their pupils spread the *Dars* throughout India. It was also adopted by the East India Company in its Calcutta madrasa. The *Dars* became popular because it enabled students to finish their education more quickly and because it prepared them well for bureaucratic posts.[104] From the nineteenth century, with the rise of Islamic reform under the leadership of the family of Shah Wali Allah (d. 1176/1762), the emphasis on the rational sciences in Indian education declined. This said, we should note that from the Ottoman through the Safawid to the Mughal empire, there was a substantial overlap in the books and commentaries taught.[105]

The work of scholars and teachers was arguably more prominent in Africa than elsewhere, but that may be because they were the prime creators of sources. In West Africa, great lineages transmitted knowledge: the Kunta in Mauritania and Senegambia, the Jakhanke in Senegambia, the Aqit and And-Argh-Muhammad in Timbuktu.[106] But we could talk equally of the Wangara communities of northern Ghana or the Nasiri Sufi brotherhood which spread through the northern Sahara.[107] In Timbuktu the sixteenth-century traveller Leo Africanus (fl. 895–933/1490–1527) noted that books were the most valuable items of trade.[108] The Shinqit of Mauritania hunted books from Fez through to the Hijaz, bringing caravan-loads back to their lands. They were noted for their learning in West Africa and generally for their high levels of literacy.[109] The library which Mahmud Ka'ti (d. 1001/1593) began in Timbuktu in the sixteenth century, numbering nearly 3,000 volumes, has been described as 'the find of the century in terms of African history'.[110] It goes without saying that the African world of scholarship was international. To begin with, the scholars of Timbuktu looked northwards to Morocco, where the Aqit Ahmad Baba (d. 1036/1627) was to acquire such a reputation. But increasingly they came to look eastwards to Egypt and the Hijaz. Al-Suyuti was engaged with Timbuktu for both political and scholarly reasons; his *Jalalayn* was widely studied. The records of that remarkable eighteenth-century Indian resident of Cairo, Murtada al-Zabdi (d. 1205/1790), reveal an astonishing network of scholarly connections across Africa from west to east.[111]

In this context Timbuktu emerged in the fifteenth and sixteenth centuries as a great 'university' city, assisted by its position at the crossroads of the north–south/east–west trade routes. It has been reckoned that there were up to 300 scholars in the city, who would have taught at the advanced level, plus 150 Qur'an schools for the elementary level. The 300,000 manuscripts or more that exist in Timbuktu are a tribute to the scholarly effort of the era and its influence.[112] Scholars usually taught in their homes and, because the size of the body of scholars permitted specialisation, students would move from scholar to scholar. At a more advanced level, students received individual tuition; it would appear that ijazas were given in this case.[113] There was an emphasis on the traditional sciences, but the rational sciences were also taught, and there is no evidence of their being prohibited.[114] More generally, 'the curricula of study in Timbuktu' we are told, 'were designed to give the scholars as wide a humanistic training as was the vogue in the Middle East at the time'. Indeed, al-Suyuti was regarded as a model.[115]

Education was not as well-developed in South East Asia. Islam had been a much more recent arrival along the trade routes of the Indian Ocean. The sultanate of Acheh in the seventeenth century was the first major centre. Scholars came from India and the Islamic heartland. 'Abd al-Ra'uf of Singkel (d. 1104/1693) was the dominant scholar of the period. In a stay of nineteen years in Mecca, Jiddah, Bayt al-Faqih, Zabid and Medina he studied with fifteen teachers, among whom were Ahmad al-Qushashi (d. 1070/1660) and the great Ibrahim al-Kurani (d. 1101–1690).[116] 'Abd al-Ra'uf's writings, in particular, and the emphasis of Malay scholarship in general, suggest that the prime concern was with the traditional sciences and with Sufism. If there was any serious tension it was not with the rational sciences, but Sufism and the appropriate interpretation of Ibn al-'Arabi. This was a matter that Ibrahim al-Kurani resolved in a magisterial work.[117] Among the more popular works studied were Baydawi's (d. 685/1286) *Tanzil* and Khazin's (d. 740/1340) *Ta'wil*. But by far the most popular work, as in many parts of the Muslim world, was al-Suyuti's *Jalalayn*.[118] There is no evidence for the transmission of knowledge being institutionalised in pesantren, the Indonesian version of the madrasa boarding school, until the late eighteenth century. There is close correspondence between the books taught in these pesantren and those at Cairo's al-Azhar and some Meccan halqas, which suggests Middle Eastern influence over their development.[119]

Spiritual Education

Mystical education, the process of learning how to know God in one's heart which was called tasawwuf, that is, the process of becoming a Sufi, was another dimension of education. We treat these dimensions separately, but more often than not they were two sides of the same Islamic personality. It was widely accepted that the best scholars were those with spiritual understanding. Equally, it was widely understood that the starting point for the Sufi was the faithful following of the injunctions of the shari'a as adumbrated by scholars. Sufis might discuss aspects of formal knowledge no less than 'ulama' might discuss tasawwuf.

To begin the process of spiritual education a man – although it could also be a woman – would have to be accepted by a master (Ar. Shaykh; Pers. Pir). The process of being accepted was not easy. The aspirant might have to undergo humiliations to prepare for the hardships of the spiritual path – cleaning latrines was a favoured test. After three years of service, providing he had performed satisfactorily and his shaykh had developed an affinity with him, he would be permitted to enter his shaykh's circle. The relationships would be formalised by an initiation which would recall the oath of allegiance that Muhammad's followers had sworn to him. Elements of the ceremony might vary from order to order, but the clasping of hands and the giving of a patched cloak, or khirqa, as a symbol of Sufi status, were common. The disciple would also receive a written shijra (tree), which would show how spiritual knowledge had come from the Prophet, through the founder of the order, down to his shaykh. One of his first tasks might be to write down his spiritual lineage and commit it to memory. We might note that, whereas the pupil received his ijaza when he finished a book, the Sufi received his shijra at the beginning of his spiritual journey.[120]

If the teacher–pupil relationship was special, the master–disciple relationship was extra-special. All knowledge, all understanding, all progress flowed from the master. 'When the sincere disciple enters under obedience of the master, keeping his company and teaching his manners,' wrote Shihab al-Din Abu Hafs al-Suhrawardi (d. 632/1234), 'a spiritual state flows from within the master to within the disciple, like one lamp lighting another.' The disciple was called a murid, one who desires, and the master, the murad, one who is desired.[121] The master oversaw the spiritual journey of the disciple as a father might a son. The reverence of a disciple for his master could go to extraordinary lengths. In fourteenth-century India one Chishti Sufi rode the long distance from Dawlatabad to Delhi facing backwards on his horse out of respect for his master who remained in Dawlatabad.[122]

In the master's company the disciple would be taught the dhikr of his order, its way of remembering God and other rituals. The disciple would follow the path or ladder to higher levels of mystical experience under his master's guidance, a process often described as 'unveiling'. He might start with tawba (repentance), a turning away from sin and worldly concerns, and embrace the struggle against nafs, the body's sensual appetites. He might move through the stage of tawwakul (complete trust in God), to mahabba (love) and ma'rifa (gnosis), achieving the state of fana' and baqa', the total annihilation of the self in the divine presence.[123] Once the disciple had achieved this level of understanding his master might make him a khalifa, or successor, who was permitted to guide others along the path. At this point his master might bestow upon him another cloak, a cloak of succession. There were many disciples and few successors.

The powerful bonds of disciple-master allegiance were often closely intertwined with those of pupil and teacher. Often it was the connections of Sufi orders that played the central role in assisting the transmission of knowledge other than tasawwuf, as the Naqshbandi Sufis did in Asia, or the Qadiri Sufis in Africa.[124] These two powerful educational bonds reinforced each other in transmitting knowledge across the Muslim world.

The Early Education of Children

Approaches to the early education of children were for the most part driven by the need to save their souls. 'The child', declared al-Ghazali, 'is by way of being "on loan" in the care of his parents... If he is made accustomed to good and is so taught, he will grow up in goodness, he will win happiness in this world and the next, and his parents and teachers will have a share of his reward.'[125] Parents were responsible before God for the education of their children, fathers were particularly responsible for protecting their sons from evil influence in their environment. The onset of the 'age of discernment' (tamyiz), when the child knew the difference between right and wrong and could begin to grasp abstract ideas, was the time for education to begin. This development was thought to take place usually between age six and seven. Indeed, education at this age was a condition for success: 'At this age', al-Ghazali said, 'learning is like engraving a stone.' Character training was part of the process; al-Ghazali was concerned that the child 'get used to modesty, respect for others, and gentleness of speech'.[126] But the desire to play was not to be neglected, as it was seen as a means to attract the child towards more serious studies. Apart from those involving chance, there was a general approval of games. Indeed, tenth-century Baghdad was known to have a toyshop.[127]

Over much of the Muslim world the curriculum of the elementary school (known as kuttab or maktab) was limited to the minimum that al-Ghazali prescribed: the tenets of faith, learning the Qur'an, traditions about the beginnings of Islam and its prominent figures.[128] Parents favoured the limitation, Ibn Khaldun tells us, because they wished to exploit fully the opportunity of youth to instil the most essential knowledge.[129] There were, however, some areas where there was support for a broader curriculum. The Tunisians added some 'scientific problems', knowledge of different readings of the Qur'an and laid much emphasis on handwriting. The Spanish went further, including poetry and composition, and making sure that children had a good knowledge of Arabic.[130]

An enduring feature of discussions of elementary education was the beating of pupils. That excessive corporal punishment was a problem is clear from the recollections of men from all parts of the Muslim world.[131] Moreover, one of the jobs of the muhtasib, the market inspector, was to oversee elementary schoolteachers to make sure they were not harming their charges.[132] In theory a teacher could only beat a pupil with the father's permission.[133] Al-Ghazali took the line that moderate force might be used, but it should be seen as part of a package of measures designed to improve the conduct and performance of the pupil.[134] Ibn Khaldun was also opposed to the severe treatment of children, in part because it led them into deceitful ways; but in part, too, because it dehumanised them, with deleterious effects for society.[135] This said, it was to be expected that pupils would get their revenge on their teachers. Arguably, the most hilarious episode in that classic of the story-teller's repertoire, *The Adventures of Amir Hamza*, which spread throughout the Asian Muslim world, described the revenge of Hamza and his sidekick, Amar, on their brutal mulla (teacher).[136]

The need to secure the child's salvation meant that kuttabs, often known as Qur'an schools, were to be found throughout the Islamic world, from the great sabil-kuttabs (fountain schools) of Mamluk Cairo through to, say, Mauritania, where women would do the teaching in desert encampments. Indeed, elementary education provided the basis on which not just higher learning might flourish, but other activities from trade to administration. In the sixteenth century Timbuktu supported between 150 and 180 elementary schools. In the late eighteenth century, Cairo had as many as three hundred.[137] There is an argument that their growth was, among other things, closely associated with that of trade.[138]

Slave Education

A good number of Muslim regimes were either dependent on slaves or, indeed, ruled by them. Classic examples were the Safawid and Ottoman empires and the Mamluk regimes of Egypt and northern India. This meant that the education and training of slaves was a matter of no small importance. In the case of the Egyptian Mamluks, they were usually imported as youths from the Eurasian steppe or the Caucasus, and converted to Islam; they learned Arabic andgatek were trained for the most part as cavalry. Once their training was completed they were freed but had to serve either the Mamluk ruler or in another Mamluk household. Because the system was replenished not by birth but by the importation of fresh batches of slaves, training in the Mamluk way had to be rigorous and intense. Mamluks followed the dictates of furusiyya, a code which valued courage and generosity as well as skills in horsemanship, archery and cavalry tactics. They lived together in garrisons. Skills were maintained by regular competitions, at least twice a week. Their first loyalty was to their Mamluk master or ustad.[139]

In the Safawid empire, slaves from the Caucasus were crucial both to asserting the power of central government and to success across a broad front. They were educated in the royal household alongside princes and the sons of noble families. They were taught both the traditional and rational sciences, horsemanship, polo and archery, as well as civility, humanity and painting. They progressed through the ranks by merit.[140]

The greatest achievement in the education of slaves, however, was that of the Palace School (Enderun), which was founded by Mehmed II soon after his conquest of Constantinople, and which operated at the heart of the Ottoman state for nearly four hundred years. The school in fact was at the apex of a cluster of schools in which slaves were trained. The *devsirme*, or levy of Christian subjects in lieu of taxes, was the main supplier of personnel – in the sixteenth century 10,000–12,000 slaves were supplied thus every three to four years. For most of its existence the school had 800–900 pupils. On arrival slaves were tested and divided into two classes: the comely and intelligent, who went into the sultan's service; and the remainder, who went into the Janissaries, the sultan's elite corps of household infantry. Of those in the sultan's service, the very able became student pages, and the remainder gardeners, gatekeepers, etc. The student pages themselves were divided between the most able, who went into the Palace School and the less able, who went into the auxiliary schools. The sultan normally took great interest in the school, watching sports, listening to debates and presiding over the admission and graduation of pupils.[141]

The curriculum was not dissimilar from that of the other slave systems, though perhaps rather more wide-ranging. The traditional sciences were studied, but of the rational sciences only arithmetic, at which the Turks excelled, and perhaps geometry. Turkish and Persian language and literature were also studied along with Turkish history and music. A well-stocked library supported wider reading, while vocational subjects such as calligraphy were also available. Within the broad curriculum it appears that pages were permitted to specialise according to inclination, only the Qur'an and Turkic and Arabic languages being compulsory. Exercise was taken very seriously, embracing weightlifting, wrestling, archery, sword practice, dart throwing and horsemanship; there were many competitions. Progress was only by merit, and punishment for breaking rules or failing in performance was severe but controlled; a pupil could not be beaten more than once a day. The aim was to produce good Muslims who were warrior-statesmen, cultivated and courteous. By the account of outsiders, the Ottomans were most successful.[142]

It should be noted how far this system – and indeed the other slave systems – differed from the normal run of education in Muslim societies. Indeed, it has been suggested that, for instance, in the division of intellectuals and artisans, the training of the body and the freedom to specialise, it owed something to the inspiration of Plato's *Republic*.[143] We should also note that, while 'ulama' and lay teachers taught the pages, they do not appear to have been offered the notable respect gained elsewhere in Muslim societies. That was reserved for the sultan,[144] as it was for the Safawid shah and the Mamluk ustad.

Popular Education

The transmission of knowledge was not just the particular work of 'ulama' and their pupils or that of specialist environments such as the Sufi Khanqah, or the Palace School; it was an activity that could touch everyone in Muslim societies. There was the view that the madrasa should be open to the whole community. 'To lock the door of a madrasa', declared Ibn al-Hajj (d. 737/1336), 'is to shut out the masses and prevent them from hearing the [recitation] of knowledge . . . and being blessed by it and its people' (i.e. the 'ulama').[145] So madrasas in late medieval Cairo arranged the recitation of the Qur'an so it might be heard by passersby in the street.[146] They provided large numbers of lower-level posts – muezzins, gatekeepers, etc. – for men in their localities who would not only be exposed themselves to the daily transmission of knowledge but might also attend classes and become transmitters themselves.[147] Madrasas provided more direct educational services to the community: some had employees to teach the Qur'an or how to write; others, along with mosques or khanqahs, might support men who would recite from memory, for popular consumption, basic books from the traditional sciences including Qur'an commentaries and accounts of the early pious Muslims.[148] However, the activity in which the general public were most involved was the transmission of hadith. They might be recited at moments of public anxiety or celebration. Some institutions held public sessions, distinct from normal classes, in the months of Rajab, Sha'ban and Ramadan. There was also the practice of mass transmission when members of the public might receive ijazas for hadith they had heard. Such large-scale transmission of knowledge, though not necessarily with ijazas, could be found in other urban environments, for instance, in eighteen- and early nineteenth-century Lucknow, where the Shi'a held majlis (assemblies for the remembrance of the imams) during Muharram and Sunni 'ulama' gave mawlid (birthday celebrations for the Prophet Muhammad) lectures on the first twelve days of Rabi 'al-Awwal.[149] At such points all could benefit from the transmission of knowledge.

One dimension of popular education was preaching and storytelling. The popular preacher (wa'iz), declared one experienced fourteenth-century teacher, 'had the responsibility of inspiring pious fear in his listeners and telling the stories of the early heroes of the Islamic faith'.[150] The storyteller, or qass, on the other hand 'would sit or stand in the streets, reciting from memory passages from the Qur'an, hadith and stories of the early Muslims and encouraging his audience to pray, fast, and fulfil their other cultic and legal obligations'.[151] These functionaries, whose roles clearly overlapped, could be found in many Muslim societies. Some preachers might be superstars, such as the visitor to eleventh-century Baghdad who drew audiences approaching 30,000.[152] Of course, the content might change according to time and context. From the thirteenth century it would appear that the themes embraced by storytellers in West Asia came increasingly to be infused by Sufi thought: the desirability of poverty and the renunciation of the world, suffering, death, judgement and salvation.[153] Scholars tended to have reservations, but were forced to acknowledge the value of the role they performed: 'The storytellers and preachers were also given a place in this order (amr) so as to exhort (khitab) the common people', declared the Hanbali jurist Ibn al-Jawzi (d. 597/ 1201) in the twelfth century; 'as a result the common people benefit from them in a way they do not from a great scholar.'[154]

That scholars had reservations about popular preachers and storytellers is worthy of note. They raised the issue of legitimate knowledge – that is, of authority – in at least two ways. First, storytellers and popular preachers tended to transmit spurious hadith and use inappropriate emotionalism. But they also had great popular support. So, when al-Suyuti issued a fatwa (legal opinion) against a storyteller for transmitting spurious hadith, the man's audience threatened to stone the scholar.[155] Second, they tended to transmit hadith and other texts without having heard them from a scholar, and therefore without the authority of an ijaza. For all the good that these functionaries might do, they also threatened the very basis of authoritative knowledge.[156]

Women and Education

It has been noted that copyists added to the well-known hadith 'the seeking of knowledge is the duty of every Muslim' the words *wa Muslima* to underline the point that this duty applied to every woman as well as man.¹⁵⁷ Throughout the Muslim world there were women who engaged with education as far as legal and social restrictions – and the latter could be very constraining – would permit. There certainly existed some prejudice against educating women. 'It is said that a woman who learns [how to] write,' went a Mamluk market inspector's manual, 'is like a snake given poison to drink'. This view tended not be shared by 'ulama', who often played a leading role in educating their own daughters, nor is there much evidence that it was shared by ruling families. It was, after all, hard to gainsay the example of the women of the Prophet's family and those of his immediate followers.¹⁵⁸

One female engagement with education was the patronage of learning. In Mamluk Cairo women endowed a range of institutions in which education might take place, as well as five madrasas, most founded by royal women. A sixteenth-century history of madrasas in Damascus suggests that the city was host to even more women's foundations.¹⁵⁹ Six of the thirteen major buildings endowed by women in Safawid Isfahan were madrasas.¹⁶⁰ In Mamluk Cairo the right to supervise the administration of a madrasa could go to the female descendants of a founder. But that was as far as their association might go. No woman held a post as a teacher or a student. Their presence, moreover, within the madrasa confines was deemed highly undesirable; they would put the students off their studies.¹⁶¹

Patronage of learning was a worthy act, but it was real learning for the individual that counted. Such learning might range from some engagement with the Qur'an, hadith and knowledge of basic religious obligations through to serious engagement with major books of advanced learning. Relatives played an important role in teaching women within the home. Thus, Zaynat al-Tukhiyya (d. 894/ 1388), who in the fourteenth century was brought up in a small town in the Egyptian Delta, memorised the Qur'an under her father, learned how to write, and studied several basic works of Shafi'i jurisprudence. After she married she continued her education, studying hadith under her husband's guidance.¹⁶² Scholars encouraged their daughters to hear the transmission of hadith and collect ijazas.[163] Moreover, it was understood that with her husband's permission a woman might attend the halqa of a scholar, at which men would be present, in a private house or a mosque.[164] Learned women could play an especially important role in enabling the learning of women. In Fatimid Cairo there were women who devoted themselves to teaching divorced and widowed women and young girls in their homes. There were, moreover, at least five Sufi khanqahs where women taught women.[165] Nothing, perhaps, is quite as remarkable as the daughter of 'Uthman dan Fodio, the creator of Nigeria's Sokoto caliphate. She sent groups of mature and intelligent women into the villages with her authority to bring girls under fourteen and women over forty-four to her. These women in groups led by the best choral singers would wend their way to Sokoto where during their stay with Asma'u they would be taught the essentials of the faith and how to apply the law. Asma'u's pupils would then return to their villages to teach others.[166]

The range of roles women had in transmitting knowledge is worthy of note. In the Timurid and Mughal royal families the early education of young boys and girls was handed over to older women in the household. Senior women of the Ottoman harem taught young women how to speak and read, and the requirements of the law, in an institution that paralleled that of the Palace School. Doubtless, the improvement in the Turkish of the personal notes sent by Hurrem, Sulayman the Magnificent's favourite consort from Poland, to the sultan is testament to their success.[167] In the Sahara, the women in the family educated young boys and girls in the Arabic alphabet, grammar, reading and basic Qur'anic knowledge.[168] In Safawid Iran, in cities where Shi'ism was particularly strong, women restricted their teaching to girls.[169] In Fatimid Cairo and also in contemporary Damascus, women played a major and respected role in transmitting hadith. So highly regarded were they in the role that leading scholars such as Ibn Hajar al-'Asqalani (d. 852/1449) and Jalal al-Din Suyuti relied on their authority in transmitting hadith.[170]

A further outcome of women's engagement with education was seriously learned women. The restrictions of the harem mean that we shall never know their number as we do for men. Nevertheless, al-Sakhawi's famed biographical dictionary tells of at least 411 women with some education, mentioning in particular the many learned women of Damascus's Bulqini family.[171] In the sixteenth century, Fakhri of Herat produced a biographical dictionary entirely devoted to the poetesses and learned women of Timurid and early Safawid Iran. Focusing on women from noble and scholarly families, it points to active women's engagement in intellectual life, which in the Timurid period was sometimes in mixed company. One notable figure was Bija Munajjima, an astrologer/astronomer renowned for her command of advanced mathematics. As a mystic she was also known for her rivalry with the Sufi thinker and poet 'Abd al-Rahman Jami (d. 898/1492).[172] The Mughal royal household was remarkable for its literary and learned women, produced in every generation from the emperor Babur's (r. 932–7/1526–30) daughter, Gulbadan Begum (d. 1011/1603), to the emperor Awrangzib's daughter Zib al-Nisa (d. 1114/1702).[173] Few, however, were likely to match the range of Nana Asma'u, who wrote in Arabic, Fulfulde and Hausa on: health, women's education, shari'a law as it applied to women, women and bori (spirit possession), women as sustainers, the family, history, eschatology, politics, theology and her father's caliphate.[174]

Conclusion

It is worth stepping back to consider the impact on the development of Muslim societies from about 1000 to about 1800 of the high value placed on the pursuit of 'ilm. Certainly, it meant that by the end of the period, despite the continuing emphasis on the oral transmission of knowledge, forms of literacy were spreading. Admittedly, 'literacy' is a slippery concept. We take it to embrace all forms from the skills of the great scholar to the techniques learned by a boy in a kuttab which were later put to use in his business in the bazaar. But the search for 'ilm was just one of the driving forces behind literacy. It intertwined with the growth of trade; there is a correlation between the intensification of international trade from the sixteenth century and literacy in the regions involved. It also intertwines with the expansion of bureaucratic and legal cultures over the same period. Arguably it is also expressed in the growing practice of letter-writing among middling folk and the keeping of diaries.[175]

Focusing on 'ilm as knowledge transmitted by 'ulama' and Sufis, we must acknowledge their role in deepening the Islamic presence in different environments. They might do so in great urban centres ruled by Muslim potentates such as Fatimid Cairo or Nawabi Lucknow. They might do so on the Islamic frontier in South and South East Asia, where, working perhaps with the expansion of arable cultivation, or more frequently with the long-distance trade, they brought the high Islamic tradition into new environments, linked them into great centres of Islamic scholarship and stimulated them with their continuing discourse on how best to be a Muslim. Nowhere, however, does their role seem to have been more prominent than in Africa.

It has been argued that the Muslim world in this period represented the world system that preceded the Wallersteinian one based on the emergence of capitalism in Europe. If the long-distance trade across land and sea was one dimension of this world system, the second was the pursuit of 'ilm. From Africa to South East Asia Arabic was the language of Islamic scholarship; Muslims learned the Qur'an, transmitted hadith and absorbed the tenets of their faith. Some of the same textbooks were used both in Timbuktu and in Sumatra. 'Ulama' and Sufis travelled freely across this world in search of 'ilm. The connections of teachers and pupils, masters and disciples, represented powerful linkages; indeed, they were the veins and arteries along which the life-giving blood of 'ilm coursed.

One important point flows from the oral transmission of authoritative knowledge and the non-institutional nature of the teacher–pupil relationship. It gave the process of transmission a flexibility which enabled it to be remarkably inclusive. Foreign elites such as Mamluks could be included, so could women, so could the urban masses. Storytellers could entertain whoever came their way, and a princess could reach out to rural villagers. 'Ilm was not locked behind the doors of institutions. It was not the sole possession of a caste of scholars, even though there was always the danger that, in fear of inaccuracy and innovation, the 'ulama' would rather that this was so.[176]

Marshall Hodgson characterised the classic systems of Islamic learning as essentially conservationist.[177] We have noted its central concern to pass down the priceless heritage of 'ilm, the Qur'an, hadith and the skills to make them socially useful, which were adumbrated in the books of great scholars of the past, in pristine form, a task that seemed more difficult with each passing generation. This did not mean that changing times were completely ignored; they were addressed in fresh commentaries on, and sometimes introductions to, the great books. More generally they might be addressed in preaching. We have noted, furthermore, the enduring suspicion of the rational sciences which meant that by the eighteenth century their study in any substantial sense had come to be confined to Iran and northern India. On its own terms the system was remarkably successful in reproducing itself and in sustaining Islamic societies. Again, on its own terms it was able to produce creative responses to the challenges of Europe, as it did in nineteenth- and twentieth-century South Asia.[178] Some have thought that, had the rational sciences been allowed to flourish, education and learning might have been able to produce a more creative response to Europe. But apart from the odd will-o'-the-wisp, such as the translation into Persian in the early nineteenth century of Newton's *Principia* by a scholar in the Farangi Mahall tradition, the areas where the rational sciences flourished seemed to offer little hope. Their study was in its way as conservationist as that of the traditional sciences.

This said, we should note the system's capacity, when transmitting knowledge construed in its broadest sense, to produce levels of intellectual development and human understanding able to support great bureaucratic empires, administer vast armies, design some of the world's most beautiful buildings, create some of the world's most loved poetry, bring a highly respected law to many human societies and, most important of all, provide large numbers of human beings with the guidance in life that offered them hope of salvation in the hereafter.

Notes

1. Franz Rosenthal, *Knowledge Triumphant: The Concept of Knowledge in Medieval Islam* (Leiden: Brill, 1970), p. 2.
2. Ibid.
3. Burhan al-Din al-Zarnuji, *Ta'lim al muta'allim-tariq at-ta'allum. Instruction of the Student; The Method of Learning*, trans. G.E. Von Grunebaum and Theodora M. Abel (New York: King's Crown Press, 1947), p. 21.
4. Jonathan Berkey, *The Transmission of Knowledge in Medieval Cairo: A Social History of Islamic Education* (Princeton, NJ: Princeton University Press, 1992), p. 1, n. 1.
5. Zarnuji, *Ta'lim*, p. 57.
6. George Makdisi, *The Rise of Colleges: Institutions of Learning in Islam and the West* (Edinburgh: Edinburgh University Press, 1981), p. 91.
7. Zarnuji, *Ta'lim*, p. 21.
8. Ibn Khaldun, *The Muqaddimah: An Introduction to History*, trans. Franz Rosenthal, 2nd ed., 4 vols (Princeton, NJ: Princeton University Press, 1967), vol. II, p. 425.
9. Berkey, *Transmission of Knowledge*, p. 4.
10. Zarnuji, *Ta'lim*, p. 33.
11. Abu Hamid Muhammad al-Ghazali, *Imam Gazzali's Ihya ulum-id-din*, trans. Al-Haj Maulana Fazul-ul-Karim (Lahore: Sind Sagar Academy, n.d.), Book 1, pp. 73–109.

12. Ibrahim Moosa, *Ghazali and the Poetics of Imagination* (Karachi: Oxford University Press, 2005), pp. 8–10.
13. William Montgomery Watt (trans.), *The Faith and Practice of al-Ghazali* (Oxford: One World, 1994).
14. Shaykh Mushrifuddin Sa'di of Shiraz, *The Gulistan of Sa'di*, trans. W.M. Thackston (Bethesda: Ibex, 2008), pp. 68, 119–23.
15. Berkey, *Transmission of Knowledge*, pp. 182–3.
16. George Makdisi, *The Rise of Humanism in Classical Islam and the Christian West with Special Reference to Scholasticism* (Edinburgh: Edinburgh University Press, 1990), p. 80.
17. Ibn Khaldun, *Muqaddimah*, vol. II, pp. 436–9.
18. Francis Robinson, *The 'Ulama of Farangi Mahall and Islamic Culture in South Asia* (Delhi: Permanent Black, 2001), pp. 221–51.
19. Ibid.; Makdisi, *The Rise of Colleges*, p. 76.
20. Makdisi, *The Rise of Humanism*, p. 88.
21. Ibn Khaldun, *Muqaddimah*, vol. II, p. 436–63, vol. III, pp. 1–75.
22. Ibid., vol. III, p. 76.
23. Ibid., pp. 99–103.
24. Ibid., p. 111.
25. Ibid., p. 139.
26. Ibid., pp. 147–52.
27. Ibid., p. 154.
28. Ibid., pp. 121–37. We should note that Ibn Khaldun acknowledges other areas of knowledge: sorcery, and the use of amulets, the evil eye, forms of letter magic and alchemy. He is profoundly aware both of their existence and of the damage that, along with metaphysics, they can do to religion. Ibid., pp. 156–246.
29. Makdisi, *The Rise of Humanism*, pp. 88–96.
30. Ibid., p. 129.
31. Ibid., p. 128.
32. Ibid., p. 131.
33. Ibid., pp. 137–8.
34. Ibid., p. 141.
35. Ibid., p. 143.
36. Ibid., p. 145.
37. Ibid., p. 152.
38. Ibid., pp. 163–7.
39. Ibid., pp. 171–2.

40. Ibid., pp. 173–200. For comment on the art of the academic sermon, and its attendant dangers, see George Makdisi, *Ibn 'Aqil: Religion and Culture in Classical Islam* (Edinburgh: Edinburgh University Press, 1997), pp. 220–8.
41. Makdisi, *The Rise of Colleges*, pp. 77–8.
42. Jonathan Berkey, *The Formation of Islam: Religion and Society in the Near East, 600–1800* (Cambridge: Cambridge University Press, 2003), p. 230.
43. Maria Eva Subtelny and Anas B. Khalidov, 'The Curriculum of Islamic Higher Learning in Timurid Iran in the Light of the Sunni Revival under Shah-Rukh', *Journal of the American Oriental Society*, 115, 2 (1995), p. 214.
44. Ibid., pp. 210–36.
45. Elias N. Saad, *The Social History of Timbuktu: The Role of Muslim Scholars and Notables, 1400–1900* (Cambridge: Cambridge University Press, 1983), p. 80.
46. Makdisi, *The Rise of Colleges*, pp. 78–9; Michael Chamberlain, *Knowledge and Social Practice in Medieval Damascus 1190–1350* (Cambridge: Cambridge University Press, 1994), pp. 83–4.
47. Makdisi, *The Rise of Humanism*, p. 90.
48. Ibid., p. 105.
49. Ibid., p. 112.
50. Ibn Khaldun, *Muqaddimah*, vol. II, pp. 427–9.
51. H.J. Fisher, 'The Eastern Maghrib and the Central Sudan', in R. Oliver (ed.), *The Cambridge History of Africa*, vol. III: *From c. 1050 to c. 1600* (Cambridge: Cambridge University Press, 1977), p. 295.
52. S.S. Pirzada, *Foundations of Pakistan: All India Muslim League Documents 1906–1947*, 2 vols (Karachi: National Publishing House, 1970), vol. II, p. 351.
53. Berkey, *Transmission of Knowledge*, pp. 22–3.
54. Ibid., p. 23.
55. Diana Ephrat, *A Learned Society in a Period of Transition: The Sunni 'Ulama' of Eleventh-Century Baghdad* (Albany: State University of New York Press, 2000), pp. 76–9; Christopher Melchert, 'The Etiquette of Learning in the Early Islamic Study Circle', in Joseph E. Lowry, Devin J. Steward and Shawkat M. Toorawa (eds), *Law and Education in Medieval Islam: Studies in Memory of Professor George Makdisi* (Cambridge: E.J.W. Gibb Memorial Trust, 2004), pp. 35–44.

56. Ephrat, *Learned Society*, p. 81
57. Ibn Khaldun, *Muqaddimah*, vol. III, p. 300.
58. J. Pedersen, *The Arabic Book*, ed. R. Hillenbrand, trans. G. French (Princeton, NJ: Princeton University Press, 1984), pp. 20–36.
59. Berkey, *Transmission of Knowledge*, p. 34.
60. Ibn Khaldun *Muaqaddima*, vol. III, pp. 316–17.
61. Ephrat, *Learned Society*, pp. 33–74.
62. Saad, *Timbuktu*, pp. 58–93.
63. Berkey, *Transmission of Knowledge*, p. 91.
64. A.J. Arberry, *Sakhawiana* (London: Emery Walker Ltd., 1951).
65. D. Stewart, 'The Doctorate of Islamic Law in Mamluk Egypt and Syria', in Lowry *et al.* (eds), *Law and Education*, p. 74.
66. Makdisi, *The Rise of Humanism*, p. 202.
67. Makdisi, *The Rise of Colleges*, pp. 99–103.
68. Makdisi, *The Rise of Humanism*, p. 202.
69. Chamberlain, *Knowledge and Social Practice*, p. 145.
70. Zarnuji, *Ta'lim*, p. 30.
71. Berkey, *Transmission of Knowledge*, p. 30.
72. Makdisi, *The Rise of Humanism*, pp. 208n9; Makdisi, *The Rise of Colleges*, pp. 128–40.
73. Makdisi, *The Rise of Humanism*, p. 214.
74. Ibid., pp. 212–27.
75. Makdisi, *Rise of Colleges*, pp. 140–52, 27–6; Stewart, 'The Doctorate'.
76. Berkey, *Transmission of Knowledge*, p. 21.
77. Ibid., pp. 31–3, Ignaz Goldziher, 'Idjaza', *Encyclopaedia of Islam*, 2nd ed. (Leiden: Brill, 1960–2009), vol. III, pp. 1020–2.
78. J. Pedersen and G. Makdisi, 'Madrasa', *Encyclopaedia of Islam*, 2nd ed., vol. V, pp. 1123–34.
79. Ephrat, *Learned Society*, pp. 28–9.
80. Richard W. Bulliet, *Islam: The View from the Edge* (New York: Columbia University Press, 1994), pp. 147–9.
81. Berkey, *Formation of Islam*, p. 137.
82. Said Amir Arjomand, 'The Law, Agency and Policy in Medieval Islamic Society: Development of the Institutions of Learning from the Tenth to the Fifteenth Century', *Comparative Studies in Society and History*, 41, 2 (1999), p. 272.
83. Ibid., p. 273.

84. Ibid., p. 276; Maria Eva Subtelny, 'A Timurid Educational and Charitable Foundation: The Ikhlasiyya Complex of 'Ali Shir Nava'i in 15th-century Herat and its Endowment', *Journal of the American Oriental Society*, III, 1 (1991).
85. Berkey, *Transmission of Knowledge*, pp. 67–9.
86. Arjomand, 'The Law', p. 275.
87. Chamberlain, *Knowledge and Social Practice*, p. 70
88. Ibid., pp. 69–70; Berkey, *Transmission of Knowledge*, pp. 15–20.
89. Berkey, *Transmission of Knowledge*, pp. 128–60.
90. Ibid., pp. 134–6.
91. Ibid., pp. 136–7.
92. Ibid., pp. 17–20.
93. Berkey, *Formation of Islam*, p. 189.
94. Ibid., p. 228.
95. Ibid., p. 189.
96. Robinson, *Farangi Mahall*, pp. 211–51.
97. Halil Inalcik, *The Ottoman Empire: The Classical Age 1300–1600*, trans. N. Irzkowitz and C. Imber (London: Weidenfeld & Nicolson, 1973), pp. 165–71.
98. Colin Imber, *The Ottoman Empire, 1300–1650: The Structure of Power* (Basingstoke: Palgrave Macmillan, 2002), pp. 228–31.
99. Cornell H. Fleischer, *Bureaucrat and Intellectual in the Ottoman Empire: The Historian Mustafa Ali; 1541–1600* (Princeton, NJ: Princeton University Press, 1986), pp. 27–9.
100. Ibid., pp. 22–4, 30–2.
101. Inalcik, *Ottoman Empire*, pp. 175–8: Robinson, *Farangi Mahall*, pp. 240–3.
102. Inalcik, *Ottoman Empire*, pp. 179–85.
103. Robinson, *Farangi Mahall*, pp. 42–53.
104. Ibid., pp. 53–4.
105. Ibid., pp. 211–51.
106. Ira M. Lapidus, *A History of Islamic Societies*, 2nd edn (Cambridge: Cambridge University Press, 2002), pp. 409–10; Lamin O. Sanneh, *The Jakhanke: The History of an Islamic Clerical People of the Senegambia* (London: International Africa Institute, 1979); Saad, *Timbuktu*, pp. 82, 240–1.
107. Ivor Wilks, 'The Transmission of Islamic Learning in the Western Sudan', in Jack Goody (ed.), *Literacy in Traditional Societies* (Cambridge: Cambridge University Press, 1968); David Gutelius, 'Sufi

Networks and the Social Contexts for Scholarship in Morocco and the Northern Sahara, 1660–183', in Scott Reese (ed.), *The Transmission of Learning in Islamic Africa* (Leiden: Brill, 2004), pp. 15–38.
108. Saad, *Timbuktu*, p. 79.
109. Ghislaine Lydon, 'Inkwells of the Sahara: Reflections on the Production of Islamic Knowledge in *Bilad Shinqit*', in Reese (ed.), *Transmission*, pp. 39–71.
110. Albrecht Hofheinz, 'Goths in the Lands of the Blacks: A Preliminary Survey of the Ka'ti Library in Timbuktu', in Reese (ed.), *Transmission*; see also John O. Hunwick and Alida Jay Boye, *The Hidden Treasures of Timbuktu* (London: Thames & Hudson, 2008).
111. Stefan Reichmuth, 'Murtada al-Zabidi (1732–91) and the Africans: Islamic Discourse and Scholarly Networks in the Late Eighteenth Century', in Reese (ed.), *Transmission*, pp. 121–53.
112. Hofheinz, 'Goths' p. 159.
113. Saad, *Timbuktu*, pp. 60–1.
114. Ibid., pp. 74–81.
115. Ibid., pp. 78–9.
116. Peter Riddell, *Islam and the Malay-Indonesian World* (London: Hurst & Co., 2001), pp. 125–6.
117. Ibid., pp. 125–38.
118. Ibid., pp. 141–7.
119. Martin van Bruinessen, 'Continuity and Change in a Tradition of Religious Learning', in Wolfgang Marschall (ed.), *Texts from the Islands: Oral and Written Traditions of Indonesia and the Malay World* (Berne: Institute of Ethnology, 1994), pp. 132–7.
120. Annemarie Schimmel, *The Mystical Dimensions of Islam* (Chapel Hill: University of North Carolina Press, 1975), pp. 101–3; Carl Ernst, *The Shambhala Guide to Sufism* (Boston: Shambhala Publications, 1997), pp. 133–43.
121. Ernst, *Sufism*, p. 124.
122. Carl Ernst, *Eternal Garden: Mysticism, History, and Politics at a South Asian Sufi Center*, 2nd edn (New Delhi: Oxford University Press, 2004), p. 124.
123. Schimmel, *Mystical Dimensions*, pp. 98–186.
124. Marc Gaborieau, Alexandre Popovic and Thierry Zarcone (eds), *Naqshbandis: Cheminements et situation actuelle d'un ordre mystique musulman* (Istanbul: Institut Francais d'Etudes Anatoliennes, 1990): Lapidus, *Islamic Societies*, p. 415; there is an excellent exposition of

the intertwining of pupil-teacher and disciple-master links in Barbara D. Metcalf, *Islamic Revival in British India: Deoband, 1860–1920* (Princeton, NJ: Princeton University Press, 1982), pp. 87–97.
125. Avner Gil'adi, *Children of Islam: Concepts of Childhood in Medieval Muslim Society* (Basingstoke: Palgrave Macmillan, 1992), p. 50.
126. Ibid., p. 58.
127. Ibid., pp. 58–60.
128. Ibid., pp. 54–5.
129. Ibn Khaldun, *Muqadimmah*, vol. III, p. 305.
130. Ibid., pp. 301–4.
131. Fleischer, *Bureaucrat and Intellectual*, p. 21; Lutfullah, *Autobiography of Lutfullah: An Indian's Perceptions of the West*, introd. S.A.I. Tirmizi (New Delhi: International Writers Emporium, 1985), pp. 14–21; I.O. Sanneh, 'The Islamic Education of an African Child: Stresses and Tensions', in Godfrey N. Brown and Mervyn Hiskett (eds), *Conflict and Harmony in Education in Tropical Africa* (London: Allen & Unwin, 1975).
132. Gil'adi, *Children of Islam*, p. 63.
133. Sherman A. Jackson, 'Discipline and Duty in a Medieval Muslim Elementary School: Ibn Hajar al-Haytami's *Taqrir al-maqal*', in Lowry *et al.* (eds), *Law and Education*, pp. 25–8.
134. Gil'adi, *Children of Islam*, pp. 163–5.
135. Ibn Khaldun, *Muqaddimah*, vol. III, pp. 305–7.
136. Ghalib Lakhnavi and Abdullah Bilgrami, *The Adventures of Amir Hamza*, introd. Hamid Dabashi, trans. Musharraf Ali Farooq (New York Modern Library, 2007), pp. 70–83.
137. Nelly Hanna, *In Praise of Books: A Cultural History of Cairo's Middle Class, Sixteenth to the Eighteenth Century* (Syracuse: Syracuse University Press, 2003), p. 51.
138. Ibid., pp. 52–64.
139. Robert Irwin, *The Middle East in the Middle Ages: The Early Mamluk Sultanate 1250–1382* (London: Croom Helm, 1986), pp. 3–10; Berkey, *Transmission of Knowledge*, pp. 9–11.
140. Sussan Babaie, Kathryun Babayan, Ina Baghdiantz-McCabe and Massumeh Farhad (eds), *Slaves of the Shah: New Elites of Safavid Iran* (London: I.B. Tauris, 2003), pp. 29–30, 129.
141. Barnette Miller, *The Palace School of Muhammad the Conqueror* (Cambridge, MA: Harvard University Press, 1941), pp. 70–94.

142. Ibid., pp. 94–125.
143. Ibid., p. 42.
144. Ibid., pp. 94–125.
145. Berkey, *Transmission of Knowledge*, p. 202.
146. Ibid., pp. 192–3.
147. Ibid., pp. 193–200.
148. Ibid., pp. 205–10.
149. Abdul Halim Sharar, *Lucknow: The Last Phase of an Oriental Culture*, ed. and trans., E.S. Harcourt and Fakhir Husain (London: Elek, 1975), pp. 215–17.
150. Jonathan P. Berkey, *Popular Preaching and Religious Authority in the Medieval Islamic Near East* (Seattle: University of Washington Press, 2001), p. 13.
151. Ibid.
152. Ibid., p. 25.
153. Ibid., pp. 45–7.
154. Ibid., pp. 23–4.
155. Ibid., p. 25.
156. Ibid., pp. 7–87.
157. Berkey, *Transmission of Knowledge*, p. 161.
158. Ibid., pp. 161–2.
159. Ibid., pp. 162–4.
160. Stephen P. Blake, 'Contributors to the Urban Landscape: Women Builders in Safavid Isfahan and Mughal Shahjahanabad', in Gavin R.G. Hambly (ed.), *Women in the Medieval Islamic World* (New York: St Martin's Press, 1998).
161. Berkey, *Transmission of Knowledge*, pp. 165–7.
162. Ibid. pp. 169–70.
163. Ibid., pp. 170–1.
164. Ibid., pp. 170–2; Suraiya Faroqhi, *Subjects of the Sultan, Culture and Daily Life in the Ottoman Empire* (London: I.B. Tauris, 2005), p. 115.
165. Berkey, *Transmission of Knowledge*, pp. 173–5.
166. Jean Boyd, *The Caliph's Sister: Nana Asma'u 1793–1665, Teacher, Poet and Islamic Leader* (London: Routledge, 1989), pp. 42–53.
167. Leslie P. Pierce, *The Imperial Harem: Women and Sovereignty in the Ottoman Empire* (New York: Oxford University Press, 1993), pp. 63–5, 139–41.
168. Lydon, 'Inkwells of the Sahara', p. 48.

169. Maria Szuppe, 'The "Jewels of Wonder"': Learned Ladies and Princess Politicians in the Provinces of Early Safavid Iran', in Hambly (ed.), *Women in the Medieval Islamic World* p. 330.
170. Berkey, *Transmission of Knowledge*, pp. 175–81.
171. Ibid., pp. 167–71.
172. Szuppe, 'The "Jewels of Wonder"', pp. 325–48.
173. Ruby Lal, *Domesticity and Power in the Early Mughal World* (Cambridge: Cambridge University Press, 2005); Annie Krieger Krynicki, *Captive Princess: Zebunissa, Daughter of Aurangzeb* (Karachi: Oxford University Press, 2005).
174. Boyd, *The Caliph's Sister*, pp. 121–35.
175. Nelly Hanna, 'Literacy and the "Great Divide" in the Islamic World, 1300–1800', *Journal of Global History*, 2, 2 (2007).
176. Berkey, *Transmission of Knowledge*, pp. 216–18.
177. Marshall G.S. Hodgson, *The Venture of Islam: Conscience and History in a World Civilisation*, 3 vols (Chicago: Chicago University Press, 1974), vol. II, pp. 37–44.
178. Francis Robinson, *Islam, South Asia and the West* (New Delhi: Oxford University Press, 2007), pp. 59–98.

4

On How Since 1800 Islamic Societies Have Been Built from Below

For one thousand years and more, as Bernard Lewis once put it, Islam walked hand in hand with power. The basic infrastructure of Islamic societies – the mosque, madrasas, the administration of the law, the wider activities of 'ulama' – was for the most part supported by Muslim political power. Some religious institutions which played an important part in popular Islamic life, for instance, Sufis and the shrines of Sufi saints, at times strove to distance themselves from the wielders of political power. On the other hand, the powerful usually sought to patronise the Sufis, and sometimes they were happy to be patronised. For a thousand years and more, Muslim power and the Islamic infrastructure of Muslim societies were closely intertwined.

This all changed with the spread of Western power and influence through the Muslim world. Key moments in this process were Napoleon's invasion of Egypt in 1798 and Wellesley's conquest of the last major Muslim power in India at Seringapatam in 1799. From now on the European tide flowed fast. The British were the hegemonic power in India by 1818 and had conquered all of it by the mid-nineteenth century. At the same time the British and Dutch completed their conquests of Malaya and Indonesia. In the thirty years before World War One the British, French, Germans and

Italians divided Muslim Africa between them. During World War One the British and French divided the Middle East between them and at the same time the Russians completed their conquest of the Caucasus and Central Asia. By 1920 in what remained of the Muslim-ruled world, the Iranians had been subjected to a humiliating treaty by the British and the remnant of the Ottoman army was fighting for its life in Anatolia as the great powers started to dismember it. The only lands free of Western power were Afghanistan, North Yemen and what is now Saudi Arabia.

Western power meant an assault on the Islamic infrastructure of Muslim societies. In South Asia British power meant an end of government support for Islamic education. The British saw no point in good revenue being used to support learning which, after their utilitarian fashion, they considered worthless. So steadily in Bengal and northern India they reclaimed the grants which sometimes for centuries had supported Islamic learning. By the same token they no longer found room in their bureaucracy for men with Islamic learning; the training of an 'alim, a Muslim learned man, was no longer a route to government service. From now on Muslims had to acquire Western knowledge and pass British exams if they were to rule. On occasion the British also removed the government grants which supported Sufi shrines, but not always; the British noted that landed Sufis in Sindh and the Punjab might be bulwarks on which their power might rest. At the same time the British imposed English law in the public sphere, narrowing down the sphere of Islamic law to the Personal Law, that involving marriage, divorce and inheritance. Even this became increasingly Anglicised, as first the advice of Islamic legal experts ('ulama' in the form of qadis) was removed from court proceedings and second the law itself became increasingly divorced from its Islamic starting point as the application of common law principles of justice, equity and good conscience were applied by British judges. South Asian Muslims came to live at an increasing distance from the sources of revelation which should inform an Islamic society.

In the Ottoman Empire and subsequently republican Turkey there was a similar development. The process began in the nineteenth-century tanzimat (reform period) as the Ottomans, heavily influenced by the Code Napoleon, reconstructed public life, most notably making all citizens, Muslim and non-Muslim, equal before the law. The process was continued with a vengeance from the 1920s in Mustafa Kemal Ataturk's Turkish Republic. The abolition of the Caliphate in 1924 was followed by the abolition of the Shaykh al-Islam – the Islamic Chief Justice – the abolition of the religious hierarchy, the replacement of shari'a law by European legal codes, which amongst other things brought about the introduction of civil marriage, and an end to polygamy and Islamic divorce. The madrasas were closed, which meant the end of education in the formal knowledge of Islam. The Sufi lodges were closed, which meant the end of training in the spiritual understandings of Islam. Government took control of all religious endowments; in the same way it took control of over 70,000 mosques. Individuals were pressed into Western dress as opposed to more modest Islamic dress, they were told to abandon the Islamic calendar in favour of the Western one, they were literally instructed by Ataturk to give up their cursive Islamic script in favour of the Roman script. The fabric of an Islamic society built up over hundreds of years was reduced to tatters.

What took place in British South Asia and in Turkey was replicated in most other Muslim societies: in Indonesia under the Dutch, in the Caucasus and Central Asia under Russia and the Soviet Union, in Iran under the Pahlawis, and in the European rule of north Africa. There is one notable exception to this, and that is northern Nigeria. Here the British, as always short of resources, rested their rule on the Hausa chiefs of this Islamic society of long standing. In consequence shari'a law was sustained by the state, as well as Islamic education.[1]

Leaving northern Nigeria to one side, the completeness of the change brought about by the presence of the West, its overwhelming nature, the way in which many of the structures, on which an Islamic society might depend, had been rubbed out is summarised by the poet, Akbar Ilahabadi, writing in India in the late nineteenth century. He declares:

> They hold the throne in their hand. The whole realm is in their hand. The country, the apportioning of men's livelihood, is in their hand . . . The springs of hope and fear are in their hand . . . In their hand is the power to decide who shall be humbled and who exalted . . . Our people is in their hand, education is in their hand . . . If the West continues to be what it is, and the East what *it* is, we shall see the day when the whole world is in their hand.

Then he makes the point even more strongly thus:

> The minstrel, and the music, and the melody have all changed. Our very sleep has changed; the tale we used to hear is no longer told. Spring comes with new adornments; the nightingales in the garden sing a different song. Nature's every effect has undergone a revolution. Another kind of rain falls from the sky; another kind of grain grows in the field.[2]

What I want to do is to examine Muslim responses to this shattering change. In particular, I want to examine their responses to the degrading or the destruction of what we might term the infrastructure of an Islamic society. We should note that these responses were informed, for the most part, by the movement of revival and reform in the Muslim world which began to gather way in the sixteenth and seventeenth centuries, and spread throughout it in the eighteenth and nineteenth centuries. It had bases in the ideas of Ibn Taymiyya of Damascus, in Ibrahim al-Kurani's school of hadith in Medina, and subsequently in the ideas of Muhammad ibn 'Abd al-Wahhab. It also had bases in the thinking of Shaykh Ahmad Sirhindi in South Asia and his spiritual successors in the Naqshbandi-Mujaddidi line, not least amongst them Shah Wali Allah of Delhi and his family. Prime features of this movement were: an emphasis on direct engagement with the Qur'an and hadith, often circumventing the considerable weight of medieval scholarship; an assault on Sufi practices, in particular those which suggest that Sufi saints might intercede for man with God; and, bound up with this, an attack on Ibn 'Arabi's concept of the unity of being. These ideas spread through the Muslim world along the connections of 'ulama' and Sufis. Recently the Indonesian scholar Asyumardi Azra has traced these connections in detail as they reach from West Asia, into North and West Africa, and also as they move into Central, South and Southeast Asia to China. I like to think of these connections as the arteries and veins of the Muslim world along which the life-giving force of Islamic knowledge travelled.[3]

I shall begin by looking at the Muslim responses in South Asia. There are good reasons for this. South Asian Muslims had arguably the largest and deepest interactions with the West. In consequence they were particularly productive in generating new ideas and new organisations to sustain them. Representing one-third of the Muslim peoples of the world, they have been most effective transmitters of these new ideas and organisations to the world beyond South Asia.

At the centre of South Asian Muslim responses was what has been called the emergence of a 'willed' or 'Protestant Islam', or a form of Islam which might, after Marshall Hodgson, be called 'shari'a-minded'.[4] At the heart of this process were the 'ulama' of the madrasa founded in the qasbah of Deoband some 90 miles northeast of Delhi in 1867. They were assisted by other groups of reforming 'ulama', who took more extreme jurisprudential positions than the Deobandis and were less widely followed – the Ahl-i Hadith and the Ahl-i Qur'an. These reformers developed a new emphasis on piety. Believers were encouraged to engage directly with scripture, which was translated into Urdu, and other Indian languages. At the same time, any idea of intercession for man with God at a saint's tomb, or through angels, or the imams, was rejected out of hand. Muslims in this tradition were reminded of the horrors of the Day of Judgement, as Ashraf Ali Thanawi did in his *Bihishti Zewar* (Jewels of Paradise), his famous handbook for women, the prescriptions of which applied equally to men. Such Muslims were required to reflect every day on whether they had done enough to follow God's guidance – to meet His high standards. The Reformist God was certainly compassionate and merciful as he had always been, but He was also to be feared. 'Fear God' was the very first practice sentence that women in the Reformist tradition confronted, as they were learning to read. Such Muslims were always agonising over whether they had done enough to be saved. Out of this newly fashioned piety there grew a heightened sense of personal responsibility towards living a good Muslim life and in the process helping to fashion an Islamic society. So, in the absence of Muslim political power the individual Muslim conscience was being shaped into the foundation on which an Islamic society would rest. This process also came to fashion an activist piety, in which Muslims knew they had to act on earth in the light of God's guidance if they were to be saved.[5]

The Reformists not only fashioned a new form of piety, they also fashioned new means of supporting it and of spreading it. At the centre of this process was the Deoband madrasa. It depended entirely on subscriptions from the people; it rejected all subsidies from government. The 'ulama' were now rooted, as never before, in society. They founded new madrasas in their tradition; by 1900 there were well over thirty. They gave religious guidance to the community in the form of fatwas, opinions on points of law. Muslims were encouraged to write from all over South Asia with their questions and the Deoband Fatwa Office would send out answers through the imperial postal service. Deobandis set to the work of translating the Qur'an, hadith and books in the classical Islamic tradition into Urdu and other vernacular languages. They wrote books which reinforced their Reformist understandings – biographies, collective biographies, pamphlets on contested issues as well as comprehensive guides to Reformist behaviour. South Asian Muslims had avoided print until the nineteenth century. Now everything was published large scale to reach the widest possible market at the cheapest possible price. Deoband was a town of printing presses and bookshops, so too was the old Nawabi capital of Lucknow, where, as Ulrike Stark has shown us, Islamic publishing was very big business.[6] These 'ulama' stood up for their faith, engaging in set-piece debates with Christian missionaries and Hindu revivalists. Moreover, as they spread into the qasbahs and local communities of South Asia, they preached their reformist vision in local mosques and illustrated what it meant by the way in which they themselves behaved.

At this point we should note that, although the tide was with them, the Reformists were not the only producers of religious leadership at this moment of Western dominance. There were the Barelwis, the followers of Ahmad Rida Khan of Bareilly. They believed in intercession at saints' shrines and followed many other practices which the Reformists condemned. Theirs was a religious practice which embraced the deeply entrenched Sufi traditions of the South Asian world. They, too, began to found madrasas and produced literature and leadership. So, too, did a totally new sect, the Ahmadiyya who emerged from a cauldron of economic change and religious competition in the late nineteenth-century Punjab. Their leader, Ghulam Ahmad of Qadian, claimed that he was the Messiah of the Christian and Muslim traditions as well as being an Avatar of Krishna. Apart from this his beliefs were not very different from those of the Reformists except that he claimed the power of prophecy. This made him anathema to most Muslims. But he gained followers who were renowned for their missionary work, and still are.[7]

Having introduced you to the early attempts of South Asian Muslims to rebuild their society from below, through the work of madrasas and through reaching out directly to society, let me now demonstrate what happened to this initiative as the twentieth century developed. In one sentence: the numbers of madrasas exploded. During the first half of the twentieth century their number would have been less than one thousand. By the end of the century there were 80,000, perhaps many more. Accurate numbers are hard to establish. Sometimes madrasas have resisted registration, at others, maktabs, or primary schools, have been registered, which would not produce fully-fledged 'ulama'. Nevertheless, although we cannot be precise about numbers we can be sure that they have vastly increased, and well out of proportion to the increase in population.

Let us consider this process in slightly greater detail. In Pakistan at independence there were just 189 madrasas. By 2002 there were at least 10,000 of which 7000 were Deobandi and 1600 Barelwi. The reasons for their growth were several: poor Pakistani families found madrasas which offered not just education but board for their sons most attractive; the state, which spent three times on defence that it spent on education, failed to provide satisfactory public education at the local level. To these factors should be added: the impact of the green revolution which brought much new wealth to agrarian society; an enabling environment under the Islamising regime of General Ziya' al-Haqq; the use made both by Pakistan and the West of madrasas, and their human materials, to resist the invasion of Afghanistan; some Saudi and Gulf funding; and the growing value they had from the 1980s as pools of supporters for those engaged in Pakistan's increasingly sectarian politics.[8]

Many were the forces driving the growth of madrasas. But before we leave Pakistan we should note one particular outcome of Deobandi activism, that is the work of their madrasas in creating a Sunni infrastructure in Eastern Iran. Stephane Dudoignon of the CNRS (Paris) has recently demonstrated how the Deobandis spread from Karachi into Iranian Baluchistan, making the Jami'a Dar al-'Ulum, Zahedan, a great centre of scholarship. From here with the support of both the Pahlawi and the revolutionary regime they spread their madrasas through the region, and into Sistan, Khorasan and Central Asia. Under Khumayni they were given permission to run their own Shari'a courts. It would appear that the central government in Tehran preferred to deal with law-abiding Sunni 'ulama' as regional representatives rather than their fractious tribal leaders. The outcome was the further spread of the infrastructure of a Sunni Islamic society.[9]

In Bangladesh madrasas have always been part of the state provision. There are two main types: the Aliya madrasas which are state-funded and teach secular subjects alongside the Qur'an and hadith, and the Qaumi madrasas, modelled after the Deobandi pattern, and therefore privately funded and focusing on a religious curriculum. Between 1972 and 2002 the Aliya madrasas grew from about 1500 to well over 8000 and the Qaumi madrasas from 1500 to nearly 12,000. Amongst the reasons for this development were: the failure of the state, as in Pakistan, to provide effective education to the lowest levels of society; the enabling atmosphere created by the Islamising regime of General Ziya' al-Rahman, as he sought legitimacy after overthrowing the founders of Bangladesh; the remittances of Bangladeshi migrant workers as they sought respectability in their villages by supporting religious education; and the work of large numbers of Islamic NGOs. As in Pakistan, some madrasas and their 'ulama' organisations became caught up in politics. Some for instance on the borders of Chittagong became involved in Rohingya militancy.[10]

In India it would appear that the number of madrasas have risen from a few hundred at Independence to over 40,000 at the beginning of this century. In explaining this we need to remember the poverty of Indian Muslims, who are for the most part an oppressed minority. As in Pakistan and Bangladesh madrasas make up for the failure of the state education system – there are said to be 30 million school-age children out of school. But for Muslims, even as they teach the classical madrasa subjects, madrasas also preserve identity by preserving Urdu, and Muslim manners. Indian 'ulama' steer well clear of politics, although right-wing Hindu politicians have not been slow to draw their madrasas into politics for their own purposes.[11]

One of the elements of an Islamic society which the madrasa world of India has supported is the Imarat-i Shari'a organisation of the states of Bihar, Jharkhand and Orissa. Founded in 1921 in the midst of the Khilafat-Noncooperation movement against the British, it established a separate legal structure outside the framework of the state to administer Islamic law. This has survived down to the present administering Islamic personal law. The organisation arbitrates between litigants, as a traditional qadi might have done. It has no power to enforce outcomes, depending on the faith of those concerned, and perhaps social pressure, for enforcement. It is a not inconsiderable organisation which so far the Indian state has permitted to exist.[12]

The number of madrasas in South Asia has therefore grown substantially. In principle this has meant a significant increase in those able to support the infrastructure of an Islamic society. How much weight we should give to this is difficult to say. The numbers of madrasas only give an indication of the possible numbers of madrasa students, which might vary from under a hundred per institution to over three thousand or more. Equally we do not know how many students persist to the end of their course and emerge as fully-fledged 'ulama'. Nevertheless, we can be sure that the numbers of those able to play a part in sustaining an Islamic society have increased substantially.

This said, the foundation of madrasas, and the education of increasing numbers of 'ulama', were not the only means of building an Islamic society from below. There were also movements designed to fashion correct behaviour and sustain piety in society at large. One of these was the Tablighi Jama'at, or Preaching Society, which focused on reforming the individual and by this means society at large. It was founded in 1927 by a Deobandi scholar, Muhammad Ilyas, who wished to rescue Muslims whom Hindus had recently converted to Hinduism. Out of this there grew a vigorous Muslim missionary movement, the basic aim of which was to call upon Muslims to improve their Islamic standards. Followers, who paid their own expenses, formed themselves in groups of ten, Jama'ats. They then went to a specific area and by what they preached, how they dressed, and how they behaved, called their fellow Muslims to Islam. All was modelled on the example of the Prophet Muhammad. Tablighis agree to give a day a week, a weekend every month, or forty days a year, to the cause of preaching. They are now said to form, although no one can be sure as membership records do not exist, the most widely followed movement in Islam with 100–150 million followers. Its annual gatherings, which are said to be sources of great blessings to attendees, attract vast numbers – over one million at Bhopal in India, over 1.5 million at Raiwind in Pakistan and over three million at Tongi in Bangladesh. The movement, moreover, attracts support from all classes; in Pakistan, for instance, from leading generals and politicians down to humble apprentices.[13]

There are other Islamic movements, for instance, the Jama'at-i Islami, founded by journalist and Islamic thinker, Mawlana Mawdudi. This organisation was to fashion an elite vanguard of the pure to transform Islamic society from within. Its branches in Pakistan, India and Bangladesh have relatively few members – prospective members have to pass vigorous tests to belong – but it does have millions of sympathisers, particularly amongst the university-educated. Having initially taken a conservative approach towards women's activism, the Jama'at now embraces their support. It runs separate women's organisations, women's reading groups, and even publishes romantic novels with Islamic messages. Its prime concern is to use the power of the state to press forward its Islamic purpose; it recognises that women have votes equally with men.[14]

Yet another movement is Farhat Hashmi's al-Huda organisation which has gained considerable purchase amongst middle- and upper-class women in Pakistan. Hashmi, an Arabic scholar who comes out of an Ahl-i Hadith background, is not popular with the 'ulama'. They do not like a woman taking the lead in religious teaching. They are also unhappy about the privileged background of the al-Huda members.[15]

I hope it is now clear how in South Asia under colonial rule, and under the independent regimes which followed, Muslims, for the most part without political power, have taken control of the business of fashioning an Islamic society. Direct knowledge of scripture working together with the individual human conscience, was the basis. Tens of thousands of madrasas, funded by popular subscription, have helped supply the infrastructure. Hundreds of thousands of students with various levels of learning have poured out of these schools to act as a leaven, particularly at the lower levels of society. The printing press has made vast numbers of Islamic works available in vernacular languages and in cheap format. The work of preaching has been carried forward with great vigour by ordinary men, and now increasingly by women.

These developments have, of course, had an impact on public life. In some cases, madrasas have been supporters of sectarian movements, and indeed Islamic militancy. The Jama'at-i Islami has achieved positions of influence and occasionally been a member of governing coalitions in both Pakistan and Bangladesh. Islamic vocabulary has increasingly become part of the political discourse. Political scientists will rightly point out that there are many factors, both political and geopolitical, behind the Islamisation of the politics of Pakistan and Bangladesh since the 1970s but I have no doubt that part of the explanation lies in the construction of Islamic societies from below that I have set out. The same processes have been at work in India, but the situation of Muslims as a relatively small and oppressed minority has meant that their expression has been different.

****

Let us now turn to Turkey. You will recall that under Ataturk much of the infrastructure of Islam was expunged from society. Yet, as in South Asia, Turkey has seen a remarkable rebuilding of its Islamic structure from below. In this case the process owed nothing to the 'ulama'; they had been destroyed by Ataturk. It was the work of Sufis who survived Ataturk and the private piety of millions of individuals.

As it happens the initial spark for this process came from South Asia. The most important Sufi order in terms of building an Islamic society in the twentieth century has been the Naqshbandiyya. In the early seventeenth century, the Naqshbandiyya in India had experienced an important renewal under Shaykh Ahmad Sirhindi, whom I mentioned earlier. His specific ideas were worked out in his resistance to the religious eclecticism of the Mughal emperors Akbar and Jahangir. They were contained in his *Maktubat*, his collected letters written to the Mughals and their courtiers. Specifically, they supported his beliefs in the unity of God against various forms of heterodoxy. He was given the title of Mujaddid, or renewer of the second millennium of Islam. The Naqshbandi line that flows from him is known as the Mujaddidi.

In the early nineteenth century Sirhindi's Mujaddidi tradition inspired Mawlana Khalid of Baghdad first to come to India to learn from Sirhindi's successors in Delhi, and then to found his own formation of the Naqshbandi-Mujaddidi, the Khalidiyya. This was focused on the renewal of Islam and resistance to Western economic and political penetration. It had followers throughout the Caucasus, Anatolia, the Crimea and Istanbul. Sirhindi's *Maktubat* remained a central work of guidance within the order. All the Naqshbandiyya manifestations of twentieth-century Turkey flowed from the Khalidiyya. We are credibly informed that Turgut Ozal, the prime minister who liberalised the Turkish economy in the 1980s, was a Naqshbandi, and that Tayyib Erdogan, the current President, is a Naqshbandi.[16]

Three offshoots of the Naqshbandiyya-Khalidiyya have been building Turkish Islam from below. The first is the Sulaymancis, the followers of the Naqshbandi Shaykh Sulayman Hilmi Tunahan (1888–1959); with four million followers they represent the second largest Islamic movement in Turkey. Their prime concern has been to sustain a traditional Hanafi/Ottoman Islamic society against both Kemalist materialism and those who wish to unite Islam to political power – Islamists. In the high Kemalist era they would meet to read classical texts, in particular Sirhindi's *Maktubat*, in order to build an inner resistance to secular developments. At the same time, although harassed by the authorities, they trained men to be Imams and preachers. From the mid-twentieth century they increasingly operated more publicly. They worked with the Democrat government in the 1950s in establishing Imam/Hatip schools, now part-funded by the state, to train prayer leaders and preachers. From the 1980s they focused particularly on youth, providing scholarships for university students and the largest and best-equipped student dormitory network in the country. Their main supporters came from the growing and increasingly wealthy Turkish middle class powered by the industrialisation of Anatolia from the 1960s and the liberalisation of the economy from the 1980s.[17]

The most powerful force in building Turkey's Islamic society from below has been the Nurcular, the followers of Sa'id Badi' al-zaman Nursi (1876–1960), a Kurd from Bitlis near Lake Van in Southeast Anatolia. A brilliant young man, he tried unsuccessfully to persuade the Ottoman Sultan 'Abd al-Hamid II to support the foundation of a university in Van teaching both modern science and Islam. He was also a supporter of the Young Turk Revolution. He had an excellent record in the First World War, fighting the Russians in E. Anatolia, and was a strong supporter of the subsequent Turkish Liberation Struggle. But from 1923 he separated from the Kemalist regime when he realised that Ataturk's aim was to divide the modern Turkish state and society from their Islamic heritage. He went through a major spiritual crisis. Assisted by reading Sirhindi's *Maktubat*, amongst other works, he came to realise that man could serve only one master, and that was God. He left the Kemalist regime in Ankara, and returned to Van to a life of contemplation, writing and spiritual leadership. He now understood that the rejuvenation of Islamic society in Turkey must be carried out at the level of the individual. He aimed to fashion a new Turkish Islamic self which would be reflective and which would be able to resist the destructive power of nationalism and materialism. Just as the Deobandi Muslims in India wanted to fashion the individual human conscience as the basis of an Islamic society under British rule, he did the same for Turkish society under Kemalist rule. He was sent into internal exile and frequently imprisoned. His means of transmitting his ideas was his *Risale-yi Nur*, his commentary on the Qur'an. As people were forbidden to read his writings, they could not be printed. Instead they were copied by hand and delivered through much of Turkish society. It is said that as many as 600,000 copies were made.[18]

From the 1960s Nursi's followers would come together in Dershanes, an apartment or single-floor building, in which they would read out loud passages from Nursi's writings and discuss them. The readings would involve a continuous process of interpretation in relation to contemporary issues and events. The make-up of groups would depend on the locality in which the Dershane was, but typically they might include small businessmen, lawyers, teachers, students. Discussion would normally be led by laymen; government-paid religious functionaries were not taken seriously. In this environment there was a club-like atmosphere, businessmen might do business. But the weekly Dershane session had the impact of fostering a shared Islamic worldview and a heightened community consciousness. In the light of the business support it is not surprising that from the 1980s the Nurcus consistently defended Turgut Ozal's liberalising policies, and the withdrawal of the state from the educational and economic spheres. By the early twenty-first century the Nurcus had five million followers and 5500 Dershanes. They had the largest number of educated supporters in Turkey and also the strongest support amongst young people. To add to this they had developed major positions in publishing and in the religious media.[19]

The third Naqshbandi offshoot, which in fact is a branch of the Nurcu movement, is that of Fethullah Gulen (b. 1941), known as the community of Fethullah Gulen, it is said to be the most influential Muslim movement in contemporary Turkey. Coming from a village near Erzerum close to Turkey's borderlands with Russia, he grew up regarding Islam and the state as the protectors of his world. The son of a religious functionary, he went to work for the Directorate of Religious Affairs. By the mid-1960s he had come to develop his vision for enabling Islam to work as a leaven in Turkish society. To put this into practice he aimed not to create a new class of 'ulama' but a new class of intellectuals, rooted in the Turkish Islamic tradition but also able to engage with European enlightenment thought. These intellectuals, moreover, were not to be the inwardly turned Islamic self-fashioners of Sa'id Nursi, but Muslims of action, Muslims who would realise their faith by action in this world. Gulen's constant theme has been action (aksyon). He invokes the mobilising concepts: hizmet (rendering service to religion and state); himmet (giving donations and protecting good work); and ilhas (seeking God's appreciation of every action). Like the Sulaymancis and the Nurcus, Gulen's supporters came from the increasingly large and wealthy Turkish middle class. Alongside the businessmen and teachers there were growing numbers of journalists. Gulen benefited greatly from the support of Prime Minister Turgut Ozal, who saw value in the fact that Gulen was a nationalist Muslim but had no desire to link Islam to the state. Ozal's liberalising of the Turkish system enabled Gulen's move into the media, his establishment of the national newspaper, *Zaman*, and the national television channel, *Samanyolu*. It also enabled him to establish business associations and most of all educational institutions. Education was at the heart of his mission; this was the way an activist Islamic piety was to be established. As it was not possible to teach religion, outside the Imam/Hatip schools, Gulen's followers taught 'Islam by conduct'. His educational network, in which this takes place, supports 6000 teachers, 200 high schools, about eighty university preparatory schools, and seven universities in Turkey and Turkic Central Asia. English is the primary language in the classroom and his students are notably successful in getting into universities. These formal institutions are supported by a widespread informal network of Dershanes, where college students provide religious, educational and social support to their peers.[20]

Such has been Gulen's success that governments have become concerned about the size of his organisation within the state. In consequence, even though he defended the military crackdown after the soft coup of 1997, the military regime moved against him and he was forced into exile in the United States. In 2015 Tayyib Erdogan, whose Justice and Development Party Gulen had supported throughout the twenty-first century, decided that Gulen's followers had too strong a position in the police and judiciary and began a witch hunt against them.[21]

So, the Turks have built a major Islamic presence in civil society, in spite of Ataturk, and in spite of the Kemalist military regimes which succeeded him. It is a presence which has nothing to do with the administration of the shari'a, which was abolished by Ataturk, although it does have something to do with Islamically trained functionaries – the numbers being trained in Imam-Hatip schools rose from about 220,000 in 1983 to 511,000 in 1997. On the other hand, it is a presence which has all to do with the internalisation of Islamic values by ordinary citizens and their expression in social action. A measure of its weight in Turkish society is the way in which Tayyib Erdogan's Islamically rooted Justice and Development Party has been able since 2002 to keep the Kemalists and the army on the margins of politics. Another measure of a slightly different kind is the way in which Erdogan was able to offer to Arab states during their 'Spring' the model of Turkey as a secular state ruled by an Islamically rooted party.

As I indicated at the beginning, the processes we can see taking place in South Asia and in Turkey, can also be seen at work elsewhere in the Muslim world, although always subject to the pressures of local political contexts. Indonesia under Dutch rule saw a similar development of madrasas and Islamic organisation. From 1912 there developed the Muhammadiyya, an organisation stimulated by the general process of Islamic reform and expressing an Islamic piety very similar to that of Deoband. Now it supports nearly 6000 schools and has 29 million members. In opposition to the Muhammadiyya a second group, the Nadlatul 'ulama' was founded in 1926; its views were very close to India's Barelwis. Now operating outside the framework of the state, it claims to have nearly 7000 schools, to own 44 universities and to have fifty million members. In the 1980s, as General Suharto began to demilitarise his New Order dictatorship, he began to court the huge Islamic presence in Indonesia's civil society. He promoted Islamic values: supporting the development of a code of Islamic law, the founding of an Islamic Bank, and lifting the ban on the veil in schools and government offices. He went on Hajj, changing his name to Hajji Muhammad Suharto. Whereas at the beginning of his reign Suharto felt able to ignore Muslim sensitivities, the sheer presence of Islam in civil society meant that as time went on he had to pay it increasing attention.[22]

Egypt offers another example of Islamisation from below. Here leadership came not from 'ulama', who were government employees, but from Muslim intellectuals. In the context of British rule in 1928 Hasan al-Banna founded the Muslim Brotherhood 'to instil the Qur'an and the Sunnah as the sole reference point for ordering the life of the Muslim family, community and state'. His aim was to drive Western influence from Egypt. This has been the aim of the Brotherhood, influenced by the ideas of the South Asian Mawlana Mawdudi from the 1950s, down to the present. Primarily funded by tithes from its members, it won widespread support amongst students and the middle classes as well as the working classes through its work in supporting poor Egyptians. Measures of its support in Egyptian society are, for instance, Egypt's referendum of 1981 which voted to make the shari'a the sole source of law, and the elections of the Arab Spring which saw the Muslim Brotherhood's political wing become by far the largest party in the Egyptian Parliament and the election of the unfortunate Muhammad Morsi as Egypt's President in 1912. As we know, the Egyptian military have overturned these results, but what they say about how Egyptians have built their Islamic society from below remains unchanged.

The capacities developed in building Islamic societies from below over the past two hundred years have meant that Islam has been particularly well-equipped to establish itself in new regions where the state is either neutral or hostile. Most of the notable organisations covered here have spread Islamic communities into Europe and North America. In Europe, where there were in 2014 roughly 44 million Muslims, the Muslim Brotherhood and all the South Asian organisations are significantly present. In North America a particular prize goes to the controversial Ahmadiyya community for being the first American Muslim community and building in Detroit the first purpose-built mosque in the United States. Turkey's Gulen community has been active in establishing Charter schools. Not a penny to my knowledge has been taken from the state, although the odd Muslim ruler has taken a hand – Saddam Husayn supplying a mosque in Birmingham, England, and the Saudis many school books.

I have tried to provide a picture of how over the past two hundred years Muslim societies without Muslim political power have built Islamic societies from below. Of course, Muslims have always contributed to the Islamic infrastructure of their societies, but the loss of power made it crucially important that they did so. The achievement of the past two centuries has often involved a turning inwards to fashion the self, to develop the individual conscience as the basis of a Muslim society. Moreover, as time has gone on there has been the requirement that this self should be an activist self. The achievement has also involved massive projects in education at all levels. A willingness to embrace new technology, in particular print, has driven the process forward, so too has the willingness of millions of individual Muslims to invest their resources of time and money. There have been many acts of courage as individual Muslims have faced imprisonment, torture or death at the hands of secular and usually dictatorial regimes. The fashioning of Islamic societies from below has been a profound achievement of piety, of humility (most of the time) and of selfless social service.

Notes

1. For the continuance of shari'a law in northern Nigeria, see John H. Hanson, 'Africa South of the Sahara in the First World War', in Francis Robinson, ed., *The New Cambridge History of Islam, vol. 5, The Islamic World in the Age of Western Dominance* (Cambridge: Cambridge University Press, 2010), pp. 627–9.
2. Ralph Russell and Khurshidul Islam, 'Satirical Verse of Akbar Ilahabadi', *Modern Asian Studies*, 8, 1 (1974), p. 9.
3. For the transmission of reforming ideas along the connections of 'ulama' and Sufis, see Azyumardi Azra, *The Origins of Islamic Reformism in Southeast Asia: Networks of Malay-Indonesian and Middle Eastern 'Ulama' in the Seventeenth and Eighteenth Centuries* (Crows Nest NSW: Allen & Unwin, 2004).
4. For the concept of shari'a-mindedness, see Marshall G.S. Hodgson, *The Venture of Islam: Conscience and History in a World Civilisation, vol. 1, The Age of Classical Islam* (Chicago: University of Chicago Press, 1974), pp. 315–58.
5. Barbara D. Metcalf, *Perfecting Women: Maulana Ashraf 'Ali Thanawi's Bihishti Zewar: A Partial Translation with Commentary* (Berkeley: University of California Press, 1990), pp. 221–30, 233–6.
6. Ulrike Stark, *An Empire of Books: The Naval Kishore Press and the Diffusion of the Printed Word in Colonial India* (Ranikhet: Permanent Black, 2007).
7. Yohanan Friedmann, *Prophecy Continuous: Aspects of Ahmadi Religious Thought and its Medieval Background* (Berkeley: University of California Press, 1989).
8. Ali Riaz, *Faithful Education: Madrassahs in South Asia* (New Brunswick: Rutgers University Press, 2008), pp. 79–115.
9. For the spread of Deobandi influence in Iran, see Stephane Dudoignon, *The Baluch, Sunnism and the State in Iran: From Tribal to Global* (London: C. Hurst & Co., 2017).
10. Riaz, *Faithful Education*, pp. 116–61.

11. Ibid., pp. 162–89; Yoginder Sikand, *Bastions of the Believers: Madrasas and Islamic Education in India* (New Delhi: Penguin Books, 2005), pp. 93–193.
12. For the Imarat-i Shari'a organisation, see https://www.imaratshariah.org/.
13. For the spread of the Tabligh, see Yoginder Sikand, *The Origins and Development of the Tablighi-Jama'at: A Cross-Country Comparative Study* (Hyderabad: Orient Longman, 2002).
14. Seyyed Vali Reza Nasr, *The Vanguard of the Islamic Revolution: The Jama'at Islami of Pakistan* (London: I.B. Tauris, 1995); Amina Jamal, *Jamaat-e-Islami Women in Pakistan: Vanguard of a New Modernity?* (Syracuse, NY: Syracuse University Press, 2012); Maimuna Huq, 'Reading the Qur'an in Bangladesh: The Politics of "Belief" Among Islamist Women', in Filippo Osella and Caroline Osella eds, *Islamic Reform in South Asia* (Delhi: Cambridge University Press, 2013), pp. 283–316; Elora Sheabuddin 'Jamaat-i-Islami in Bangladesh: Women, Democracy and the Transformation of Islamist Politics', ibid., pp. 445–71.
15. Sadaf Ahmad, *Transforming Faith: The Story of Al-Huda and Islamic Revivalism Among Urban Pakistani Women* (Syracuse, NY: Syracuse University Press, 2009).
16. M. Hakan Yavuz, *Islamic Political Identity in Turkey* (New York: Oxford University Press, 2003), pp. 133–45.
17. Ibid., pp. 145–9.
18. Sukran Vahide, *Islam in Modern Turkey: An Intellectual Biography of Beduzzaman Said Nursi* (Albany: State University of New York Press, 2005).
19. Yavuz, *Islamic Political Identity*, pp. 162–78.
20. Ibid., pp. 175–202
21. Ibid., pp. 202–5.
22. Robert W. Hefner, 'Southeast Asia from 1910', in F. Robinson, ed., *New Cambridge History of Islam*, vol. 5, pp. 591–622.

5

Crisis of Authority
Crisis of Islam?

OVER THE PAST TWO HUNDRED years there has been a growing crisis of authority in the Muslim world. This crisis was set in motion by the European conquest of this world between 1800 and 1920, a process, which was part of that first great moment of globalisation powered by industrial capitalism. In the second half of the twentieth century it was intensified by the next great movement of globalisation, powered by finance, communications and increasingly large movements of people. Throughout this period the crisis has been exacerbated by the measures taken by Muslims to resist the challenges of Western domination. It is a crisis which has been felt through all aspects of Muslim societies: their modes of wielding power, their sense of justice, their culture, their values, their literature, their forms of art, in some cases their especial forms of medicine, but in all cases, in the area of religious authority.[1]

No area could be more important. From the outset Islamic civilisation was fashioned primarily by God's revelation to humankind through the Prophet Muhammad, the Qur'an. The business of interpreting God's will as law, from place to place, and from day to day, has been a central activity in moulding both Muslim lives and Muslim societies. But, the past two hundred years have seen great changes, indeed massive transformations, in this process. The authority of much scholarship from the past, has been rejected; the authority of the traditional interpreters, the 'ulama', has been marginalised. New claimants to authority have come forward with none of the finely honed skills of traditional scholarship; indeed, for growing numbers of Muslims Islam has become a matter of individual conscience, individuals have come to interpret the faith for themselves. No one knows any longer, as the saying goes, 'who speaks for Islam'. There is, in fact, a crisis of authority. This essay explores this crisis. It does so in the belief that some understanding of the crisis will give us an insight not only into some of the problems of the contemporary Muslim world but also into some of the strands of hope it offers for the future.

****

To understand this crisis of authority we need to know first how authority was established and sustained in the Islamic world. The process begins, of course, with the emergence of Muhammad as a charismatic prophet in early seventh-century Arabia, and with his successful assertion of his authority against the traditional Arab order. He succeeded in doing so because he came to be widely recognised as the messenger of an omnipotent God, indeed, as that God's last messenger to humankind, who succeeded through His revelation in fashioning the first Muslim community. The Qur'an is quite explicit about how Muhammad's role as messenger translates 'the omnipotence of Allah [God]', as Hamid Dabashi has shown, 'into the comprehensive authority of Muhammad':

> Say [O Muhammad] O mankind! Lo! I am the messenger of Allah to you all – [the messenger of] Him unto whom belongs the sovereignty of the heavens and the earth. There is no God save Him. He quickeneth and he giveth death. So believe in Allah and His Messenger, the Prophet, who can neither read nor write, who believeth in Allah and His word, and follow him that haply ye may be led aright. (VII.158)[2]

After Muhammad's death the succession to his authority was bitterly contested amongst those whom Marshall Hodgson termed the 'piety-minded', followers of 'Ali, the Prophet's cousin and son-in-law, Kharijis, who broke with 'Ali because he appeared to be willing to compromise with the first Umayyad caliph, indeed, numerous groups usually divided over the means by which authoritative understandings of revelation were to be achieved.[3] Eventually, as what Hodgson termed the Jami'a-Sunni consensus emerged under the Abbasid caliphate, Muhammad's authority, if you will permit a Weberian moment, came to be routinised for the majority Sunni community in several forms. His political authority came to be institutionalised in the office of the caliphate, an office which was finally abolished by Mustafa Kemal Ataturk in 1924; his judicial authority in the office of the qadis or judges; his military authority in that of the amirs, or military commanders; his spiritual authority in the roles of the Sufi saints, the Islamic mystics; and finally, and most important from our point of view, his religious authority in the roles of the 'ulama' or learned men.[4] The term 'ulama' is the plural of 'alim, meaning learned man, which is derived from the Arabic root 'ilm meaning knowledge. It was the task of the 'ulama' to transmit the essence of knowledge, the Qur'an, God's revelation to humankind, and the hadith, the reported sayings and doings of his Messenger, from generation to generation. Alongside this they had to transmit the skills which would enable future 'ulama' to understand this essence of knowledge, such as Arabic grammar and syntax, and the skills, such as jurisprudence and rhetoric, to make this knowledge socially useful in the form of law.

Of course, these routinised splinters of Muhammad's charismatic authority did not through time remain completely independent spheres of authority: the caliphs and sultans, the rulers, were always trying to subordinate the authority of the 'ulama' to their purposes; Sufis, in many different circumstances from Indonesia to West Africa, might also be military leaders; moreover, as Islamic history developed, it became commonplace for 'ulama' also to be

Sufis; indeed, it came to be understood, as was so wonderfully recorded by the eleventh-century scholar al-Ghazali in his autobiography, *The Deliverance from Error*, that there was little point to formal learning unless it was imbued with spiritual meaning.[5] This said, in spite of these often overlapping spheres of routinised authority, the 'ulama', the transmitters of the central messages of Islam, were at the heart of the process of shaping Muslim societies, then sustaining them, and then, as necessary, reshaping them.

At this point we should note the area of the Muslim community where 'ulama' had enhanced authority derived from Muhammad's charisma, that is, the Shi'a, the party of 'Ali, who contested the leadership of the Muslim community with the first three elected caliphs. The followers of 'Ali came to argue that irfan, the divine light with which God had graced Muhammad, flowed down through 'Ali and his bloodline, who became Imams or leaders of the Shi'a Muslim community. Thus, Muhammad's charismatic (and comprehensive) authority persisted in the Shi'i Imams, the Shi'i leadership until, as the Twelver Shi'as maintain, the Twelfth Imam disappeared, or occulted (became hidden), in AD 874. This created the possibility of continuing charisma in Shi'i history, as the leaders of the Safawid Sufi order, who created Iran's Safawid empire in the sixteenth century, claimed to be reincarnations of the hidden Imam, and as the Shi'i 'ulama' later claimed to be representatives of the hidden Imam. The greater authority to which the Shi'i 'ulama' can lay claim has led to greater flexibility in their jurisprudential tradition as compared with the Sunnis. Moreover, it is this greater potential for authority which has bolstered, not wholly but certainly in part, the authority of Mulla Hassan Nasr Allah's leadership of the Shi'i Hizb Allah movement in the Lebanon, that of Grand Ayat Allah 'Ali Sistani in Iraq, and of course that of Ayat Allah Khumayni in Iran. The continuing force of the idea of a charismatic Imamate was demonstrated, as in the years of the Iranian revolution from 1978 to 1979 Khumayni came to be called no longer Ayat Allah Khumayni but Imam Khumayni.

****

We now turn to considering the way in which authority, and by implication authoritative interpretation, was sustained amongst the 'ulama', Shi'i and Sunni, down to the nineteenth century. At the heart of authority in learning was the system for transmitting the Qur'an, the very essence of knowledge. For Muslims the Qur'an is the word of God, His very word. It is the divine presence, the mediator of divine will and grace. Qur'an itself means recitation, al-Qur'an, the recitation or the reading out aloud. It is through being read out aloud that the Qur'an is realised and received as divine. Pious Muslims strive to learn most of it by heart; its words are forever on their lips.

Authoritative transmission of the Qur'an was always oral. This was how the Prophet transmitted the messages he had received from God to his followers. And when a few years after His death they came to be written down, it was only as an aid to memory and oral transmission. Telling evidence for the authority of the orally transmitted Qur'an comes from the 1920s when the Egyptian standard edition was produced, not from a study of the variant manuscript versions but from a study of the fourteen different traditions of recitation.[6]

Receiving the Qur'an orally, learning it by heart, and then reciting it out aloud, has traditionally been the first task of young Muslim boys and girls. The usual method of learning was that each day the teacher would recite some verses, write them on the pupil's slate, and then the pupil would spend the rest of the day learning them. Those able to recite them successfully the next day, in addition to those they already knew, would be entitled to wash their slates, hear more verses, and have them written down for them. Those who succeeded in remembering and reciting the whole Qur'an were celebrated with joy and received much respect.

The methods of learning and transmitting the Qur'an laid their impress on the transmission of all other knowledge. 'The Qur'an', declared the great fourteenth-century Muslim historian, Ibn Khaldun, in a discussion of the art of teaching, 'has become the basis of instruction, the foundation of all habits that may be acquired later on.'[7] So, when a book was published in the early Islamic centuries, its writing down was merely an aid to oral publication. The author would dictate his first draft, either from memory or from his own writing; the copyist would then read it back to him. Publication would then take place through the copyist reading the text to the author in public, often in a mosque. During this process the author might make additions and emendations, and several readings might be required before it was given his authorisation. This was known as the ijaza, which means 'to make lawful'. Thus, the author gave permission for the work 'to be transmitted from him'. Further copies had real authority only when they had been read back and approved.[8]

A similar process took place when a member of the 'ulama' transmitted some of the great Islamic texts to his students. The teacher would dictate the text to his pupils, who might write it down, and frequently commit it to memory. Subsequently, depending on its nature, there might be an explanation of the text. The completion of the study of the book would involve a reading back of the text with an explanation. If this was done to the teacher's satisfaction, the student would be given an ijaza, an authority to teach the text. On that ijaza would be the names of all those who had transmitted the text going back to the original author. The student knew that he was in his generation the trustee of part of the great tradition of authoritative Islamic learning handed down from the past.

You may wonder why in a society where beautiful writing, calligraphy, was deemed to be the highest of the arts, and where in great cities like medieval Baghdad or Cairo paper was widely available, authoritative knowledge had to be orally transmitted. The fact is that Muslims were fundamentally sceptical of the written word. 'Language', declares Ibn Khaldun, 'is merely the interpretation of ideas that are in the mind . . . Words and expressions are media and veils between the ideas . . . The student of ideas must extract them from the words that express them.' 'But', Ibn Khaldun goes on, 'when a student has to rely on the study of books and written material and must understand scientific problems from the forms of written letters in books, he is confronted with another veil . . . that separates handwriting and the form of letters found in writing from the spoken words found in the imagination.'[9] To understand the words properly, the student must read them out aloud. As the Qur'an gained full realisation only by being recited out aloud, so too did the academic book give of its full meaning by being read aloud. Muslims got at the truth in speech.

Thus, person-to-person transmission was at the heart of authoritative transmission of knowledge. The best way of getting at the truth was to listen to the author himself. Muslim scholars constantly travelled throughout the Islamic world so that they could receive authoritative transmission of knowledge. And, when a scholar could not get knowledge from the author in person, he strove to get it from a scholar whose 'isnad', or chain of transmission from the original author, was thought to be the most reliable. The preference for the oral over the written text may be explained by the central concern for the transmission of the author's meaning – for the transmission of the most authoritative understanding of the text. Person-to-person transmission through time was the most reliable way of making up for the absence of the original author in the text. It enabled the students to read the white lines on the page, as the 'ulama' used to say, as well as the black lines.[10]

Symptomatic of the anxieties of the 'ulama' about person-to-person transmission and authority was the criticism which the formidable fifteenth-century scholar of Cairo, Jalal al-Din al-Suyuti, attracted because he did not sit at the feet of other scholars enough, taking his knowledge directly from books.[11] Symptomatic again was the custom of taking very young boys to listen to the transmission of hadith from very old men, so that the line of transmission would be shorter, the chance of error be less, and their authority as transmitters thereby greater.[12] A powerful demonstration, moreover, of the anxiety over person-to-person transmission and authority was the notable literary/historical genre developed by the 'ulama' in the classical Islamic era, and continued virtually down to the present, of collective biographies, the tabaqat or tadhkirah. These might deal with the scholars of a particular discipline, place, family or time. They recorded, after family details, who a man's teachers were, what he learned, and who his pupils were. His own contributions to knowledge would be listed along with anecdotal evidence bearing on his reliability as a scholar and transmitter of knowledge. These collective biographies were ways in which 'ulama' set out their contributions to sustaining Islamic civilisation and bolstered their authority.[13] Nothing, however, was more symptomatic of the relationship between person-to-person transmission of knowledge and authority than the way in which the 'ulama' for centuries rejected print. From the sixteenth century print was known about through much of the Muslim world but, apart from a brief dalliance in Istanbul in the 1730s, it was ignored. Print undermined directly, and explicitly, the authority of person-to-person transmission. It also promised to undermine the monopoly over the interpretation of religious knowledge which belonged to the 'ulama'.[14]

So, let us consider the location of religious authority as it was to be found in Muslim societies in general around 1800, nearly 1200 years after the beginning of the Islamic era. Religious authority, and the capacity to produce authoritative interpretation, derived from the Qur'an and the life of the Prophet, lay with the 'ulama'. They were the recipients of the traditions of Islamic scholarship which had built up through time. They were proud of the many ijazas they possessed, permitting them to transmit the great scholarly works of the past. They relied on the authority of these and other works as they strove to make revelation in the form of law relevant to the problems of their time. Throughout they strove to prevent others muscling in on their monopoly, whether they were Sufis or sultans.

Of course, the general authority of the 'ulama' was subject to specific social, political and personal conditions. It helped if they could claim to be Sayyids, and therefore descendants of the Prophet. It helped, too, if they came from a well-known family of scholars; learning could be regarded as being in the blood. If they did not, it helped to have studied with the best scholars of the day. Moreover, 'ulama' needed to behave like men who corporeally embodied the word of God and the capacity to interpret it. They should not behave like the young Mawlana 'Abd al-'Ali of the great Farangi Mahalli family of Lucknow, who later in the eighteenth century was to become the foremost scholar of his day. Soon after his father's death he attended the most important Sufi ceremony in Lucknow over which his father would normally have presided. He wandered through the crowd in dandyish fashion carrying a quail cage. Someone gave him a shove and asked him where he thought he was going. 'Don't you know me,' 'Abd al-'Ali said, 'I am Mulla Nizam al-Din's son.' 'By God,' the man replied, 'if you are the son of Ustad al-Hind, you would be presiding over the assembly and not carrying around quail cages.'[15] And, of course, 'ulama' needed to have a reputation for avoiding those with power. 'The worst of scholars is he who visits princes', went an oft-quoted hadith, 'and the best of princes is he who visits scholars.' Nothing should stand between the authority of God and the authority of the scholar.

****

Over the past two hundred years this system for the authoritative transmission of Islamic knowledge, and for its authoritative interpretation, has broken down. Lay folk have come forward to challenge the authority of the 'ulama' as interpreters, indeed, increasingly each individual Muslim has come to arrogate to himself or herself the responsibility for interpretation. Lay folk and some 'ulama' have come to challenge the authority of past Islamic scholarship. Scholarly authority has become fragmented; old hierarchies have been flattened; the old interpretative disciplines have been sidelined. All kinds of new interpreters of the faith have come forward; all kinds of new interpretations have been promulgated.

As I declared at the beginning of this lecture, no one now knows who speaks for Islam with authority. Let us see how this has come to pass.

The first source of this change was the Western conquest of the Muslim world. For nearly 1200 years Islam walked hand in hand with power. The Muslims who had burst out of seventh-century Arabia to conquer within a century much of the known world, had gone on to create a world system. This was based on the long-distance trade by land across Asia and Africa, and by sea across the Indian Ocean to the China Sea. It shared the great books of Islamic civilisation, alongside Arabic as a language of learning, and Islamic law. In a few decades in the nineteenth and twentieth centuries, this world system was overwhelmed by Europe. The symbolic beginning was Napoleon's invasion of Egypt in 1798, followed in 1799 by the snuffing out of Mysore, the last significant Muslim opponent of British power in India. Between 1800 and 1920, the British, the French, the Russians, the Dutch, the Italians and the Germans annexed, or asserted influence over, almost the entire Muslim world. In 1920 the only areas largely free of European influence were Afghanistan, North Yemen, and Central Arabia. Iran enjoyed a much qualified freedom; Ataturk was fighting for Turkish freedom and respect in Anatolia.

Let us consider the impact on the Indian subcontinent, home to nearly one-third of the world's Muslims. British rule transformed its economy, making it, as far as possible, a producer of commodities and receiver of finished goods. India was also fashioned into a great military base, whose huge resources of men and material would support the military operations of the British Empire in Asia, Africa and Europe. British policy came to display utter contempt for Indian learning, which of course included the sources of Muslim civilisation. 'A single shelf of a good European library', declared Macaulay in his notorious Minute on Education of February 1835, '[is] worth the whole native literature of India and Arabia.'[16] It was not surprising that the grants made by Muslim rulers to support the scholarship and teaching of the 'ulama' were abolished.

Now, new forms of knowledge had to be mastered for success in the world of Western dominance. Able Muslims from India went less to the great Muslim madrasas of Arabia and Egypt and more to London, Paris, Oxford and Cambridge. Power had seeped away from the old Muslim heartlands in northern India, from the former centres of Muslim civilisation like Delhi and Lucknow, to the new European cities of the coast – Calcutta, Madras, Bombay. When the old centres of Muslim power were caught up in revolt, as they were in the Mutiny Uprising of 1857, the British slaughtered many, laid them waste, and reshaped them to their purpose.

One outcome was a pervading sorrow at the passing of Muslim greatness. Two decades after the destruction of Delhi, the poet, Altaf Husayn Hali, wrote his *Musaddas*, or elegy entitled *The Flow and Ebb of Islam*. This was a great set-piece on the rise and decline of Islam and its causes. It was replete with nostalgia for past Muslim greatness. Full of criticism of the failures of Muslims in the present, along with admiration for the achievements of the British.[17]

Over the next forty years the poem had many imitators. The mood, of course, was felt widely throughout the Muslim world. Recently it has been well expressed in the concept of huzun, which pervades the chapters of Orhan Pamuk's autobiographical work, *Istanbul*.[18] To experience this in the European context we need to go to Giuseppe di Lampedusa's paean on the decline of Sicilian aristocratic life, *The Leopard*.[19]

There was also anger at the destructiveness of Europe. 'Against Europe I protest', wrote Muhammad Iqbal, the finest Indo-Muslim poet of the twentieth century:

> And the attraction of the West.
> Woe for Europe and her charm,
> Swift to capture and disarm!
> Europe's hordes with flame and fire
> Desolate the world entire.[20]

Crisis of Authority: Crisis of Islam?

This anger and protest can be seen growing from the late-nineteenth century in the lively arena created by the newspaper press. From the Russo-Turkish war of the late 1870s and the British invasion of Egypt in the early 1880s through to the Italian occupation of Cyrenaica and the European conquest of Ottoman territories in the Balkans just before World War One, Muslims expressed anguish and protest. At the same time, from 1912, the British imperial capital of New Delhi became a theatre for imperial display against the much smaller Old Delhi, which the Mughal emperor Shah Jahan had built for the same purpose. New Delhi became a symbol of the declining position of Muslims in the world. All came to a head as Britain and her allies dismembered the Ottoman Empire during and after World War One. This led to the Khilafat movement of the Indian Muslims, which was the greatest protest against British rule before the Quit India movement of 1942. I have often wondered from where the energy and psychic resources for this extraordinary movement came. Certainly, they came from the economic disruption caused by World War One. Certainly, too, from the impact of hundreds of thousands of returning soldiers. The political fluidity caused by the introduction of the Montagu-Chelmsford form of democracy also played its part. But I have absolutely no doubt that a crucial driving force was a psychological response to the loss of power and authority of Muslim civilisation, and one most deeply felt in India where the impact of the West had been greatest. This verse by the satirist, but most sensitive poet, Akbar Ilahabadi, says it all:

> The minstrel, and the music, and the melody have all changed.
> Our very sleep has changed; the tale we used to hear is no longer told.
> Spring comes with new adornments; the nightingales in the garden sing a different song.
> Nature's every effect has undergone revolution.
> Another kind of rain falls from the sky; another kind of grain grows in the field.[21]

When one civilisation is overcome by another, it is hard not to think that what the former contains and represents might lose authority. It is hard not to think, too, that in this context there might not be concern for the authority of the Qur'an and the Prophet. Indeed, ever since, Muslims have been deeply sensitive to failures to show respect to these founding sources of their civilisation. Thus, when Mawlana 'Abd al-Bari, the head of Lucknow's Farangi Mahall family of 'ulama', discovered at the foundation ceremony of a new college for 'ulama', the Nadwat al-'Ulama', in 1907 that the Qari reading the Qur'an was placed at a level lower than the Lieutenant-Governor, he had the Qari stand on a table so that the word of God would come down from on high to the representative of British power.[22] This was nearly a century before the Rushdie crisis or the cartoon crisis. There was an overwhelming feeling that Muslims had failed, and particularly that their 'ulama' had failed. Indeed, there was the feeling that, if things had come to this pass, they had not been good enough Muslims.

****

This loss of power, which was so very deeply felt, precipitated a crisis of authority. But this crisis was much exacerbated by the responses of the 'ulama', and of other Muslims, as they sought answers to the questions set by Western power. I shall examine this crisis once more primarily in the context of the Indian subcontinent.

First, numbers of 'ulama' began to shred the old basis of authority by rejecting much past scholarship. Not all did this. The 'ulama' of Lucknow's Farangi Mahall family and those in the traditions of Bareilly's Ahmad Rida Khan continued to draw on the full panoply of classical scholarship. But others in the tradition of Shah Wali Allah, the eighteenth-century reformer of Delhi, revised their relationship to past scholarship in ways which varied from the moderate to the extreme. Thus the 'ulama' of Deoband, founded in 1867, which has grown to become the second most important traditional Muslim university in the world, continued to follow much classical scholarship in the revealed sciences, but rejected large quantities of the rational sciences, the great achievements of Greek and Persian civilisation which had flourished in the Islamic tradition. They also rejected all aspects of Sufi practices which suggested that there might be intercession for man with God. Then, a group of 'ulama' called the Ahl-i Hadith, like the Salafis of the Middle East, rejected almost all Sufism. A further group, called the Ahl-i Qur'an, used just the Qur'an as their authority. At the same time in the nineteenth century, a lay Muslim who was also influenced by the tradition of Shah Wali Allah, Sayyid Ahmad Khan, developed the trajectory of Islamic modernism. Like the Ahl-i Hadith, he rejected classical Islamic scholarship, going straight to the Qur'an and Hadith. Much influenced by Christian Biblical criticism, he made the achievements of Western science the benchmark of authority for interpretation. His dictum was that the 'word of God and the work of God must be in harmony'. If they were not, it was because Muslims had not exerted themselves enough to discover that harmony. Yet another new source of authority was experimented with in the Punjab, where Muslims found themselves competing with Christian missionaries and Hindu and Sikh revivalism. Here, one Ghulam Ahmad of Qadian declared himself a minor prophet with a messianic mission to revive Islam. He used the messianic traditions of Islam to boost his authority: as some might know, because his actions tended to undermine the finality of Muhammad's prophethood, Ghulam Ahmad and his followers are reviled throughout the Muslim world. Just these few brushstrokes are enough to suggest how by the mid-twentieth century groups of Indian Muslims had become increasingly selective about where they derived authority from. Indeed, authority itself had begun to fragment.[23]

Second, the 'ulama' attacked the heart of their authority, the oral, person-to-person transmission of knowledge. From the beginnings of reform in the nineteenth century they began both to use print and to translate the Qur'an, the hadith, and the texts of classical scholarship from Arabic into the vernacular languages. Thus, they themselves began to destroy the closed shop which gave them the monopoly over transmission and interpretation of knowledge.[24]

You may well ask, why should the 'ulama' so damage their position? It was a matter of survival. With the removal of government support after the British conquest, the 'ulama' found themselves needing to build a constituency in Indo-Muslim society at large, and to do so both in competition with missionaries from other faiths and with the secular Western system of education supported by the government. Print and translation, alongside a considerable expansion of their madrasa system of education, was their means of doing so. The 'ulama' were right at the heart of the Urdu printing revolution of nineteenth-century northern India, from the very first reforming pamphlets of the 1820s and 1830s through to the late nineteenth century, when religious publications dominated the print trade, and Deoband, the centre of reform, was growing into the town of printing and bookshops it has now become.[25] 'Ulama' tried to limit the damage to their authority caused by this uncontrolled transmission of knowledge by insisting that no one should read a work of scholarship without their supervision. But it was a lost cause. Men and women could not resist the opportunity to engage with the sources of their faith themselves. 'Increasingly from now on', as I have argued elsewhere, 'any Ahmad, Mahmud or Muhammad could claim to speak for Islam. No longer was a sheaf of impeccable *ijaza*s the buttress of authority. . . . The force of 1200 years of oral transmission, of person-to-person transmission, came increasingly to be ignored.'[26]

Third, the reforming 'ulama' began to develop what some have called a 'Protestant' or willed Islam. Some of you, I am sure, can see the various elements coming together. There was the attack on all ideas of intercession for men at saints' shrines, indeed amongst some reformers an attack on all forms of Sufism: at the same time individual consciences were primed with an increased awareness of the horrors of the Day of Judgement. There was a new emphasis on personal engagement with texts in languages people could understand, in particular the Qur'an. Then there was the role of print in making texts widely available, combined with a growth in literacy encouraged both by the 'ulama' and by British rule.

What the 'ulama' were doing was – in the absence of any Islamic political power – developing and informing the individual human conscience as the force which would fashion a Muslim society. Muslims in the reforming tradition knew that they must act on earth in the light of God's guidance if they were to be saved. Many Muslims thus became those activists for the faith that we see all over the world today.[27]

One consequence of these changes was the emergence of interpreters of Islam from outside the ranks of the 'ulama'. We have noted the emergence of Sayyid Ahmad Khan, whose Islamic modernism did much to fashion the people and the institutions which were to create the state of Pakistan. We should also note Mawlana Mawdudi, who was educated for the most part outside the world of the 'ulama', and who came to create both a vision of Islam as a system, an ideology, and the institution, the Jama'at-i Islami (or Islamic Society), which was to carry it forward. Mawdudi's totalitarian understanding of Islam, which it is said was influenced by his reading of Western social science, was particularly popular with the growing Muslim bourgeoisie. He and his followers were to play the major role in pressing for the Islamisation of Pakistan down to the introduction of such a programme by General Ziya' al-Haqq in the late 1970s. He was the ideal type of the Islamist thinker. The of lay interpreters of this kind was a feature of the Muslim world in the twentieth century. And frequently they drew inspiration from the West, as for instance Sayyid Qutb of Egypt's Muslim Brotherhood did from the French fascist thinker, Alexis Carrell, and 'Ali Shari'ati of Iran did from Frantz Fanon, Jean Paul Sartre and Louis Massignon.

A second consequence was the emergence of Muslims who felt personally responsible for making God's revelation live on earth. They felt empowered by this sense of personal responsibility; they also felt empowered by the capacity to engage with the central message of Islam themselves. They were the modern Muslims, as envisaged by Muhammad Iqbal, the leading Indo-Muslim poet-philosopher of the twentieth century, who realised themselves in the creative work of shaping and reshaping the world. As the Ottoman Caliphate died, Iqbal, drawing on the Qur'anic reference to Adam as God's Caliph or successor on earth, came increasingly to emphasise the dynamic role of man, by referring to man as God's Caliph, or successor on earth. This was an idea taken up by reformers, 'ulama' and lay alike, across the Muslim world. It is one full of potential, and not least for the fashioning of a new system of authority.[28]

What does this mean for religious authority in the Muslim world by the middle of the twentieth century? The authority of the 'ulama' has fragmented as they have come to pick and choose from the authority of the past. Moreover, the authority of the 'ulama' is no longer central to the working of Muslim societies as new lay interpreters have risen from outside the traditional systems for transmitting knowledge. This said, we should note that the introduction of print did not totally undermine the authority of the 'ulama'; they were able to use print to bolster their authority while others came forward to rival them.[29] Nevertheless, we can see a new type of Muslim beginning to emerge, who might note what the 'ulama' say, who might note what the Islamists say, but increasingly he, and those like him, will engage with the texts themselves. They will form their own conclusions and pursue what their conscience dictates. Thus, the individual human conscience, that most uncomfortable bedfellow for all forms of authority, began to work its way more fully in the life of Muslim societies.

****

Crisis of Authority: Crisis of Islam?

Let us now address the fate of religious authority in the second half of the twentieth century. There are several developments we need to note, which lead to further fragmentation of authority and what has been described as a 'spectacularly wild growth of interpretation.'[30]

The first is that in many Muslim societies religious authority continues to be exercised in the context of Western domination. Muslim states may have received their independence between the late 1940s, when Pakistan and Indonesia did, and the early 1990s, when the states of Central Asia and the Caucasus did, but through this period many were entangled first in the Cold War, and then increasingly with global capitalism, as it sought commodities and markets, alongside great-power assertiveness. Ordinary Muslims knew that the elites of their societies were often deeply engaged with the political and economic interests of outside forces. Many of you will recall the notable instances of Western bullying, and I include Russia as part of the West in this context: the overthrow of Musaddiq in Iran in 1953 by Britain and the US; the British invasion of Egypt in 1956; the Russian invasion of Afghanistan in 1979; the Russians in Chechnya in the 1990s; and the US and Britain in Iraq since 2003. Rulers who were subservient to the West risked losing authority. Listen to Ayat Allah Khumayni's scorn in June 1963 after the Shah's Israeli-trained security forces had attacked a madrasa:

> Shah . . . I don't want you to become like your father [who was forced to abdicate by the British and Americans]. Listen to my advice, listen to the ulama of Islam. They desire the welfare of the nation . . . Don't listen to Israel . . . You miserable wretch, forty-five years of your life have passed; isn't it time for you to think and reflect a little . . .[31]

Listen to Osama bin Laden's cheeky upbraiding of bin Baz, the Chief Mufti of Saudi Arabia, and its leading scholar, after he failed to criticise both the establishment of US bases in Saudi

Arabia after the first Gulf War and the Oslo Accords of 1993 between Israel and Palestine.[32] Bin Laden, a man of no scholarly credentials, declared:

> Honorable Shaikh you have reached a good age, and you have achieved much in the service of Islam, so fear God and distance yourself from these tyrants and oppressors who have declared war on God and His Messenger and stand with the righteous men . . . the most prominent characteristic of these righteous scholars was the way they dissociated themselves from sultans.

In many, though not all, Muslim societies 'ulama' are paid functionaries of the state. Thus, their authority suffers.

A second agent transforming the nature of authority has been the growth of mass education. Mass primary education only began in Egypt in the 1950s and in the Arabian peninsula in the 1970s. Now literacy in Egypt is 71 per cent, in Bahrain 85 per cent and in Qatar 87 per cent. We might note, too, that the literacy rate in the country with the largest Muslim population, Indonesia, is 83 per cent, but nearly 100 per cent amongst those of schoolgoing age.[33] And we might also note that Iran plans to have 40 per cent of the age cohort in higher education by 2010, a target just 10 per cent below that of the UK.[34] The context in which authority operates is very different from fifty years ago.

Not surprisingly the growth of mass literacy has stimulated the mass development of print media. In the religious arena the typical product is the small-format printed booklet, which would have been called a chapbook in early modern England. Some are written by 'ulama', but many by lay folk. They might give basic guidance as to how to live a good Muslim life, or present biographical models of such a life, that of the Prophet or a great figure from the Islamic past.[35] Alternatively, popular culture might be bent to didactic purpose, as in Bangladesh where a Mills & Boon tradition of romantic novels has been turned into a vehicle for religious teaching.[36] The great Turkish reformer, Sa'id Badi' al-Zaman Nursi, would send out his disciples with sacks of such booklets saying, 'they are my gazis [warriors for the faith]'.[37] Go to any major mosque or shrine, or small-town bookshop, throughout the Muslim world and you will find stalls full of such booklets.

The emergence of this new audience and the vibrancy of the market in religious print matter has been accompanied by the emergence of more and more interpreters – new authorities – from outside the world of the 'ulama': the schoolteacher, Rashid Gannushi of Tunisia; the lawyer, Hasan al-Turabi of the Sudan; the engineers, Mehdi Bazargan of Iran and Mahamed Shahrour of Syria. As these men, and others like them, spoke the language of those educated in secular systems, they continued the marginalisation of the 'ulama'. Then, particularly among women, the phenomenon of reading groups has sprung up to discuss the Qur'an and other texts.[38] Increasingly individuals, driven by conscience and by the requirements of much of the reforming movement that believers should engage directly with the sources of the faith, have insisted on their right to interpret. And in doing so they have brought to the process the repertoire of skills they have learned outside the Islamic tradition.[39]

The third agent transforming the nature of authority has been the growth of new media, by which I mean, in particular, cassettes, audio and video (and of course CDs), television, terrestrial and satellite, and the internet. All play their part in the democratisation of knowledge. They work, of course, for the 'ulama' as well as lay interpreters. It is well known how audio cassettes helped to project Ayat Allah Khumayni's authority in Iran in the years before the revolution of 1979. In the same way, the layman, Osama bin Laden, has used video cassettes, allied to satellite television, to project his message across the Muslim world, and beyond. The al-Jazeera Arabic satellite television channel of Qatar has given a great boost to the authority and reach of the traditionally educated Islamic scholar, Shaykh Yusuf al-Qaradawi. On his show he answers religious questions just as a traditional scholar might.[40] On the other hand, Sa'udi terrestrial television has made a huge success of the layman and popular preacher, Amr Khaled, who does not wear the traditional beard and turban, but is clean-shaven, dressed in a suit and adopts a style that unites Billy Graham and Oprah Winfrey.[41] The internet, however, is the great democratising force, which I sense must in time push authority further from the reach of the 'ulama'. So far, its main impact has been amongst Muslims in the West. In the rest of the Muslim world, internet penetration has been achieved for between 20 per cent and 40 per cent of the population only in Malaysia, Turkey, the Lebanon, the UAE and Qatar.[42] Nevertheless, its spread, with its ready access to key sources, and its host of different opinions, more or less neutrally presented, means further fragmentation of authority and further opportunities for individuals to decide for themselves.

Finally, transnational developments also undermine authority. In Western Europe, for instance, a feature of the Muslim experience has been that first-generation immigrants have tended to replicate the world from which they have come by bringing over 'ulama', usually in the form of Imams, from their countries of origin. More often than not these Imams have little understanding of the environment to which they have come. They are unable to offer informed and authoritative advice to often highly-educated second- and third-generation Muslims. It is a problem of authority painfully set out in Ed Husain's informative autobiography, *The Islamist*, which was published last year.[43] The second issue is that, along with the gulf which lies between the generations, all the fragmentations of authority which have taken place in the Muslim world, as it strove to respond to the West over the past two centuries, have been replicated in Muslim communities in the West. This is one of the reasons why in Britain and France, and doubtless elsewhere, there has been such difficulty in finding authoritative representatives with whom government could discuss religious issues.[44]

****

In the middle of the twentieth century we noted that religious authority was being fragmented, that lay interpreters were emerging to challenge the 'ulama', and that individuals were coming to interpret texts for themselves. Over the past half century, we have seen a massive increase in these processes aided by the growth of literacy, new communications technology, transnational movements of peoples, and the context of continuing Western dominance. The outcome has been a further fragmentation of authority in which 'ulama' have become just some amongst the many voices clamouring to be heard. In this world of democratic access to religious knowledge, and widespread capacity to use it, religious authority, in the helpful image of the French political scientist, Olivier Roy, has become a 'bricolage', a do-it-yourself-project. Increasingly every individual's view comes to have the same value as everyone else's. Arguably, the Muslim world has returned to the interpretative anarchy which marked its early years.[45]

This development created problems, but also helped to foster encouraging possibilities. One of the problems has been the lack of authoritative religious leadership to counter those who wish to serve their faith, and to do so at the extremes, with violence and terror. This was clearly the case for the young Moazzam Begg of Birmingham, whose naivety and good intentions saw him imprisoned in Guantanamo Bay.[46] It was also the case of Ed Husain, who only began to see the light when the activities of the London Muslim circles in which he moved embraced violence.[47] No traditional scholar, not one amongst the 'ulama', had the respect of the civil engineer, Abu Hamza, the so-called Imam of the Finsbury Mosque, who radicalised numbers of young Muslims and now moulders at Her Majesty's pleasure in Belmarsh Prison: 'the people who have been bestowed *ijaza* give us nothing but headache', he complained. 'What's the point of all this "Islamic knowledge" if it is not bringing anything positive to Muslim people and Islam?'[48] I have already told you of the contempt which that other civil engineer, Osama bin Laden, had for the Chief Mufti of Sa'udi Arabia. There is no doubt about the problems which come with the lessening of the traditional forms of authority and the empowering of individuals.

On the other hand, the weakening of traditional authority has also created possibilities, and opened spaces in which new interpretations, which might in time have authority, can emerge. I think of the creative Islamic modernism of Fazlur Rahman of Pakistan and of Nurcholish Madjid of Indonesia. But I think in particular of the brilliant Khaled Abou el-Fadl, educated traditionally in Kuwait and Egypt, also at Princeton and Yale, and currently a Professor of Law at UCLA. Working from within the Islamic intellectual and jurisprudential tradition, he has been able to produce powerful arguments for democracy, pluralism, and gender equality.[49] A second possibility takes off from the very last point. It is the growing movement by women scholars to unpick, indeed to shred, the traditional patriarchal interpretation of the Qur'an, demonstrating instead how the Qur'an affirms the complete equality of the sexes. At the head of this most important movement is the Afro-American Islamic scholar, Amina Wadud, who caused a stir in March 2005 when she led a mixed congregation in prayer. As the bourgeoisie expands in Muslim societies, as more women in many societies enter higher education than men, and as they also enter the world of work, I expect more and more women to argue against patriarchal interpretations of the faith.[50]

So, there is most certainly a crisis of authority. But does this mean there is a crisis of Islam? In one sense, yes, because that 'spectacularly wild growth of interpretation' has allowed through some understandings that are against the spirit of the faith. But, in another sense I would argue that this crisis is the making of modern Islam, the making of modern Muslim societies. The destruction of old forms of authority is empowering hundreds of millions of Muslims as individual believers, as individual trustees/successors/caliphs of God. The human conscience is getting a lot of exercise. It flourishes best in expanding bourgeoisies. We may reflect that it was the often inconvenient workings of the human conscience, operating in these very social locations, which helped democracy develop in the West. We may also reflect that it is the Islamist parties, the parties of the rising bourgeoisie, which have driven forward the development of democracy in the advanced Muslim countries of Indonesia and Turkey. Out of religious change in the Muslim world there may just be prospects for social and political development.

Notes

1. For a brief but excellent survey of issues and scholarship relating to religious authority and authorities, see Gudrun Kramer and Sabine Schmidtke, 'Introduction: Religious Authority and Religious Authorities in Muslim Societies: A Critical Overview', in Gudrun Kramer and Sabine Schmidtke (eds), *Speaking for Islam: Religious Authorities in Muslim Societies* (Leiden: Brill, 2006), pp. 1–14.
2. Hamid Dabashi, *Authority in Islam: From the Rise of Muhammad to the Establishment of the Umayyads* (Piscataway, NJ: Transaction Publishers 1989), p. 2.
3. Marshall G.S. Hodgson, *The Venture of Islam: Conscience and History in a World Civilisation*, vol. I (Chicago: Chicago University Press,1974), pp. 187–279.
4. *Ibid.*, pp. 71–93.
5. Al-Ghazali, *al-Munqidh min ad-Dalal*, W. Montgomery Watt (trans.), *The Faith and Practice of Al-Ghazali* (Oxford: One World, 1994).
6. William A. Graham, *Beyond the Written Word: Oral Aspects of Scripture in the History of Religion* (Cambridge: Cambridge University Press, 1987), pp. 96–7.
7. Ibn Khaldun, *The Muqaddimah: An Introduction to History*, trans. Franz Rosenthal, ed. N.J. Dawood (Princeton, NJ: Princeton University Press, 1967), p. 421.
8. J. Pedersen, *The Arabic Book*, trans. G. French, ed. R. Hillenbrand (Princeton: Princeton University Press, 1984), pp. 20–36.
9. Ibn Khaldun, *Muqaddimah*, pp. 431–3.
10. Pedersen, *Arabic Book*, p. 35; Timothy Mitchell, *Colonizing Egypt* (Cambridge: Cambridge University Press, 1988), pp. 150–4; Michael Chamberlain, *Knowledge and Social Practice in Medieval Damascus 1190–1350* (Cambridge: Cambridge University Press, 1994), pp. 137–8; Sayyed Hossein Nasr, 'Oral Transmission and the Book in Islamic

Education: The Spoken and the Written Word', *Journal of Islamic Studies*, 3, 1, January 1992, pp. 1–14.
11. E.M. Sartain, *Jalal al-Din al-Suyuti*, vol. 1 (Cambridge: Cambridge University Press 1975), p. 74.
12. Chamberlain, *Knowledge and Social Practice*, p. 139.
13. Sir Hamilton Gibb, 'Islamic Biographical Literature', in B. Lewis and P.M. Holt (eds), *Historians of the Middle East* (London: Oxford University Press, 1962), pp. 54–8 and Wadad al-Qadi, 'Biographical Dictionaries as the Scholars' Alternative History of the Muslim Community', in G. Endress (ed.), *Organizing Knowledge: Encyclopaedic Activities in the Pre-Eighteenth Century Islamic World* (Leiden: Brill, 2006), pp. 23–75.
14. Francis Robinson, 'Islam and the Impact of Print in South Asia', in Francis Robinson, *Islam and Muslim History in South Asia* (Delhi: Oxford University Press, 2000), pp. 66–104.
15. Mawlana Mawlwi Muhammad, 'Inayat Allah, *Tadhkira-yi 'Ulama-i Farangi Mahall* (Lucknow: Ishaat al-'Ulum, 1928), pp. 137–8.
16. Minute recorded in the General Department by Thomas Babington Macaulay, law member of the governor-general's council, dated 2 February 1835, in Lynn Zastoupil and Martin Moir, *The Great Indian Education Debate: Documents Relating to the Orientalist–Anglicist Controversy, 1781–1843* (London: Routledge, 1999), p. 165.
17. Christopher Shackle and Javed Majeed, trans. and introd., *Hali's Musaddas: The Flow and Ebb of Islam* (Delhi: Oxford University Press, 1997).
18. Orhan Pamuk, *Istanbul: Memories of a City* (London: Faber & Faber, 2005), pp. 79–96, 137–54.
19. Giuseppe di Lampedusa, *The Leopard* (London: Everyman, 1991)
20. A.J. Arberry (trans), *Persian Psalms (Zabur-i Ajam) . . . from the Persian of the late Sir Muhammad Iqbal* (Karachi: Sh. Muhammad Ashraf, 1968), p. 76.
21. Ralph Russell and Khurshidul Islam, 'The Satirical Verse of Akbar Ilahabadi (1860–1921)', *Modern Asian Studies*, 8, 1, 1974, p. 9.
22. Mawlana Mawlwi Muhammad, 'Inayat Allah, *Risala-i hadrat al-afaq ba wafat majmua al-akhlaq* (Lucknow: Nami Press, 1348/1929–30), p. 35.
23. For this diverse interpretative response, see Francis Robinson, "Ulama of South Asia from 1800 to the Mid-Twentieth Century', in Francis

Robinson, *Islam, South Asia and the West* (Delhi: Oxford University Press, 2007), pp. 59–98.
24. Idem.
25. Barbara D. Metcalf, *Islamic Revival in British India: Deoband, 1860–1900* (Princeton: Princeton University Press, 1982), pp. 198–215; Ulrike Stark, *An Empire of Books: The Naval Kishore Press and the Diffusion of the Printed Word in Colonial India* (Delhi: Permanent Black, 2007).
26. Robinson, 'Impact of Print', pp. 80–1.
27. Francis Robinson, 'Other-Worldly and This-Worldly Islam and the Islamic Revival', in Robinson, *Islam, South Asia,* pp. 171–88.
28. Ibid., pp. 179–82.
29. Francis Robinson, 'Impact of Print', pp. 80–1. Other professions were also able to rebuild their authority through print, not least medical hakims for whom authority was essential, see G.N.A. Attewell, *Refiguring Unani Tibb: Plural Healing in Colonial India* (Hyderabad: Orient Longman, 2007).
30. Fazlur Rahman, 'Approaches to Islam in Religious Studies: Review Essay' in Richard C. Martin, ed., *Approaches to Islam in Religious Studies* (Oxford: One World, 2001), p. 195.
31. Speech delivered by Khumayni at the Fayziya Madrasa in Qum on 3 June 1963, in Hamid Algar (trans. and ed.), *Islam and Revolution: Writings and Declarations of Imam Khomeini* (Berkeley: Misan Press, 1981), p. 179.
32. Bruce Lawrence, *Messages to the World: The Statements of Osama Bin Laden* (London: Verso, 2005), p. 12.
33. For the general argument, see Dale F. Eickelmann and Jon W. Anderson, 'Redefining Muslim Publics', in Dale F. Eickelmann and Jon W. Anderson (eds), *New Media in the Muslim World: The Emerging Public Sphere* (Bloomington and Indianapolis: Indiana University Press, 2003), pp. 1–18.
34. Personal communication from Dr Hasan Kaleghi, Iranian Minister for Higher Education, 21 January 2005.
35. For examples of these booklets, see Francis Robinson, ed., *Cambridge Illustrated History of Islam* (Cambridge: Cambridge University Press, 1996), p. 247.
36. Maimuna Haq, 'From Piety to Romance: Islam-Oriented texts in Bangladesh', in Eickelmann and Anderson, *New Media,* pp. 129–57.

37. Serif Mardin, *Religion and Social Change in Modern Turkey: The Case of Bediuzzaman Said Nursi* (Albany, NY: State University of New York Press, 1984), p. 4.
38. See, for instance, M. Hakan Yavuz, 'Nur Study Circles (*Dershanes*) and the Formation of New Religious Consciousness in Turkey', in Ibrahim M. Abu-Rabi (ed. and intro.), *Islam at the Crossroads: On the Life and Thought of Bediuzzaman Said Nursi* (Albany, NY: State University of New York Press, 2003), pp. 297–316, and Maimuna Haq, 'Reading the Quran in Bangladesh: The Politics of "Belief" Among Islamist Women', *Modern Asian Studies*, 42, 2–3, March/May 2008, pp. 457–88.
39. Suha Taji-Farouki (ed.), *Modern Muslim Intellectuals and the Qur'an* (Oxford: Oxford University Press/Institute of Ismaili Studies, 2004), pp. 18–19.
40. Jakob Skovgaard Petersen, 'The Gobal Mufti', in Birgit Schaebler and Leif Stenberg, *Globalisation and the Muslim World* (Syracuse, NY: Syracuse University Press, 2004), pp. 153–65. For the views of some 'ulama', and in particular Qaradawi, on how a new consensus might be formed out of fragmented religious authority, see Muhammad Qasim Zaman, 'Consensus and Religious Authority in Modern Islam', in Kramer and Schmidtke, *Speaking for Islam*, pp. 153–80.
41. Peter Mandaville, *Global Political Islam* (Abingdon: Routledge 2007), pp. 329–30.
42. Mandaville, *Islam*, p. 323.
43. Ed Husain, *The Islamist: Why I Joined Radical Islam in Britain, What I Saw Inside and Why I Left* (London: Penguin, 2007); Mandaville, *Islam*, pp. 320–1; Olivier Roy, *Globalised Islam: The Search for a New Umma* (New York: Columbia University Press, 2004), pp. 164–7.
44. Roy, *Globalised Islam*, pp. 201–20.
45. For an excellent discussion of individualisation and the decline of religious authority, particularly amongst Muslims in the Western world, see ibid., pp. 148–84.
46. Moazzam Begg, *Enemy Combatant: A British Muslim's Journey to Guantanamo and Back* (London: Free Press, 2006).
47. Husain, *Islamist*, pp. 129–53.
48. Speech of Abu Hamza, December 2000, cited in Roy, *Globalised Islam*, p. 166.
49. Khaled Abou El Fadl, Joshua Cohen and Deborah Chasman (eds), *Islam and the Challenge of Democracy* (Princeton: Princeton University Press,

2004); Khaled Abou El Fadl, *The Place of Tolerance in Islam* (Boston: Beacon Press, 2002); *Speaking in God's Name: Islamic Law, Authority and Women* (Oxford: One World, 2001).

50. Amina Wadud, *Qur'an and Women: Rereading the Sacred Text from a Woman's Perspective* (New York, 1999); Asma Barlas, *Believing Women in Islam: Unreading Patriarchal Interpretations of the Qur'an* (Austin: University of Texas Press, 2002).

6

Strategies of Authority in Muslim South Asia in the Nineteenth and Twentieth Centuries

AUTHORITY, IF YOU WILL forgive an obvious statement, is a fascinating phenomenon. You know it when you see it; you know, too, when it is not there. It can be deeply rooted in time; it can be destroyed in a matter of a few minutes. Who can forget how Mikhail Gorbachev's authority drained away publicly and instantly when, after the August coup of 1991, Boris Yeltsin challenged him before the television cameras? Authority is rooted in time and in context. It is constantly being made and remade, as the players in the game draw on the changing social, cultural and political resources available to them. It is always, even in the most apparently static societies, a work in progress.

If we move to a situation where one society rules another, and yet further to one where ruler and ruled come from different civilisations, as in nineteenth- and twentieth-century Muslim India, the business of constructing authority becomes yet more interesting. It might be thought that players would adopt strategies of authority which rigorously excluded the cultural resources of the other side, but this was certainly not so; the record shows rulers and ruled exploiting resources from each other in developing their strategies. Then extra spice is introduced to the mix, when technological changes, in particular in communications, and structural changes in power, make popular support, however expressed, an increasingly important bulwark of authority. This paper looks at the ways in which religious leaders, in particular the 'ulama', Unani hakims (the doctors of Mughal high culture), writers of poetry and prose, and those wielding power itself, constructed and reconstructed their authority in the nineteenth and twentieth centuries: The evidence is taken for the most part from the former centres of Muslim power in the north of the subcontinent. In conclusion some of the common themes in their strategies will be highlighted.

Religious Leaders

Here I am concerned with the strategies of authority of those who, from the nineteenth century, strove to provide religious leadership, most of whom were 'ulama'. The issue was, of course, how to fashion an Islamic society without power; the connection between din and dawla, which had existed from the first Muslim community at Medina, had been spectacularly broken. The key changes in the scene are well known. The British reclaimed many revenue-free grants which supported families of 'ulama'; they stopped funding madrasa education; they increasingly insisted on government servants having qualifications from government schools; and from 1865 administered their Anglo-Muhammadan form of the shari'a without the advice of muftis. From the annexation of Awadh in 1856, the Shi'a mujtahids of Lucknow faced the same prospect. These were desperate times.

One response was to develop a new relationship to the authority of the past. Not all religious leaders followed this route. The 'ulama' of Farangi Mahall, those following Ahmad Rida Khan Barelwi, and, as far as I understand them, the Shi'a mujtahids of Lucknow, maintained the full panoply of classical scholarship, the transmitted sciences and the rational sciences, those that hailed from the great Arab traditions and those which had come from the Greeks and had been elaborated by the Persians. Their authority, moreover, was authenticated in the traditional way of oral transmission, certified by an ijaza with its isnad, going back to the original author of the book, and indicating how this piece of knowledge was deeply rooted in the Islamic past.

Other religious leaders made the following two changes in whole or in part. The first, supported by all those involved in reform from the Deobandis and the Ahl-i Hadith through to the modernist Sayyid Ahmad Khan and the Islamist, Mawdudi, was a significant shift in learning from the rational sciences to the transmitted sciences, that is, to those which specifically surrounded and supported the Qur'an and Hadith. This was part of a significant shift taking place in Indo-Muslim civilisation away from the great traditions developed in the Iranian, Timurid and Mughal worlds, and towards the pristine inspiration of Arabia and the first community at Medina. It was a process which arguably had its early phases in the work of 'Abd ul-Haqq Muhaddith and the family of Shah Wali Allah, and for which the destruction of Mughal rule and the coming of British power created the opening for success.

The second change, which arguably was even more significant than the first, involved the complete rejection of the scholarship of the past, as the Ahl-i Hadith, Sayyid Ahmad Khan and his modernist followers, and Mawdudi and the Islamists focused once more, like the founders of the schools of law, just on the Qur'an and Hadith. The rejection of the authority of classical scholarship, and the ijazas that came with it, meant that authority would have to be found elsewhere: for the Ahl-i Hadith in their aristocratic background, their high levels of education, their Arabian connections, and perhaps their emotional and sectarian devotion to their maslak; for Mawdudi in his aristocratic background, his reputation for scholarship, his vast output of published work and his personal courage in pursuing his ends; for Sayyid Ahmad Khan in his aristocratic background and his abundant sincerity, but his flank was left wide open by his reliance on Western science. These qualifications, relied on to exercise ijtihad on the sources of the faith, seem a poor replacement for the authority of a great scholarly past. It would be interesting to know how the traditional 'ulama' rated the authority of Mawdudi. Sayyid Ahmad Khan from the point of view of many had no authority; he attracted fatawa of kufr from Mecca.

The new emphasis on hadith was a symptom, although a mighty one, of the way in which the Prophet as the perfect model for human life came to play a larger part in South Asian Muslim piety. One example was the Sirat movement which Iqbal tells us was kicked off by the influence of the Ahl-i Hadith. 'Probably', Cantwell Smith informs us, 'more lives of Muhammad appeared in every one of the years between the two World Wars than in any of the centuries between the twelfth and the nineteenth.'[1] It was to be expected that the authority of the Prophet would have a heightened presence in the thought and practice of religious leaders.[2]

This was almost as much the case for those who resisted reform as for those who espoused it. In the nineteenth century, for instance, Farangi Mahallis became much involved in mawlid ceremonies (ceremonies, often lectures, recalling the qualities of the Prophet given in the days leading up to his birthday) during the first twelve days of Rabi al-Awwal; by the twentieth century these ceremonies had come to attract large gatherings. Moreover, a Dar al-Hadith had been constructed in the Farangi Mahall muhalla. Family biographies reveal the growing centrality of the Prophet in their piety. Moving to the Barelwis the evidence suggests that the Prophet was even more central to the piety of Ahmad Rida Khan. For him, as Barbara Metcalf tells us, the Prophet was 'pre-eminent'. He wrote sixteen books on his life, composed Urdu verse in his praise, wrote on hadith and on the Prophet's family and companions. He made much of the Sufi doctrine of *nur-i Muhammadi*, the idea that there was a light of Muhammad, derived from God's own light, which had existed from the beginning of creation. Of course, he gave great importance to mawlid ceremonies.[3]

For modernist thinkers, from Sayyid Ahmad Khan through to Iqbal and beyond, the Prophet was central both to their piety and their thought. For Sayyid Ahmad Khan, Muhammad was the 'uniquely qualified guide for giving *tawhid* (the oneness of God) adequate expression in practical life'.[4] His love of the Prophet was expressed in much of his writing from his early tract designed to improve mawlid practices through to his defence of Muhammad against the wanton attacks of William Muir. Who can forget his *na't* which begins 'Oh my God, give me a burning breast!/ Oh my God bestow on me weeping eyes!/ Oh my God, keep me utterly intoxicated with the love of Ahmad!'?[5] Ameer Ali in his *Life and Teachings of Muhammad or the Spirit of Islam* made Muhammad both a man to be proud of and a truly modern man, bringing his authority to support change and progress.[6] For Iqbal the Prophet lay at the heart of his thinking from his early nationalist poem, *Tarana-i Milli* – 'The caravan leader for us is the prince of Hijaz,/ By his name our soul acquires peace.'[7] – through to his very last collection of poems entitled *The Gift of the Hijaz*. The Prophet's authority came to be deployed in support of new visions of life from the socialist through to the bourgeois capitalist.

It goes without saying that the authority of the Prophet was particularly important for the Muslim reformers. Barbara Metcalf has left us in no doubt as to the reverence for the Prophet which existed in the early Deobandi community; one story has Muhammad Qasim Nanawtwi walking barefoot the whole way from Mecca to Medina.[8] But more important was the central role of Hadith in Deobandi education and in their constructions of authority. So all six canonical collections of Hadith were taught to students in the space of one year, a practice which continues to this present day in Pakistan, and which has given South Asia a particular prominence in hadith scholarship in the modern Muslim world.[9] Hadith commentaries might be used, as Muhammad Qasim Zaman has shown, as a powerful way of bringing an author's voice from the past into the present.[10] Or yet more pertinently they might be used, as in the case of a 21-volume commentary by Zafar Ahmad Uthmani, to demonstrate, against the charges of the Ahl-i Hadith that they were based on mere opinion, that the legal doctrines of the Hanafi school were firmly based on the traditions of the Prophet.[11] Or, as in the case of one volume of this mighty work, Zafar Ahmad might use hadith to refute the arguments of his colleague, Husayn Ahmad Madani, in favour of composite nationalism. The example of the Prophet was too powerful a resource to ignore.

The elitism of this type of hadith scholarship should not blind us to the major change for most institutions, practices and cultural forms in this era, and that is the need to find roots in society at large. Muslim religious leaders, whose financial support the utilitarian British were concerned to reduce in every possible way, were not exceptions to this rule. The key means for doing this, as Barbara Metcalf has shown us, were the translation of the Qur'an, the collections of Hadith and the great books of the classical Islamic era into Urdu and the making of them widely and cheaply available through print, which was adopted by Muslims only from the early nineteenth century. As we know, the process began with the writings of Muhammd Isma'il Shahid of the mujahidin, who wrote in his introduction to the *Taqwiyat al-Iman* that he had translated the key quotations from the Qur'an and Hadith, supporting his argument, into 'simple and easy Urdu so that they would be comprehensible to all who read or heard.'[12] The process continued into the late nineteenth century and beyond with religious publications in Urdu forming a large proportion of all published work. The newspaper press operated most powerfully in support, as it has done to the present day. This shift from the elite language of Arabic and Persian into Urdu (and indeed other vernaculars) represented a profound indigenisation of the classical materials of the Islamic tradition.

Further means of building a constituency were by education, and in the case of the reforming Deoband tradition we know that by its centenary in 1967 it had taught 7417 students in its own Dar al-'Ulum, but claimed to have established or affiliated a further 8,934 institutions. All of this, moreover, was achieved by popular subscription; Deobandi education, as with that of the other nineteenth-century 'ulama' traditions, only survived if it provided a service which people wanted. One of those services was religious guidance, which came from its Dar al-Ifta, its Fatwa Office, and the regular publication of collections of fatwas. In meeting this popular demand for guidance Deoband was not only broadcasting its authority widely but also bolstering the concern of its 'ulama' that Muslims should follow their understandings of the shari'a and not those of their rivals or of the British courts. In this great revolution in the basis of Islamic society in India, from primarily a top-down one to a bottom-up one, the authority of individual 'ulama' remained supported by their ijazas, but it was now increasingly supported by a brand, and the public recognition of that brand, the Deobandi brand, the Barelwi brand, or perhaps at a stretch for the modernists, the Aligarh brand.

A similar development can be seen amongst the Sh'ia 'ulama', who have been too-long neglected. I base my comments on the excellent recent work of Justin Jones on the Shi'a of nineteenth- and twentieth-century India, in particular Lucknow. The Shi'a mujtahids, that is those who had been given an ijaza to exercise ijtihad by an established mujtahid, had in principle much greater authority than their Sunni colleagues. The victory of the Usulis over the Akhbaris in West Asia and India in the eighteenth century enabled them to use reason and consensus, as well as the Qur'an, hadith and the guidance of the Imams, in reaching legal decisions. Under the Awadhi regime they exercised considerable public functions, in addition to their religious roles, and were closely tied to the interests of the nobility and the state. This elite position was destroyed by the annexation of Awadh and the subsequent Mutiny Uprising. They were stripped of their offices, lost much of their financial support, and suffered the humiliation of having their premier religious site, the Bara Imambarah with its Asafi mosque, turned into a barracks for British soldiers. Like their Sunni colleagues they had to find new ways of bolstering their authority.

One way was serious scholastic endeavour. But more important, and also driven by financial need, they began for the first time to reach out to the Shi'a community at large and fashion a constituency for themselves. Mujtahids began to pay especial attention to their personal followers, their muqallids; they paid serious attention to gathering as many students as possible; they devoted much time to issuing fatwas, subsequently published by the Newal Kishore Press. Towards the end of the nineteenth century they founded two madrasas, negotiated successfully with the British for the return of the Bara Imambarah and the reinstatement of Friday prayer at the Asafi mosque. Then, in 1901 they founded the Anjuman-i Sadr-i Sudoor, whose purpose was to provide worldly as well as religious leadership for Shi'as throughout India, its purposes embracing everything from madrasa foundation to business support. By the 1890s, Jones argues, the mujtahids had gained an 'unprecedented level of public exposure and authority . . . [indeed] public involvement replaced scholarly reputation or the familial name as the crucial basis of clerical authority.'[13]

At the same time as the Shi'a mujtahids were adding to their authority by forming an organisation, and by playing once again a prominent role in public life, so were the Sunni 'ulama'. The three decades from the 1890s saw their attempts to develop organisations in order to assert their authority. The first was the foundation of the Nadwat al-'Ulama' in 1894. At its very first meeting Shibli Nu'mani declared: 'a very large part of the national life is in the ulama's right of ownership . . . and they alone have or can have absolute sway . . . over it.'[14] The process continued through 'Abdul Bari of Farangi Mahall's revival of the Majlis Mu'id al-Islam in 1910 to the foundation of the Jami'at al-'Ulama'-yi Hind, of which he chaired the first meeting in 1919 and which has remained the authoritative representative body of the Indian Sunni 'ulama'. Since Independence one might ask: how far did the authority of the 'ulama' come to be transferred to the two Personal Law Boards? Moreover, we should also note that the authority of the Islamists

(Mawdudiyat) has come to be embodied in Mawdudi's Jama'at-i Islami organisation. This said, the migration of religious authority from the late 1890s is evident, not in total but certainly in part, from the ijazas of the 'ulama' to the organisations they founded and the brands they represented. Indeed, these organisations played a key role in expanding the reach and weight of their authority.

The politics and actions of the 'ulama' organisations illuminate this purpose. Their overwhelming concern was to ensure their control over the shari'a. Their mastery of the jurisprudential traditions of Islam needed to interpret the shari'a lay at the heart of their claims to authority. This is what Shibli meant when he said that 'a very large part of the national life is in the ulama's right of ownership ... and they alone have or can have absolute sway ... over it.' This concern of the 'ulama' was manifest, as we might expect, whenever the state came to address aspects of the shari'a. So, in the colonial period the 'ulama' ran successful campaigns to achieve the amendment of the Waqf Validation Act in 1913 and to remove customary law from shari'a practice, a process culminating in the Shari'a Application Act of 1936. They were less successful, however, in the Child Marriage Restraint Act of 1929 and the Dissolution of Muslim Marriages Act of 1939. After Independence their concern was displayed in 1985 in Sayyid Abul Hasan 'Ali Nadwi's intervention as President of the All-India Muslim Personal Law Board in the Shah Bano case, and also by the view of the Pakistani 'ulama' that they had no objection to the codification of the shari'a, providing they were in charge of the process.[15]

The overwhelming concern of the 'ulama' for the shari'a is also manifest in their political vision and the practical actions they press forward. Their proposals for political progress under the British, whether it was those made by the Majlis Mu'id al-Islam to Montagu in 1917 or the Badaun proposals of the Jamiy'at al-'Ulama'-yi Hind of 1921, or their Saharanpur formula of 1931 – all sought what Peter Hardy called a 'shari'a protectorate', a form of jurisprudential apartheid.[16] This vision has also been echoed in the practical measures they urged and adopted from time to time. It is present in the *Imarat-i Shari'a* organisation, a legal system apart from the colonial state which, following the Badaun proposals, was established in Bihar by the Khilafat-Non-cooperation movement.[17] It is present in Ashraf 'Ali Thanawi's attempt to devise a structure of Islamic legal authority under colonial rule, which has its legacy, so Muhammad Qasim Zaman tells us, in the *Compendium of Islamic Law* published by the All-India Muslim Personal Law Board in 2001 and the Board's insistence that Muslims should resort to privately constituted shari'a courts.[18]

The relationship between the shari'a and 'ulama' authority as its interpreters is also revealed in their responses to madrasa reform. In Pakistan, government reports of 1962 and 1979 recommended that madrasas should be brought within the educational mainstream, certainly regulated and perhaps even integrated into the state educational system. Such proposals were resisted, in part because of the danger of subordinating the religious sciences to Western sciences, but in part, too, because 'ulama' argued that religion was part of a separate sphere which needed to be preserved. An attempt to devise a curriculum for all sectarian affiliations – Deobandi, Barelwi, Shi'a and so on – was further resisted on the grounds that the authority of scholars was in part dependent on sectarian identity – their brand. The bottom line, of course, was that the emasculation of the madrasas would lead to the emasculation of the authority of the 'ulama' as interpreters of the shari'a.[19]

I now turn to two further strategies of authority adopted by religious leaders. The first involves forms of oppositional engagement with other groups ranging from well-structured debates through to vicious sectarian struggles. Public debate was a feature of nineteenth-century north India, as Barbara Metcalf has demonstrated in an excellent section in *Islamic Revival*. Their functions, however, were not genuine intellectual exchanges; little attempt was made to listen to the other point of view or understand it. The major object was to build up the authority of the leading contenders, say Muslim, Arya Samajist or Christian, in the eyes of their followers.

It was the same for sectarian divisions within a particular faith. So Barelwis, Deobandis and Ahl-i Hadith assailed each other with accusations of kufr and their followers took pride in the combative role of their leaders.[20] Examining the *Madh-i Sabha* and *Tabarra* conflict in 1930s Lucknow, Justin Jones has concluded that, alongside the political and social changes of that decade, the key dynamic behind the outbreaks of Shia–Sunni animosity was generational change in the leading two families. So 'Abd al-Shakoor Faruqi stoked up the Madh-i Sabha agitation to be able to claim his father's authority as champion of Sunni polemics and a younger Kinturi mujtahid kept the tabarra agitation going to enable him to seize the lead from the senior Kinturi mujtahid.[21] Turning to Pakistan, Sayyid Vali Reza Nasr has argued that sectarianism was the outcome of one group of Deobandi 'ulama' trying to assert their authority in the country's religion and politics. These were the followers of Husayn Ahmad Madani, who had opposed the creation of the state. To rehabilitate themselves and to assert their authority, they played leading roles first in the agitation against the Ahmadiyya and then in that against the Shi'a.[22]

The final strategy involves authority and relationships with the government, which I shall restrict in this case to the colonial government. I am not concerned here with the Islamic modernists, who derived important dimensions of their authority from engagement with Western scholarship, and who, although in some cases willing to speak the truth to power, were also willing to accept honours from the British. Again, I am concerned with the 'ulama' and what I must describe as a somewhat ambivalent relationship to the British as a source of authority. I well remember Barbara Metcalf's horror when I mentioned to her that I had seen a file in the National Archives of India about the award of Shams al-'ulama' titles to two Deobandi 'ulama'. This could not be; Deobandis rejected all such baubles from the colonial power. In this case they did so; the file was just a record of the government's consideration of the matter. Indeed, Deobandi authority rested on their keeping their distance from the colonial power, accepting no grants from it, urging their followers not to use the British courts, and in the last thirty years of British rule going openly into opposition. The main group of Farangi Mahalli 'ulama' adopted a similar policy; they had only contempt for those members of the Bahr al-'Ulum faction in the family who accepted titles of Shams al-'ulama' during the Khilafat-Non-cooperation movement.[23] But matters were not quite so simple. When in the 1890s a faction in Deoband town tried to take over the Dar al-'Ulum, making a series of accusations in the process, the school council called in a retired Hindu government servant and the British collector of Saharanpur to testify to its integrity.[24] When in 1908 the Nadwat al-'ulama' opened in Lucknow, the Lieutenant Governor, Sir John Hewitt, presided over the ceremony with the leading Farangi Mahalli of the day present.[25] Moreover, the new style of madrasa education provided in Deoband from 1867 with its classrooms, central library, students admitted for a fixed course of study, with regular examinations, prize-givings, and annual reports on institutional performance, as well as that offered in the new Farangi Mahall madrasa from 1905, derived its authority from the colonial model which it followed.[26]

Two further points need to be made about religious leadership and authority. The first involves Sufi leadership. I recognise that many 'ulama' derived their authority in part from the spiritual dimensions of their lives, but here I am focusing on those leaders who are primarily Sufi. As compared with the 'ulama' they have been less troubled by the challenges and disruptions of colonial rule. They did not break, as some 'ulama', modernists and Islamists did, the chains of authority reaching back into the Islamic past; their shijras still take their line of authority back through the founding saints of their order, to 'Ali, and thence to the Prophet. Secondly, they did not have to realign the bases of their support under colonial rule. While some Sufis benefited from government patronage, the majority have always depended on popular support. As the saying goes: 'It is not the saints that fly, but their disciples who make them fly.' Also, like the 'ulama', they have had little difficulty in adopting forms of modernity to their causes, whether it be print in the early twentieth century or the internet in the late twentieth century. On the other hand, the past two centuries have brought some serious challenges to their authority; the assault of Islamic reform on many Sufi practices, indeed, on Sufism itself. In response, Ashraf 'Ali Thanawi, arguably the most influential South Asian Sufi of the twentieth century, set out to anchor Sufi doctrines in the hadith, and spent much of his career in demonstrating the concordance between Sufi and shari'a norms. Indeed, such were the elaborate rules, order and disciplines he required of his disciples that he was described as having an 'English' sense of organisation.[27] In a similar way the Chishti-Sabiri Sufis of Pak Pattan, in navigating the harsher, often Wahhabi-inspired, rhetoric of contemporary Pakistan, insist that theirs is the path rooted in the Prophet's sunna and the shari'a. They, and not the Ahl-i Hadith, the Wahhabis, the Jama'at-i Islamis and the Tablighi Jama'atis, are the rightful heirs to the Prophet's legacy.[28] Their strategy of authority is that they have the greatest right to speak for Islam, a claim with particular resonance in the Islamic Republic.[29]

The second point involves one of the ironies of the strategies of the religious reformers. The fracturing by some of them of the traditional systems for establishing authority; their translation of the Qur'an, collections of hadith, and many other works into vernacular languages; their encouragement of literacy so that individuals could engage with the sources themselves; their assault on all ideas of earthly intercession for man with God; their great emphasis on the individual moral responsibility of each believer, summed up in the idea of man as the Khalifat Allah, God's trustee on earth, which gained wide currency in the twentieth century; indeed, the fashioning of the individual human conscience as the platform on which an Islamic society would be built, opened the way towards a 'priesthood of all believers' and a reduction in the authority of religious leaders, in particular the 'ulama'. It is a moot point how far such developments have gone, or may go. Arguably, they are well developed amongst Muslim communities in the West, but in South Asia they are surely confined to the highly educated, for instance, those who might participate in preaching or reading groups.[30] Nevertheless, this strategy of authority may in time weaken what it set out to support.

At this point, let us review the strategies adopted in the religious sphere: there is the rejection of the Mughal/Persian inheritance (amongst the Sunnis); there is an embracing of Arab sources of authority represented in enhanced engagement with hadith; and more particularly there is the focus on the Prophet as the model. Alongside there is the revolutionary shift towards rooting authority in society at large; part of this process was the development of organisations which might embrace society and project a brand; with the development of brands there came oppositional styles, sectarianism, and its role in boosting the authority of brands, or indeed individuals; and finally, there was that ambivalent relationship with the authority of colonial rule.

Unani Hakims, Medical Leaders

Authority was just as central to the role of the medical doctor as it was to the religious leader. In considering the strategies of the Unani hakims we find many echoes of those adopted by the religious leaders. Excellent recent research on Unani hakims in nineteenth- and twentieth-century India has indicated the richness and complexity of the strategies adopted. I draw out three main strands.

The first involved a shift towards Arab cultural resources and the authority of religion and ultimately community. Thus, as Seema Alavi has shown so well, we note the abandonment of Mughal understandings of Unani Tibb supporting health as an aristocratic virtue, with its copious literature in Persian, in favour of the envisioning of Unani Tibb as a science, supported by a growing Arabic literature, often of a doctrinal sub-Wahhabi nature.[31] In the late-eighteenth and early-nineteenth centuries this shift was enhanced by the East India Company, which welcomed Unani Tibb as a science. One would have thought that it would be but a short step for leading Unani hakims, working in an Arabic-dominated discipline, to incorporate the authority of that increasingly powerful contemporary model, the Prophet. But no, the drive here came from those Alavi terms 'new hakims', those from outside the great medical families, major users of newspapers to advertise their wares. They really needed the extra authority which the Prophet could bring to their work. Once the door was open, however, the Prophet's authority was quickly incorporated into Unani practice as a whole.[32] By the twentieth century Shibli Nu'mani had taken the possible sources of authority one stage further, describing Unani Tibb as 'Islamic Medicine'. This latter development was strongly resisted by the greatest hakims of the day, the 'Azizi hakims, the founders of the Lucknow school of modern Unani practice, and Hakim Ajmal Khan, the founder of the Delhi school of modern Unani practice. Their opposition, however, was not enough to prevent a medical tradition, once widely shared by Hindu and Muslim, becoming an icon of Muslim identity and receiving its authority substantially from a Muslim past.[33]

The second strand of strategies flowed, as in the case of the religious leaders, from the decline of aristocratic and government patronage under the British, and the need to root Unani Tibb more firmly in Indian society – to indigenise it. Alongside this there was the need to defend it against Western biomedicine and the rationalising practices of the colonial state. Print, newspaper and book publishing, played an enormously important role in mediating these changes, creating a medical public sphere in Urdu; indeed, it became a source of authority itself. So, Unani Tibb became the ancient medicine of Hindustan, its methods and prescriptions closely aligned to the local environment and Hindustani constitutions, as mulki medicine, so much more sympathetic to Indians than that offered by the British.³⁴ So, hakims set out to root their prescriptions much more deeply and widely in the wealth of medicinal plants offered by India. By the twentieth century, they were, like the 'ulama', forming All-India organisations, first in 1910 as a joint organisation with the Ayurvedic practitioners, and then from 1911 in a breakaway conference led by the 'Azizi hakims of Lucknow and focused solely on Unani hakims. Both organisations had the same basic purpose of rationalising their traditions and promoting their interests to government. Of course, the all-India Unani Tibb Conference of the 'Azizi hakims was soon captured by Muslim communitarian purposes. The outcome was that a set of medical practices handed down through great families of hakims, from which they derived authority, came to be part of a national brand linked to the Muslim community, with much of its authority derived from its supposed indigenous roots, its national organisation and its Islamic impress.

The third strand involves the relations of the hakims with the authority of their colonial rulers. They had in general a much easier and closer relationship than the religious leaders. From early on they worked effectively with the British in public health matters.³⁵ The Ajmal Khan family of Delhi and the 'Azizi hakims of Lucknow, like the 'ulama' of Deoband and Farangi Mahall, both institutionalised the teaching of their disciplines after British models by creating, as Barbara Metcalf has shown us in the case of Ajmal Khan, 'formal schools with paid staff and fixed requirements to replace their personalistic informal settings of family homes and apprenticeship'.³⁶ Anatomy and surgery were added to the disciplines covered by the Unani hakims, certificates marked the successful completion of the course, and inspection by government was encouraged. Powerful drivers for the reshaping of the medical tradition were not just the knowledge that government was increasingly concerned to regulate medical practice, but the need of the elite hakims to assert themselves over a host of 'new hakims' who had begun to practice. Most striking was the way that both these great families of hakims drew on British authority to augment their own. British officials, as Barbara Metcalf tells us, graced every significant occasion in Ajmal Khan's institutionalisation of Unani reform down to 1916 when Viceroy Hardinge laid the foundation of his Tibbi College in Delhi.[37] Hakim 'Abd al-'Aziz purposely aligned the inauguration of his Takmil al-Tibb College in Lucknow with the days of the coronation of Edward VII in 1902.[38] This said, while noting the extent to which these elite hakims had reconfigured their authority, and drawn on their imperial rulers in doing so, we should note, as Guy Attewell has emphasised, that a degree from one of the new colleges did not entirely displace the traditional forms of authority represented by the teacher's ijaza or by belonging to a great family of hakims. The fullest authority now rested on several pillars.[39]

Literary Leaders

Moving into the literary sphere we find further echoes of the strategies of religious leaders and Unani hakims, as Muslim writers, robbed of aristocratic patronage and forced to relate to a more prosaic English-dominated world, set out to find authoritative modes of expression. At the heart of the process were those dominant figures in late-nineteenth-century Urdu literature, Muhammad Husayn Azad and Altaf Husayn Hali. There was a reaction against Persian models, against the ornate and flowery products of a failed courtly culture. So, in the 1870s, Azad laments the heritage of artifice which Persian has left with Urdu and the problems it gives Indians in writing and translating English.[40] So, too, Hali, while working on English-Urdu translation in Lahore, talks of his growing feeling for English literature as that for Persian 'began gradually to diminish'.[41] In these same years Nadhir Ahmad produced in his *Taubat-an-Nasuh* what C.M. Naim has described as one of the most appalling scenes in Urdu literature, when Nasuh piles his son's collection of old Persian and Urdu literature into the courtyard and burns it.[42]

There is also that shift towards Arab inspiration, which is well expressed in Hali's great *Musaddas*, his elegy on the rise and fall of Islam. 'Poetry', he wrote in his introduction to the first edition, 'has been bequeathed to the Muslims as a legacy by the Arabs for the purpose of awakening the community'.[43] He forsook Persian rhetorical style in fashioning the elegy, as Shackle and Majeed suggest, for 'the more virile model of Arabic', favouring a distinctive (and unusual) Arabic metre.[44] He filled the poem with quotations from the Qur'an and hadith and adorned it with many Arab names, for instance, the great centres of Arab culture in Spain. He talks of the 'rain of the Arabs' making the desert green, as of course, he suggests, the British were also doing in contemporary India.[45] The Prophet appears at the heart of the elegy as the active agent fashioning a new social and moral order.[46] The model of the Prophet Hali presents, as Shackle and Majeed have astutely observed, owed 'as much to Victorian values as to any putative Islamic ones'. Important was valuing frugality, cleanliness, sobriety, self-discipline, self-improvement and most importantly time. Thus, the Arab inspiration was deployed to reawaken the community, and that of the Prophet to support a vision of the ideal Muslim as a Weberian Protestant.[47]

Hali may have stressed Arab inspiration in literature and life, but both he and Azad were no less keen in their field, indeed embarrassingly keen, on English models, much more so than were the religious leaders and Unani hakims. So, in a famous lecture given in Lahore's Anjuman-i Punjab in May 1874 Azad called for a new Urdu poetry based on English models.[48] And in his masterwork of 1880, *Ab-i Hayat* (Water of Life) refers to the 'English language [as] . . . a magic world of progress and *islah* for our literature'.[49] What Azad particularly valued was the directness of English literature (dare I say its Anglo-Saxon quality) which would enable Urdu literature to break out of tradition, artifice and self-reflexivity.[50] Hali in his *Introduction to Poetry and Poetics* of 1893, in which he intended to transform Urdu poetry, advocated the development of simple 'natural' poetry, drawing on the authority of English writers, among them Milton and Macaulay. We do not know if he knew of Macaulay's notorious Minute on Education of 1835, with its lofty dismissal of all Asian literature. We do know, however, that in all the eighty-three chapters of his *Introduction* he does not refer once to the achievements of Persian poetry. Authority was only to be found in the West, and this was to continue to be the case into the twentieth century as 'natural' poetry metamorphosed into the socialist realism of the Progressive Writers Movement.[51]

Rulers

Finally, I turn to rulers, where we can see many of the same strategies of authority adopted but with one or two interesting twists. Let us consider the imperial British. After the Mutiny Uprising of 1857 their pretext of exercising power in the name of the Mughal emperor, whom they had held a virtual hostage, was stripped bare. They needed a source of authority greater than the declaration of November 1858, in which Queen Victoria, now Queen of India, undertook to mind the traditions and seek the improvement of her subjects. So, paradoxically, at a time when all forward-looking Indians were rejecting Mughal/Persianate forms, and embracing Arab, Islamic or Western models, the British chose the Mughal model as the face of their authority.[52] The Mughal durbar, as Bernard Cohn explained in one of his most influential articles, became the arena in which British political authority was expressed, although its rituals were transformed from those of incorporation to those of hierarchical subordination. Durbars were held at all levels throughout India. Then, in the 1870s Victoria was aligned more specifically with the great Mughal/Timurid heritage of power, being made Queen-Empress at a huge durbar, not in Calcutta, the British capital, but in Delhi, the old Mughal capital. The coronations of Edward VII and George V were celebrated at similar Delhi durbars in 1903 and 1911.[53] Viceroys, like Indian royalty of the past, would at ceremonial moments ride elephants; it was doing so, while entering Delhi in 1912, that

Viceroy Hardinge was nearly killed by a terrorist bomb. With the adoption of Mughal forms to express authority, there came, as Tom Metcalf has shown us so well, the casting aside of European classical style in architecture and the adoption of the Indo-Saracenic style, as the means to represent political authority in stone. Arguably, the ultimate British claim to Mughal authority from the past was the decision, announced at the 1911 Coronation Durbar, to move the capital of British India to Delhi. The irony was that Indo-Saracenic, the architecture of British appropriation of Mughal authority, was not found to be suitable for New Delhi.[54]

In the post-colonial states of Pakistan and Bangladesh most of the strategies of authority we have reviewed come into play. Both Ziya'al-Haqq in Pakistan and Ziya'al-Rahman in Bangladesh, generals with the blood of their predecessors on their hands, sought legitimacy in programmes of Islamisation, opening the door to vastly increased Arab influences and in the case of Pakistan's Awqaf department, a Sunnification of its monuments.[55] Both Ziya'al-Haqq and Ziya'al-Rahman annexed the authority of the Prophet to their cause, the former gracing his Islamisation programme with the title Nizam-i Mustafa, the Prophet's System, and the latter making Eid un-Nabi, the Prophet's birthday, a national festival. Leaders have also sought to root their regimes more deeply in society. Thus, from the beginning of Ayub Khan's reign in Pakistan Sufi shrines, as Robert Rozehnal tells us, came to be 'celebrated as sacred national spaces while pre-modern Muslim saints . . . [were] publicly embraced as poets, social reformers and proto-nationalists'.[56] And then, between bouts of martial law, they have sought the authority of the people through the ballot box. There has been some resort to Western models of authority. Jinnah, in everything from his Savile Row suits to his constitutionalism, supported them. Arguably, so did Bangladesh's Mujibur Rahman in his vigorous secularism. But then, towards the end of the twentieth century, as politics indigenised and geo-political frameworks shifted, the authority of Western models seemed to fade, as they have been appropriated and reshaped by Muslim societies.

Conclusion

How might we conclude? I reiterate my statement at the beginning of this essay that authority, however monolithic its expression may seem to be, is constantly a work in progress. Observing the strategies of religious leaders, Unani hakims, writers and rulers, we have noted in a very broad-brush way the following cultural resources in play: Mughal/Persianate models speedily being rejected by most Muslims but embraced, for the purposes of expressing power at least, by the British; Arab inspiration/Islamic models, involving increasing emphasis on hadith and on the example of the Prophet, which have grown in strength as time has gone on; Western models, which have been embraced with varying degrees of enthusiasm, but whose impact may be waning, as they are appropriated and transformed by Muslim societies; and finally, society, or the people themselves, as in the context of colonial rule and the commodification of aspects of culture, authority in South Asia went through its great tectonic shift from a top-down to increasingly a bottom-up process. In this change authority migrated from belonging largely to individuals to increasingly being enfolded in organisations which represented brands. In all of this there are many complexities, which forgive me for ignoring, although I must mention the tendency of multiple forms of authority to exist side by side like, for instance the individual human conscience in piety alongside the ijaza of the 'alim and the noble birth of the Sayyid. But I hope there is enough here for readers to appreciate the range of the cultural resources drawn upon, and the changing balance in the use of those resources.

Notes

1. Wilfred Cantwell Smith, *Modern Islam in India* (London: Victor Gollancz, 1946), p. 65.
2. Not all religious leaders were willing to accept the authority of Hadith. For an excellent discussion of the rejection of Hadith as a source of

authority by Khwaja Ahmad al-Din Amritsari, the founder of the Ahl-i Qur'an, see Ali Usman Qasmi, 'Islamic Universalism: The "Amritsari" Version of the Ahl al-Qur'an', *Journal of Islamic Studies*, 20, 2, May 2009, pp. 159–87.
3. Barbara Daly Metcalf, *Islamic Revival in British India: Deoband, 1860–1900* (Princeton: Princeton University Press, 1982), pp. 300–12.
4. Annemarie Schimmel, *And Muhammad is His Messenger: The Veneration of the Prophet in Islamic Piety* (Chapel Hill and London: University of North Carolina Press, 1985), p. 229.
5. Ibid., p. 229.
6. Ibid., pp. 230–1.
7. Ibid., p. 256.
8. Metcalf, *Islamic Revival*, p. 166.
9. Muhammad Qasim Zaman, *The Ulama in Contemporary Islam: Custodians of Change* (Princeton: Princeton University Press, 2002), p. 39.
10. Ibid., pp. 50–2.
11. Ibid., p. 41.
12. Metcalf, *Islamic Revival*, p. 200.
13. Justin Jones, 'Religion, Community and Shi'a Islam', forthcoming.
14. S.M. Ikram, *Modern Muslim India and the Birth of Pakistan (1858–1951)*, second edition (Lahore: Shaikh Muhammd Ashraf, 1965), p. 134.
15. Zaman, *The Ulama*, pp. 97–9.
16. Peter Hardy, *Partners in Freedom and True Muslims: The Political Thought of Some Muslim Scholars in British India 1912–1947,* Monograph no. 5 of the Scandinavian Institute of Asian Studies (Lund: Studentlitteratur, 1971), pp. 32–43.
17. Francis Robinson, *Separatism Among Indian Muslims: The Politics of the United Provinces' Muslims, 1860–1923* (Cambridge: Cambridge University Press, 1974), pp. 329–30.
18. Muhammad Qasim Zaman, *Ashraf 'Ali Thanawi: Islam in Modern South Asia* (Oxford: Oneworld, 2008), pp. 111–15.
19. Zaman, *The Ulama*, pp. 74–80.
20. Metcalf, *Islamic Revival*, pp. 232–3.
21. Jones, 'Religion, Community and Shi'a Islam'.
22. Zaman, *The Ulama*, p. 133.
23. Francis Robinson, *Islam, South Asia, and the West* (New Delhi: Oxford University Press, 2007), pp. 78–9; and see biographies of Abdul Hamid

and Abdul Majid Farangi Mahalli, Robinson, *Separatism*, pp. 421, 423–4.
24. Metcalf, *Islamic Revival*, pp. 119–20.
25. Mawlana Mawlwi Muhammad 'Inayat Allah, *Risala-i Hadrat al-afaq ba wafat majmua al-akhlaq* (Lucknow, 1348/1929–30), p. 35.
26. Metcalf, *Islamic Revival*, pp. 102–5; Francis Robinson, *The 'Ulama of Farangi Mahall and Islamic Culture in South Asia* (Delhi: Permanent Black, 2001), pp. 152–3.
27. Zaman, *Ashraf*, pp. 89–92.
28. Rozehnal, *Islamic Sufism*, pp. 34–6.
29. Ibid., pp. 37.
30. For this process at work amongst a women's preaching group in Sri Lanka, see Farzana Haniffa, 'Piety as Politics amongst Muslim Women in Contemporary Sri Lanka', *Modern Asian Studies*, 42, 2/3 (2008), pp. 347–75; and amongst a women's reading group in Bangladesh, Maimuna Huq, 'Reading the Qur'an in Bangladesh: The Politics of "Belief" Among Islamist Women', ibid., pp. 457–88.
31. Seema Alavi, *Islam and Healing: Loss and Recovery of an Indo-Muslim Medical Tradition, 1600–1900* (Basingstoke: Palgrave Macmillan, 2008), pp. 43–53 ff.
32. Ibid., pp. 216–28.
33. Ibid., pp. 321–33.
34. Ibid., pp. 265–78.
35. Ibid., pp. 100–53.
36. Barbara D. Metcalf, 'The Nationalist Muslims in India: The Case of Hakim Ajmal Khan', in Barbara D. Metcalf, *Islamic Contestations: Essays on Muslims in India and Pakistan* (Delhi: Oxford University Press, 2004), p. 123.
37. Ibid., p. 128.
38. Alavi, *Islam and Healing*, p. 296.
39. Guy Attewell, *Refiguring Unani Tibb: Plural Healing in Colonial India* (Hyderabad: Orient Longman, 2007), pp. 145–6.
40. Frances W. Pritchett, *Nets of Awareness: Urdu Poetry and Its Critics* (Berkeley: University of California Press, 1994), p. 141.
41. Ibid., p. 33.
42. Nazir Ahmad, *The Repentance of Nussooh (Taubat-al-Nasuh)*, transl. M. Kempson, ed. C.M. Naim (Delhi: Permanent Black, 2004), pp. 58–60; C.M. Naim, 'Prize-Winning Adab: A Study of Five Urdu Books

Written in Response to the Allahabad Government Gazette Notification' in Barbara Daly Metcalf, ed., *Moral Conduct and Authority: The Place of Adab in South Asian Islam* (Berkeley: University of California Press, 1984) pp. 311–12.

43. The first introduction to the *Musaddas* is reproduced in Christopher Shackle and Javed Majeed (trans. and introd.), *Hali's Musaddas: The Flow and Ebb of Islam* (Delhi: Oxford University Press, 1997), pp. 88–97. The precise reference is on p. 93.
44. The metre was a variety of mutaqarib, which was not favoured by large-scale poems in Persian and Urdu. Shackle and Majeed, *Hali's Musaddas*, pp. 29–30.
45. Ibid. pp. 60–2.
46. See the *Musaddas*, verses 21–54, ibid., pp. 109–23.
47. Ibid., pp. 76–7.
48. Pritchett, *Networks*, p. 34.
49. Ibid., p. 47.
50. Ibid., p. 143.
51. Ibid., p. 168 and Khizar Humayun Ansari, *The Emergence of Socialist Thought Among North Indian Muslims (1917–1947)* (Lahore: Mustafa Waheed, 1990).
52. David Washbrook, 'After the Mutiny: From Queen to Queen-Empress', *History Today*, 47, 9, September 1997, pp. 10–15.
53. Bernard S. Cohn, 'Representing Authority in Colonial India', in T. Ranger and E. Hobsbawm (eds), *The Invention of Tradition* (Cambridge: Cambridge University Press, 1983), pp. 165–210.
54. Thomas R. Metcalf, *An Imperial Vision: Indian Architecture and Britain's Raj* (Berkeley: University of California Press, 1989) and *Ideologies of the Raj: The New Cambridge History of India*, III.4 (Cambridge: Cambridge University Press, 1994), especially pp. 153–9.
55. Khan deals with this process most effectively in the latter stages of his thesis devoted to Shi'a-Isma'ili motifs in Indus Valley architecture. Hasan Ali Khan, 'Shia-Ismaili Motifs in the Sufi Architecture of the Indus Valley AD 1200–1500 (University of London, Ph.D. thesis, 2009).
56. Robert Rozehnal, *Islamic Sufism Unbound: Politics and Piety in Twenty-First Century Pakistan* (New York: Palgrave Macmillan, 2007), p. 24.

7

Islamic Reform and Modernities in South Asia

FROM THE BEGINNING OF the Islamic era Muslim societies have experienced periods of renewal (tajdid).[1] Since the eighteenth century Muslim societies across the world have been subject to a prolonged and increasingly deeply felt process of renewal. This has been expressed in different ways in different contexts. Amongst political elites with immediate concerns to answer the challenges of the West, it has meant attempts to reshape Islamic knowledge and institutions in the light of Western models, a process described as Islamic modernism. Amongst 'ulama' and Sufis, whose social base might lie in urban, commercial or tribal communities, it has meant 'the reorganisation of communities . . . [or] the reform of individual behaviour in terms of fundamental religious principles', a development known as reformism.[2] These processes have been expressed in movements as different as the Iranian constitutional revolution, the jihads of West Africa, and the great drives to spread reformed Islamic knowledge in India and Indonesia. In the second half of the twentieth century the process of renewal mutated to develop a new strand, which claimed that revelation had the right to control all human experience and that state power must be sought to achieve this end. This is known to many as Islamic fundamentalism, but is usually better understood as Islamism. For the majority of Muslims today, Islamic renewal in some shape or other has helped to mould the inner and outer realities of their lives.

This great movement of religious change in the Muslim world coincided with a Western engagement with that world of growing intensity. It should be clear, of course, that the movement of reform precedes the Western presence, its roots lying deep in the Islamic past, and being represented classically in the eighteenth century by the teaching of Muhammad ibn 'Abd al-Wahhab in Arabia and Shah Wali Allah in India. Nevertheless, from the beginning of the nineteenth century Western imperial powers surged across the Muslim world so that by 1920 only Central Arabia, the Yemen, Anatolia, Afghanistan and Iran were free from formal Western control. The process of decolonisation which spanned the period from the mid-twentieth century to the 1990s made little difference. The end of formal political control, more often than not, left elites in Muslim societies with strong external allegiances which, for a period, were made to serve the Cold War rivalries of the great powers, and throughout played their part in submitting their societies, to a greater or less extent, to the influence of global economic forces. Thus, over two hundred years, the old ways of getting and spending of nomadic and agrarian societies were supplanted by those of industrialising ones, often driven by global capitalism. The old social hierarchies, which brought order to many a locality, gave way to new classes. The old knowledge, hallowed from the Islamic past, was challenged by new knowledge from what often seemed to be a godless West. Powerful material symbols of these changes were the new Western-style cities, with broad boulevards, apartment blocks and shopping streets, with banks and cinemas and perhaps an opera house, which grew up alongside the old Islamic cities, often walled cities with a sultan's palace, a Friday mosque, a grand bazaar, sinuous lanes and gated quarters.

It was in this context of change, of the increasingly rapid erosion of old ways and cherished values, that the process of renewal took place. If the drive came from the inner compulsion of Muslims to make their faith live to the best possible effect, it was shaped in constant interaction with the changing material world in which it existed. Moreover, while Islamic reform often defined itself, in part at least, through its opposition to Western cultural and political hegemony, at the same time it made use, where appropriate, of Western knowledge and technology to drive forward its purposes and came to be fashioned in part by its interaction with it.

There were, associated with the workings of Islamic reform in these circumstances, changes which, taking into account the Western experience and noting the trajectories of Western social science, might be associated with modernity – admittedly always a relative concept. They were: the ending of the total authority of the past as Muslims sought new ways of making revelation and tradition relevant to the present; the new emphasis on human will as Muslims realised that in a world without political power it is only through their will that they could create an Islamic society on earth; the transformation of the self, achieved through willed activity, leading to self-reflectiveness, self-affirmation and growing individualism; the rationalisation of Islam from scripturalism through to its formation into an ideology; and finally a process of secularisation involving a disenchantment of the world which arguably has been followed by a 're-enchantment'.

These changes will be considered primarily in the context of the working of Islamic reform in South Asia. The focus will be on those in the tradition of Shah Wali Allah; some mention will be made of Sayyid Ahmad Khan and his modernist strand, but the main concern will be with the Deoband School, the Ahl-i Hadith, the Ahl-i Qur'an and the Tablighi Jama'at. Attention will be paid to the evolution of reform into the Islamism of Mawlana Mawdudi's Jam'at-i Islami. Moreover, the insights of that extraordinarily perceptive poet-philosopher, Muhammad Iqbal, who was admired by Muslims as different as Mawdudi, Sayyid Abul 'Ali Hasan Nadwi and Ayat Allah Khumayni, will be kept firmly in view. This is by no means a comprehensive list of those figures engaged in reform more generally; significant individuals such as Ghulam Ahmad of Qadian, 'Inayat Allah Mashriqi, Shibli Nu'mani and the remarkable Abul Kalam Azad are left out. Particular attention is paid to those in the Wali Allah tradition, however, because they embrace a religious change, aspects of a 'Protestant reformation' perhaps, which arguably helped to drive a broader set of changes in the Muslim world that we might associate with modernity. This position is adopted on the grounds that there is value in taking a Weberian perspective, while at the same time being prepared to recognise its limitations.

Let us identify the key aspects of reform in nineteenth- and twentieth-century India. First, it is crucial to remember the colonial context. British rule brutally removed much of the financial and institutional support for Islamic society. This helped to create a general anxiety about how a Muslim society might be sustained without power. Specifically, it meant that 'ulama', who had once received land grants and jobs in government, now turned to society at large to sustain them in their role. They would survive only if they provided services society wanted.

The theme of emphasising tawhid (the unity of God) and condemning shirk (actions which compromised the unity of God) ran through all the movements of the time. There was a running attack on all Sufi customs which, following Ibn al-'Arabi, suggested that God might be immanent rather than purely transcendent, which was expressed most frequently and forcibly in attacks on any practices which suggested that Sufi saints might be able to intercede for man with God. At their most extreme these attacks aimed to wipe out Sufism altogether.[3] By the same token, there were assaults on indigenous customs which had come to be incorporated into Islamic practice, for instance, following the Hindu custom of not marrying widows.

A major concern of all reformers was to review the knowledge handed down from the past to see what should be used to enable them to operate effectively in the present. At one level, that of the Deoband School, it meant no more than a shift in emphasis in the madrasa curriculum from theology and philosophy, and the triumphs of medieval Persian scholarship, to the Qur'an and hadith and those subjects which made these central messages of Islam socially useful. 'Ulama' in this tradition firmly followed the precedent of medieval scholarship in these fields, that is, observed taqlid. At another more exacting level, 'ulama' circumvented medieval scholarship and the schools of law to exercise ijtihad (independent reasoning), on the Qur'an and Hadith, if they were Ahl-i Hadith, or on just the Qur'an, if they were Ahl-i Qur'an. As the stream of reform flowed into ever more challenging contexts from an Islamic point of view, the demand for ijtihad became even stronger. It was used, after the mode of the Ahl-i Hadith, by both Islamic modernists and Mawdudi's Islamists.

A major concern of all movements was to spread knowledge of their reforming message as widely as possible. All to a greater or lesser extent founded madrasas or other educational institutions. The Deoband madrasa, founded in 1867, and supported by public subscription alone, was the model. By 1967 it claimed to have founded over 8,000 madrasas in its image. From these institutions came the teachers and scholars who provided the knowledge and the guidance to enable Muslim society not just to survive but also to entrench itself further. One important development at Deoband was the establishment of a Dar al-Ifta ready to receive questions and to issue fatawa all over India. A key development in supporting this self-sustaining community of Muslims was the introduction of print and the translation of the Qur'an and large numbers of important texts into the regional languages of India. The reforming 'ulama' were amongst the very first to use the printing press; rightly they saw it as the means to fashion and to consolidate their constituency outside the bounds of colonial rule.[4] Reform, moreover, reached beyond the world of the literate. From the 1920s, it was carried forward by the Tabligh-i Jama'at, or preaching society, in which the devout set aside a period each year to work in teams which transmitted the reforming message orally to small town and village communities.[5] The Tabligh-i Jama'at is said now to be the most widely followed society in the Muslim world. Thus, the reformers created a broad constituency for reform in Indo-Muslim society at large, and amongst the literate a growing body of Muslims who, without the constraints of a madrasa education, reflect upon the sources of their faith and interpret them for themselves.

The impact of the growing availability of knowledge of how to be a Muslim was only enhanced by the way in which the reforming movement made it clear that there was no intercession for man with God. Muslims were personally responsible for the way in which they put His guidance to them into practice on earth. Thus, the leading Deobandi reformer, Ashraf 'Ali Thanawi, in his guide for women (but also men) in the tradition, *Bihishti Zewar* (Jewels of Paradise), which is said to be the most widely published Muslim publication on the subcontinent after the Qur'an, paints a horrific picture of the Day of Judgement and the fate that will befall those who have not striven hard enough to follow God's guidance. To help believers avoid this fate, he instructs them in regular self-examination, morning and evening, to ensure purity of intentions and to avoid wrongdoing.[6] Thus, those in the Deobandi way, which was at the heart of India's reforming movement, were made powerfully conscious that they must act to sustain Islamic society on earth, if they were to be saved.

Emphasis on personal responsibility before God, and on the need to act on earth to achieve salvation, ran through the many manifestations of reform in India.[7] It was a central issue for Sayyid Ahmad Khan (d. 1898), who hailed from the reforming tradition but, in his development of the principles of Islamic modernism, travelled far beyond it: 'I regard it as my duty to do all I can, right or wrong', he said of his striving to realise his faith on earth, 'to defend my religion and to show the people the true, shining countenance of Islam. This is what my conscience dictates and unless I do its bidding, I am a sinner before God.'[8] This sense of personal responsibility was, if anything, even more enhanced in Muhammad Ilyas

(d. 1944), the founder of the Tablighi Jama'at. He was oppressed by fear of Judgement and by whether he was doing enough to meet God's high standards. 'I find no comparison between my anxiety, my effort and my voice', he wrote, 'and the responsibility of Tabligh God has placed upon my shoulders. If he shows mercy, He is forgiving, merciful, and if He does justice, there is no escape for me from the consequences of my guilt.'[9] Barbara Metcalf has cast doubt on the levels of anxiety amongst Islamic reformers.[10] But anxiety does seem to be abundantly present amongst its leaders, at least.[11] It is reflected, moreover, into life in general. In his autobiography, the nephew of Ilyas, Muhammad Zakariyya Kandhlawi, shows himself to be constantly aware of time, concerned about punctuality, worried about wasting resources (on marriages for instance), punctilious in all money matters and delights in the story of a colleague who kept a note of the minutes taken up by visitors when he was teaching in the madrasa so that he could repay an appropriate amount from his salary at the end of the month. His is witness to a life lived anxiously in the sight of God.[12]

The sense of personal responsibility and the centrality of action on earth to the Muslim life was expressed most completely by that sensitive and remarkable thinker, Muhammad Iqbal (d. 1938). For Iqbal, man was chosen by God, but equally free to choose whether he followed God's guidance or not. Man realised himself in the creative work of shaping and re-shaping the world. The reality of the individual was expressed most explicitly in action. 'The final act', he declares in the closing sentences of his *Reconstruction of Religious Thought in Islam*, 'is not an intellectual act, but a vital act which deepens the whole being of the ego and sharpens his will into creative assurance that the world is not just something to be seen and known through concepts, but to be made and remade by continuous action.'[13] Man was the prime mover in God's creation. As the prime mover, man was God's representative on earth, his viceregent, the Khilafat Allah. Thus, Iqbal draws the Qur'anic reference to Adam as his vice-regent, or successor, on earth, which had been much discussed by medieval commentators on the Qur'an, and not least among them, Ibn Taymiyya and Ibn al-'Arabi, into the modern politico-Islamic discourse of South Asia. In doing so, he both emphasises the enormous responsibility of each individual human being in the trust he/she has received from God and encapsulates that relationship in the concept of the caliphate of each individual human being.[14] The idea was taken further by Mawlana Mawdudi who added his considerable weight to its acceptance.[15] Indeed, the idea is present in much of the movement of reform in the Shi'a as well as the Sunni world.[16]

Taken together these key aspects of reform come close to that mix of aspects of 'Protestantism' which Eisenstadt argued some years ago gave it transformative potential. They were: its 'strong combination of "this-worldliness" and transcendentalism', its 'strong emphasis on individual activism and responsibility', and 'the direct relationship of the individual to the sacred and the sacred tradition', which in South Asia becomes stronger the closer reform moves into the modes of the Ahl-i Hadith and the Islamists.[17]

****

Let us turn to those new facets of Muslim life and thought which seem to spring, in part at least, from the religious changes of reform and represent aspects of what we might associate with modernity.

The Assault on the Authority of the Past

There is the assault on the authority of the past. While never forgetting that Islam expresses itself in different ways in different contexts, we may assert that a pervasive feature of Muslim societies has been what Bill Graham has termed the isnad paradigm.[18] At the heart of this, of course, is the system for the transmission of hadith in which the authority of a tradition lies in the isnad or chain of individual transmitters from the Prophet, or his companions, down to the most recent receiver. The defining elements of the paradigm are that authority is derived from linkage to the origins of the tradition through an unbroken chain of personal transmission. Central is the belief that truth does not reside in documents, however authentic, ancient, or well preserved, but in 'authentic human beings and their personal connections with one another.' Authoritative transmission of knowledge through time was by people both learned and righteous, the person-to-person transmission of 'the golden chain of sincere Muslims'. This was a model which expanded to embrace Sufis, the Shi'a, and the descendants of the Prophet in general. It was also a model which applied to all forms of learning. So, when a pupil had finally demonstrated his mastery, say, of Suyuti's *Jalalayn* he would be given an ijaza or permission to teach which would have all the names of those who had transmitted the book going back to Suyuti himself.[19] Should he wish, he could consult the tadhkirahs, or collective biographies, and see how many like him had received the central messages of Islamic knowledge from their teachers and transmitted it to their pupils. It was thus that authoritative knowledge was passed to the present.

Reform assaulted this authority from the past in two main ways. First, there was the jettisoning by the reformers of much of the medieval scholarship of the Islamic world. If the Deobandis cut out much of the great Persianate traditions of scholarship in ma'qulat, the rational sciences, the Ahl-i Hadith, the Ahl-i Qur'an, the modernists and the Islamists cut out the great traditions of Islamic scholarship altogether. In their concern to make contact with the Qur'an and Hadith afresh, in making them relevant to the modern world, they cast aside a thousand years of intellectual effort in fashioning a Muslim society, and the authority that came with direct connection to that effort.

Second, there was reform's vigorous support for the adoption of print. From the very beginning print was the weapon of reform. Amongst the first printed works in Urdu were two tracts of the 1820s, the *Sirat al-Mustaqim* and the *Taqwiyat al-Iman* of Muhammad Isma'il, who died with Sayyid Ahmad Barelwi in 1831 on the latter's jihad in the Northwest Frontier. During the nineteenth century, religious titles formed the largest category of Urdu books.

The town of Deoband was renowned for the number of its bookshops. Certainly, reformers insisted that readers should only consult religious books in the company of an 'alim, a learned man, so that the possibility of proper understanding and authoritative transmission could be maintained. But in practice anyone could now read the sources and, as they came to be translated into Indian languages, read the great textbooks of the past and decide, without the benefit of a great sheaf of ijazas, what they meant for Islam in the present.[20]

It is difficult for us, so profoundly moulded by our 'modern' experience, to grasp the psychological impact, indeed the pain, of jettisoning so much of the past, the special connectedness this gave to the work of fashioning the community through time, and the authority that came with it. This, moreover, was just one amongst a series of challenges to Muslim civilisational authority at the time, to be seen alongside that of Western science to theology, Western biomedicine to Unani Tibb, that of Western literary forms to Muslim ones, that of Western manufactured goods to the output of Muslim craftsmen, and that of Western powers to remnants of Muslim might. Arguably, all was brought to a head in the outpouring of emotion which accompanied the ending of the Turkish Khilafat between 1919 and 1923, the breaking symbolically of the continuous chain of leadership of the Muslim community back to the Prophet, an event which resonated at a deep psychological level. All was summed up by the poet Akbar Ilahabadi:

> The minstrel, and the music, and the melody have all changed.
> Our very sleep has changed; the tale we used to hear is no longer told.
> Spring comes with new adornments; the nightingales in the garden sing a different song.
> Nature's every effect has undergone revolution.
> Another kind of rain falls from the sky; another kind of grain grows in the field.[21]

In the outcome the revolution was not quite so complete as Akbar suggests. The old style of authority rooted in connectedness to the past has remained in the 'ulama' of the Deobandi tradition, as in those of the followers of Ahmad Rida Khan Barelwi (d. 1921). But the breaking of the continuous link with the past has enabled new forms of religious authority to emerge, an authority which could be made and remade in each generation, and make use of the new resources of the times – a very modern kind of authority. Arguably, Mawlana Mawdudi was representative of this new form. He had been educated outside the madrasa system and vigorously attacked the 'ulama' for their attachment to old forms of authority. Indeed, his only claim to authority derived from Islamic tradition was his assertion that he was a mujaddid, a renewer of the faith, in the mould of al-Ghazali (d. 1111), Ibn Taymiyya (d. 1328), or Shaykh Ahmad Sirhindi (d. 1624). Otherwise, Mawdudi's authority was derived from the following: his character – a man of principle, self-reliant, dedicated and courageous, quite unmoved when condemned to death by the Pakistani authorities in 1953; his style – his aristocratic manners and his beautiful Urdu, deploying reason rather than rhetoric; and his life in which he defined himself in opposition to traditional authority – 'I recognise no king or ruler above me', he declared, 'nor do I bow before any government; nor do I view any law as binding on me . . . nor do I accept any tradition or custom.'[22] Thus, the reformers, the Deobandis apart, drove a coach and horses through the old authority resting on a connectedness to a 'sacred' past and created new forms, future-oriented forms, which could be regularly remoulded with the materials then available.

The New Emphasis on Human Will

The second outcome of reformism was the new emphasis on human will. In the absence of Muslim power it was the will of each individual Muslim which was to fashion an Islamic society.

Knowledge of the central messages of the faith was made accessible and widely spread, and it was the individual human conscience, working with this knowledge, which now had sole responsibility to ensure rightly guided behaviour. Thus, reformed Islam was a willed faith, a 'Protestant' faith, a faith of conscience and conviction.

In the reformed world the will of women was emphasised no less than that of men. Indeed, under colonial rule, the responsibility for fashioning a Muslim society fell particularly heavily on women. As non-Muslims dominated public space, women moved from their earlier position of being threats to the proper conduct of Muslim society to being the mistresses of private Islamic space, key transmitters of Islamic values and symbols of Muslim identity. It was for this reason that Ashraf 'Ali Thanawi wrote *Bihishti Zewar* for women so that with the learning of a 'mawlwi', as he put it, they could play their parts in asserting tawhid and in fashioning an Islamic society.[23] It was for this reason, too, that Mawdudi insisted that women should acquire the same level of Islamic knowledge as men, and examine their consciences in the same way. This said, their task was to be the rulers of domestic space, sealed off from all those elements of kufr which polluted public space. 'The harim', he declared, 'is the strongest fortress of Islamic civilisation, which was built for the reasons that, if it [that civilisation] ever suffered a reverse it [that civilisation] may then take refuge in it.'[24]

The new emphasis on human will heightened ideas of human instrumentality in the world. Indeed, it runs through all the manifestations of reform, often laced with a sense of urgency. The very life of Sayyid Ahmad Khan is testament to his belief that he, as an individual, must take action for the good of the community and of Islam.[25] Reformers from Ashraf 'Ali Thanawi to Mawdudi emphasised that if a man knew what he should do, he must do it. Knowing meant doing. They were depicted as terrified by the thought that they might not be doing enough to be saved. Thus, Husayn Ahmad Madani, Principal of Deoband in the mid-twentieth century, would weep at the thought of his shortcomings. And, of course, no one laid as much emphasis on the Muslim as a man of action as Iqbal. Man, as the prime mover in God's creation, would by his repeated effort bring the world closer and closer to being a Qur'anic society. Thus, the reforming vision empowered Muslims on earth.[26] Thus, too, that most sensitive observer, Wilfred Cantwell Smith, in his *Islam in Modern History* (1957) referred to the extraordinary energy which had coursed through the Muslim world in the nineteenth and twentieth centuries, talking of 'dynamism, the appreciation of activity for its own sake, and at a level of feeling a stirring of intense, even violent, emotionalism . . .'[27]

Women, too, have felt empowered although almost invariably it has been at the cost of enduring the tensions generated between their desire and capacity to act, on the one hand, and the demands of patriarchy and the symbolic requirements of community on the other. Historically, these tensions have been most acute amongst women from well-off families, but as time has gone on they should, in all likelihood, have become more widely spread. In his recent book, Yoginder Sikand has surveyed some of the women's madrasas which have come up in India since Independence. They range from madrasas in the Deobandi tradition through those of the Jama'at-i Islami to those of the Mujahids, an Ahl-i Hadith-style group in Kerala. The outcomes were different in different reforming traditions and environments. Deobandi women's madrasas in north and central India, while insisting on strict purdah and patriarchal control, do enable women to become both teachers in girls' madrasas in India and abroad and to set up their own madrasas.[28] In the case of the less conservative Jama'at-i Islami madrasas, girls study traditional and modern subjects, including English. The aim is that they should become religious authorities in their own right as well as teachers, founders of madrasas, or even practitioners of Unani medicine.[29] In the Mujahid madrasas of Kerala the empowerment of women has gone much further. The senior Mujahid leader, 'Abd al-Qadir, made it clear that women could be the teachers of men. In fact, Mujahid women work outside the home alongside men, including being elected to local councils, the main restriction being that they should not be left alone with a man. 'Islam', declared Zohra Bi, a leading figure in Mujahid education, 'is wrongly thought of as a religion of women's oppression. Through our work in the college we want to show that Islam actually empowers Muslim women to work for the community at large.'[30]

Transformation of the Self

A third outcome of reformism was a crucial transformation of the self which, under the guidance of Charles Taylor and others, we have come to associate with modernity. This transformation involves in part an inward turn, the growth of self-consciousness and reflectiveness which Taylor argues is an important part of the constitution of the modern self,[31] and in part the affirmation of ordinary life which Taylor asserts 'although not uncontested and frequently appearing in secularised form, has become one of the most powerful ideas in modern civilisation.'[32]

We have noted that self-examination was a key aspect of Islamic reform; a willed Islam had to be a self-conscious one. This stimulated an inward turn and the growth of a reflective habit. Muslims had to ask themselves regularly if they had done all in their power to submit to God and to carry out His will in the world. In book seven of *Bihishti Zewar* Ashraf 'Ali Thanawi has a charming way of illustrating the process of regular self-examination to ensure purity of intention and avoidance of wrongdoing. He suggests to the believer that she sets aside a little time in the morning and the evening to speak to her lower self, her nafs, as follows:

> O Self, you must recognise that in this world you are like a trader. Your
> stock-in-trade is your life. Its profit is to acquire well-being for ever, that is,

salvation in the afterlife. This is indeed a profit! If you waste your life and

do not gain your salvation, you suffer losses that reach to your stock-in-trade.

That stock-in-trade is so precious that each hour – indeed, each breath – is valuable beyond limit.

O Self, recognise God's kindness that death has not yet come.

O Self, do not fall into the deception that Almighty God will surely forgive you.[33]

This theme of self-consciousness and self-examination is to be found in many religious thinkers of the late nineteenth and twentieth centuries, whether we look at Muhammad Ilyas and Mawdudi or Sayyid Ahmad Khan and Iqbal. In Reformation Europe the process was accompanied by the emergence of the spiritual diary.[34] Something similar, though not directly comparable, exists from the India of Islamic reform. There is, for instance, Mawlana Mahomed 'Ali's semi-spiritual *My Life a Fragment*, which was written while he was interned during World War One, or Dr Syed Mahmud's record of his spiritual reflections while in jail after the Non-cooperation movement.[35] There is also a great deal of correspondence with Sufis, which often contains processes of self-examination. With such evidence for the reflective habit, alongside the widespread exhortation to examine the self, it is arguable that the development of Islamic reform helped to open up an interior landscape. Whereas in the past the reflective believer, the mystic, might have meditated on the signs of God, the new type of reflective believer reflected on the self and the shortcomings of the self. Now the inner landscape became a crucial site where the battle of the pious for the good took place. Doubtless, there had been Muslims in the past, in particular times and in particular contexts, for whom this had been so. Who can forget the anguished reflections of that great eleventh-century scholar, al-Ghazali, in his autobiography, *The Deliverance from Error*?[36] Nevertheless, the importance of Islamic reform was that self-consciousness and self-examination were encouraged to become widespread. Moreover, once the window on the inner landscape had been thrown open by reform, it could stay open for purely secular purposes.[37]

With the inward turn, there also came the affirmation of the things of the self, the ordinary things of daily life. We can see this process at work in the new trends which emerge in the biographies of the Prophet, whose number increase greatly in the twentieth century. Increasingly, Muhammad is depicted not as the 'Perfect Man' of the Sufi tradition, but as the perfect person. Less attention, as Cantwell Smith has pointed out, is given to his intelligence, political sagacity and capacity to harness the new social forces in his society and much more to his qualities as a good middle-class family man: his sense of duty and his loving nature, and his qualities as a good citizen, his consideration for others and in particular those who are less fortunate.[38] The transition is also mirrored in changes which take place in biographical writing generally; the concern is less with what the individual might have contributed to Islamic civilisation and more on his life in his time and his human qualities. Even in the writings of the 'ulama' it is possible to see them responding to the humanistic preferences of their times and depicting much more rounded lives to support their didactic purpose. Another dimension of this process was the growing discussion of family and domestic issues, and particularly women, in public space. This discourse was begun by men such as Nadhir Ahmad, Hali and Mumtaz 'Ali in the late-nineteenth century, but in the twentieth century it was increasingly taken up by women, and not least by the tens of women who aired their views in those remarkable journals, *Ismat* and *Tehzib un-Niswan*. All matters were discussed in public, from education, diet and dress to love marriages, divorce and sources of women's inferiority. The writing is often assertive in style, demanding that women be given respect. Alongside these developments, there came the rise of the short story and the novel, which indicated the new value being given to understanding human character and the many ways of being human. The themes, often shocking in their day, which were taken up by leading practitioners such as Manto and Ismat Chughtai – family life, relationships, feelings, sex – indicate the new areas in which Muslims were finding meaning. Of course, not all of these striking changes can, by any means, be laid at the door of Islamic reform; the influence of the West and developments in wider Indian society all had their part to play. Nevertheless, such was the importance of these profoundly human matters that religious thinkers could not afford to ignore them.[39] 'The Islamic pattern of life', declared the religious philosopher Syed Vahiduddin, 'finds expression in religious and moral acts, in prayer, in love, in forgiveness, in seemingly mundane activities such as sex and domestic life, which should be radiated by the glow of the world beyond.'[40]

Rationalisation

Rationalisation of religious belief and practice was a further outcome of Islamic reform. In using the term, however, it is not given the full weight of the Weberian concept in which areas of modern life, from politics to religion to economics, become increasingly marked by the impact of science, technology and bureaucracy, though there is much of value in the rationalising trajectory.

By emphasising the development of a scriptural faith focused on the Qur'an and hadith, by attacking local custom around which many superstitions revolved, and by attacking all idea of intercession at Sufi shrines, indeed at times by attacking Sufism itself, Islamic reform rationalised belief and practice. Print was ever the handmaid as it made available the Qur'an in forms that believers could read, and as it produced guides which specifically stated what practices should be followed and what customs abandoned.[41] Reforming 'ulama' used their organisations developed through the Deoband madrasa and its political wing, the Jamiy'at al-'ulama'-yi Hind, to put pressure on the colonial state to remove all elements of custom from the personal law. Thus between 1918 and 1920 reforming 'ulama' successfully pressed the state to remove Hindu custom which persisted in law governing Muslims in the Punjab, Memons in Western India and Mapillas in Kerala. Then from the 1920s the Jamiy'at waged a campaign to impose shari'a law over custom in the personal law throughout India, a rationalising campaign crowned with success in the Shari'at Application Act of 1937. Through this work of rationalisation, which began to reorient Muslims from local cults towards widely shared practices and symbols, Islamic reform helped to prepare Muslims for the world of the modern political party and the modern state.

Side by side with this there went the reification of Islam. The reforming impulse, in which submitting to God became an act of will rather than an unquestioning following of the folkways of the faith, drove the development, although some responsibility must be attributed to the impact of the colonial state. Men and women consciously embraced a particular set of beliefs and practice that they identified with 'true' Islam, and abandoned others which could not be so identified.[42] But this reification process stemmed in part, too, from two additional influences: the distancing impact of print which enabled Muslims to stand apart from their faith, analyse and conceptualise it, and their growing consciousness, which was especially strong in India, that they were living alongside other faiths, at times real competitors, which were also reified, or being so. For the first time, in the late-nineteenth century, Muslims begin to use the term 'Islam' not just to describe their relationship to God, but to describe an ideal religious pattern, or a mundane religious system, or even just Islamic civilisation. Thus, it appears in the title of the poet Hali's masterwork, *Musaddas, Madd-o jazr-i Islam* (1879) or Ameer Ali's *Spirit of Islam* (1891). It does not appear in the title of Ashraf 'Ali Thanawi's *Behishti Zewar*, although the contents of the book are very much the forerunners of the host of how-to-be-a-proper-believer books which have followed, for instance, Mawdudi's *Towards Understanding Islam* of 1940, Muhammad Hamidullah's *Introduction to Islam* of 1959 or Manzoor Nomani's *What Islam Is* of 1964.[43] In the latter part of the twentieth century, along with mass education, this reification of Islam in Muslim consciousness has become widespread.[44]

The final stage in the reification of Islam, but arguably also in its rationalisation, was its conceptualisation as a system. This was the particular achievement of Mawdudi, growing out of his concern to establish an Islamic vision of life to set against that of the West, and which was to be protected against the West. He describes Islam as a nizam, a system which was comprehensive, complete and covered all aspects of human existence. These aspects, moreover, were integrated as the human body was integrated into one homogeneous whole. God in another image was the great engineer in his workshop; he had created the world and in the shari'a had given man a complete set of principles on which to conduct himself in that place. 'It is his explicit Will', Mawdudi states:

> that the universe – this grand workshop with its multifarious activities – should go on functioning smoothly and graciously so that man – the prize of creation – should make the best and most productive use of all his powers and resources, of everything that has been harnessed for him in the earth and in the high heavens . . . The *Shari'ah* is meant to guide the steps of man in this respect.[45]

This vision of Islam as a system, which may also be seen as an ideology, meant that the shari'a must be united to power on earth. Mawdudi described the pursuit of power, by which he meant capturing the machinery of the modern state, as a jihad obligatory on all his followers. In fact, he was not particularly effective in politics. But he did set a standard against which the conduct of the first thirty years of government in Pakistan might be set, and a model which from February 1979 General Ziya' al-Haqq tried to introduce into that country.

Secularisation

Finally, let us turn to the relationship between Islamic reform and secularisation. This is, of course, a much-disputed concept, For the founding fathers of sociology, as science and technology increasingly controlled and explained the social and physical world, and as the modern state grew to provide security within it, religion was due to become more and more marginalised. On the other hand, strong critics of the concept have emerged amongst sociologists, arguing that religion remains an important force in modern societies, though often expressed in new forms.[46] The impact of Islamic reform supports the latter view.

At one level we can see Weber's secularisation at work. We see his process of disenchantment of the world, or using his term *entzauberung*, the driving of magic out of things: the attack on all ideas of intercession for man with God, the rationalisation of belief and practice, and the emphasis on action on earth to achieve salvation. We can also see a further process associated with disenchantment, which is a fragmentation of human understandings of the world, though this outcome owes as much to the impact of the West as to Islamic reform. We can see it, for instance, in the way in which the Muslim modernists make Western science the measure of Islamic belief, and that in which Muslim socialists, Progressive Writers and their ilk, come to think in terms of a godless world.[47] This said, while noting how Islamic reform would seem to have driven matters down a Weberian secularising path, we should also note that, as in the West, this has not resulted in a complete eradication of magic. Deobandi 'ulama' at the heart of the reforming process prepared amulets for followers to use in case of illness.[48]

One criticism of a focus on disenchantment in Weberian thought is that it is a trajectory derived from the European Christian experience. Arguably the process of secularisation should be considered in Islamic terms, indeed, as Weber might have done, in terms of the unique developmental history of Islam, that is, in terms of its development as a rationalisation of worldviews. In this light it has been suggested that, as Islam has always had a considerable interest in this world, being more concerned with how men behave than in what they believe, the developmental criterion must rest with Muslim behaviour. The shari'a, ideally the distilled essence of the Qur'an and the life of the Prophet, which offers guidance for every aspect of human life, represents the criterion. So Muslim society is Islamic to the extent that it follows the shari'a and Muslim states are Islamic to the extent that they support the shari'a. Here we have a possible criterion of secularisation in Muslim societies and states.

If we apply this criterion to India, on the one hand we can reasonably argue that Islamic reform led to scriptural knowledge becoming more widespread and more widely followed than before. On the other hand, the pressure brought by Islamic reformers on the state led to the shari'a, at least in its personal law aspects, being more completely imposed by the state than before. Of course, if this trajectory is taken through into the history of Pakistan, it is possible to see a continuing expansion of the realm of the shari'a and an Islamisation of the state. Alongside this theme stands the ideal created by Mawdudi and his Islamist followers of an ideological system in which the shari'a is asserted over all of human life and backed by all the authority of the modern state. We conclude by noting a paradox. If we take the Weberian trajectory of disenchantment, we can see Islamic reform driving magic out of the Indo-Muslim world, to some degree at least. But, if we take the developmental approach, arguably the pressure of reform on society and on the state, in British India and Pakistan at least, has led to greater levels of shari'a application/Islamisation than ever before.[49]

****

Before concluding we need to note the broader context in which religious reform amongst South Asian Muslims was taking place. In the nineteenth and twentieth centuries, across the Muslim world, there were moves towards this-worldly faith, or forms of Islamic 'Protestantism', expressed in varying ways.[50] Similar processes were also taking place at the same time amongst other

Islamic Reform and Modernities in South Asia   225

South Asians; the faiths of Hindus, Sikhs and Buddhists were all acquiring this-worldly 'Protestant' forms, and were in time to develop fundamentalist dimensions.[51]

So where does this leave the relationship between Islamic reform and modernity? Much as the vision and brio of Weber's *Protestant Ethic and the Spirit of Capitalism* is to be admired, and although the impact of Islamic reform is full of Weberian echoes, there is no evidence for the emergence of some quasi-Calvinistic group, whose this-worldly moral energy and ascetic self-discipline have stimulated a continued capitalist development, not even among the Ahl-i Hadith.[52] This is said, moreover, in spite of the success of Islamic reform among the Muslim merchant classes. Arguably Weber's friend, the religious historian Ernst Troeltsch, gives us helpful direction when he argues that Protestantism had a unique role in fashioning the modern religious spirit: this 'religion of personal conviction and conscience', he declared, 'is the form of religion which is homogeneous with and adopted to modern individualistic civilisation, without, however, possessing in detail any very close connexions with the creations of the latter.'[53] Ernest Gellner, in considering some thirty years ago the impact of Islamic reform in North Africa came to a similar conclusion: 'the severe discipline of puritan Islam', he declared, far from being incompatible with modernisation might be 'compatible with, or positively favourable to modern social organisation.'[54]

In the arguments already surveyed, there is plentiful evidence of the way in which Islamic reform both opened the way to modernity, and then worked with it. Islamic Reform destroyed much of the authority of the past, making possible a more creative engagement with the present. It emphasised human will, preparing the way for the modern understanding of undiluted human instrumentality in the world. It set off transformations of the self that we associate with modernity, the emergence of an internal landscape and the affirmation of the ordinary things of life. It helped set off a rationalisation and reification of Islam which, amongst other things, prepared Muslims to engage with a broad-based political identity and conceive of their faith as an entity, even a system. And finally, it set going processes which offered both a disenchanted world and one in which paradoxically the transcendent was reasserted, indeed, the world itself was re-enchanted.

This, then, is the relationship between Islamic reform and modernity in South Asia, one of preparing the way and then engagement with the worldwide forces of modernity, shaping them to its particular purposes. This said, should not the Islamist insistence on reasserting the transcendent over all creation give us pause for thought? This is, after all, not the outcome of the modernising process which the founding fathers of sociology anticipated. Now, it is a commonplace of modern scholarship on Islamism, or any other form of religious fundamentalism, that it is a profoundly modern phenomenon, being fashioned by modernity, as it strives to shape it – protesting against the outcomes of Enlightenment rationalism, what Bruce Lawrence terms 'the heresies of the modern age.'[55] It seeks to assert the moral community, the transcendent, and moral absolutes, in order to confront the uncertainties, and relativisms of the time. It raises the question of whether modernity should necessarily be dominated by Enlightenment rationalism.

In an excellent recent work Roxanne Euben has juxtaposed the critique of the nature and limits of modern rationalism by a series of Western social theorists (Hannah Arendt, Charles Taylor, Alasdair MacIntyre, Richard Neuhaus, Robert Bellah and Daniel Bell) with that of Sayyid Qutb, who was with Mawdudi the most influential Islamist thinker of the twentieth century. She notes that, although coming from different angles of vision, all see in modernity 'a crisis due to rupture with tradition, the dual rejection of theology and teleology inaugurated by Enlightenment rationalism and the subsequent diminishment of meaning in authority, morality and community . . .'[56] Turning to Qutb she finds similar anxieties, similar analysis. Where, of course, he differs from the Western theorists is in insisting on divine sovereignty as the answer to the crises of authority, morality and community.[57]

These arguments proposed in relation to Qutb could be applied no less to Mawdudi. Thus, Islamism, which is the current end point of Islamic reform, is not only a profoundly modern phenomenon but also offers an answer to widely shared modern anxieties. Research devoted to Islamism in West Asia has demonstrated its modernising impact,[58] as do the papers in Filippo Osella's recent collection of papers on Islamic reform in South Asia.[59] Indeed, if we accept that the Islamist concern to build a moral community, to reassert the transcendent, and to re-enchant the world is one possible answer to the problems of modernity, it is arguable that Islamic reform not only helped to prepare the way for modernity but in its Islamist form has become a modernising force in its own right. As Haniffa states, 'the promise that feminism . . . holds for transforming women's lives does not necessarily require a secular framework within which to flourish'.[60]

This leads us to a final reflection. It is clear that there is no *one* modernity, as once Western modernisation theorists vainly believed, but many or multiple modernities. Societies fashion their modernities differently as arguably do different individuals. The reforming traditions of Muslim South Asia from Shah Wali Allah to the Islamists of the present are powerful strands amongst Muslim modernities. But they form only one set of strands amongst Muslim modernities, just as those modernities are a larger set of strands amongst those fashioned by humankind in general.[61]

Notes

1. This article draws on attempts to consider aspects of Islamic reform and modernity over the past twenty years. See Francis Robinson, 'Secularisation, Weber, and Islam', first published in Wolfgang Schluchter (ed), Max Weber's *Sicht des Islams. Interpretation und Kritik* (Frankfurt, Germany: Suhrkamp, 1985), and republished in slightly amended form in Toby E. Huff and Wolfgang Schluchter (eds), *Max Weber and Islam* (New Brunswick, NJ: Transaction Books, 1999), pp. 231–46; Francis Robinson, 'Islam and the Impact of Print in South Asia' in Francis Robinson (ed.), *Islam and Muslim History in South Asia* (Delhi: Oxford University Press, 2000), pp. 66–104; Francis Robinson 'Other-Worldly and

This-Worldly Islam and the Islamic Revival', in *Journal of the Royal Asiatic Society,* 3rd series, vol. 14, 1, April 2004, pp. 47–58.
2. Ira M. Lapidus, *A History of Islamic Societies,* 2nd ed. (Cambridge: Cambridge University Press, 2002), p. 457.
3. It should be noted, however, that Sufis adjusted their practices not just to take account of reform but also to embrace its transformative processes. Nile Green, 'The Politics of Meditation in Colonial South Asia', *Modern Asian Studies,* 42, 2/3, March/May 2008, pp. 283–316, is a good example of the former. The classic study of reform led by a Sufi and his Naqshbandi followers is Serif Mardin, *Religion and Social Change in Modern Turkey: The Case of Bediuzzaman Said Nursi* (Albany, NY: State University of New York Press, 1989).
4. Barbara Daly Metcalf, *Islamic Revival in British India: Deoband, 1860–1920* (Princeton, NJ: Princeton University Press, 1982), pp. 46–260.
5. Muhammad Khalid Masud, ed., *Travellers in Faith: Studies of the Tablighi Jama'at as a Transnational Islamic Movement for Faith Renewal* (Leiden: Brill, 2000); Yoginder Sikand, *The Origins and Development of the Tablighi Jama'at (1900–2000): A Cross-Country Comparative Study* (Hyderabad: Orient Longman, 2002).
6. This is done in Book 7 titled: 'On Comportment and Character, Reward and Punishment'. Barbara Daly Metcalf, *Perfecting Women: Maulana Ashraf 'Ali Thanawi's Bihishti Zewar: A Partial Translation with Commentary* (Berkeley: University of California Press, 1990), pp. 177–239.
7. Haniffa emphasises the indissoluble connection between piety and social action. Farzana Haniffa, 'Believing Women: Piety and Power amongst Muslim Women in Contemporary Sri Lanka', *Modern Asian Studies,* vol. 42, 2/3, March/May 2009, pp. 317–46.
8. Speech of Sayyid Ahmad Khan quoted in Altaf Husain Hali, *Hayat-i-Javid,* K.H. Qadiri and David J. Matthews trans. (Delhi: Idarah-i Adabiyat-i Delli, 1979), p. 172.
9. S. Abul Hasan Ali Nadwi, *Life and Mission of Maulana Muhammad Ilyas,* Mohammad Asif Kidwai trans. (Lucknow, 1979), p. 108; Huq emphasises the seriousness with which a contemporary women's Islamic student organisation in Bangladesh takes the Day of Judgement. Maimuna Huq, 'Reading the Qur'an in Bangladesh: The Politics of "Belief" Among Islamist Women', *Modern Asian Studies,* vol. 42, 2/3, March/May 2009, pp. 457–88.

10. Barbara D. Metcalf, *Weber and Islamic Reform*, in Huff and Schluchter eds, *Weber*, pp. 217–29.
11. Robinson, 'Religious Change', pp. 108–10; Metcalf, *Deoband*, p. 269.
12. Maulana Muhammad Zakariyya Kandhlawi, *Aap Beeti: Autobiography*, 2 vols (Delhi: Idarah Isha'at-e-Diniyat, Pvt. Ltd, 1993).
13. M. Iqbal, *The Reconstruction of Religious Thought in Islam* (Lahore: Sh. Muhammad Ashraf, 1954), p. 154.
14. For a discussion of this see Robinson, 'Other-Worldly and This-Worldly Islam', p. 54 and note 22.
15. S.A.A. Maudoodi, *Fundamentals of Islam* (Delhi: Markazi Maktaba Islami, 1979), p. xviii, and for a disquisition on the role of man as God's trustee on earth, see pp. 29–30.
16. Robinson, 'Other-Worldly and This-Worldly Islam', pp. 54–6.
17. S.N. Eisenstadt, 'The Protestant Ethic Thesis in an Analytical and Comparative Framework', in S.N. Eisenstadt, ed., *The Protestant Ethic and Modernisation: A Comparative View* (New York: Basic Books, 1974), p. 10.
18. William A. Graham, 'Traditionalism in Islam: An Essay in Interpretation', *Journal of Interdisciplinary History*, XVIII, 3, Winter 1993, pp. 495–522.
19. Ibid., pp. 511–22.
20. Robinson, 'Islam and the Impact of Print', pp. 80–1.
21. Ralph Russell and Khurshidul Islam, 'The Satirical Verse of Akbar Ilahabadi (1861–1921)', *Modern Asian Studies*, 8, 1, 1974, p. 9.
22. Seyyed Vali Reza Nasr, *Mawdudi & the Making of Islamic Revivalism* (New York, Oxford University Press, 1996), p. 138; for a general discussion of Mawdudi's authority, pp. 126–38.
23. Metcalf, *Perfecting Women*, pp. 1–38.
24. Cited in Faisal Fatehali Devji, 'Gender and the Politics of Space: The Movement of Women's Reform, 1857–1900', in Z. Hasan, ed., *Forging Identities: Gender, Communities and the State* (New Delhi: Kali for Women, 1994), pp. 35–6.
25. Hali, *Hayat-i-Javed*; C.F.I. Graham, *the Life and Work of Sir Syed Ahmed Khan, K.C.S.I* , new and rev. ed. (London: Hodder and Stoughton, 1909).
26. Robinson, 'Religious Change', p. 9.
27. W.C. Smith, *Islam in Modern History* (Princeton, NJ: Princeton University Press, 1957), p. 89. In harmony with Smith's insight, Haniffa

emphasises how the women's piety movement in Sri Lanka has made its Muslims into 'a highly energised force of some magnitude within Sri Lanka's polity.' Haniffa, 'Piety as Politics', pp. 347–75.

28. Yoginder Sikand, *Bastions of the Believers: Madrasas and Islamic Education in India* (New Delhi: Penguin India, 2005), pp. 218–21.
29. Ibid., pp. 221–2.
30. Ibid., p. 136.
31. Charles Taylor, *Sources of the Self: The Making of the Modern Identity* (Cambridge: Cambridge University Press, 1989), p. 111.
32. Ibid., p. 14.
33. Metcalf, *Perfecting Women*, p. 234; Haniffa, 'Piety as Politics', and Huq, 'Reading the Qur'an', are both excellent studies of projects designed to construct a new Islamic selfhood amongst women.
34. See, for instance, Tom Webster, 'Writing to Redundancy: Approaches to Spiritual Journals and Early Modern Spirituality', *The Historical Journal*, 31, 1, 1996, pp. 35–6.
35. Mohamed Ali, Afzal Iqbal, ed., *My Life: A Fragment – An Autobiographical Sketch* (Lahore: Sh. Muhammad Ashraf, 1942). Syed Mahmud's spiritual reflections may be found in the Farangi Mahall Papers, Karachi.
36. W. Montgomery Watt, *The Faith and Practice of al-Ghazali* (Oxford: One World, 1994).
37. Robinson, 'Religious change', pp. 24–5.
38. Wilfred Cantwell Smith, *Modern Islam in India: A Social Analysis* (London, 1946), pp. 64–7. See also Amit Dey, 'The Image of the Prophet in Bengali Muslim Piety, 1850–1947' (Ph.D. thesis, University of London, 1999).
39. Robinson, 'Religious Change', pp. 10–11.
40. Christian W. Troll, ed., *Islam in India: Studies and Commentaries, 3: The Islamic Experience in Contemporary Thought* (Delhi: Chanakya Publications, 1986), p. 153.
41. Book VI of Thanawi's *Bihishti Zewar*, for instance, specifically discusses the whole issue of custom. Metcalf, *Perfecting Women*, pp. 89–161.
42. 'At every turn', Haniffa records, 'I was told by members of Al-Muslimaat that they were Muslims by choice as well as by birth.' Haniffa, 'Piety as Politics', pp. 347–75.
43. Robinson, 'Islam and the Impact of Print', p. 91.
44. Dale F. Eickelman and James Piscatori, *Muslim Politics* (Princeton, NJ: Princeton University Press, 1996), pp. 37–45.

45. Sayyid Abul A'la Maududi, *Towards Understanding Islam*, Khurshid Ahmad, trans. and ed. (London: UK Islamic Mission, 1980), pp. 138–9.
46. Anthony Giddens, *Sociology*, 4th ed. (Cambridge: Cambridge University Press, 2001), p. 545.
47. Robinson, 'Secularisation, Weber, and Islam', pp. 236–7.
48. Kandhlawi, *Aap Beeti*, 2, pp. 314–16; Marsden makes a similar point about reform-minded Muslims in Chitral. Magnus Marsden, *Living Islam: Muslim Religious Experience in Pakistan's North-West Frontier* (Cambridge: Cambridge University Press, 2005), p. 241.
49. Robinson, 'Secularisation, Weber, and Islam', pp. 239–41.
50. Robinson, 'Other-Worldly and This-Worldly Islam', pp. 54–8.
51. Francis Robinson, 'Fundamentalism: Tolerance and India's Heritage', *Journal of the Asiatic Society*, XLV, 3, 2003, pp. 5–13.
52. For a sceptical approach to Islamic 'Protestantism' as a preparation for modernity, see Martin Reixinger, 'How Favourable is Puritan Islam to Modernity? A Case Study on the Ahl-i Hadith (late 19th/early 20th centuries)', unpublished paper, 2004.
53. Troeltsch put this argument to the ninth conference of German historians at Stuttgart in April 1906 when he gave the lecture which Weber had been supposed to give on the meaning of Protestantism for the rise of the modern world. Ernst Troeltsch, *Protestantism and Progress; The Significance of Protestantism for the Rise of the Modern World* (Philadelphia, PA: Fortress Press, 1986), p. 100.
54. Ernest Gellner, *Muslim Society* (Cambridge: Cambridge University Press 1981), p. 170; twenty years later the argument is put much more forcibly by Lapidus, *History of Islamic Societies*, pp. 817–22.
55. Bruce B. Lawrence, *Defenders of God: The Fundamentalist Revolt Against the Modern Age* (London: I.B. Tauris, 1990).
56. Roxanne L. Euben, *Enemy in the Mirror: Islamic Fundamentalism and the Limits of Modern Rationalism: A Work of Comparative Political Theory* (Princeton: Princeton University Press, 1999), p. 124.
57. Ibid., pp. 45–92, 154–67.
58. See, for instance, B.O. Utvik, 'The Modernising Force of Islamism', in J.L. Esposito and F. Burgat, eds, *Modernising Islam: Religion in the Public Sphere in the Middle East and Europe* (London: Hurst, 2003), pp. 43–68; B.O. Utvik, *The Pious Road to Development: Islamist Economics in Egypt* (London: Hurst, 2006); Geneive Abdo, *No God But God: Egypt and the Triumph of Islam* (Oxford: Oxford University Press,

2000); F. Adelkhah, *Being Modern in Iran* (London: Hurst, 1998); Jenny B. White, *Islamist Mobilisation in Turkey: A Study in Vernacular Politics* (Seattle, WA: University of Washington Press, 2002).
59. Filippo Osella, guest editor, *Modern Asian Studies*, 42, 2/3, March/May, 2008.
60. Haniffa, 'Piety as Politics'; this point has also been made at length and to great effect by Saba Mahmood, *Politics of Piety: The Islamic Revival and the Feminist Subject* (Princeton: Princeton University Press, 2005).
61. S.N. Eisenstadt, 'Multiple Modernities', *Daedalus*, 129, no. 1, Winter 2000, pp. 1–30; Amit Chaudhuri, *Clearing a Space: Reflections on India, Literature and Culture* (Oxford: Peter Lang, 2008).

8

Iranian Influences on South Asia

THERE HAS BEEN CULTURAL exchange between Iran and South Asia for thousands of years. There are close resemblances between the Avestan and the Vedic Sanskrit languages. Under the Sassanians South Asia gave Iran the *Panchtantra* and chess, while the Sassanians ruled its northwestern region. From the ninth century CE the Saffarids brought a new Perso-Islamic culture to Sind. Towards the end of the tenth century the Isma'ilis strengthened this culture in Sind and extended it into Multan and the Punjab. As you will know Firdawsi wrote the *Shahnama* at the court of Mahmud of Ghazna, so it was not surprising that Ghaznawid expansion towards Lahore and further east represented a further extension of Persian literary culture: the cities of the Punjab became destinations for scholars and literary figures from Iran, Khorasan and Mawarannahr. From the early thirteenth century the establishment of the Delhi Sultanate created the base from which Perso-Islamic culture could spread east into Bengal and south into the Deccan. The poet and musician, Amir Khusraw (1252–1325), who is buried alongside the Sufi saint Nizam al-din Chishti in Delhi, represents one of the peaks of the new Indian-based Perso-Islamic culture. The latter half of the fourteenth century saw regional Sultanates develop, for instance, the Bahmanid in the Deccan and those of Bengal, Jawnpur and Kashmir in the north. They were all great centres of

Perso-Islamic culture, their courts destinations for Iranians in search of patronage.

My aim in this lecture is not to talk about the emergence of Perso-Islamic culture in South Asia in the medieval period. I want to address its high point which stretches from the early years of the Mughal empire through to the mid-nineteenth century, when the British annexed the rich Shi'a-ruled state of Awadh. This was a period in which South Asia was an Eldorado for Iranians in very much the same way that, in the nineteenth and twentieth centuries, the USA was for European artists, businessmen and scholars. It is worth reflecting that the Safawid empire at its height ruled 6.5 million while the Mughal empire at its height ruled 100 million. Moreover, the Mughals developed a system of land taxation which generated, from the late sixteenth to the late seventeenth century, steadily increasing quantities of revenue. [1]

Power, People and Iranian Influence in South Asia

It was the assertion of Mughal power which made possible the massive extension of Iran's influence in South Asia. You will know the names of the Great Mughals, that extraordinary line of men who ruled India from 1526 to 1707 – Babur, Humayun, Akbar, Jahangir, Shah Jahan and Awrangzib. But, what kind of worldview did they represent? One of the problems of much history written over the past two centuries is that, whether written in British India, or in the independent countries of South Asia, it has come to be confined within the boundaries of the modern state. So, in the textbooks of South Asia, and I fear in the monographs of scholars who should know better, Mughal history is seen to begin when the Mughals entered South Asia. But Mughal, as you know, is the Persian for Mongol. The Mughals saw themselves as Timurids; thus, they were part of a tradition of power which went back to Genghis Khan. Babur saw himself as descended on his father's side from

Timur and on his mother's side from Genghis Khan.² The *Akbarnama*, Abul Fadl's record of Akbar's reign, traces Akbar's ancestry back to the divine light which, in an Annunciation-like scene, entered the Mongol goddess Alanquwa.³ In the seventeenth century there was a genre of one-off Mughal paintings which portrayed the crown being handed down from Timur through his descendants, to the Mughal rulers and ending with the Mughal ruler of the time.⁴ Shah Jahan, when he constructed his Peacock Throne, had a large ruby placed in the centre of its breast which he had been given by the Safawid, Shah Abbas. On that ruby were inscribed the names of Timur, Shahrukh, Ulugh Beg and Shah Abbas, as well as those of Akbar, Jahangir and Shah Jahan. The Mughals came out of the Persianate cultural florescence patronised by Timur and his descendants in Samarqand and Herat. This was a period of cultural vitality comparable to the Florentine Renaissance. It is not for nothing that my colleague, Stephen Dale, has compared the emperor Babur to Italian renaissance figures including Benvenuto Cellini.⁵

The Mughals brought with them the memory not only of great power but also of the highest Persianate cultural production. The *Shahnama* of Muhammad Juki, which belongs to the Royal Asiatic Society, Britain, and which represents a high point of book painting in the Persian style, was a treasured item in the Mughal library as we know from the seals of the Great Mughals in the book.⁶ Babur's famous description of Hindustan in the *Baburnama* tells us of how he thought he had taken a step down culturally in establishing himself there: It 'is a place of little charm', he wrote, 'there is no beauty in its people, no etiquette, nobility or manliness. The arts and crafts have no harmony or symmetry . . . the one nice aspect of Hindustan is that it is a large country with lots of gold and money.'⁷

Iran, in the form of the Safawids, was intimately involved both in the rise of the Mughals and in the politics of the dynasty; in the form of the Afsharids it was closely involved in its fall. The emperor Babur, in his attempts to recapture his family patrimony of Samarqand from the Shaybanid Uzbeks, was helped by Shah Isma'il. Once in power in Hindustan he kept two Caucasian slave girls sent to him by Shah Tahmasp. The emperor Humayun, after he had been defeated by the Suri Pathans, took shelter with Shah Tahmasp, an event memorably recorded in the murals of Isfahan's Chihil Sutun.[8] He returned to India at the head of an army of mainly Iranians. The emperor Jahangir had the Safawids very much in mind: two of the great paintings he commissioned show him in close relationship with the Safawid Shah 'Abbas.[9] Moreover, he made a note in his memoirs the day he received news of the Shah's assassination of his eldest son, Muhammad Baqir.[10] The Afghan city of Qandahar, which commanded the route from the Mughal to the Safawid empire, was constantly changing hands between the two dynasties. When the ambitious prince, Awrangzib, failed to recapture the city twice in 1649 and 1652, Shah Jahan humiliated him, feeding the Prince's resentment, which led to Awrangzib's overthrow and humiliation of his father, and his killing of his brother and nephew. When Awrangzib's eldest and favourite son, Prince Akbar, son by his Safawid wife, Dilras Banu, failed to overthrow his father he fled to the Safawid court. In 1736, it was Nadir Shah Afshar who gave the effective *coup de grâce* to the Mughals. He invaded Hindustan, sacked Delhi, massacred its citizens, and carried vast quantities of wealth, Mughal princesses, and the Peacock Throne back to Iran. The implosion of Mughal authority in the early eighteenth century made Nadir Shah's victory possible. The event announced to Indians and Afghans that the days of Mughal power were over. From now to the overthrow of the dynasty in 1858 they were men of straw to be manipulated by others.

A key source of Iranian influence in the Mughal world was the large number of Iranians which flocked to serve at the Mughal court. The emperor Humayun brought many Iranians with him on his return from exile in the Safawid court, amongst them leading painters from Shah Tahmasp's studios, who were to have a major influence on the development of Mughal art.[11] The emperor Akbar in the 1560s specifically encouraged Iranians to join his imperial service; he needed them to help him overcome the ambitions of his Chaghatay Turki nobles. But, moving beyond politics, Akbar was concerned that his court should be a home for leading Iranian scholars and poets. Illiterate, or dyslexic, we do not know, Akbar had large numbers of works in prose and poetry read to him – always in Persian. He himself composed verses in Persian and Hindi, although only his Persian verses have been recorded. Akbar was probably the first Muslim ruler in South Asia to institute the office of poet laureate (Malik al-Shu'ara). All the poets laureate, bar one, up to the end of Shah Jahan's reign were Iranians. Fifty out of the fifty-nine top-rated Persian poets at Akbar's court were Iranian. According to the historian, Badauni, Akbar and his nobles patronised 168 Iranian poets.[12]

The life of one Iranian family demonstrates how the Mughal court offered opportunities to rise from rags to riches. In the late sixteenth century one Mirza Ghiyas Beg, originally from Tehran, turned up destitute at Akbar's court. He had come in a caravan from Yazd but had been robbed close to Qandahar and left with nothing but two mules. Akbar found him a place in his household and, although the Mirza got into difficulties over embezzlement and backed the wrong horse in court politics, he rose to become wazir under Jahangir. He is buried in that jewel of a tomb by the river Jumna at Agra, known as Itimad Dawlah's tomb, after his official title. The tomb was built, and probably designed, by his daughter Nur Jahan, a woman whose many gifts ranged from the arts through hunting, through business to politics. A great beauty, Jahangir married her when he was 42 and she was 34; his memoirs reveal that he was completely besotted by her. Towards the end of his reign he increasingly handed over the government to her: firmans were issued in her name; coins were also struck in her name. She lost the succession struggle which broke out as Jahangir neared death because her brother, Afzal Khan, changed sides to support Shah Jahan. She went into retirement in Lahore, supported by the vast wealth she had accumulated, and with the project of building her husband's mausoleum.[13] But the influence of this Iranian family did not end here. Nur Jahan's niece, Afzal Khan's daughter, Arjomand Begum, married Shah Jahan. While she was alive, she was his only wife to whom he was passionately devoted. Her palace name was Mumtaz Mahal and it was for her burial that Shah Jahan built – and he was involved in the process on a daily basis – that wondrous mausoleum, the Taj Mahal.[14] Thus Iranian blood ran in the veins of Shah Jahan's four sons and three daughters, several of whom had great gifts. Not many Iranian immigrants' stories glitter as this one does. But up to the nineteenth century, Hindustan continued to be a place where Iranians could fulfil their ambitions and, if they wished, become rich.

At this point I shall step aside from the Mughal world, for a moment, to consider the impact of some other Iranian immigrants on South Asia. The first are the Parsis, who settled on India's west coast around the tenth century CE. Nowadays a small community of no more than 100,000 they have had a disproportionate impact on Indian life. They have been prominent in music and the arts, especially in music, ranging from Zubin Mehta to Freddie Mercury. They have headed all three of India's military services. Homi Bhabha and Homi Sethna played a major role in developing India's atomic energy programme. Parsi names – Tata, Godrej and Wadia – figure amongst India's greatest industrial families. The Tatas were, indeed, the founders of India's industry and the saviours of some of Britain's, for instance, steel in the form of Corus and motor manufacture in the form of Jaguar/Land Rover. Parsis in the form of Pherozshah Mehta and Dadabhai Naoroji were amongst the founders of the Indian National Congress – the Indian nationalist movement. The Parsi blood of Feroze Gandhi ran through India's assassinated prime minister, Rajiv Gandhi, and today runs through his son, Rahul, who hopes one day to be prime minister.

There are two further stories of Iranian immigrant impact which I shall take together. The first involves Aga Khan I who in the early nineteenth century was more Iranian provincial notable than Isma'ili

Imam. After losing out in Iranian politics he moved to India, eventually settling in Bombay, where with great skill he managed to persuade the British to address him as 'His Highness' and the British courts to recognise him as the leader of the Khoja Isma'ili community.[15] This was the beginning for his family of great wealth and of national and international political careers reaching from the Government of India, through the highest ranks of British society, to the League of Nations. In narrow South Asian political terms Aga Khan III played a major role in getting Muslim separatist politics off the ground in India, amongst other things leading the delegation to the Viceroy in 1906 which asked for, and was granted, special privileges for Muslims. The second story of Iranian immigrant impact involves men who played a leading role in the final success of Muslim separatist politics. They were the Ispahanis, businessmen who settled in Bombay, Madras and Calcutta. They were leading supporters of the campaign for Pakistan in its last ten years, and important public servants in the new country.[16] Just as the Tatas founded the airline which eventually became Air India, so did the Ispahanis found Orient Airways which became PIA.

The Two Pillars of Iranian Influence in South Asia

So much for the roles of power and peoples. I now want to turn to the two great pillars of Iranian cultural influence, the two great supports of Perso-Islamic culture. I mean the Persian language and religious knowledge.

Let us consider the impact of Persian. In the two hundred years before 1600 Hindawi had been widely used in north India by court circles in administration and by Sufis when they wanted to communicate with their constituencies at large. The emperor Akbar changed this. He formally declared Persian to be the language of administration at all levels. The proclamation was issued by his Khatri Hindu revenue minister, Raja Todar Mal. At the same time all government departments were reorganised by the Iranian polymath, Fadl Allah Shirazi. 'Earlier in India the government's accounts were written in Hindi according to the Hindu rule', declared the eighteenth-century Muslim historian Ghulam Husayn Tabatabai, 'Raja Todar Mal acquired new regulations from the scribes of Iran, and the government offices then were reorganised as they were in wilayat [Iran].'[17] We should be clear that this was not just a change in the royal court and household; it went down to the lowest levels of government. Persian became the language used by small-town officials and village-based revenue officers. All Mughal government papers, from royal firmans down to the acceptance letters of village Chaudhuris, were in Persian. Persian was the language of the zamindar classes no less than the Muslim literati. Even the common soldier was expected to understand simple Persian.[18]

This meant that Persian spread beyond the purely Muslim world to embrace all those who worked in the imperial service. The large number of Hindu munshis expert in accountancy (siyaq) and draftsmanship (insha') – Khatris, Kayasths and Kashmiri Brahmins – became expert in Persian, lovers of its literature and producers of it. A famous letter of Chandra Bhan 'Brahman' to his son gives an idea of Hindu love and mastery of Persian:

> Initially, it is necessary to acquire training in *akhlaq* [good manners/ethics]. It is appropriate to listen always to the advice of elders and act accordingly. By studying the *Akhlaq-i Nasiri, Akhlaq-i Jalali, Gulistan,* and *Bustan* one should accumulate one's own capital and gain the virtue of knowledge. When you practice what you have learnt, your code of conduct too will be firm . . .
>
> Although the science of Persian is vast, and almost beyond human grasp, in order to open the gates of language one should read the *Gulistan, Bustan,* and the letters of Mulla Jami to begin with. When one has advanced somewhat one should read key books on norms and ethics as well as history books such as the *Habib al-Siyar, Rauzat al-Safa, Rauzat al-Salatin, Tarikh-i Guzida, Tarikh-i Tabari, Zafarnama* and *Akbarnama.* The benefits of these will be to render your

language elegant, also to provide you knowledge of the world and its inhabitants . . . of the master-poets, here are some whose collections I read in my youth . . . Hakim Sana'i, Mulla Rum, Shams Tabriz, Shaikh Farid al-din 'Attar, Shaikh Sa'di, Khwaja Hafiz, Shaikh Jami . . . [plus 50 others].[19]

He then goes on to list a large number of contemporary poets he thinks his son should read. This is a man, and there were many like him, who was completely drenched in Persian.

Let us turn to that second pillar, Islamic knowledge both formal and mystical. Under the Mughals, formal learning, by which I mean crudely madrasa learning, was given a powerful injection of Iranian learning. Classically, madrasa learning had two main halves, manqulat, the revealed sciences (Qura'n, hadith, etc. . . . .) and ma'qulat, the rational sciences (logic, philosophy, theology, maths, etc.). Until the late sixteenth century the revealed sciences had been dominant in South Asia. This began to change with the arrival of Fadl Allah Shirazi at the court of Akbar in 1573. He promoted the study of the philosophical traditions of his countryman Jalal al-Din Dawwani (d. 1502/03), which led to great interest in the contemporary philosophers, Mir Baqr Damad of Isfahan (d. 1631) and his gifted pupil, Mulla Sadra of Shiraz (d. 1642). The study of the ma'qulat subjects gained an extra boost in the seventeenth century from the migration into South Asia of many scholars fleeing from the rigorous Sunni orthodoxy of the Shaybanid Uzbeks in Central Asia. Both Sialkot in the Punjab and Jawnpur in the centre of the Ganges valley became major centres of ma'qulat skills. The emperor Awrangzib, a great believer in good administration, supported 'ulama' expert in ma'qulat subjects with revenue-free grants. When one 'alim, Mulla Qutb al-Din Sihalwi, who was at the centre of the ma'qulat revolution, was killed in 1691 in a squabble over land, Awrangzib compensated his four sons by granting them the sequestered property of a European Indigo merchant in Lucknow – Farangi Mahall. At Farangi Mahall, Mulla Qutb al-Din's third son, Mulla Nizam al-Din, fashioned a new style of teaching known as the *Dars-i Nizami*. This drew on the ma'qulat traditions of Iran to encourage students to think rather than learn by rote. The training both brought a greater flexibility in jurisprudence and enabled students to finish their madrasa course with greater speed. Thus, Iranian philosophical traditions came to be established in the Sunni scholarship of South Asia. This said, a glance at the books, commentaries and super-commentaries taught by South Asian scholars would tell you that almost all of them had been written in either Iran or Central Asia between 1100 and 1600 CE. Those great rivals at the court of Timur, Sa'ad al-Din Taftazani and Sayyid Sharif Jurjani were the most widely represented.[20]

Sufism, Islamic mysticism, was no less a projection of Iranian cultural power into the subcontinent. The Chishti order, the major South Asian order and one only to be found there, had been brought by Mu'in al-Din Sijzi from the area around Herat at the end of the twelfth century. The Qadiri path was first introduced by Muhammad Ghawth, who travelled through much of the Perso-Islamic world before establishing himself in fifteenth-century Uchch. The Suhrawardis, founded by the Iranian Sufi, Ziya 'al-Din al-Suhrawardi (d. 1168), developed their most important bases in South Asia, most notably at the shrine of Baha al-Din Zakariyya in Multan, while in the late sixteenth century the Naqshbandiyya were brought from Central Asia. The letters of these Sufis, their maktubat, were in Persian, as were their sayings, their malfuzat. Moreover, the monistic teachings of that most influential Spanish Sufi, Ibn al-'Arabi, which even some Naqshbandis followed, were to be found everywhere in the work of the greatest Persian poets. It was not possible to recite the verse of Rumi, of Hafiz, of Jami or Nizami, as the ashraf ruling classes loved to do, without absorbing the ideas of this great mystic. Moreover, although this high Sufi culture can be treated separately from the South Asian world in which it moved, at saints' shrines Sufism embraced that world. To survive, Muslim holy men had to build bridges to the languages and religious customs of the primarily non-Muslim society in which they moved. Non-Muslims came to see these shrines and their holy men as sources of relief from the uncertainties of daily life.[21]

The Pillars of Iranian Influence in the Eighteenth and Nineteenth Centuries

Now, you might think that the events of the eighteenth century meant the end of Iranian cultural influence. I refer to: the destruction of effective Mughal power by the mid-eighteenth century; the reduction of Muslim power itself by the early nineteenth century to the Mughal successor states of Awadh in the north and Hyderabad in the south; the rise of confident non-Muslim powers – the Sikhs in the Punjab, the Marathas across a great swathe of territory from Gujarat in the West to the Bay of Bengal in the East; the rise of the British in Bengal, most of the Gangetic Basin, and Madras; the consequent decline of the highest levels of patronage; and the subsequent slackening of the tide of Iranians coming to seek their fortune. All these developments might have quickly brought Iranian cultural influence to an end. Far from it. There continued to be patronage and creativity throughout the eighteenth and early nineteenth centuries. Indeed, the German art historian, Herman Goetz, was to describe it as the period of 'highest refinement' of Persian culture, a period to be compared with the late Renaissance in Italy, the golden age of Spain, and the era of French rococo.[22]

Consider the first pillar of Iranian cultural influence – Persian. Until the 1830s Persian was the language of government in most of the subcontinent. This was the case not just in the provincial Muslim courts which sprang up as Mughal power ebbed – Murshidabad, Hyderabad, Arcot, Mysore, Awadh, Shahjahanpur, Rampur – but also under the Sikhs, the Marathas and the British. All the successor states rested on the established systems of Mughal administration and the skills of its service classes. Indeed, as government functions began to expand in this period so did the Persian-speaking bureaucratic class. The British, in fact, were in the forefront of maintaining government-sponsored learning for this class when in 1782 they set up the Calcutta Madrasa. Gifted administrators were able to travel throughout the land in order to deploy their Persianate skills. Thus, when Muslim administrators, but also Kashmiri Brahmins with names like Dar, Chak, Sapru and Nehru, were forced out of the northwest by the rise of Afghan and Sikh rule, they were readily able to find posts in northern India. Such were the talents of these people that Mirza Qatil (d. 1817), a Hindu converted to Islam, was able to find work and make a home for himself in Iran, in Shiraz, Isfahan, Tehran and Azerbayjan.[23] The East India Company official, Sir William Jones, became a great lover of Persian and a major channel by which the language and its messages were to travel to Europe.[24]

Arguably, Persian came to be more widely used in the eighteenth and early nineteenth centuries than ever before. Hindu involvement in the language now reached its peak. The Hindu Raja of Benares gave substantial patronage to the distinguished Iranian scholar Shaykh Muhammad 'Ali 'Hazin' Gilani (1692–1760) to migrate to South Asia in the eighteenth century.[25] Hindus now came to use Persian forms of mystical verse, for instance, the mathnawi, to express religious themes. Hindus dominated the study of Persian grammar and lexicography. Insha' now became a Hindu Kayasth monopoly and the considerable Hindu tradition of historiography in Persian reached its peak.[26] In the 1820s the leading Hindu intellectual of Calcutta, Raja Ram Mohan Roy, expressed his advanced views not in Bengali but in Persian. Indeed, in some areas Persian came to be used by the common people. 'Knowledge of Persian language in the later eighteenth and nineteenth centuries', declared the Lucknow literary historian 'Abd al-Halim Sharar, 'was greater in India than in Persia itself . . . this was particularly the case in the last century [nineteenth] when Lucknow was famed throughout the world for its progress and education, when every child could speak Persian, when ghazals were on the lips of all, even the uneducated courtesans and bar workers, and when even a bhand [entertainer] would jest in Persian.'[27]

Let us now consider the fate of the second pillar of Iranian influence – religious knowledge. In formal learning the rational sciences, that is, ma'qulat, seemed powerful.[28] Until the mid-nineteenth century they were cultivated most vigorously in Awadh, which Shah Jahan had described as the 'Shiraz of India'. Almost all the scholars involved were Farangi Mahallis or their pupils. Such was the reputation of their scholarship that it came in the early nineteenth century to be used in Cairo's Al-Azhar to try to revive the rational sciences.[29]

Again, the *Dars-i Nizami* syllabus, with its emphasis at the time on the rational sciences, a vehicle of Iranian intellectual influence, was carried by the Farangi Mahallis and their pupils throughout South Asia, into towns and qasbahs across the plains of northern India and into Hyderabad and Arcot in the south. The family's pupils came to be scattered throughout India and the wider Muslim world. Most of the chains of teaching, declared Ghulam 'Ali Azad Bilgrami, towards the end of the eighteenth century, go back to Mulla Qutb al-Din Sihalwi; all the [traditional] educational centres from Calcutta to Peshawar, declared Shibli Nu'mani at the beginning of the twentieth century, are mere offshoots of the *Dars-i Nizami*.[30] The East India Company's patronage of the *Dars-i Nizami* only helped to consolidate its dominance in South Asia, and by the same token the influence of Iranian scholarship that went with it.

In mystic knowledge the orders closest to those Persian Islamic mystical traditions, which stretched back through Mughal to pre-Mughal South Asia, seemed to revive and spread themselves more widely. The Chishti-Nizamis, through the energy of Shah Kalim Allah and his successors, became once more a vigorous all-India order, their khanqahs springing up most thickly in the region from Awadh to the Punjab. The Chishti-Sabris became extremely active in the qasbahs of the Ganges–Jumna Doab, eventually producing Haji Imdad Allah (d. 1899), spiritual inspiration of more than one nineteenth-century reformist movement and the most influential Sufi of his time. The Qadiris also displayed new vitality in the Awadh and the Punjab. With this new vitality there also came some important new practices. Sufis began to be initiated in more than one order; they also began to place greater emphasis on formal Islamic knowledge while 'ulama' acknowledged the importance of spiritual development. All was part of a coming together of the transmitters of the central messages of Islam at a time of growing weakness. But the Sufi aspect of these messages remained firmly in the Persianate tradition. Bahr al-'Ulum Farangi Mahalli's magisterial study of Rumi's *Mathnawi* in the light of Ibn al-'Arabi's *Fusus* and *Futuhat* is a representative classic of the period.[31]

In addition to the strengthening of the acknowledged pillars of Iranian influence in the eighteenth century there was also the establishment of a new one. This took the form of the emergence of a powerful and self-confident Shi'ite culture in constant interaction with the Shi'a heartlands in Iraq and Iran. The platforms of this development were the Shi'a satrapies which, as Mughal power declined, came forward as increasingly independent states. First, Murshidabad arose as a major commercial centre, and the seat of the governors of Bengal; at the same time Bengal's Hughli river came to be favoured by long-distance traders from Iran. Iranians began to settle there. When the East India Company took power in Bengal in the 1760s, these Iranians turned to Awadh where from 1722 another Shi'a satrapy had begun to flourish. This court, which had been established by Sayyids from Nayshapur, grew steadily more Shi'ite in its institutions and its culture. From the 1760s the Nayshapuri nawabs began to gather Shi'a 'ulama' around them. In May 1768 Shi'a congregational prayers were held for the first time. By the early nineteenth century 2,000 imambaras and 6,000 ta'zia khanas were said to have been built in Lucknow alone, many of whose citizens threw themselves into Mohurram celebrations of a distinctly Safawid kind. Shi'a 'ulama' led prayers, acted as muftis, collected the khums tax and distributed it as charity. The evolution of this Shi'a state reached its climax in the 1840s when a formal

Shi'a judicial system was established and a royal madrasa set up. By this time the Shi'a nawabs of Awadh had long since claimed that they were the true successors of the Safawids.³²

The Shi'a worlds of Murshidabad and Lucknow were regularly refreshed by emigrants from the cultural centres of Iran and the shrine cities of Iraq. Shaykh Muhammad 'Ali 'Hazin' Gilani, as we have seen, fled the wreck of the Safawid empire to finish his life teaching the rational sciences and verse composition in Benares. Descendants of the great Majlisi family of Isfahan came to serve 'Ali Wardi Khan in Murshidabad, their descendants moving on to Lucknow. Such men had vast networks of cousins who were scholars in the shrine cities of Iraq or high religious officials in the towns of the Iranian plateau. From the early nineteenth century the migration from Iran to northern India dwindled, but physicians, poets and architects still came in numbers and settled with success.³³

With these men there also came ideas. When, for instance, the millenarian Shaykhist movement developed in early-nineteenth-century Iran its impact was soon felt in Awadh. When the Akhbaris amidst the ruins of the Safawid empire came to dominate amongst the Iranian 'ulama' so they did in India. When from the 1760s the rationalist Usulis rose to prominence, supported by the Zand peace, Usulism came to the fore in Lucknow, led by the city's most famous Shi'a 'alim, Sayyid Dildar 'Ali Nasirabadi 'Gufran Ma'ab'. In these circumstances Shi'ism emerged as a new carrier of Iranian influence, which it has been down to the present. Lucknow was its centre. And from Lucknow it has created new centres, most especially in Hyderabad Deccan.³⁴

The Swift Decline of Iranian Influence from the Mid-Nineteenth Century

Arguably, the late eighteenth and early nineteenth centuries were the high point of Iranian cultural influence in South Asia. Then from the 1820s and 1830s this influence declined with almost shocking speed. Part of the reason was the imposition of a self-confident British imperial power over most elements of Persianate Mughal institutions and culture. But another part lay in the increasingly vigorous rejection of Iranian models by most of the people of South Asia. What was happening was (1) that South Asian elites knew that to find a way forward under British rule they must abandon the old Mughal ways, which no longer had the authority of power and success, for British, or in aspects of religion, Arab models; (2) at the same time, in this context of British rule, elites knew for the first time that they needed to build bases – constituencies – in South Asian society, and that to do this they needed to use Indian languages.

Let us consider the process in the cases of the pillars of Iranian influence. First, the Persian language. In the eighteenth century, indigenous languages came increasingly to be cultivated and to challenge the cultural sway of Persian outside government. By the end of the eighteenth century, Bengali, whose development had been held back by the dominance of Persian, was beginning to develop new and vigorous Sanskritised forms; Punjabi had produced its two greatest poets, Bulhe and Warith Shah; and Sindhi, under the patronage of the Kalhora and Talpur dynasties, was flourishing as never before. But it was the rise of Urdu which represented the real challenge to Persian. Urdu was the creation of Muslims in India; it was the language they had created to communicate with the Indian world about them. It combined regional grammar and syntax with Persian nouns, adjectives and images, all written in nastaliq. Two streams had developed over the centuries of Muslim rule, one in the Deccan, the other around Delhi. After Awrangzib's conquest of the Deccan these two streams came together to create a medium which the Mughal service classes found more satisfactory for the expression of their poetic genius than an increasingly artificial Persian style. Within a generation, so Aziz Ahmad, the scholar of South Asian Islamic culture tells us, the Muslims of Delhi had discarded Persian as their main poetic language for Urdu.[35]

Changes in the preferred poetic language were important, but arguably the major blow to Persian came in the 1830s when the British abandoned it as the language of government and the law courts for English at the higher levels and the vernacular languages at the lower. At a stroke the main reason for learning Persian was wiped out. There were still jobs open in Persian in the Sikh Punjab and Awadh, that is, until they were annexed by the British in 1849 and 1856. Only in the state of Hyderabad, until 1883, and the state of Kashmir, until 1889, did Persian continue as a language of government. The evidence of the impact of these changes is salutary. Before 1857, Ghalib, the greatest poet of the nineteenth century, thought Persian the only fit literary language. But, in the following decade it was the loss of his Urdu verse in the chaos of the Mutiny Uprising that he regretted the most. In his MAO College founded in the 1870s, Sayyid Ahmad Khan tried to teach Persian language and Persian subjects. He quickly stopped; students only wanted English. In the final decade of the twentieth century a mere 281 Persian books were published in the United Provinces, the heartland of Perso-Islamic civilisation, as compared with 3547 Urdu books. There was, moreover, just one newspaper in Persian, as opposed to 116 in Urdu.[36]

Urdu might have supplanted Persian, but this language, which was itself a carrier of Persian words, images and sensibilities, in its turn found itself on the defensive. It was increasingly attacked from two sides. The first was from Hindu revivalists who wished to purge Urdu of its Persian elements and Sanskritise it instead. In fact, they wanted to assert Hindi over Urdu and at the same time replace the Persian script with their own Nagri script. Pressure was put on the imperial government and by 1900 in the united Provinces Nagri had been given equal standing with the Persian script in the courts. The end of Urdu as a widely shared literary language was signalled in 1915 when the leading north Indian novelist of the day, Premchand, switched from Urdu to Hindi.[37]

But the assault on the Persianate dimensions of Urdu also came from Muslims. In the second half of the nineteenth century leading figures of the Urdu literary world, like Muhammad Husayn Azad and Altaf Husayn Hali, were waging war against Urdu's Persianate heritage of artifice, what they felt to be the ornate and flowery products of a failed courtly culture. Instead, they now looked to Arabic for inspiration, as Hali tells us in the introduction to his *Musaddas*, his masterpiece on the rise and fall of Islam. Or alternatively both Hali and Azad also turned to English models; indeed, these provided models for most of the great Urdu writers of the late-nineteenth century. By the twentieth century, as they adopted models of socialist realism, they had left Persian far behind.[38]

Let us consider the fate of the second pillar of Iranian influence, that is, religious knowledge. In formal learning you will recall Iranian influences were mediated through the prominent position of the rational sciences. In mystical knowledge they were mediated through the predominance of Ibn 'Arabi's ideas in Sufi practice. From the eighteenth and nineteenth centuries these Persianate elements in religious knowledge came increasingly under attack from Islamic reform.

In formal learning we can see the beginnings of the attack in a new emphasis on the study of hadith which comes to be formalised in the curriculum taught at the madrasa established in Delhi at the end of the seventeenth century by Shah 'Abd al-Rahim. Rahim's son, Shah Wali Allah, driven by the need to strengthen Islam in South Asia in an age of political decline, continued the process. He attacked the rationalist scholastic traditions of Iran as a source of arid intellectualism and confusion. Muslims, he said, should return to the study of the revealed sciences; only these would bring them closer to the central teachings of the faith. But this line of thinking did not catch fire until Muslims were confronted from the 1820s by the realities of British rule – namely, a government which was removing all the grants which supported Islamic learning; a government which supported Islamic law only in a partial and bastardised form; and a government which no longer had places in its bureaucracy for madrasa students. 'Ulama' realised that their role had shifted from supporting a political power which maintained the shari'a to one of trying to preserve Muslim society altogether. The role of the rational sciences became devalued; that of the revealed sciences upgraded. 'Ulama' knew that in the absence of political power they must transfer to Muslims as a whole the knowledge and skills to fashion a Muslim society for themselves. This led to direct engagement with scripture (Qur'an and Hadith), the growth of self-interpretation, and a new emphasis on the Prophet as a model. It also led to the foundation of a host of reforming organisations from the Deoband School to the Tablighi Jama'at. It meant a major downgrading of Persian intellectual influences in Islamic scholarship.[39]

Sufism saw a similar decline in Persian influences. As in the case of formal learning its beginnings in South Asia can be dated back to the early seventeenth century when, in the context of Mughal religious eclecticism, Shaykh Ahmad Sirhindi attacked the monism of Ibn al-'Arabi. For the next two centuries this attack was carried in the Naqshbandi Sufi line which flowed from Sirhindi. In the late eighteenth century, it flourished in the circles surrounding the descendants of Shah Wali Allah. Then again, from the 1820s and 1830s with the realisation of the full impact of British rule, and with Wahhabi influences having their impact from Arabia, it became a growing presence in Indian Sufism. There was a great attack on all ideas of magic. There was a great attack on any idea that there could be intercession for man with God at saints' shrines. There was a new emphasis on the Day of Judgement. Islamic reform wanted to focus attention more fully on Revelation and the shari'a; it was with these forms of guidance that the individual human conscience must work. There could be no escape clause through intercession. Thus, the old inclusive Persianate Sufism came to decline; some wished that Sufism would disappear altogether. This said, forms of magic continued to exist in South Asian Sufi practice, but they did so without necessarily having the support which could be found in Persian literature, and they did so, too, in an environment in which their practices were strongly contested.[40]

Thus, these two pillars of Iranian influence came to crumble into the South Asian soil. By the twentieth century, Iranian influences were for the most part confined to traces: in the Persian script, in the Persian words in South Asian languages, in the remaining Parsi and Isma'ili communities, in the Islamicate culture of Bollywood; in some aspects of Sufi thought; in the landed cultures of Awadh and the Indus Valley, and of course in the sometimes imperilled but vibrant Shi'a communities, whose numbers of 60–70 million, we should note, match those of contemporary Iran. Beyond this, there are elements of culture and material artefacts to which I have not yet referred: South Asia's Sufi musical tradition of qawwali; its many Islamic gardens, most of them in ruins, and its great shrines, amongst them the peerless Taj Mahal.

Two Final Reflections

This said, I have a couple of final reflections on Iranian influences, admittedly felt at some distance, on the most dramatic event of twentieth-century South Asia: its division into India and Pakistan. The first reflection relates to Muhammad Iqbal, the poet-philosopher of the Pakistan movement. He was steeped in Iranian influences. His first work, his Munich Ph.D. thesis, was on the Development of Metaphysics in Persia. Most of his poetry was in Persian; he hoped to reach a wider audience than a purely Indian one. He loved the forms of classical Persian poetry, the mathnawi and the ghazal; he enjoyed those contrasting pairs – roses and nightingales, moths and candles; while he hated what he termed the Persian encrustations of Sufism, which mixed in the manner of Hafiz the profane with the divine, he acknowledged the prophetic example of Zarathustra, and the inspiration of Jamal al-Din al-Afghani, al-Hallaj and Rumi. We are credibly informed that Ayatollah Khumayni enjoyed his verse; we know that 'Ali Shari'ati was influenced by him. This was the man who in his Presidential speech to the All-India Muslim League in 1930 identified the northwest of British India as the future site of a Muslim state.[41] This was the man, too, whose Islamic thinking led to the conclusion that the individual Muslim self could only be fully realised in an Islamic order.[42]

My second reflection is connected to the first. It involves the Muslim element of the former Mughal governing class, a class shaped in many different ways by Iranian culture. In the nineteenth and twentieth centuries they had great difficulty in coming to terms with their loss of power and status. They mourned the passing of greatness and did so in ways certainly influenced by the Shi'a marsiya tradition, and typified by Hali's *Musaddas*, his elegy on the rise and fall of Islam of 1879, and Iqbal's *Shikwa-i Hind* of 1909.[43] 'The footprints in the sands of India still say,' as Hali wrote in his *Shikwa-i Hind* of 1888, 'a gracious caravan has passed this way.'[44] This sense of past greatness, of special 'political importance', as they argued, meant that this sharif class demanded separate representation and reserved seats in the developing constitutional arrangements of British India. Here again, arguably, lingering Iranian influences pointed in the direction of Pakistan. Here we have a final irony. While Persianate Sufi traditions were inclusive, Iranian legacies of power pointed towards the division of British India.

Notes

1. For the extraordinary increase in Mughal revenues under the Great Mughals, see John F. Richards, *The Mughal Empire; New Cambridge History of India*, 1, 5 (Cambridge: Cambridge University Press, 1993), pp. 75–8, 138–41, 185–90.
2. For the argument about the continuities and connections between the worlds of the Il Khans, Timurids and Mughals, see Francis Robinson, *The Mughal Emperors and the Islamic Dynasties of India, Iran and Central Asia, 1206–1925* (London: Thames & Hudson, 2007), pp. 14–74, 112–79.

3. Abu'l Fadl, *The Akbar Nama of Abul-Fazl*, trans. H. Beveridge (Delhi: Low-Price Publications, 1989), I, pp. 178–83.
4. Ibid., pp. 7, 121.
5. Stephen Frederic Dale, 'Steppe Humanism: The Autobiographical Writings of Zahir al-Din Muhammad Babur 1483–1530', *International Journal of Middle East Studies*, 22, 1990, pp. 37–58.
6. The picture facing the title page of Barbara Brend's edition of the Juki *Shahnamah* contains the seals of the Great Mughals. There is also a fascinating discussion of the regular engagement of the Mughals and the librarians with the book by A.H. Morton. Barbara Brend, *Muhammad Juki's Shahnamah of Firdausi* (London: Philip Wilson for the Royal Asiatic Society, 2010), pp. 163–75.
7. Babur, *Babur-Nama (Memoirs of Babur)*, trans. Annette S. Beveridge (New Delhi: Oriental Reprint Corporation, 1979), pp. 518–19.
8. Humayun's sister Gulbadan was present at the meetings between her brother and Shah Tahmasp. She described them when in later life she wrote a memoir of her brother. She tells of the entertainments they had together and charmingly summed up the relationship of the two monarchs thus: 'The friendship and concord of these two high-placed pashas was as close as two nut-kernels in one shell.' Gulbadan Begam, *The History of Humayun: Humayun-Nama by Gul-Badan Begam*, ed. and trans. Annette S. Beveridge (London: Royal Asiatic Society, 1902).
9. To see these two paintings together on one page, see Amina Okada, *Indian Miniatures of the Mughal Court* (New York: Harry N. Abrams Inc., 1992), p. 56. Both these paintings are representations of Jahangir's dreams which in the Islamic context would be regarded as a source of prophecy. Moin suggests for one of these paintings which shows Jahangir embracing Shah Abbas, Jahangir standing on a lion and the Shah on a lamb, that it is the submission of the Shah which is being depicted. As two of his forefathers, Babur and Humayun, had had to submit in various ways to the Safawids, now through his dream Jahangir was showing that the relationship had been reversed. As Moin says: 'Shah 'Abbas was now the recipient of Timurid charisma and *barakat*.' A. Azfar Moin, *The Millennial Sovereign: Sacred Kingship and Sainthood in Islam* (New York: Columbia University Press, 2012), pp. 204–6.
10. Jahangir, *The Tuzuk-i-Jahangiri or the Memoirs of Jahangir*, trans. Alexander Rogers, ed. Henry Beveridge 3rd ed. (Delhi: Munshiram Manoharlal, 1978), vol. I, p. 294.
11. Two painters from the atelier of Shah Tahmasp accompanied Humayun

on his return to India, 'Abdus Samad and Mir Sayyid 'Ali. They both played a key role in the development of Mughal painting under Akbar.
12. Muzaffar Alam, *The Languages of Political Islam in India c. 1200–1800* (New Delhi: Permanent Black, 2004), pp. 124–7.
13. For Nur Jahan, her father's tomb, her relationship with Jahangir and her husband's tomb, see Robinson, *Mughal Emperors,* pp. 145–7.
14. For a presentation and analysis of the Taj Mahal and its context conducted at the highest levels of scholarship, see Ebba Koch, *The Complete Taj Mahal and the Riverfront Gardens of Agra* (London: Thames & Hudson, 2006).
15. For the fashioning of the beginnings of modern Ismailism by Aga Khan I, see Nile Green, *Bombay Islam: The Religious Economy of the West Indian Ocean 1840–1915* (Cambridge: Cambridge University Press, 2011), pp. 155–78.
16. Haji Mohammed Hashem (1789–1850), the founder of the house of Ispahani, moved from Isfahan to Bombay in 1820. Under his descendant M.A. Ispahani (1898–1986) the business became a major corporation; Ispahani was a major figure in the industrial development of Pakistan. His younger brother, M.A.H. Ispahani, was particularly close to Jinnah, the leader of the movement for Pakistan, becoming the first Pakistani ambassador to the US.
17. Quoted in Alam, *Languages,* p. 128.
18. Ibid., p. 129
19. Ibid., pp. 130–1.
20. Francis Robinson, *The 'Ulama of Farangi Mahall and Islamic Culture in South Asia* (Delhi: Permanent Black, 2001), pp. 42–55.
21. Ibid., pp. 15–16, 18–19.
22. H. Goetz, *The Crisis of Indian Civilisation in the Eighteenth and Early Nineteenth Centuries* (Calcutta: University of Calcutta Press, 1938), pp. 6–7.
23. Robinson, *Farangi Mahall,* pp. 20–1.
24. Michael J. Franklin, *'Orientalist Jones': Sir William Jones, Poet, Lawyer and linguist, 1746–1794* (Oxford: Oxford University Press, 2011).
25. Abdul Halim Sharar, *Lucknow: The Last Phase of an Oriental Culture,* trans. and ed. E.S. Harcourt and Fakhir Husein (London: Elek, 1974), p. 99.
26. Aziz Ahmad, *An Intellectual History of Islam in India* (Edinburgh: Edinburgh University Press, 1969), pp. 234–8.
27. Sharar, *Lucknow,* p. 100.

28. Saiyid Athar Abbas Rizvi, *Shah Wali Allah and His Times: A Study of Eighteenth Century Islam, Politics and Society in India* (Canberra: Maʻrifat Publishing House, 1980), p. 398.
29. Peter Gran, *Islamic Roots of Capitalism: Egypt 1760–1840* (Austin: University of Texas Press, 1979), p. 146.
30. Muhammad Rida Ansari, *Bani-yi Dars-i Nisami* (Lucknow, 1973), p. 31; Shibli Nuʻmani, *Maqalat-i Shibli*, vol. I (Aʻzamgarh: Dar Mutbah Muʻaraf, 1955), p. 104.
31. Robinson, *Farangi Mahall*, pp. 23–4.
32. Ibid., pp. 24–5.
33. Ibid., p. 25.
34. J.R.I. Cole, *Roots of North Indian Shiʻism in Iran and Iraq: Religion and the State in Awadh, 1722–1859* (Berkeley: University of California Press, 1988), pp. 145–220.
35. Robinson, *Farangi Mahall*, p. 27; Aziz Ahmad, *Studies in Islamic Culture in the Indian Environment* (Oxford: Oxford University Press, 1964), p. 252.
36. Robinson, *Farangi Mahall*, pp. 32–3.
37. Ibid., p. 34.
38. Ibid., p. 35; Hali, *Hali's Musaddas: The Flow and Ebb of Islam*, ed. and trans. Christopher Shackle and Javed Majeed (Delhi: Oxford University Press, 1997).
39. Ibid., pp. 35–7.
40. Ibid., pp. 29–31, 37–8.
41. Syed Sharifuddin Pirzada, ed., *Foundations of Pakistan: All-India Muslim League Documents: 1906–1947* (Karachi: National Publishing House Limited, 1970), vol. II, pp. 153–71, but especially p. 159.
42. Aziz Ahmad, *Islamic Modernism in India and Pakistan 1857–1964* (London: Oxford University Press, 1964), pp. 141–67.
43. Hali, *Musaddas*; Iqbal Singh, *The Ardent Pilgrim: An Introduction to the Life & Work of Mohammed Iqbal* (Delhi: Oxford University Press, 1997), pp. 39–41.
44. Translation by Gail Minault, in G. Minault, 'Urdu Political Poetry during the Khilafat Movement', *Modern Asian Studies*, 8, 4, 1974, pp. 459–71. N.B. – The attribution in Minault's article is not quite correct. The quotation is from Hali's *Shikwa* of 1888. I am grateful to Eve Tignol for pointing this out.

9

South Asia and West Asia from the Delhi Sultanate to the Present

Security, Resources and Influence

THE ARAB, TURKISH AND Persian invasions of South Asia, which began in the eighth century, set off a process of Islamisation which has led to the fact that now the subcontinent contains one-third of the world's Muslims – half a billion – and India has one of the world's largest Muslim populations. The development is one of great geopolitical importance. It means that South Asia, which has always had important connections with West Asia, has taken those connections to a new level, embracing religion, scholarship, the arts, statesmanship, worldview, family history, the emotions and so on.

I intend to examine the interactions of South Asia and West Asia from the emergence of the Delhi Sultanate in the thirteenth century down to the present. Over such a long time, you will say? It is bound to be a very broad-brush treatment. Yes, I fear it will be, but I believe that there are things to be learned from the broad overview, in which the slow movement of history's tectonic plates can be observed, no less than from the fine-grained treatment of one process or one event.

I shall divide this 800-year period, if you will forgive divisions which will have the taint of old imperial ones, into the Sultanate and Mughal period, the British period, and the post-Independence period. Several interesting themes will run through them: West Asia and the security of South Asia; resources broadly construed – cultural, ideological, economic; and influence, that of West Asia on South Asia and vice versa. Amongst the processes we will see at work are: the expanding horizon of South Asian security in West Asia; the shift from primarily Persianate influence on Muslim South Asia to primarily Arab influence, at least in religious terms; and that great change from South Asia as a receiver of West Asian influences to (increasingly) South Asia as a transmitter of influences to the West.

From the Delhi Sultanate to the British

From the period of the Delhi Sultanate to the eighteenth century, West Asia, broadly construed as those parts of Asia to the west of South Asia, was the prime threat to the security of regimes established in north India. It is true that these regimes could be challenged by Sultanates elsewhere in India, as they in turn could challenge regional Sultanates, but the prime threat always came from the northwest. It was from the northwest that the Turkish Ghaznawids had invaded South Asia in the eleventh century. It was from the northwest that the Turkish Ghorids invaded India in the twelfth century and eventually established the Delhi Sultanate.

By the thirteenth and fourteenth centuries much of the energy of the Delhi Sultanate was consumed in fighting the Mongols. It was thus that Muhammad, Balban's son, was killed in 1285, inspiring a great qasida from Amir Khusraw, but also precipitating the death of the 80-year-old Sultan.[1] Ala al-Din Khilji was so successful against the Mongols in the early fourteenth century that according to the historian, Barani, they 'conceived such a fear and dread of the army of Islam that all fancy for coming to Hindustan was washed clear out of their breasts'.[2] Ghazi al-Din Tughluq, who ruled from 1321, came to the throne with twenty-nine victories over the Mongols behind him.

When there was a strong regime in north India, it was possible to prevent armies from West Asia from penetrating the region. But when power in north India was weak, or divided, it was hard to resist invading forces, and the collapse of Tughluqid power after Firuz Shah's death left the way open for Timur to invade India and sack Delhi. In the same way, divisions amongst the Afghan rulers of India in the early sixteenth century left the way open for a series of invasions from the Mughal, Babur, culminating in his great victory over Ibrahim Lodi in 1526. So also the weakness of Muhammad Shah's Mughal regime in the 1730s, which was underlined by Maratha raids into the outskirts of Delhi, prompted Nadir Shah of Iran's invasion of 1739, when the city's fabulous treasure was looted and the Peacock Throne taken to Iran. In the mid-eighteenth century, the continuing weakness of central power led to regular invasions from the Afghan, Ahmad 'Abdali, and the massive defeat of Mughal and Maratha forces at Panipat in 1761.

Finally, the ambitions of a West Asian power could make it possible for a prince, down on his luck, to relaunch his regime from West Asia. So, Shah Tahmasp of Safawid Iran, thinking that he had persuaded the fugitive Mughal, Humayun, to convert to Shi'ism, lent him the troops which enabled him to begin his reconquest of India in 1555. In the late seventeenth century, the emperor Awrangzib's son Akbar fancied that he might overthrow his father with Safawid help. From the thirteenth to the eighteenth century, when power weakened in northern India, the region was seriously exposed to invasion by West Asian forces.

Resources

The establishment of Muslim power in India, both in the north and in the Deccan, opened the way to the spread of Islamic culture across the region. Arguably, from now on, South Asia had a rich extra resource to add to that which flowed from Sanskritic civilisation. It was a resource which brought powerful links to West Asia, as well as to the wider Muslim world. Thus, India became part of a world of Perso-Islamic culture, which reached from Istanbul and Anatolia through to Bengal.³

Amongst the cultural resources which linked South Asia to West Asia were the following. There was the authority to rule. Delhi Sultans made a point of acknowledging the Caliphate in their titles and on their coinage. In 1229 Iltutmish was delighted to receive an embassy from Baghdad, bearing robes of honour and formal confirmation of his authority over the lands he had conquered – not a bad achievement for a man who had once been a slave in Baghdad. In 1343, Muhammad bin Tughluq was similarly delighted to receive an embassy and recognition from the Caliph, who now lived in exile in Egypt.⁴

The Mughals tended not to acknowledge the Ottoman caliphate, seeing themselves as Caliphs of India. But they still drew their authority from the lands west of South Asia. In this case it was from the Mongol and Timurid traditions of sovereignty which was made very clear both in the early chapters of Abul Fadl's *Akbarnama* and in the Mughal tradition of lineage portraits in which, for instance, Timur might be seen handing down the right to rule through his descendants down to Awrangzib.⁵

Crucially important was the Persian language and its literature. Persian became the language of government almost everywhere except the far south. Throughout, Hindus as well as Muslims came to explore the riches of Perso-Islamic civilisation; it became the main language of intellectual and artistic life. The main forms of Persian literature came to be widely cultivated: history, biographical dictionaries, Sufi malfuzat, and insha', the art of official letter writing. Most important, of course, was poetry. Hafiz, Sa'di, Jami, Nizami, the great poets of Persia were much loved; in the late sixteenth and seventeenth centuries poets from Iran and Central Asia created a golden age at the courts of both the Mughal emperors and the Deccan Sultans.⁶

No less important in linking South to West Asia was Islamic knowledge, both formal and mystical. It is striking how much in the Mughal period its various forms were rooted in West Asia.

Almost all the books and commentaries normally used in transmitting Islamic learning had been written in Iran or Central Asia between 1100 and 1600. To list some of their names is to parade the great scholars of the Perso-Islamic world: 'Abd Allah Nasafi (d. 1312), Burhan al-Din al-Marghinani (d. 1197), Jalal al-Din Dawwani of Shiraz, and those great rivals at the court of Timur, Sa'ad al-Din al-Taftazani (d. 1389) and Sayyid Sharif al-Jurjani (d. 1413). In the same way the Sufi orders and their teachers were all intrinsic parts of Perso-Islamic civilisation on the subcontinent. The Chishti way which had been brought to India by Mu'in al-Din Sijzi from the area round Herat at the end of the twelfth century; the Qadiri path, first introduced by Muhammad Ghawth, who travelled through much of the Perso-Islamic world before establishing himself at Uch; and that of the Naqshbandis, brought from Central Asia in the sixteenth century by Khwaja Baqi Billah, and thence to flourish vigorously in the Mughal world.[7]

The courts of India were rich sources of patronage for thousands of men from West Asia, whether they just sought patronage or were fleeing oppression. This was as much the case of Ibn Battuta and 'Abd al-'Aziz Ardabili, the pupil of Ibn Taymiyya, who found employment at the fourteenth-century court of Muhammad bin Tughluq, as it was for Mir Muhammad Amin from Nayshapur, who arrived in India in 1708 and went on to found Awadh's Nawabi dynasty, or Shaykh 'Ali 'Hazin', who fled Iran for India in 1734 and became one of the great Persian poets of the eighteenth century under the patronage of the Raja of Benares. The third volume of the Mughal historian, 'Abd al-Qadir Badauni's *Muntakhab al-Tawarikh*, is a monumental record of the movement of gifted men from West into South Asia.[8] Moreover, the arrival of some figures marked notable new directions in their fields: Mir Sayyid 'Ali and 'Abd al-Samad arrived with Humayun from Safawid Iran in 1555 and set new directions for Mughal painting; the arrival of Fadl Allah Shirazi, also from Iran via Bijapur, in 1583 brought a great flowering of scholarship in the rational sciences.[9]

It is worth stopping for a moment to consider how the more

ordinary person might have experienced this connection with West Asia, how might it have played a part in their mental and emotional worlds. The young scholar who completed learning one of the great texts of the Islamic tradition would see on his ijaza, his licence to teach that text, how he had become part of a chain of transmission which reached back to the original author in West Asia. The freshly made Sufi murid, or disciple, would see on the shijra, or record of succession which his Shaykh gave him, how he had become part of a tradition of spiritual understanding which went back through the founder of his order in West Asia to the Prophet's nephew and son-in-law, 'Ali. It is most unlikely that the ordinary man would have been able to perform the Hajj to Mecca as, for instance, the ladies of the Mughal royal family did in 1585, much as he might have dreamed of it. But he might easily enjoy the storytelling of the Dastan-i Amir Hamza. This book, so loved by the emperor Akbar that he had 1200 illustrations made to accompany its telling, would take him into a James Bond-like world of magical realism, embracing amongst other things Sassanian Ctesiphon, and seventh-century Mecca and Medina.[10]

Influence

For almost all the period from the thirteenth to the eighteenth century, influences flowed one way, from West Asia to South Asia. The Mughals had some diplomatic engagement with West Asian powers which reached as far as the Ottoman Empire and Ethiopia. Part of this diplomacy was designed to curb the power of the Safawid empire. But in effect little was achieved, and West Asia's neglect of the Mughals, almost bordering on contempt, illustrated to their chagrin the limited influence they were able to wield.[11]

Nor were the Mughals able to project military power into West Asia. Throughout the dynasty they lost control of Qandahar more often than they held it. Their one major military expedition westward to conquer the family's former heartland of Central Asia ended ignominiously when their army under Awrangzib had to retreat in the snow from Balkh in 1647.

The one point where the Mughals had some impact was in facilitating the Hajj to Mecca. For this purpose, Akbar negotiated deals with the Portuguese and made major donations to Mecca and Medina. In later years the pattern was followed by the Muslim princes of India: the Nawabs of Arcot, for instance, endowed lodging houses for pilgrims, the Arcot Rubats, and the Begums of Bhopal did so too. In the same way the Shi'a Nawabs of Awadh channelled huge sums to an-Najaf both to support scholars and to build a canal from the Euphrates to the city.[12]

The matter of Hajj and holy places apart, it is not until the eighteenth century that we begin to see an increasing two-way traffic between South and West Asia, and one can begin to talk, in ideas at least, of growing South Asian influence. In the realm of Persian poetry there is the influence of sabk-i Hindi, that is, of the Indian School, with 'Abd al-Qadir Bedil of Azimabad at its head. In the eighteenth century this came to have considerable influence in Iran, and subsequently in Afghanistan and Central Asia. In this matter, Bedil was, in a way, the forerunner of Iqbal. Since the 1980s Bedil's influence has seen a significant revival in Iran.

Arguably, the more striking influence is to be found in scholarship and mysticism. The flourishing of scholarship in the Islamic rational sciences, which Fadl Allah Shirazi was said to have inspired, gained a great head of steam in Awadh in the seventeenth and eighteenth centuries, so that Shah Jahan described the region as the 'Shiraz of India'. The Farangi Mahall family of 'ulama', and their pupils, were right at the heart of this scholarly development.[13] In the late eighteenth century Awadhi scholarship in the rational sciences came to have a major influence in West Asia. When the Shaykh al-Azhar, Shaykh Hasan al-Attar left Cairo in 1802 to study the rational sciences in Turkey and Syria, he found that most of the post-classical scholars were Indian, and devoted much time to the works of the Awadhi school. When he returned to Cairo in

1815 he stimulated a revival of the rational sciences. More generally, it seems that both scholars in Turkey in support of the *Tanzimat* and those in Egypt in support of Muhammad 'Ali drew on the rationalist scholarship of India when they needed to use scholastic theology as a vehicle of defence against orthodoxy rooted in the transmitted subjects.[14]

A further dimension of Indian influence lies in the spread of the Naqshbandi Sufi order from India to West Asia. You will recall that, under the influence of Shaykh Ahmad Sirhindi, his reaction against the religious eclecticism of Akbar and Jahangir, and his rejection of Ibn al-'Arabi's philosophy of the Unity of Being, the Naqshbandi Sufi way entered its Mujaddidi phase in which Sirhindi's collected letters, his maktubat, was a key book.[15] One important mujaddidi silsila went through Mecca, the Yemen and thence to Egypt. A second more important line was extended by Murad al-Bukhari, a Khalifa of one of Sirhindi's sons, into the elite of Damascus and the circle of that pivotal eighteenth-century West Asian intellectual, Shaykh 'Abd al-Ghani Nabulusi. But arguably the most fascinating line was the connection made by Mawlana Khalid Baghdadi with the Naqshbandi khanqah of Shah Ghulam 'Ali, which he visited in Delhi in 1809. On returning to West Asia he launched the Khalidiyya phase of the Naqshbandi order which was marked by aims of Islamic revival, popular mobilisation, and concerns to fight both Western imperialism and processes of imitative Westernisation. His influence was felt widely, from Algeria to Indonesia, but especially in Damascus, Baghdad, Istanbul, Kurdistan and eastern Anatolia.[16] The Naqshbandi–Khalidiyya provided the context in which that remarkable man, Sa'id Badi' al-Zaman Nursi, developed the Nurcu movement, in which his Turkish followers embraced forms of scripturalism, indeed of 'Protestantism', in which Sirhindi's maktubat played an important part.[17] As many of you will know, it is men from this movement who in the 1960s drove the industrialisation of Central Anatolia from below.[18] It is men from this movement who have been at the heart of the rise of Islamist politics in modern Turkey, the politics of the

National Salvation Party, the Rifa Party and now the AKP which has formed the government in the twenty-first century.[19] In my wilder fantasies, I see 'Abd Allah Gul, President of Turkey, and Tayyib Erdogan, Prime Minister, with Sirhindi's maktubat on their bedside tables. It is in the context of the spread of South Asian Islamic ideas to West Asia in the nineteenth century that Albert Hourani demonstrated several decades ago that India began to take an intellectual lead in the Muslim world.[20]

The British Period

Security

I now turn to the British period, stretching from roughly 1800 to 1947. In terms of the security of South Asia, West Asia remained the key area but, as this period went on, a new twist was added. Security became less an issue of threats from West or Northwest Asia than of the impact which the actions of the British Empire in West Asia might have on Muslim opinion in South Asia.

Alongside this, considerations of the security of India also became bound up with Great Power competition in Europe and the Mediterranean. Calcutta, and later Delhi, would from time to time find themselves either in competition or disagreement with policies enunciated by Whitehall. This tension was demonstrated right from the beginning in 1809, when both Whitehall and India sent envoys within weeks of each other to the Qajar Shah in Tehran, down to 1922 when the Secretary of State for India, Edwin Montagu, resigned because he could no longer navigate the tensions which existed between the Foreign Office's policies for West Asia as opposed to those of a Government of India deeply sensitive to Indian Muslim opinion.

Napoleon's invasion of Egypt in 1798 made the point about the new interconnection between the rivalry amongst European powers and the security of South Asia. The British saw this thrust as a threat to India and were mightily relieved to have cut off his army's move into Syria at Acre in 1799. A major French diplomatic and military mission to Tehran in 1807 was seen as a further threat, which led to the two competing British missions of 1809. Indeed, French competition was seen as a threat down to 1815, but never really far away.[21] One of the reasons for the Balfour declaration of 1917 was that the Jewish homeland, which the British proposed to support in Palestine, would act as a buffer between the French-controlled territories of Lebanon and Syria, and that key artery of Britain's Indian empire, the Suez Canal.[22]

From the 1820s the British became increasingly concerned about a Russian threat and focused their attention on bolstering Iran. When in the 1830s this policy seemed unsatisfactory, they moved towards promoting Afghanistan as a buffer, a policy which collapsed in the disaster of the retreat from Kabul in 1842. The British response was now to fashion security in the northwest by annexing Sindh and the Punjab, beginning the life of the latter as a semi-militarised region which has lasted down to the present.[23] The frontier was taken up to the Hindu Kush and then from 1893 finally drawn, after a fashion, as the British and the Afghans established the Durand Line. Throughout this period, down to 1919, Afghanistan was treated as a buffer state to which from time to time the British issued orders, but with limited effect, as Viceroys Lytton and Curzon discovered. By the twentieth century Russian power had reached the northern fringes of Afghanistan and Iran. The British endeavoured to secure their interests in India and Iran by means of the Anglo-Russian Convention of 1907, which divided Iran into spheres of influence, the drawing of the British sphere in Southeast Iran clearly underlining Britain's Indian interest. Noting these various security stratagems, commonly known as the 'Great Game', we should remember the extent to which they were dictated by financial constraints.[24]

A second front of rather less importance for the security of India, at least for most of the period, existed in the Persian Gulf. From the beginning the British presence in the Gulf was a function of their commercial interests in the Indian Ocean region. From 1763 there was a British Resident in Bushihr who in the nineteenth century was first subordinate to the Governor of Bombay, and then from 1873 to the Viceroy. Curzon described him as the 'uncrowned king' of the Persian Gulf. And so he was, having responsibility for the Persian coast, including the suppression of piracy, and from 1853 for the Trucial States on the Arabian Coast, which by 1892 had become British protectorates. The Resident's authority was reinforced first by ships of the Indian Navy and then from 1867 by those of the Royal Navy. Although the opening of the Suez Canal somewhat reduced the strategic importance of the Gulf, this was in part compensated for by the routing of the international telegraph through the region, then more than compensated for by the discovery of oil in Iran, which could only be marketed through the Gulf, as also by Churchill's decision in 1913 to power the Royal Navy by oil rather than by coal. By 1914 the Gulf region had acquired a strategic importance which would make it the focus for a major projection of military power from India during and after World War One.[25]

Resources

By the beginning of the twentieth century, British activities in West Asia, and those of other European powers were coming to have an increasing impact on the politics of India. The security of government in South Asia had come to be more and more affected by what took place in West Asia. We need to step aside for a moment to see why this was so. We need to see, in effect, what new resources (or elements) had come to link West Asia and South Asia.

In the nineteenth century West and South Asia came to be linked in new ways and with new intensity. One new way was the great shift in the focus of cultural inspiration, particularly amongst north Indian Muslims, away from Mughal and Persianate sources towards Arab sources. The prime reason was the loss of Mughal power and the need, under the British, to find some new and vigorous cultural resource on which to rebuild Muslim society. For some aspects, literature and Unani Tibb for example, Muslims drew on both Arab and Western inspiration. But in matters of their faith they turned increasingly to Arab inspiration. In scholarship reforming 'ulama' came increasingly to focus on the transmitted subjects as opposed to the rational subjects, the original works of Arab guidance as opposed to the Persianate skills of interpretation. Reforming 'ulama' increasingly attacked the influence of Ibn al-'Arabi, all ideas of intercession at saints' shrines, and what Iqbal termed the 'Persian encrustations' of Sufism. And so reforming 'ulama' increasingly focused on a scriptural faith in which the conscience of the individual believer came to engage with the word of God, often found in translation. The Prophet himself came to move much closer to the centre of piety. Hadith, the traditions relating to the Prophet, became an increasingly important focus for scholarship, leading South Asia to what it is today, the centre of Hadith scholarship in the Islamic world. This 'Arab turn' in inspiration continues down to the present, much to the sorrow of some.[26]

In this context the worlds of South Asia and West Asia came to be increasingly closely linked – by steamship, by the telegraph and by the post. It is notable, for instance, that the scholar and Sufi in the north Indian reforming tradition, Hajji Imdad Allah, who fled India after the Mutiny Uprising, was able to counsel his disciples for many years from Mecca, as his maktubat reveals. In the same vein, 'Abd al-Bari of Lucknow's Farangi Mahall family, in the early twentieth century, corresponded regularly with Sharif Husayn of Mecca and Anwar Pasha, the Young Turk leader.

Of course, the new connectedness and ease of communication was accompanied by a substantial growth in the Hajj from South Asia. It was also accompanied by a greater Indian presence in the region. At the high point of Indo-Omani commerce in the nineteenth century, as many as 4,000 Indians, Hindu and Muslim, lived in Muscat. Major fugitives from India ran transnational networks which linked West Asia to Asia further East. Seema Alavi has shown how the Hadhrami 'alim, Sayyid Fadl, who led Kerala's Mapillas in revolt against the new taxation system introduced by the British, ran a network of contacts which reached from Istanbul, through Kerala to Acheh in Sumatra. She has also shown how Rahmat Allah Kayranawi, who had debated with Christian missionaries at Agra in 1854, established his Madrasa Sawlatiyya in Mecca, a destination for Indian Muslims but with links that reached both to Istanbul and to Deoband. In the same way the reputation of Siddiq Hasan Khan, husband of Begum Shah Jahan of Bhopal and Ahl-i Hadith scholar, whose work circulated widely in West Asia both in Arabic and in Turkish translation, attracted a stream of Arab scholars to Bhopal and other centres.[27]

Most important in building this new connectedness, at least from the South Asian point of view, was the press, which from the mid-nineteenth century grew steadily in Muslim India. There came to be a symbiotic relationship between the advance of European power in West Asia and the expansion of Muslim consciousness and emotion to embrace that region. When, in the late 1870s, Russia and the Ottoman Empire went to war, the press boomed. When, in 1882, Britain invaded Egypt, it boomed again. From 1911 onwards, when the Ottoman Empire entered its terminal stages, it boomed as never before. Newspapers flourished on the news of West Asia: Abul Kalam Azad's *al-Hilal*, Muhammad 'Ali's *Comrade*, and Zafar 'Ali Khan's *Zamindar*. Novels of the time indicate how West Asia had entered Muslim imaginative life, for instance, Sarshar's *Fasana-yi Azad*, which is set in the context of the Russo-Turkish war of the 1870s, or the many historical romances of 'Abd al-Halim Sharar. Fashion in dress indicated forms of West Asian identity, as Aligarh College adopted the fez of the Ottoman reformers or the 'ulama' of Lucknow followed the clothing fashions of Egypt, Syria and Iran. By the early twentieth century there was an important dimension of the intellect and emotion, of some Muslims at least, which was engaged with West Asia.[28]

Influence

Let us consider the issues of power and influence. The first point to note is that the play of power which in the Sultanate and Mughal periods had for the most part moved from West Asia to South Asia now moved firmly in the opposite direction, and South Asian influences in various forms were coming to be more widely felt in West Asia.

The most striking demonstration of the new dispensation in the first half of the twentieth century was the role South Asia played in projecting British power into West Asia. A substantial number of the million Indians who fought in World War One fought in West Asia. They suffered in the British defeats at Gallipoli in Ottoman Rumelia and Kut in Mesopotamia, but also played the central role in the subsequent drives through Mesopotamia, Sinai and Palestine which pushed the Ottoman forces back into Anatolia. India's role in the War led to its representation at the Versailles Peace Conference. Between the wars it was Indian troops who helped sustain British authority in Iraq and Palestine, which was often grievously challenged. In the Second World War, the British Indian army, which mobilised over 2.5 million men, played the central role in resisting the Axis powers in Syria, the Lebanon and Iraq, the Anglo-Soviet invasion of Iran, in the campaign against Rommel in North Africa, and the Allied drive up through Italy. Indian military power had been deployed in West Asia and beyond, as never before.

It is instructive to note the influence wielded by India in decisions made about West Asia during and after World War One. West Asia was a key point where the Government of India interacted, not always harmoniously, with the British Foreign Office. It was the Government of India's strategic concern to command the Persian Gulf in general and Basra and its Iraqi hinterland in particular, which led to the reservation of the wilayats of Basra and Baghdad to Britain in the Husain–McMahon correspondence of

1915–16. This meant, of course, that the French insisted on having Syria for their part, and that the area available for an Arab national state, should there ever be one, was much reduced. In the 1920s the Government of India had the satisfaction of seeing Ibn Sa'ud, who for a decade had been their candidate to rule in Central Arabia, take power in the Hijaz, displacing the Foreign Office's candidate, Sharif Husayn.[29]

But there were other positions taken by the Indian government which were the outcome of the strength of Muslim feeling in India and fears for the security of the Raj. As you will know, that Indo-Muslim emotional engagement with West Asia, which had been fostered by the great changes in communication during the nineteenth century, became channelled, as the British threatened the Hijaz and the Ottoman Caliphate, into the Khilafat movement, the greatest movement of opposition to British rule between the Mutiny Uprising and the Quit India movement of 1942. The movement was powerful in part because the Khilafat leadership won over Gandhi and the national movement to their side for nearly three years, but also because the Western threat to the Caliphate – no more than an empty shell in its late Ottoman form – reached deep into Muslim concerns about their loss of power, their capacity to maintain their civilisation, indeed, their relationship to the authority of their revelation.

Government of India nervousness about Muslim feeling in India meant a complete ban on any deployment of British troops in the Hijaz in support of Sharif Husayn in World War One (a point that the USA might have noted in 1990).[30] It was amongst the reasons which required the clandestine nature of the undertakings made with the Arabs and the French in 1915 and 1916.[31] Moreover, it was the reason why in 1922 Secretary of State, Montagu, published the Government of India's proposals for the revision of the Treaty of Sevres, an act which restricted the Foreign Office's negotiating hand and forced his resignation.[32]

After the upheaval of World War One and its aftermath, South

Asian influence in West Asia flowed increasingly from its burgeoning national movements. Nehru and the Congress gave their support to all anti-colonial movements in the region. In 1927, for instance, the Congress passed a resolution demanding the withdrawal of Indian troops from all Arab lands. The Muslim League tended to focus on specific developments, most especially the issue of Palestine which was the subject of much comment and many resolutions from the 1920s to the 1940s.[33] Two developments deserve further attention. The first was when the Jewish Agency, in the context of the Arab Revolt in Palestine and the dangers it held for the Zionist project, sent Herman Kallenbach to India to seek Gandhi's aid. The Zionists did not get the reply from Gandhi they were hoping for: 'In my opinion', declared a message from Gandhi to Chaim Weizmann, 'the Jews should disclaim any intention of realising their aspiration under the protection of arms and should rely wholly on the goodwill of Arabs.'[34] A second Zionist envoy, after twenty minutes' exposure to Gandhi's worldview, declared him 'ein lammel', a simpleton.[35] Gandhi's statement after Kristellnacht on 9/10 November 1938 that 'Palestine belongs to the Arabs in the same way that England belongs to the English' brought an end to any thought that he might mediate in Palestine.[36] This said, the Jewish Agency's approach is an indication of how some Zionists regarded Gandhi.

A second development was the involvement of the rump of India's Khilafatists, in particular Muhammad and Shawkat 'Ali, in the international Muslim Congress movement from the 1920s, for instance, that which considered Sharif Husayn's claim to the Caliphate in 1924, or that which considered the Egyptian claim in 1926, or that which tried to win general support for the Palestinian Arabs, and the establishment of an international Muslim university, in 1931. Indian Muslims were major players on all these occasions, but the Muslim Congress movement, rather like the Islamic Conference Organisation, which is arguably its successor, always found difficulty in raising a common Islamic interest above specific national interest.[37] The fate of the views of Gandhi and the Khilafatists in West Asia, while pointing to some future concerns of South Asia in West Asia, only serves to underline the limitations of their influence at this time.

Post-Independence

What themes can we pick up from this long overview which continue to resonate in the post-Independence period? The first is, of course, the fact that the main security threat to India continued to come from the northwest, and was arguably more pressing, and at times more dangerous, than it had been before. The creation of Pakistan by partitioning British India left a large chunk of the semi-militarised province of the Punjab in the new state. Just as the Mughals used diplomacy in West Asia to limit the Safawid threat so independent India used diplomacy in West Asia, and further afield, to counter the Pakistan threat.

As in the British period the threat to India from the northwest was further complicated by the great power conflict of the time. Now it was not the rivalry of European powers but the Cold War rivalry between the Soviet bloc and the West. The signing of the Baghdad Pact in 1958 and the inclusion of Pakistan in the 'northern tier' of countries (Turkey, Iraq and Iran alongside Britain and the USA) made it inevitable that India should tilt in a pro-Soviet direction.

The last twist of the Cold War brought Afghanistan into play. Afghanistan, you will recall, was in the Mughal period a launch pad for invasions of India, while under the British it came to be seen as a key buffer against Russian expansion. Russia's invasion of Afghanistan in 1979 realised the nightmare which had haunted British players of the 'great game' for a century. The Russians were in striking distance of the Indian Ocean. The outcome, as we know, was the militarisation and Islamisation of Pakistan's northwest frontier, as the West, Saudi Arabia and Gulf countries poured money and arms into the region to resist the Russian presence. Ten years later, after the Russians retreated, there remained a vacuum, in which Afghan warlords competed for power, in which Pakistan and India competed for influence, and from which Osama bin Laden and al-Qaʻida were able to launch their jihad against the 'distant' enemy in the West. The result has been military action by the West, waged for some time without due attention, which may or may not bring stability to Afghanistan, and which may destabilise Pakistan. As ever, Afghanistan remains crucially important to the security of South Asia.

We noted, when dealing with the British period, the way in which the British were constantly concerned about the impact of their foreign policy on Indian Muslim opinion, and therefore the security of the Raj. We have noted how manifestations of the Islamic revival also gave rise to security scares. Now, I am credibly informed that the government of independent India, like its colonial predecessor, most of the time conducts its policy in West Asia with an eye to Indian Muslim opinion. On the other hand, the Islamic revival in West Asia and elsewhere over the past thirty years has had its impact on India. There have been concerns about money coming into the country from Saudi Arabia and the Gulf; there have been concerns about madrasas; there have been concerns about terrorist networks. I do not doubt that there is a real basis for some of these concerns as assaults on Parliament in Delhi and on the Taj Mahal hotel in Mumbai bear out. But I sense that there might also be a fear, even a paranoia, about the Muslim militant which bears comparison to similar, usually groundless, fears under the British.

A striking feature of the British period in South Asia was the way in which the Gulf came to be included first of all in its commercial network and then in its security network. Since Independence the process has been continued and enlarged. It did not happen straight away. Until 1970 the Gulf remained a British lake. But, after the British left, the massive growth of oil wealth in the region, fuelled by both rising prices and rising demand, created great synergies with South Asia. The Gulf is the major source of India's oil and gas supplies; roughly a quarter of India's exports go there, and more than quarter of her imports come from there; four million Indian nationals work in the Gulf, remitting *c*. $12bn a year.[38] Gulf states are increasingly important destinations for Indian project and IT services; Gulf money is seen as a major source for Indian infrastructure projects. It is not surprising that the Gulf falls within the Indian security parameter, and within the operating radius of the Indian navy. It is a vital limb of the Indian economy.[39]

One feature of nationalist politics under the British, as we have noted, was objection to Zionism, which Nehru described as 'the child of British imperialism'. In 1950 India formally recognised Israel but refused to open diplomatic relations. Indian sympathies remained firmly with the Arabs in general and with the Palestinian Arabs in particular, a fact which worked greatly to India's benefit during the Arab oil embargo following the 1973 Arab-Israeli war. Matters changed in the early 1990s: the end of the Cold War and the opening of a new era of US domination; the divisions amongst the Arabs revealed by the 1991 Gulf War; the opening of the Middle East Peace Process in Madrid; and consistent Israeli support for India's position on Kashmir brought a reassessment of the Indian position. Diplomatic relations were opened with Israel. One benefit was access to Israel's advanced technology, access to its advanced military weapons, and access to its anti-terrorist expertise. Another benefit, perhaps, was leverage in the Peace Process and the capacity to moderate Israeli actions.[40] But, I do wonder how without a successful peace process this policy will play amongst the peoples and states of West Asia who are so crucial to India's future. It will certainly be difficult to maintain if the peoples of West Asia come to have a greater say in the politics of their states. Former Prime Minister Manmohan Singh's outright condemnation of Israel's Operation Cast Lead in Gaza in January 2009 underlines the stresses and tensions of the current policy towards Israel.[41]

Let us conclude by considering India's influence in West Asia since Independence. You will recall that an important change in South Asia's relationship to West Asia began to take place from the eighteenth century when South Asia became less a receiver of influences from West Asia and more a transmitter of influences to it. That historic change has accelerated since Independence. The new levels of Indian influence in West Asia that derived from the enormous authority of Nehru as a world statesman and leader of the Non-Aligned movement have been reinforced since his death by the growing synergies between West Asia's resources and opportunities and the Indian economy. Indian ideas have inspired major West Asian political movements: I think of the influence of Mawlana Mawdudi's concept of jahiliyya on Sayyid Qutb and the second phase of the Muslim Brotherhood;[42] I think of the influence of Muhammad Iqbal's vision of the Khilafat of Man on 'Ali Shari'ati and a fashioning of a dynamic Shi'a theology of modernity which enabled many young people to contribute to the Iranian revolution.[43] Then in the cultural sphere there is the film industry which wins friends for India throughout West Asia, including Israel. One day, perhaps, we will even see cricket as a cultural export reaching beyond the Indian communities of the Gulf. Such are the levels of Indian dependence on the Gulf that it is hard to imagine that it is not prepared to project military power into the region, should it be necessary, as it did under the British in the last century. We should also note that India's rise to great power status is bound to make it a competitor for influence in West Asia with a declining United States and a rising China. West Asia is rapidly emerging as India's extended neighbourhood, an essential component of her great power status and, arguably, the region in which that status will be most fully expressed.

Notes

1. Mohammad Wahid Mirza, *The Life and Works of Amir Khusrau* (Delhi: Idarah-i Adabiyat-i Delli, 1974), pp. 55–64; Ziya al-Din Barani, Tarikh-i Firoz Shahi in H.M. Elliot and J. Dowson, eds, *The History*

of India as told by its own Historians, vol. III (Delhi: Low Price Publications, 1990), pp. 122–3.
2. Ibid., p. 199.
3. See 'Perso-Islamic Culture in India from the Early Seventeenth to the Twentieth Century', in Francis Robinson, *The 'Ulama of Farangi Mahall and Islamic Culture in South Asia* (Delhi: Permanent Black 2001), pp. 9–40.
4. Aziz Ahmad, *Studies in Islamic Culture in the Indian Environment* (Oxford: Clarendon Press, 1964), pp. 6–9.
5. See for instance chapters XV to XXVI of the *Akbarnama* in which Abul Fadl describes Akbar's ancestry from the mythical Mongol queen, Alanquwa, through Chinghiz Khan down to his birth in Sind in 1541. Abul Fadl, *Akbarnama*, trans. H. Beveridge, vol I, reprint (Delhi: Atlantic Publishers, 1989). For pictorial evidence, see Francis Robinson, *The Mughal Emperors and the Islamic Dynasties of India, Iran and Central Asia 1206–1925* (London: Thames & Hudson, 2007), pp. 7, 121, and for evidence on Timur's sarcophagus, p. 49.
6. 'Perso-Islamic Culture', in Robinson, *Farangi Mahall*, p. 13.
7. Ibid., pp. 13–18.
8. Abdu-l-Qadir al-Badaoni, *Muntakhabu-t-Tawarikh*, ed. and trans. T. Wolseley Haig, vol. 3, reprint (Delh: Idarah-i Adabaiyat-i Delli, 1973).
9. S.A.A. Rizvi, *A Socio-Intellectual History of the Isna' Ashari Shi'is in India*, vol. II (Canberra: Ma'rifat Publishing House, 1986), p. 206.
10. Ghalib Lakhnavi and Abdullah Bilgrami, *The Adventures of Amir Hamza* trans. Musharraf Farooqi (New York: Modern Library/Random House, 2008).
11. Ahmad, *Islamic Culture*, pp. 22–47.
12. J.R.I. Cole, *Roots of North Indian Shi'ism in Iran and Iraq: Religion and State in Awadh, 1722–1859* (Berkeley: University of California Press, 1984), pp. 153–4, 257–72.
13. Robinson, *Farangi Mahall*, pp. 41–55.
14. Ibid., pp. 226–7.
15. H. Algar, 'Said Nursi and Risala-i Nur: An Aspect of Islam in Contemporary Turkey', in Khurshid Ahmad and Zafar Ishaq Ansari, ed., *Islamic Perspectives: Studies in Honour of Mawlana Sayyid Abul A'la Mawdudi* (Jeddah: Saudi Publishing House, 1980), p. 329.
16. Albert Hourani, 'Sufism and Modern Islam: Mawlana Khalid and

the Naqshbandi Order', in Albert Hourani, ed., *The Emergence of the Modern Middle East* (London: Macmillan, 1981), pp. 75–8.

17. It was through reading Sirhindi's maktubat that Nursi came to realise that his only guide should be the Qur'an. Sukran Vahide (ed. and intro., Ibrahim M. Abu-Rabi, *Islam in Modern Turkey: An Intellectual Biography of Bediuzzaman Said Nursi* (Albany, NY: State University of New York Press, 2005), pp. 163–6.
18. European Stability Initiative, 'Islamic Calvinists; Change and Conservatism in Central Anatolia', Berlin/Istanbul, 19 September 2005, www.esiweb.org/index.php?lang=en&id=156&document_ID=69.
19. For the close relationship between the Naqshbandi followers of Nursi and the rise of Islamist parties and politicians in Turkey, see M. Hakan Yavuz, *Islamic Political Identity in Turkey* (New York: Oxford University Press, 2003).
20. Hourani, 'Sufism and Modern Islam'.
21. M.E. Yapp, *Strategies of British India: Britain, Iran, and Afghanistan, 1798–1850* (Oxford: Oxford University Press, 1980), pp. 14–15 ff.
22. Elisabeth Monroe, *Britain's Moment in the Middle East 1914–1956* (London: Chatto & Windus, 1963), pp. 38–43.
23. Yapp, *Strategies*, pp. 463–580.
24. Yapp argues that the Anglo-Russian Convention was the logical outcome of strategies of British Indian defence from 1841. Ibid., p. 586.
25. Denis Wright, *The English Amongst the Persians* (London: Heinemann, 1977), pp. 10–11, 62–74.
26. Francis Robinson, 'Strategies of Authority in Muslim South Asia in the Nineteenth and Twentieth Centuries', *Modern Asian Studies*, 47, 1, January 2013, pp. 1–21.
27. Seema Alavi, '"Fugitive Mullahs and Outlawed Fanatics": Indian Muslims in 19th Century Trans-Asiatic Imperial Rivalries', *Modern Asian Studies*, 45, 6, November 2011, pp. 1337–82.
28. Francis Robinson, 'Islam and the Impact of Print in South Asia', in Francis Robinson, *Islam and Muslim History in South Asia* (New Delhi: Oxford University Press, 2000), pp. 78–80.
29. B.C. Busch, *Britain, India, and the Arabs, 1914–1921* (Berkeley: University of California Press, 1971).
30. Ibid., pp. 167, 171, 324, 326, 330, 476.
31. Ibid., pp. 164–214, 476.
32. S.D. Waley, *Edwin Montagu: A Memoir and an Account of his Visits to India* (London: Asia House, 1964), pp. 271–7.

33. See S.S. Pirzada, ed., *Foundations of Pakistan: All-India Muslim League Documents, 1906–1947, vol. II: 1924–1947* (Karachi: National Publishing House, 1970).
34. Simone Panter-Brick, *Gandhi and the Middle East: Jews, Arabs and Imperial Interests* (London: I.B. Tauris, 2008), p. 63.
35. Ibid., p. 25.
36. Ibid., p. 164.
37. For the Muslim Congress movement and the considerable involvement of Indians, see Martin Kramer, *Islam Assembled: The Advent of the Muslim Congresses* (New York: Columbia University Press, 1986). As a tribute to the contribution which Muhammad 'Ali had made to pan-Islamic activity, after his death – while attending the Round Table Conference in London in 1931 – he was buried in Jerusalem in the compound of the Dome of the Rock. The inscription labels him 'Muhammad 'Ali Hindustani'.
38. This figure is based on 2009 Reserve Bank of India calculations. http.//economictimes.indiantimes.com/news/news-by-industry/services/travel/visa-power/Gulf-NRIs-send-more-money-home/articleshow/5710064.cms.
39. A.K. Pasha, 'India's Policy towards the Arab World in the 21st Century', in V.D. Chopra, ed., *India's Foreign Policy in the 21st Century* (Delhi: Kalpaz Publications, 2006), pp. 215–16; the importance of the Gulf to Indian security is reinforced by a recent Indian naval strategy document, *Freedom to Use the Seas: India's Maritime Military Strategy* (New Delhi: Ministry of Defence, 2007).
40. Rajendra M. Abhyankar, 'India's West Asia Policy: Search for a Middle Ground', in Atish Sinha and Madhup Mota, eds, *Indian Foreign Policy: Challenges and Opportunities* (Delhi: Academic Foundation, 2007), pp. 321–50.
41. Statement of Manmohan Singh, 9 January 2009, http://www.nhatky.in/manmohan-condemns-Israeli-strikes-on-gaz-12317132.
42. Emanuel Sivan, *Radical Islam: Medieval Theology and Modern Politics* (New Haven: Yale University Press, 1985), p. 23.
43. 'Ali Shari'ati, *Ma wa Iqbal* (Tehran, 1979); 'The Ideal Man – The Viceregent of God', in Hamid Algar, trans., *On the Sociology of Islam: Lectures by Ali Shari'ati* (Berkeley: Misan Press, 1979), pp. 121–5, makes clear the extent to which Shari'ati had taken on board and developed Iqbal's vision of the Khilafat of Man.

10

The Memory of Power, Muslim 'Political Importance' and the Muslim League

THE MUSLIM MEMORIAL which was presented by a deputation of Muslims to the Viceroy Lord Minto in Simla on 1 October 1906 is – because it summed up so much and portended so much – one of the more important documents in the history of British India. The ideas in the memorial were not very original; elements of them had been presented before in various forms from the MA-O College Fund Committee circular of 1872 to the abortive Muslim Memorial of 1896.[1] But the memorial did set out more fully than ever before the view that Muslim descendants of the former Mughal service elite had of their political position, the pressures to which they were exposed (in particular their difficulties in keeping control of their young men), and the price of their continued support. They wanted no further decline in their position in government service; they wanted more Muslim high court judges; if Indians were to join the Viceroy's Executive Council one of them was to be a Muslim; they stressed their desire to found a Muslim University; and most important they wanted Muslims to be elected to municipal and district boards, to university senates, and to legislative councils by separate electorates, the numbers of Muslim representatives being calculated not just according to their proportions in the population but also according to the contributions they made to the defence of the empire and to their 'political importance'. Most distinctively, in a phrase which never fails to strike me, they reminded the Viceroy that they had once been the governing class; they asked for due consideration to be given 'to the position they had occupied in India a little more than a hundred years ago, and of which the traditions have naturally not faded from their minds.'[2] In this formulation they summed up the origins of their 'political importance' and pressed home their special claims for government consideration.

Minto, as we all know, responded directly to the central point. 'The pith of your address', he replied, 'is a claim that in any system of representation . . . the Mohammedan community should be represented as a community . . . and you justly claim that your position should be estimated not merely on your numerical strength but in respect to the political importance of your community, and the service it has rendered the empire. I am entirely in accord with you . . .'[3] Thus a phrase came to be embedded in the discourse around Muslims and the devolution of power in British India which was to have a continuing impact from the Morley-Minto Reforms through to the 1930s.

The Muslim Memorial was the work of descendants of the old Mughal service elite who had been gathered into the Aligarh movement. Imad al-Mulk, Sayyid Husayn Bilgrami, who was primarily involved in drafting the document, was from the Sayyids of Bilgram, a family with a great record of learning and service under the British and the Nizams of Hyderabad going back to the eighteenth-century scholar and star of the court of Nizam al-Mulk at Aurangabad, Ghulam 'Ali Azad Bilgrami. He was assisted by Muhsin al-Mulk, Nawab Mahdi 'Ali Hasan, distinguished Hyderabadi civil servant, secretary to the Aligarh Trustees, and orchestrator of the Simla deputation. Mahdi 'Ali Hasan was descended from the Barha Sayyids (Etawah branch), who in the second decade of the eighteenth century did so much to harm central Mughal authority. That they put forward a view which represented their

Aligarh and UP perspective was underlined by their refusal to accept the demands made by the leading Bengalis, Nawab Salim Allah and Nawab 'Ali Choudhury, at the Lucknow conference on the Memorial on 15–16 September 1906 that the Memorial should seek assurance that the partition of Bengal would be maintained.[4] Perhaps the reminder that the memorialists represented the former governing class and were 'politically important' was a clever political spin designed to create the most favourable context for Muslim claims to separate electorates plus extra seats in those Muslim-minority provinces in which they were deemed politically important. But a much stronger case can be made that this claim was one in which the descendants of the former Mughal service classes deeply believed. It is the purpose of this essay to explore, first, how the mindset of Muslim 'political importance' had been developed and cultivated and second, to consider its impact on politics down to the 1930s.

The Memory of Power, Its Cultivation and the Values that Went with It

For the descendants of the Mughal service classes the key element in establishing their 'political importance' was the memory of their former power.[5] The elaboration of the memory of power was primarily the work of Sayyid Ahmad Khan and the Aligarh movement. It was to be expected that this remarkable man, whose father was a favourite at the court of Akbar II, whose maternal grandfather was one of the last prime ministers of the Mughal regime, and who had vivid memories of his own attendance at court, should be sensitive to the greatness of former Muslim power in India. His first attempt to recover that greatness in his immediate world of Delhi was, of course, his *Athar al-Sanadid*. In the first edition of 1847, containing four chapters, he described the structures and recorded the inscriptions of 180 buildings outside Delhi, 32 buildings in the Red Fort, 70 in the walled city of Shahjahanabad, and the lives of 120 famous men of Delhi who preceded his time.

'As we read through the first three chapters', Hali tells us in his *Hayat-i-Javed*, 'we catch a glimpse of the dignity and splendour of former times and for a moment we forget our own miserable plight. The fourth chapter brings us face to face with the last days of Delhi's greatness and as we turn the pages we are astonished to find that only sixty years ago there were so many pious men, erudite scholars and skilful artisans in our midst.'[6] Thus, Sayyid Husayn Bilgrami's reference to the strong position of Muslims not much more than one hundred years ago echoes the spirit of Sayyid Ahmad's *Athar al-Sanadid* and almost the very words of Hali's biography of the Sayyid published just five years before. Sayyid Ahmad reinforced the memory of past greatness with his three published editions of major manuscripts relating to Muslim rule in India: Barani's *Tarikh-i Firoz Shahi* (1862), Abul Fadl's *Ain-i Akbari* (n.d.), and Jahangir's *Tuzuk-i Jahangiri* (1864).

Nothing brought home the changed circumstances of Muslims more vividly than the Mutiny Uprising of 1857 and its brutal suppression. The British were savage. Roughly 30,000 people were killed in the sack of Delhi, many just slaughtered out of hand. Muslims were driven out of the city for nearly two years; its great buildings were put to humiliating purposes; a vast tract of land in front of the Red Fort was cleared, demolishing famous bazaars, distinguished madrasas, and the houses of many nobles. The fate of Lucknow was similar. The population of this city of 400,000 was halved; two-fifths of it in a swathe four miles long and half a mile wide by the River Gumti was destroyed; and its religious buildings great and small filled with demeaning activities. The desolation created is starkly revealed in the panoramic photographs of Felice Beato of 1858.[7]

Sayyid Ahmad, who experienced the Mutiny in Bijnor and Delhi, was deeply shocked by the experience. 'I could not even bear to contemplate the miserable state of my people', Sayyid Ahmad told the Muslim Educational Conference in 1889 as it celebrated the foundation of Aligarh. 'For some time, I wrestled with my grief and, believe me, it made an old man of me. My hair turned white. When I went to Muradabad, the ruin which had befallen the nobles of that town made my sorrow all the greater.'[8] As we know, it was this experience which persuaded Sayyid Ahmad to devote all his energies to the good of the descendants of the Mughal service class. Many of those who were to help him in his project to help Muslims engage with modernity under British rule, while not forgetting their glorious past, had also had taxing and at times horrific Mutiny experiences, among them: Altaf Husayn Hali, Munshi Zaka Allah, Muhsin al-Mulk, Mawlwi Nadhir Ahmad and Mawlwi Sami Allah Khan.[9] The record of these events, experienced by some of the brightest lights of post-Mughal culture in northern India, entered literature: in Ghalib's *Dustanbuy*, his record of events in Mutiny Delhi, in his elegies on the fate of the city in the genre of *Shahr-e Ashob*, in his letters which record week by week the humiliation of the former Mughal capital, and in Hali's marsiya on the 'Devastation of Delhi' – 'Hearken to me', he told a musha'ira at Lahore in 1874, 'do not go into the ruins of Delhi. At every step priceless pearls lie buried beneath the dust ... times have changed as they can never change again.'[10]

It was Hali who more than anyone else established the dominant narrative of past grandeur and present decline in the Urdu literary canon. In his *Musaddas*, 'The Flow and Ebb of Islam', commissioned by Sayyid Ahmad, and first published in 1879, he writes in elegiac mode of the glorious advance in civilisation which the Prophet's message brought to a hitherto dark world and how in the present that mission had fallen into such a state of decay that Muslims were as men asleep in a boat in a whirlpool. The overall tone is well conveyed in the following lines which appear not in his *Musaddas* but in his *Shikwa-i Hind* of 1888:

> When autumn has set in over the garden,
> Why speak of the springtime in flower?
> When shadows of adversity hang over the present,
> Why harp on the pomp and glory of the past?
> Yea, these are things to forget;

> But how can you with the dawn
> Forget the scene of the night before?
> The assembly has just dispersed;
> The smoke is still rising from the burnt candle;
> The footprints on the sands still say
> A graceful caravan has passed this way.[11]

The extraordinary reception of the *Musaddas,* and subsequently his *Shikwa,* indicated that Hali had articulated a widespread feeling. Sayyid Ahmad himself was delighted: 'I was the cause of this book,' he wrote to Hali in June 1879, 'and I consider that my finest deed. When God asks me what I have done, I will say: nothing, but I had Hali write the *Musaddas.*'[12] By its second edition in 1886 the *Musaddas* had made its way throughout India, there were pirated editions in northern India, the North Western Provinces' government had made it a school text on account of its popularity, stanzas were recited at celebrations of the Prophet's birthday, the 'ulama' were quoting it, plays were being performed based on it, and those hearing it could be relied upon to burst into tears.[13]

Such was the impact of the *Musaddas* that it spawned many imitators, 'a mass *Musaddas* mania' Shackle and Majeed term it. 'The *Musaddas* created an entire new poetic universe of its own', they continue, 'within which writers from often quite surprisingly diverse sections of Indian society felt it natural to explore issues which Hali had opened up in the verse format he had created.'[14] Some were opposed to his 'nature-ism' and to his new style with its disregard for long-respected conventions of rhyme. Others disapproved of his outspoken loyalty to the British Empire. But the majority took up the main theme of dwelling on past glory and present weakness. Of these the *Qaumi Musaddas* recited to the students of Aligarh in 1890 by the young Shibli Nu'mani (1857–1914) was typical and contained this verse in characteristic spirit:

> Those fine views of Marv, Shiraz and Isfahan,
> Those palaces, walls and gates of the Alhambra

Every stone of Egypt, Granada and Baghdad,
And the decayed ruins of our lamented Delhi –
All still have jewels glittering in their dust,
All still remember their stories by heart.[15]

Alongside the 'mass *Musaddas* mania', writers were using other literary forms to focus attention on the grandeur of the Muslim past. Thus, Muhammad Husayn Azad (1830–1910) had already engaged with the achievements of Urdu poets of the past and the greatness of Delhi as a literary centre in his *Ab-e-Hayat*;[16] thus, the great satirist, Akbar Ilahabadi (1846–1921), revered the past for its own sake, finding the present degraded and degrading by comparison;[17] thus, Shibli Nu'mani, the founder of modern history in Urdu, set out both to defend Islamic history against attacks on it from the West and to place before his contemporaries that history, and the lives of leading figures in it, such as 'Umar and al-Ghazali, in the best possible light;[18] and thus, too, 'Abd al-Halim Sharar (1860–1926), as a writer of historical romances clearly inspired by Walter Scott, set out to tell the history of the Islamic world from the time of the Prophet to the eighteenth century in a large number of historical novels.[19] Sharar was often the first point of contact for his readers with, say, the Muslim conquest of Spain or the Crusades, and was particularly popular, and remained so with children and others, at least until the mid-twentieth century.[20] Sharar's celebration of the past was not restricted to novels; he wrote historical biographies, Islamic history, and most importantly did in his own distinctive way for Lucknow what Sayyid Ahmad had done for Delhi in his *Athar al-Sanadid*, when he began to publish in *Dil Gudaz* his articles on the past of Lucknow, which were later collected under the title *Hindustan Men Mashriqi Tamuddin ka Akhri Namuna* (The Last Example of Oriental Culture in India).[21]

It is in the development between 1908 and 1913 of the young Iqbal, the greatest poet of the generation after Hali, that we can see the end of just harping on the glories of the past and the problems of the present and the beginnings of charting out a way forward. Passing Sicily on the way back from England to India in August 1908 he responded in what was now traditional mode:

> Weep to thy heart's content, O blood-weeping eye,
> Yonder is the grave of Muslim culture . . .
> I am the dust raised by that caravan which once broke its journey here.
> Paint for me that picture of the old,
> Rouse me by telling the tale of bygone days;
> I shall carry thy gift to India,
> And make others weep as I weep now.[22]

But in the *Shikwa* (The Complaint), which was first recited at a meeting of the Anjuman-i-Himayat-i-Islam in Lahore in 1909, and in his *Jawab-i Shikwa* (Answer to the Complaint), which was recited at a musha'ira in Lahore in 1913 to raise funds to help the Turks fight the Bulgarians, we find a combination of a celebration of the achievements of Muslims in history, a lament at their decline in power, and a promise of a new way forward, if Muslims remain faithful to Muhammad. He was, of course, to spend the rest of his life elaborating in a number of contexts his Islamic theory of progress.

****

Alongside this process of being made especially conscious of their glorious past, the descendants of the former Mughal service class had to confront continuing evidence of Muslim decline both inside and outside India. Inside India, and particularly in northern India, there was a host of developments which disadvantaged or threatened Muslims: the rise of a new and largely Hindu commercial class; the requirement of examination success to enter public service; the introduction of elections to municipal and district boards; the manifestation of increasing Hindu assertiveness across many social and political arenas; the emergence of the Indian National Congress pressing for the devolution of power; and then in 1906 the announcement by Secretary of State, Morley, that there would be a further phase of Council Reform which raised the spectre of majority rule. From the world outside India there was a continuing stream of news vigorously reported in the lively Urdu press: of the steady overwhelming of the Muslim world by European powers in the late nineteenth century; of the advance of the Russians in Central Asia; of the advance of the British in Egypt and the Sudan; and in the years up to 1914, of the assertion of the Bulgarians in the Balkans, of the Greeks in Macedonia, and the Italians in Tripolitana; and in the years after 1914, of the loss of the Arab territories of the Ottoman Empire, and finally the threatened partition of that Empire's Anatolian heartland.

Together with the carefully cultivated memory of past glory in the context of louring present threat, there were also the carefully cultivated aristocratic values of sharif culture of the descendants of the Mughal service classes which David Lelyveld has so ably analysed.[23] Several elements contributed to them. There was the 'Mongol–Mughal' tradition that the sharif class formed part of a superior race whose noble foreign origins entitled them to a degree of deference beyond that given to indigenous Muslim groups.[24] To such people the idea of one-man one-vote was anathema. There were the norms of Mughal political culture which stressed the importance of socially established individuals as interpreters between rulers and ruled. These were not tasks for Johnny-come-latelies; they were for the sharif class which as a 'political' class in the late-nineteenth century embraced both aristocratic Hindus as well as Muslim members of the 'Urdu-speaking elite'.[25] It was this class which in 1888 Sayyid Ahmad drew together in the short-lived United Patriotic Association designed to resist Congress clamour for the extension of representative government.

These aristocratic understandings were well expressed by Sayyid Ahmad's famous Lucknow speech of 28 December 1887:

> It is very necessary that for the Viceroy's Council the members should be of high social position. I ask you – Would our aristocracy like that a man of low caste or insignificant origin, though he be a B.A.

or M.A., and have the requisite ability, should be in a position of authority above them and have power in making the laws that affect their lives and property? Never! . . . Think for a moment who you are. What is this nation of ours? We are those who ruled India for six or seven hundred years [Cheers]. From our hands the country was taken by Government into its own . . . Is Government so foolish as to suppose that in seventy years we have forgotten all our grandeur and our empire?

Then Sayyid Ahmad moved on to develop an idea which could only appeal to the Muslim members of the descendants of the Mughal service elite: 'Our nation is of the blood of those who made not only Arabia, but Asia and Europe, to tremble. It is our nation which conquered with its sword the whole of India.'[26]

A further element in their self-image was not just a 'Mongol–Mughal' right to rule but also a Muslim one. There was a sense of the moral superiority of those who had the privilege of carrying Muhammad's message through history.[27] 'I was wholly given to religious fanaticism', Hali wrote of himself in the 1860s, 'I considered the Muslims the very cream of creation . . .'[28]

Putting the Memory of Past Glory to Work in Politics

It was in the context of a heightened consciousness of past glory, of a belief in the Muslim right to rule, and of a real sense of current threat that the Muslim memorialists reminded the Viceroy that they had been the former rulers of India and that they were, therefore, politically important. Reminding audiences of past Muslim conquest and rule was a feature of early Muslim League meetings. The message came in different ways. At Dacca in December 1906 Wiqar al-Mulk reminded his listeners, presciently, of the importance of being extremely wary of 'the time when we become subjects of our neighbours, and answer to them for the sins, real or imaginary, of Awrangzib who lived and died two centuries ago, and other Musalman conquerors and rulers who went before him.'[29] At Amritsar in December 1908 Sayyid 'Ali Imam spoke of how 'wave upon wave of Muslim conquest has rolled over the entire length and breadth of India. In serried ranks, Musalman Royal Houses rose and fell, but Muslim domination of the country remained a more or less unbroken chain . . .' until the British conquest of recent time.[30] He went on to say 'the Mohammedans may be weak in anything you please, but they are not weak in cherishing the traditions of their glorious past.'[31] The very first thing that Hakim Ajmal Khan did in welcoming delegates to the League's third annual session at Delhi in January 1910 was to remind the assembly of Delhi's glorious past and enjoy the conceit that the organisation which had been founded at Jahangirabad (Dacca) should 'complete its infancy' at Shahjahanabad (Delhi).[32] At the fifth session in Calcutta in March 1912, Nawab Salim Allah of Dacca, while bemoaning the impact of the repartition of Bengal, hoped that the transfer of the capital to Delhi would lead to a revival of the ancient glories of Islam and evoked the past 'when the mighty flag of the Musalman Emperors floated triumphantly over the walls of Delhi.'[33] At the eighth session in Bombay, December/January 1915/16, Mazhar al-Haqq asked delegates to consider how the Muslims of India had grown from the 'naval expedition sent by the third khalifa in the year 636 AC', how their number had been swollen both by fresh blood from 'Arabia, Persia and other Muslim lands' and by the conversions of Indians.[34] After the Lucknow Pact, leading speakers at League sessions, if they mentioned the Indian Muslim past at all did so in a subdued fashion, except for Sir 'Abd al-Rahim in his presidential speech at Aligarh in 1925, when he used the glorious Muslim past of Bengal and its present decline as a metaphor for the position of Indian Muslims as a whole.[35]

The glorious Indo-Muslim past, for reasons largely obvious, does not seem to have been referred to again until after the Lahore Resolution. In Madras in April 1941, delegates were reminded of the remarkable career of Tipu Sultan and of the how Mawlana 'Abd al-'Ali Bahr al-'Ulum of Farangi Mahall had come from Lucknow in the eighteenth century to bring about an intellectual awakening in the south.³⁶ At Delhi in April 1943 delegates were welcomed with reminders of the Slave Kings, the Suris and how Delhi had been the cradle and grave of many empires.³⁷ At Karachi in December 1943, G.M. Syed waxed eloquent on the history of Sind, Islam, and the artificial unity of India.³⁸ But there were now different reasons for recalling the glorious Muslim past. Whereas, in the early years of the League's existence, it was to bolster the claims of the descendants of the Mughal service elite for serious attention, now it was to furnish the history of a new nation.

****

As with the focus on the glorious Muslim past, so with the use of the concept of Muslim 'political importance': it was used primarily in the first decade of the League's existence, and in particular in arguing the League case as the Morley-Minto legislation went through Parliament. It was used in the League's response to the Government of India's reform plans announced on 24 August 1907. To the government's clear failure to meet the demands of the Muslim Memorial in either the legislative council or the provincial councils, the League made it clear that it wanted a reserved number of seats that took into account both their numerical proportion of the population and their 'political importance', and that in these seats only Muslims were to vote for Muslims.³⁹ It was used in their response to Secretary of State, Morley's, Electoral College plan of 27 November 1908, which acknowledged neither of the key principles of separate electorates and 'political importance'. Sayyid 'Ali Imam, in addressing the Muslim League as President in December 1908, emphasised that Morley's scheme did not meet Minto's promise of 1906: 'the political importance of the community and other reasons demand that the number declared for seats on the councils be more than the ratio of the total number of Mohammedans to the total population of the provinces . . .'⁴⁰

The same provision was applied to the Legislative Council. It was used in the massive protests by Muslims in April and May 1909, especially in the United Province, when the Indian Councils Bill then in Parliament failed to meet Minto's promise. 'No system of Muhammedan representation in the Provincial and Imperial Councils', declared one typical resolution, in this case of a mass meeting in Lucknow, 'will be effective in itself or acceptable to them that does not provide for an adequate number of seats in excess of their numerical strength, and for all seats to be filled by election by exclusive Muhammedan electorates.'[41] The Government gave way and the principle of Muslim 'political importance' in the form of seats above their numerical proportion of the population became enshrined in India's developing democratic constitution.

After the climacteric of 1909, far less was heard of Muslim 'political importance'. But it was well understood that recognising it was the price which the Indian nationalist movement would have to pay to gain Muslim cooperation over the next stage in the devolution of power. Thus it became embedded for those provinces where Muslims were in a minority, in the Lucknow Pact, which preceded the Montagu-Chelmsford reforms. The one significant point at which the argument was brought out was when the Joint Report on Indian Constitutional Reform of 1918 suggested that the representation given to Muslims by the Lucknow Pact was too generous. This brought Dr Ansari to a vigorous defence of the principle of Muslim 'political importance' at the Delhi session of the Muslim League in December 1918.[42]

After this the argument of Muslim 'political importance' was barely heard. It was not suited to the Khilafat-Congress alliance of the 1919–23 period. It was certainly not suited to the politics of the provinces of the 1920s and early 1930s, which were dominated by class groupings of landlords. It was a difficult argument to press forward in the bitter discussions of the Round Table conferences because it could only work against the interests of Muslims in the Punjab and Bengal who saw themselves at last having the possibility of making their majorities in the population count in terms of Council seats. It was, however, used by Muhammad Shafi in arguing for one-third Muslim representation in the Central Legislative Assembly, as opposed to their 25 per cent of the population. His argument however was not based on the imagined rights of a former ruling class but on the fact that the major burden of the defence of the country fell on Muslim shoulders.[43]

****

It remains for us to consider briefly why the early Muslim League was able to make its claim of Muslim 'political importance' to the British with success. This is well-trodden ground. Briefly, an explanation of this issue, which is undeniably complex, should contain the following elements. It should rest primarily on the assumptions the British made about Indian society: 'First the assumption that Indian society was a collection of classes and interests – of traders, landlords, government servants, castes and communities. Of all these groups, the Muslims formed the largest and by far the most important. About them . . . the British made a further series of assumptions: that they were a separate and distinct community, a potential danger to the Raj, and an important conservative force. All these notions contributed to the belief that they deserved special treatment.'[44]

These assumptions about Indian society in general and Muslims in particular profoundly influenced the way in which the British ruled in the second half of the nineteenth century. Thus, they drew together powerful groups such as the Oudh taluqdars or the Urdu-speaking elite to consult with them and rule through them. Thus, too, they constructed the Council Reforms of 1892 on these principles. Assumptions of this nature influenced those in India and in Britain who confronted the Muslim claim for weightage on account of their 'political importance' in the seats reserved for them in their separate electorates.

In India we can see these views at work amongst those advising the Viceroy and the Government of India, in 1906: Archbold, Lancelot Hare, Harcourt Butler and Dunlop Smith.[45] We can see them at work again in the first half of 1909 when Minto who, despite his Simla promise, had set his face against Muslim 'political importance' being acknowledged in the number of seats reserved for them, was forced to capitulate to the extraordinary Muslim protest of that spring, acknowledging the seriousness of Muslim dissatisfaction, and perhaps remembering his dictum delivered to Morley in the previous year 'that though the Mahomedan is silent he is very strong'.[46]

In Britain Morley as Secretary of State declared himself unwilling to challenge the principle 'that Indian society lives, thinks and acts according to castes, races and religions',[47] and appeared to endorse in his Despatch of 17 May 1907 the view that the Muslim community was entitled to special representation on Councils ' commensurate with its numbers and historical importance'.[48] But when, strongly opposed to making religion the basis of Indian constituencies, he tried to realise this promise through his Electoral College scheme, he found himself opposed first by a strong group of Old-India hands in his Council (Walter Lawrence, James LaTouche, William Lee Warner, Sayyid Husayn Bilgrami and Theodore Morison), then by British public opinion which tended to be pro-Muslim, and then by the conservative majority in the House of Lords led by Ampthill, Lansdowne and Curzon. The Liberal government, voted into power in 1906, faced a conservative majority in the House of Lords, which had made a point of destroying or emasculating its legislation. Morley knew that if his Indian Councils Bill was to succeed, he had to damp down Muslim opposition so that the conservatives in the Lords could not make use of it. For this reason, when in autumn 1909 the Bill was threatened with being killed in the Lords because it did not meet the pledges made to Muslims regarding their 'political importance', he raised the number of Muslim reserved seats on the Imperial Legislative Council from six to eight. Muslims thus had 26.6 per cent of the reserved seats on the Council as compared with their 22.9 per cent of the population.[49] After the first election under the new act, when Muslim successes in the general electorates were added to their reserved seats, they had 40 per cent of the representation on the Council. We are left with the delicious thought that the House of Lords, in which the principle that an aristocracy of birth had the right to play a part in democratic government was enshrined in the British constitution, played a key role in ensuring that the idea of Muslim 'political importance', which enshrined the view of the descendants of the Mughal service classes of their hereditary right rule, was embedded in India's emerging democratic system.

Subsequently, British views on whether Muslim 'political importance' was to be taken into account or not were not to count for very much. In the case of the Montagu–Chelmsford reforms, the Lucknow Pact, which embraced ideas of weightage for Muslims in minority provinces, relieved them from having to take a view, apart from the throwaway line in the Joint Report on Indian Constitutional Reforms of 1918, which sparked Dr Ansari's uncharacteristic defence of Muslim 'political importance', a defence probably less out of principle than out of the need to defend the Lucknow Pact. In the case of the Communal Award, arguably there was some continued reflection of 'political importance' in the weightage in seats reserved for Muslims in the minority provinces, particularly in the UP.[50] This said, this imposed Award was calibrated less to embrace political ideologies than to achieve the best chance of acceptance on the part of all concerned.

****

The assertion of the principle of Muslim 'political importance' showed the enduring quality of the memory of power and a sense Muslims had of themselves as the former ruling class of the descendants of the Mughal service elite. That it was accepted owed something to British views of Indian society, something to their views of Muslims, and, somewhat curiously, something to the continuing existence of the hereditary principle in British politics. The exigencies of nationalist politics under imperial rule kept alive the principle of weightage for Muslim minorities in terms of extra reserved seats if not much in terms of rhetoric, into the fourth decade of the twentieth century. By this time, however, it was increasingly unsustainable as the era of mass politics dawned and as Muslims from majority provinces wanted their majorities to count. Intriguingly, this form of the hereditary principle died with independence in South Asia, while in Britain it has been sustained to the present, even if in much emasculated form. However, as the currency of a hereditary right to rule declined, another idea, implicit for some at least in Muslim 'political importance', gained new force. It was the notion of a Muslim community destined to carry forward the civilising mission of God's revelation through Muhammad. Although this mission had faltered, as Hali's *Musaddas* had stated, because Muslims had not been good enough Muslims, it was to find new direction, as Iqbal charted out his vision of progress towards a Qur'anic state, and as the Muslim League in the federal end game of empire fought for some form of Muslim state or states. Thus, the descendants of the Mughal service elite, who turned the memory of the traces of Hali's graceful caravan on the sands of India into a demand for special concessions in India's developing electoral system, came to be able once more to command a real caravan of power in South Asia.

Notes

1. See Francis Robinson, *Separatism Among Indian Muslims: The Politics of the United Provinces' Muslims 1860–1923* (Cambridge: Cambridge University Press, 1974), pp. 108, 121–3.
2. The Muslim address 'To His Excellency the Right Honourable the Earl of Minto . . .' Harcourt Butler Papers (65), India Office Library.
3. Lord Minto's Reply to the Address from the Mohammedan Deputation, 1 October 1906, Sharif al-Mujahid (ed.), *Muslim League Documents 1900–1947: vol. 1, 1900–1908* (Karachi: Quaid-i-Azam Academy, 1990), p. 105.

4. Robinson, *Separatism*, p. 144.
5. It should be noted that the memory of lost power was most acute amongst the intellectuals of the two greatest gunpowder empires of the Muslim world, the Ottoman and the Mughal. Amongst the Ottomans, in particular of Istanbul, it was summed up in the concept of *huzun*, the melancholy contemplation of past greatness, but also a deeply nuanced concept which has been wonderfully evoked by Orhan Pamuk in *Istanbul: Memories of a City* (London: Faber & Faber 2005), pp. 81–96, 22–8.
6. Altaf Husain Hali, *Hayat-i-Javed*, trans. K.H. Qadiri & David J. Matthews (Delhi: Idarah-i Adabiyat-i Delli, 1979), pp. 35–6.
7. Rosie Llewellyn-Jones, *Lucknow: City of Illusion* (London: Prestel, 2006), pp. 90–9.
8. Hali, *Hayat*, p. 56.
9. Francis Robinson, 'The Muslims of Upper India and the Shock of the Mutiny', in Francis Robinson, *Islam and Muslim History in South Asia* (New Delhi: Oxford University Press, 2000), pp. 138–55.
10. Narayani Gupta, *Delhi Between Two Empires 1803–1931: Society, Government and Urban Growth* (Delhi: Oxford University Press, 1981), pp. xviii–xix.
11. Syed Abdul Latif, *The Influence of English Literature on Urdu Literature*, cited in Gail Minault, 'Urdu Political Poetry during the Khilafat Movement', *Modern Asian Studies*, 8, 4 (1974), p. 462. This attribution in Minault's article is not quite correct; the excerpt is from Hali's *Shikwa*. I am grateful to Eve Tignol for pointing this out.
12. Christopher Shackle and Javed Majeed, trans. and intro., *Hali's Musaddas: The Flow and Ebb of Islam* (Delhi: Oxford University Press, 1997), p. 36.
13. So wrote Hali in introducing his second edition of 1886. He actually refers to 'seven or eight editions in various districts of northern India', which could be interpreted either as pirated editions as above or perhaps as reprints. Shackle and Majeed, *Musaddas*, p. 99.
14. Ibid., p. 37.
15. Ibid., p. 40n.43.
16. Muhammad Sadiq, *A History of Urdu Literature*, 2nd ed. (Delhi: Oxford University Press, 1984), pp. 382–4.
17. Ibid., p. 287.
18. Ibid., pp. 361–6.

19. R. Russell, 'The Development of the Modern Novel in Urdu', in T.W. Clark, ed. and intro., *The Novel in India: Its Birth and Development* (London: George, Allen & Unwin, 1970), pp. 122–32.
20. This was the judgement of Faiz Ahmad Faiz, ibid., p. 132.
21. Abdul Halim Sharar, *Lucknow: The Last Phase of an Oriental Culture*, ed. and trans. E.S. Harcourt and Fakhir Hussain (London: Elek Books, 1975).
22. S.M. Ikram, *Modern Muslim India and the Birth of Pakistan 1858–1951* 2nd ed. (Lahore: Sh. Muhammad Ashraf, 1965), p. 175.
23. David Lelyveld, *Aligarh's First Generation: Muslim Solidarity in British India* (Princeton: Princeton University Press, 1978).
24. These and other aspects of sharif values are explored in Farzana Shaikh, *Community and Consensus in Islam: Muslim Representation in Colonial India, 1860–1947* (Cambridge: Cambridge University Press, 1989), pp. 76–118.
25. For the concept of 'Urdu-speaking elite', see Robinson, *Separatism*, pp. 31–2 ff.
26. Sayyid Ahmad's speech, Lucknow, 28 December 1887, Al Mujahid, *Documents*, 1, pp. 190–201.
27. Shaikh, *Community and Consensus*, pp. 117–18.
28. Sadiq, *Urdu Literature*, p. 346.
29. Nawab al-Mulk, speech as chair of the inaugural session of the All-India Muslim League, 30 December 1906, Syed Sharifuddin Pirzada, ed., *Foundations of Pakistan: All-India Muslim League Documents 1906–1947* (Karachi: National Publishing House, 1970), vol. 1, p. 4.
30. Presidential address of Saiyid 'Ali Imam at the second session of the All-India Muslim League, Amritsar, 30 December 1908, Pirzada, *Foundations*, 1, p. 43.
31. Ibid., p. 52.
32. Speech of Hakim Ajmal Khan as president of the reception committee of the third session of the All-India Muslim League, Delhi, 29 January 1910, ibid., pp. 87–8.
33. Presidential address of Nawab Salim Allah of Dacca to the fifth session of the All-India Muslim League, 3 March 1912, ibid., p. 234.
34. Presidential address of Mazhar al-Haqq to the eighth session of the All-India Muslim League, Bombay, 30 December 1915, ibid., p. 332.
35. Presidential address of Sir 'Abd al-Rahim to the seventeenth session of the All-India League, Aligarh, 30 December 1925, Pirzada, *Foundations*, vol. 2, p. 47.

36. Address of 'Abd al-Hamid Khan, chairman of the reception committee, twenty-eighth session of the All-India Muslim League, Madras, 12 April 1941, ibid., p. 351.
37. Address of Hussayn Malik, chairman of the reception committee, thirtieth session of the All-India Muslim League, Delhi, 24 April 1943, ibid., p. 400.
38. Address of G.M. Syed, chairman of the reception committee, thirty-first session of the All-India Muslim League, Karachi, 24 December 1943, ibid., pp. 442–6.
39. Robinson, *Separatism*, pp. 152–3.
40. Presidential address of Saiyid 'Ali Imam at the second session of the All-India Muslim League, Amritsar, 30 December 1908, Pirzada, *Foundations*, vol. 1, p. 68.
41. Robinson, *Separatism*, p. 159.
42. Address by Dr M.A. Ansari, chairman of the reception committee, eleventh session of the All-India Muslim League, Delhi, 30 December 1918, Pirzada, *Foundations*, vol. 1, pp. 473–4.
43. Khalid B. Sayeed, *Pakistan: The Formative Phase 1857–1948*, 2nd ed. (London: Oxford University Press, 1968), p. 77.
44. Robinson, *Separatism*, pp. 164–5.
45. Ibid., pp. 165–7.
46. Ibid., pp. 167–8.
47. Note by W. Lee Warner, dated 19 April 1907, Morley Papers (32), quoted in S.A. Wolpert, *Morley and India 1906–1910* (Berkeley: University of California Press, 1967), p. 191.
48. Robinson, *Separatism*, p. 168.
49. Ibid., pp. 168–71.
50. For a table setting out the Award, see Sayeed, *Pakistan*, p. 78.

11

The Modern State

Citizenship, Multiculturalism and Globalisation

I ADDRESS THE THEMES OF citizenship, multiculturalism and globalisation in the context of the rise and, in part, the decline of the modern nation-state.[1] In doing so I shall first, and briefly, explore the existence of cosmopolitan worlds before the emergence of the modern nation-state. This will be a preliminary to understanding how the often sharply defined identity of the nation-state, with its associated ideas of sovereignty and territorial integrity defended by international law, undermined and often destroyed old cosmopolitanisms. The outcomes were oppressed minorities and stateless citizens. I then turn to globalisation in the latter half of the twentieth century and the challenges it brought the modern nation-state. Amongst them was the fashioning of multi-ethnic and multicultural populations with the subsequent undermining of the imagined homogeneities of national identity. Multiculturalism has been one of the policies adopted to address this challenge. I shall consider its success. Of course, there have been instances when multiculturalism, whether the outcome of state policy or as a pragmatic response to historical developments, has broken down. This will lead me to consider issues of human rights, humanitarian interventions and the emergence of mental and legal spaces beyond the nation-state. Indeed, as nation-states come to be constrained by the international community, and as major challenges emerge which affect all of humankind, we come to glimpse a new aspect of human existence, although it is one of which Muslims in a religious, or umma-conscious, sense have long been aware, that is, a citizenship which exists beyond the nation-state.

Cosmopolitanism before the Nation-State

Let us consider the world before it came to be divided into nation-states. It is a world which often accommodated difference. It embraced cosmopolitanism in the sense that it was generally hospitable to people of varied ethnicities and cultures. As a historian of the Muslim world I am very aware of the Islamic world system which preceded the Wallersteinian Western world system. Opened up by the rapid spread of Muslim power from the seventh century, this system was supported by the long-distance trade across land and sea: the silk route from China into West Asia, the caravan routes east-west across the Sahara from Cairo to Timbuktu, and north-south between the Maghreb and Timbuktu; and of course the Indian Ocean trade routes stretching from East Africa and the Hadhramawt through to South and Southeast Asia and China. Arabic was used widely throughout the region, as was Islamic law. It was this which enabled the fourteenth-century Moroccan traveller, Ibn Battuta, to travel for twenty-four years, from Guangdong in China to Timbuktu in Mali, often gaining employment as a qadi. But much more convincing evidence of the cosmopolitan nature of the Islamic world system is the way in which from the classical Islamic era down to the nineteenth century tens of thousands of 'ulama' and Sufis travelled through the world in search of knowledge and the extra authority which knowledge from many different sources might bring. We know of these travels through the plentiful records which 'ulama' and Sufis have left of how formal and spiritual knowledge came to be passed down through time. In addition to the cosmopolitan connectedness of the Muslim world there were also particular sites where powers presided over the formation of notably cosmopolitan worlds of learning and the arts. I think of Muslim Andalusia with its rich integration of Arab and Jewish learning, of Abbasid Baghdad where Byzantine, Persian and Arab strands of inspiration came together, and the sixteenth- and seventeenth-century Mughal court in India where Persians, Turks and Arabs mingled in one great dynastic enterprise with Hindus, Armenians and Western Christians.

The advance of the European empires into the Muslim world from the early-nineteenth century added new cosmopolitan possibilities to those which already existed. The British Empire through its rule of South Asia helped to fashion a new South Asian cosmopolitanism as Indians who had rarely, if ever, interacted before, and who spoke many different languages, came together to create a political movement to seize power from the British. British power in the Indian Ocean region greatly enhanced links, old and new, between Bombay, South and East Africa, the Hadhramawt and Iran, as Nile Green has so wonderfully demonstrated in his *Bombay Islam*.[2] British imperial purposes created new cosmopolitan regions like the islands of the West Indies. At the same time the workings of empire began the fashioning of London into the great cosmopolitan city it is today. The French empire created its own distinctive world, cosmopolitan in terms of its many ethnicities but definitely not cosmopolitan in its insistence that much of this empire should assimilate to French culture. Thus, Paris also set out on its journey to become in its own way a cosmopolitan city. So, too, did Vienna for the Austro-Hungarian Empire and St Petersburg for the Russian Empire.

Side by side with the European empires there also flourished the last great manifestation in political terms of cosmopolitanism in the Muslim world – the Ottoman Empire. Ewliya Chelebi, the seventeenth-century Ottoman scholar, spent forty-one years travelling throughout the Ottoman dominions from Budapest to

Baku, and from Belgrade to Baghdad. Almost everywhere he found society with which he could engage. He demonstrated his own openness and curiosity by learning the languages of each new region he entered.[3] In the nineteenth century, the Ottoman Empire was of course home to several cosmopolitan cities – Cairo, Alexandria, Smyrna, Salonica, but most of all Istanbul.[4] Ariel Salzmann has uncovered a telling example of the cosmopolitanism of the late Ottoman world. It is in a Jewish Society lottery ticket of 1874. The printed text is Ladino and the numerals are Western; these are framed by translations in Ottoman Turkish, French, Armenian and Greek.[5] The world up to the early twentieth century was full of cosmopolitan possibilities.

The Onset of the Modern Nation-State

This world of cosmopolitan possibilities was ripped apart by the rise of the modern nation-state. In 1919, the South Asian poet, Muhammad Iqbal, who was himself to play a role in the creation of Pakistan, railed against the way in which the concept of country was dividing humanity, though in his case there was an important religious dimension to this thinking:

> Now brotherhood has been so cut to shreds
> That in the stead of community
> The country has been given pride of place
> In man's allegiance and constructive work;
> The country is the darling of their hearts,
> And wide humanity is whittled down
> Indo dismembered tribes . . .
> Vanished is humankind; there but abide
> The disunited nations.[6]

The emergence of modern nation-states was a feature of Europe and the Americas in the nineteenth century. Fostering the further development of the nation-state model was a guiding principle of the peace settlement after World War One, whether it meant building such states on the basis of language in Eastern Europe and the Balkans or giving the colonial powers mandates to help give birth to such states in the Middle East. The emergence of these states from the old European empires continued through the age of Afro-Asian independence between the 1940s and 1960s through to the end of the Soviet Asian empire in the 1990s. Today 193 nation-states are recognised by the United Nations.

What was it about the modern nation-state which generally was so inimical to the diversities which might sustain cosmopolitanism? We need first to look at the modern state dimension of the problem, setting the nation element for the moment to one side. Bred in war and economic competition from the nineteenth century onwards, and powered by the industrial revolution, the modern state was the most powerful institution yet evolved for the organisation of humankind. With carefully mapped frontiers, often for the first time, its territory acquired a certain sort of magic; it was not easily surrendered. Territorial integrity acquired a particular force in political and legal thinking. The movement of people across frontiers came to be carefully monitored. The days of the freewheeling nomadic tribesman were numbered. Increasingly the state's capacity to defend its frontiers against unwanted aliens became a measure of its efficiency. At the same time, and again generally in the second half of the nineteenth century, the state came to count all its peoples in censuses. The state also came to develop a direct relationship with each individual citizen; each one came to have his or her social security number and, if they wished to travel, they could only do so with a state-issued passport. Crucial in developing the relationship was a centralised bureaucracy, supported by the telegraph, the printing press and a network of rail and road communications, all backed up by the state's monopoly of force. With these tools the state swept away intervening elements between itself – tribal chiefs, landlords, local notables and religious institutions – and society. The state developed systems of education, health and welfare to strengthen itself, and taxed its citizens heavily for this purpose. Systems of national service were developed which, as in the case of modern Turkey, were hailed as a 'school for the nation'. The supreme measure of the state's power was conscription, its ability to require in time of war its citizens to risk their lives for the state.

In some states one way of making this new and intense relationship between state and citizen tolerable was the development of forms of democracy. But in all states, forms of ideology also played this role, in particular nationalist ideology. Sometimes nationalism preceded the development of the modern state structure, sometimes it followed it. But, almost invariably, it meant the use of history and geography to develop a national story, the recognition of a national language and literature, the recognition of a national territory, and the identification of specific symbols of the state, its majesty and purpose.

I have come to learn that citizenship is a slippery concept, if ever there was one. I hope, nonetheless, that you will see that the addition of the idea of national identity to the modern state meant a new idea of citizenship. National identities built on the materials of language, culture, and perhaps religion and race, in turn made entitlement to citizenship much more clearly defined ideologically and territorially. It made it possible to exclude, or at least disadvantage, those who did not possess the required attributes, even though they might belong to the state by birth. Such developments might herald the immediate expulsion of minorities whose faces did not fit. And, if expulsion did not take place immediately, their future status would always depend on the play of power.

The decades from the 1880s are filled with the stories of growing numbers of refugees in Europe and in Asia Minor, the stories of those who did not fit into the new world of national identities. In his major work, *The Bridge on the Drina*, Ivo Andric, the Bosnian writer who won the Nobel Prize for literature in 1961, has telling, if distressing, evocations of the way in which the rising nationalisms of the late nineteenth century broke up the old cosmopolitan harmonies of the late-nineteenth-century Balkans.[7] This is what British foreign secretary Lord Curzon called the great 'unmixing of peoples'[8] – which was to continue to take place as the Romanov, Habsburg, Wilhemine and Ottoman empires broke up in the years down to 1918. Arguably Jews, who in Eastern Europe had little opportunity to assimilate, were amongst the largest groups to feel threatened by rising nationalisms. Between 1880 and 1914, 2.4 million fled Eastern Europe for the West. Further hundreds of thousands fled the tsarist empire after its breakup in 1917. Some of these were to be behind the Zionist movement, which eventually decided on Palestine as its territorial focus and under the shelter of the British Mandate set out to create a state which could only exist by displacing Palestinians. In the years before 1914 the Balkans were awash with refugees, a process which was seen as a function of the state-building processes then taking place and their associated crises of integration.[9] The Versailles peace settlement, by moving state boundaries and through the shifting of populations, enabled the number of people living under 'alien' rule in Eastern Europe to be reduced from 60m to 20m.[10] The consolidation of modern Turkey in Anatolia had its own destructive problems: the genocide of the Armenians as they were expelled from sensitive areas in the south and east of the land; the exchange of 1.5m people between Greece and Turkey under the Lausanne Convention of 1923; and a Kurdish problem, concealed under the euphemism 'Mountain Turks', which has not gone away, and will not do so.[11] New nation-states, and citizenships stamped with the new nationalist brands, usually meant a resort to forms of ethnic cleansing.

After World War Two the emergence of new nation-states from former British colonies left further problems of tension between citizen identity and hegemonic national identity. I give you three examples. The first concerns the emergence of the Israeli state after the British handed over the final decision on the outcome of the mandate to the United Nations in 1947. Arab resistance to the UN decision which gave the Zionists 11 per cent of the former mandate led to the Zionists acquiring a larger proportion, the conversion of large numbers of Palestinians into refugees as Zionist forces advanced and deliberate acts of ethnic cleansing took place, and an outcome which left an Arab minority of *c.* 20 per cent in the land which became Israel, a minority which now likes to be called Palestinian Israelis. Palestinian refugees and their descendants, who currently number five million, have had the hardest burden to bear, as a result both of the assertion of Zionism and the failures of their own leadership. The Palestinian Israelis, who currently number 1.5m, although they have equal legal rights in Israel, have found themselves in many ways to be second-class citizens in the Zionist state.

The second example concerns the East African Asians. These were successful, largely Gujarati communities, Hindu and Muslim, which at the time of Ugandan and Kenyan independence in 1962 and 1963 had lived in these countries for at least three generations. As you will know, they came to be forced out of East Africa by post-independence policies of Africanisation which reached their peak in 1972 when Idi Amin ordered all remaining Asians out of Uganda. Thus, African nationalists asserted their vision for the citizenship of their countries. But the process was to have consequences in Britain, too. Up to 1962 Commonwealth citizens had free access to the UK. But from now on more and more restrictions were imposed. The flood of migrants raised the issue (1) of whether the UK which had always envisaged itself, rightly or wrongly, as a monochrome country could cope, and (2) even if it could cope did it want to become a multi-ethnic, polychromatic country. It was in this context in 1968 that the right-wing Conservative politician, Enoch Powell, gave his notorious 'rivers of blood' speech.

The final example concerns the two states which emerged from the British Empire in India. British India contained two major nationalisms; one was focused on the idea of the essential unity of India, it was inclusive of India's great diversity of peoples, and was marshalled in politics by the Indian National Congress. The second sought a homeland for Muslims, which some envisaged as an Islamic state; it was driven forward by the Muslim League. As you will know, these competing visions of nationhood led to the division of the subcontinent into two separate states of India and Pakistan at independence in 1947. Fifteen million refugees were created as Hindus, Sikhs and Muslims strove to find themselves on the right side of the border, and nearly one million were killed. Yet again forms of ethnic cleansing accompanied the emergence of new nation-states.

It is instructive to see what happened to citizenship in the two successor states of India and Pakistan. Here, it is important to make a distinction between what was legally the case and what was possible given the constraints of politics. India began as a society aspiring to a principled inclusiveness; there were Muslims amongst the heroes of its freedom movement. True, the 15 per cent of its population which were Muslims always had the thought of possible disloyalty attached to them. They were disadvantaged, but not hugely so. But from the 1980s Hindu nationalists, promoting a programme of Hindutva, or Hinduness, began to assert themselves in national politics. Their rhetoric involved demonising the Muslim past of the subcontinent, and demonising Muslims in the present. Their rise was associated with the destruction of former symbols of Muslim power, and the increased slaughter of Muslims in communal riots. Between 1998 and 2004 these Hindu nationalists led the coalition government which ruled India. All this happened alongside a growing move across the world to see Muslims as a threat to security. I must emphasise nothing changed legally in the position of Muslims in India. But the outcome, to put it mildly, was that it became less pleasant to be a Muslim citizen of India. Muslims were more likely than others to be picked up by the police; Muslims found it easier to move to live together in ghettos.[12]

In Pakistan citizenship also became subject to politics. On the establishment of the state Jinnah, its founding father, in his first speech to its Constituent Assembly declared that all were equal citizens before the law. Religion was a purely private matter. However, there were those who thought that Pakistan should become an Islamic state, that religion should be a public matter. In pursuing this end, they regularly raised the issue of whether the Ahmadiyya, a sect that believes that there could be forms of prophecy after the death of the Prophet, were Muslims or not. In 1953, after rioting and martial law, they succeeded in forcing Ahmadis out of government, most notably Muhammad Zafar Allah Khan, the Foreign Minister. In 1974 Prime Minister Bhutto, as a sop to the religious extremists, had Ahmadis declared non-Muslims in Pakistan's new constitution. In 1984 Ziya' al-Haqq, moved by the same purpose, declared any attempt by the Ahmadiyya to practise their faith illegal. Thus, the play of politics led to the steady reduction of the rights of the Ahmadiyya as citizens. Other minorities, Shi'as, Christians and Hindus, were exposed to a similar contraction in their rights. But in their case, it was not a formal stripping of rights by legislation but a more subtle process in which the workings of religious extremism, the corruption of the state apparatus, and the apathy, and on occasion the fear, of ordinary citizens made it increasingly difficult for these minorities to exercise their rights in full as citizens. Those who spoke out about these matters did so at the risk of their lives. Some were assassinated. Whatever the law may say about the rights of minorities, they only exist if citizens in general support them, and the state is willing to enforce them.

Globalisation, Citizenship and the Modern Nation-State

Up to now I have been talking about citizenship when the modern nation-state was at its height. I now turn to consider citizenship in the era of globalisation, a period which may lead to the reinforcing of the nation-state, but which in my view is more likely to lead to its weakening. Globalisation has resisted easy definition. This said,

I am happy to work with one adopted by the sociologists Albrow and King in 1990 which defines globalisation as 'all those processes by which the peoples of the world are incorporated into a single world society'.[13] These processes, in general terms, involve: the growth of international trade and transactions; increasing flows of international capital and investment; the movement of growing numbers of people from economy to economy; and the spread of knowledge, broadly construed. Major drivers of these developments have been technological changes, for instance, the transport revolution from the mid-nineteenth century to the present which has enabled the movement of goods and peoples at increasingly low prices, and the communications revolution which has enabled the increasingly cheap movement of knowledge and culture by electronic means. The impact of these changes was supported by international action from the Bretton Woods system launched in 1944 down to the recent Doha negotiations to facilitate trade, economic growth and the increasing integration of the world economy. In this context I want to consider two developments which have worked substantially to modify citizenship in the modern nation-state: (1) the movement of peoples and (2) the growing power of supra-national forms of culture, ideas, organisation, and the emergence of global legal norms supported by UN Charters and Conventions.

Migration to live better, or just to survive, has been an enduring feature of human history. We have already noted the migrations, usually out of fear, associated with the exclusive nationalism of the modern nation-state. The migrations of the era of globalisation have had a different emphasis. Fear and endangered life may still be a spur, but contemporary reasons are primarily economic. In 2010 international migration was estimated to be 214m. If the number continues to grow at the pace of the past twenty years, by 2050 it could reach over 420m.[14] I shall not consider the impact of migration on citizenship in the case of states which have been built virtually from scratch by migration — such as the USA and Australia; in principle the absorption of migrants should not be too destabilising for established identity. Nor shall I consider it in the context of the Gulf Cooperation Council countries, whose labour force can consist of as many as 80 per cent migrants; migrants are only rarely permitted to become citizens. I shall consider it in the context of the states of Western and Central Europe where currently 45m members of the workforce come from either outside the EU or from other countries within it. Many seek and gain citizenship in the states in which they work.

The outcome has been the emergence of European nation-states of growing ethnic diversity. In 2010, 9.4 per cent of European peoples were foreign-born. Austria had the largest proportion at 15.2 per cent, but the most populous European societies were not far behind with Germany at 12 per cent, the UK at 11.3 per cent and France at 11.1 per cent.[15] In 2012 the citizens of the UK learned the outcome of their 2011 national census. Over the previous decade net immigration had been at 250,000 p.a. Over the same period, the number of foreign-born residents had risen from 4.6m to 7.5m. Over the same period, again, the percentage of those identifying themselves as 'white' British had fallen from 87 per cent to 80.5 per cent. London emerged as one of the most ethnically diverse cities on earth. Less than 45 per cent of London's population identified themselves as 'white' British. Over 300 languages were spoken in the metropolitan area and there were more than fifty non-indigenous communities with populations of more than 10,000.[16] Such diversity was bound to be a challenge to social inclusion, and at the local level a challenge to the institutions of the state.

Not surprisingly the discovery of how fundamentally and how rapidly the population of Britain seemed to be changing brought a political response. Immigration is probably the biggest issue behind the rise of the extreme right-wing United Kingdom Independence Party. It also helps to drive the opposition of the right-wing of the Conservative Party in general towards Europe. But, whatever the political rhetoric, there are at least two powerful reasons why this inward labour migration will continue to take place, not just in the UK but in the countries of Western Europe as a whole. The first is the 'push' factor, the major contribution of migrant worker remittances to economies and quality of life in the developing world. In 2004, $126bn was registered as being transferred home by migrant labourers, although we may be sure that the actual sum was much greater. In 2008 the registered sum from the EU countries was 32bn Euros.[17] The 'push', however, comes not just from migrant workers but also from policy-makers who see remittances, the total of which far exceeds that of development aid, as a major opportunity to relieve world poverty in ways that are more effective than official development aid.[18] Of course, from time to time, official attempts will be made to curb labour migration but, whatever may be done officially, such is the leaky nature of Europe's thousands of miles of border, and such is the desperate need of the poor in developing countries, that illegal migration will remain hard to contain. The second reason behind a continuing labour migration to Europe is a powerful 'pull' factor. It is the demographic revolution which is taking place throughout the industrialised world. Japan, where the population is expected to fall from 127m in 2000 to 105m in 2050, is in the lead. Declining fertility rates in all Western European countries suggest that the basic trend is in a similar direction. This places a time bomb under existing arrangements and existing expectations in society. The welfare state in Western European societies was built on the understanding that the ratio between those aged 15–65 and those over 65 would be 5:1. It is already down to 4:1 and heading fast towards 2:1. It has been worked out that to keep Europe's ageing population at its current level up to 2050 would mean admitting 25m immigrants a year.[19] I am sure that immigration will not be seen to be the only answer to this problem, but is it very likely to be part of the mix, in which case we can expect the consolidation of increasingly diverse European populations to continue.

This diversity has been reinforced by the second development working to modify citizenship in the modern nation-state. I think of the supra-national connections of family, culture, religion and organisation which help to reduce communal solidarities based on territory and increase those built on shared (supra-national) interests. Thus, modern communications enable the migrant worker to maintain a relationship with the village or regional culture from which he or she came. Often a partner will be taken from the village. Their children, if they are Muslims, may well be expected to marry their cousins. Village values will in all probability be sustained in the host nation-state: marriage, if necessary, may be forced; disobedient children, children who are deemed to threaten the honour of the family, almost invariably girls, will be killed. The likelihood of continuing to sustain alien values in the host society may be judged from the fact that the UK Census of 2011 revealed that 3m lived in households where not one person spoke English.[20] As the publicity machine of the High Commission of Pakistan in London reveals, diplomatic representatives of particular ethnic groups can work to intensify their relationship to their country of origin.

Religious networks provide another layer of transnational connectivity. Since the nineteenth century all the great religions of the world have developed into what have been termed 'religious internationals'.[21] These processes have taken place both at the level of the sect, for instance the Isma'ilis or the Ahmadiyya, or the Sufi order, for instance, the Qadiriyya or the Naqshbandiyya, or modern-style organisations, for instance, South Asia's Tablighi Jama'at, Turkey's Gulen movement and the Muslim Brotherhood of the Arab world. At another level we can note how representatives of great religions have tried to reach out to their faithful as a whole on a transnational basis, as the Hindu Sangh Parivar has done and as Osama bin Laden did in his 'Statements to the World' which were designed to appeal to his fellow Muslims as a 'community of conscience'.[22]

All this suggests that the experiential space of individuals in the nation-state may increasingly be less within the territorial unit and more within particular interest groups – a process fostered by modern social media, the internet and niche media services, which operate at all levels from the local to the global. The Canadian sociologist, Robert Wolfe, has noted that city-to-city connections in Canada are less between Canadian cities than between Canadian cities and other world cities.[23] The rise of dual citizenship strikes at the heart of nation-state loyalty; the increasing use of tax havens betrays a growing failure to respect the obligations of nationally defined citizenship. The new diversity is badly corrosive of modern understandings of state-centred citizenship.

Multiculturalism

Nation-states have seen this diversity, which increases with every passing year, as a challenge to social cohesion. Early responses were often to adopt policies of multiculturalism, which has been defined in various ways but which I shall define as 'integration with retention of identity'. Eighteenth-century Canada, confronted by the challenge of integrating its English- and French-speaking peoples, was arguably the first society formally to adopt such a policy. Multiculturalism is regarded as a founding principle of the state. From the mid-twentieth century multiculturalism was the default response in many Western societies to growing diversity. But, over the past twenty years it has become increasingly subject to criticism, and not least because of the challenges which Muslim communities have been thought to present to Western lives and Western values. The criticisms were telling: multiculturalism is oriented to the past; it tends to assume that different cultural groups might not have a shared horizon of modernity; while multiculturalism might be recognised by migrant groups as a symbol of acceptance, it helps to fashion parallel societies and ultimately acts as a barrier to social integration; and finally multiculturalism fosters an undesirable legal pluralism which tends to privilege the rights of communities over the rights of individuals, in particular women, living in these communities.[24] At an Anglo-Canadian discussion some six years ago, while Canadians for understandable reasons struggled with criticisms of multiculturalism, most British opinion was that multiculturalism needed to be abandoned in favour of more positive moves towards shared citizenship. Policy should not trap citizens in their ethnicities but give them choice. There was a feeling, which interestingly most of the Muslims present shared, that fundamental human rights should come before culture.[25] In a strange way, although this is not strictly what they mean, this is the direction of argument of the Hindu revivalists in India when they say that India's Uniform Civil Code must have precedence over shari'a law.

The idea expressed in the Anglo-Canadian discussions that universal human rights should have precedence over individual cultures points in an interesting direction. It is the growing tendency of the international community to elevate individual human rights and responsibilities above the claims of sovereign states. This would appear to have begun with the decisions of the Nuremburg Tribunal of 1945–6 which stated that individuals had duties to humanity – some would call them cosmopolitan duties – which were greater than their obligations either to their fellow-nationals or to the commands of their nation-states. The intent of the Nuremburg decision was echoed, this time over the broad span of human activity, by the United Nations Universal Declaration of Human Rights of 1948 and its baby sister the European Union Convention on Human Rights of 1953 with its very specific focus on helping individuals achieve justice. As you will know, states have chosen to follow or to ignore the Universal Declaration at will. The Soviet Union rejected the Declaration from the beginning. Islamic countries also rejected the universal claims of the UN Declaration, saying that it failed to take into account the cultural and religious contexts of non-Western countries. In 1990 the Organisation of the Islamic Conference responded with the Cairo Declaration of Human Rights in Islam. This said, the Western declarations of human rights, and the courts which support them, offer the hope of justice for many. They also predicate a new idea of citizenship existing beyond the nation-state.

We can find some fashioning of this new idea of citizenship in the growth of humanitarian intervention. This process, which has rarely been free of state self-interest, goes back at least to Western interventions in the Ottoman Empire from the early-nineteenth century onwards and has continued through India's intervention in 1971 in what is generally accepted to have been a genocide in East Pakistan and Vietnam's intervention in Cambodia in 1978 to end Pol Pot's genocidal regime. Since the end of the Cold War there has been growing enthusiasm amongst statesmen and diplomats, as well as the general public, for intervention to protect human rights. The process began with UN Resolution 688, which amongst other things established a no-fly zone in the Kurdish areas of Iraq and which also led the UN Secretary General of the time to declare that there had been a shift in public attitudes towards the idea that the defence of the oppressed in the name of morality 'should prevail over frontiers and legal documents'.[26] This was followed by a series of interventions in the 1990s – Bosnia, Somalia, Kosovo, Sierra Leone (some far too long delayed) – which culminated in Prime Minister Blair's Chicago speech of 1999 in which he qualified the UN Charter principle of non-interference in the affairs of other states, arguing that genocide, or other forms of oppression, could never be a purely internal matter; it should also be viewed as a threat to international peace and security.[27] Carried along by a continuing stream of international conventions and declarations, which supported the rights and duties of individuals rather than states, the international community has come to place a higher value on human life, threatening regimes which failed to respect it with the loss of the right to rule.[28] Developments such as these, which have also meant that individuals as well as states might have an international legal personality, have been creating a space for some form of 'citizenship' beyond the nation-state.

The realists of this world would probably say that citizenship without the nation-state is impossible. I am not sure that as time goes on this will be a sustainable position. The processes of globalisation are steadily carving out a supra-national space for citizenship. Individuals in nation-states are daily more and more aware of how full of significant activity the spaces are beyond the nation-state. They are also aware of challenges to humankind – climate change, food security, pressures on planetary resources of all kinds – which will require a supra-national response. Citizenship in our world is beginning to acquire a global dimension. This said, given the likely tenacity of nation-states, perhaps we should think of citizenship for the foreseeable future as having the dual form espoused by the Stoic philosopher, Epictetus: 'Each human being is primarily a citizen of his own commonwealth; but he is also a member of the great city of gods and men.'[29]

Notes

1. I am grateful to my colleague, Klaus Dodds, for comments on this lecture.
2. Nile Green, *Bombay Islam: The Religious Economy of the West Indian Ocean, 1840–1915* (Cambridge: Cambridge University Press, 2011).
3. Robert Dankoff and Sooyong Kim (trans. and commentary), *An Ottoman Traveller: Selections from the Book of Travels of Evliya Celebi* (London: Eland, 2010).
4. There are several recent books which describe the lost cosmopolitan worlds of the old Ottoman cities. Two of the best are: Mark Mazower, *Salonica, City of Ghosts: Christians, Muslims and Jews 1430–1950* (London: Harper Perennial, 2005), and Giles Milton, *Paradise Lost: Smyrna 1922 – The Destruction of Islam's City of Tolerance* (New York: Basic Books, 2008).
5. Ariel Salzmann, 'Islampolis, Cosmopolis: Ottoman Urbanity Between Myth, Memory and Postmodernity', in Derryl N. MacLean and Sikeena Karmali Ahmed, eds, *Cosmopolitanisms in Muslim Contexts: Perspectives from the Past* (Edinburgh: Edinburgh University Press in association with the Aga Khan University, 2012).
6. Muhammad Iqbal, *Rumuz-i Behkhudi* (The Mysteries of Selflessness) in Wm. Theodore de Bary *et al.*, eds, *Sources of Indian Tradition* (New York: Columbia University Press, 1958), p. 756.

7. Ivo Andric, *The Bridge on the Drina*, trans. Lovett F. Edwards (London: George Allen & Unwin, 1959).
8. Michael R. Marrus, *The Unwanted: European Refugees in the Twentieth Century* (Oxford: Oxford University Press, 1985), p. 41.
9. Ibid., p. 49
10. Ibid., p. 69.
11. Ibid., pp. 74–81, 97–105.
12. Laurent Gayer and Christophe Jaffrelot, eds, *Muslims in Indian Cities: Trajectories of Marginalisation* (Delhi: HarperCollins, 2012).
13. M. Albrow and E. King, eds, *Globalisation, Knowledge and Society* (London: Sage, 1990), p. 8.
14. *World Migration Report 2010 – The Future of Migration: Building Capacities for Change*, International Organisation for Migration, 2010, http://publications.iom.int/bookstore/ibndex.php?main_page=product_info&cPath=37aproducts_id+653&language=en.
15. Immigration to Europe. http://en.wikipedia.org/wiki/Immigration_to_Europe#2010_data_for_European_Union
16. *Guardian*, 23 December 2012; Ethnic Groups in London. http://en.wikipedia.org/wiki/Ethnic_groups_in_London
17. Paul Scheffer, *Immigrant Nations* (London: Polity Press, 2011), p. 93.
18. Nigel Harris, *Thinking the Unthinkable: The Immigration Myth Exposed* (London: I.B. Tauris, 2002).
19. Scheffer, *Immigrant Nations*, pp. 83–5.
20. *Guardian*, 23 February 2012.
21. Abigail Green and Vincent Viaene, eds, *Religious Internationals in the Modern World: Globalisation and Faith Communities since 1750* (Houndmills, Basingstoke: Palgrave Macmillan, 2012).
22. Francis Robinson, 'The Islamic World: From World System to Religious International', in Green and Viaene, pp. 111–38.
23. Francis Robinson, *Social Inclusion: New Challenges to the Established Order: Rapporteur's Report*, The Canada-UK Colloquium, 15–18 November 2007 (Ontario: School of Policy Studies, Queen's University, 2008), p. 12.
24. Robinson, *Social Inclusion*, pp. 5–6, 11–15; Scheffer, *Immigrant Nations*, pp. 197–203.
25. Robinson, *Social Inclusion*, pp. 10–11, 17, 19.
26. Matthew Jamison, 'Humanitarian Intervention since 1990 and "Liberal Interventionism"', in *Humanitarian Intervention: A History*, ed. Brendan

Simms and D.J.B. Trim (Cambridge: Cambridge University Press, 2011), p. 367.
27. Ibid., p. 376.
28. Andrew Linklater, 'Cosmopolitan Harm Conventions', in *Conceiving Cosmopolitanism: Theory, Context, and Practice*, ed. Steven Vertovec and Robin Cohen (Oxford: Oxford University Press, 2002), pp. 254–67.
29. Linklater pointed me in this direction: Linklater, 'Cosmopolitan Harm Conventions'. The precise reference can be found in Christopher Gill, ed., trans. and revised, Robin Hand, *Epitectus, Discourses* (London: Dent, 1995), II, 5, p. 2.

12

What Ralph Russell Meant and Means to Me

RALPH RUSSELL, ALTHOUGH he most certainly would not have seen it this way, belonged to that extraordinary generation of British scholars who became Marxists at Oxford and Cambridge in the 1930s, and acted as a leaven in British intellectual life for the rest of the twentieth century. He shares the company of, amongst others: Eric Hobsbawm, the historian of social banditry and industrial capitalism; E.P. Thompson, historian of the working class and nuclear disarmament activist; Rodney Hilton, historian of the late medieval peasantry; Christopher Hill, historian of the seventeenth-century Puritan Revolution; Victor Kiernan, polymath, translator of Iqbal and Faiz, and critic of European empire; and Joseph Needham, gifted biochemist, but even more gifted creator of the extraordinary *Science and Civilisation in China* in many volumes. Ralph shared with Hill, Kiernan, Hilton, and Thompson the background of religious nonconformity (i.e. religious positions which differentiated themselves from the Anglican Church) which from the seventeenth century has been such a rich source in Britain of social and political action, and of creativity in general. Ralph shared with Joseph Needham the distinction of having opened up an important aspect of a major world culture so that it came to be better understood, indeed valued, in the West.

I can only recall meeting Ralph – and my memory usually serves me well – on three occasions, which some may feel is strange for colleagues in the same university but the federal university of

London was a strange institution. The first was when Peter Reeves, then at the University of Sussex, held a weekend workshop in the early 1970s for those interested in the world of north India. The second was when I reviewed the first volume of Ralph's autobiography, *Findings, Keepings: Life, Communism and Everything*, at a launch in London's Nehru Centre in London in February 2002. The third was at the Ralph Russell Day, held at SOAS in June 2007, when (aged 89) Ralph performed for the whole of a morning and an afternoon.

However, I always felt that I knew Ralph well. We kept in touch through the occasional letter and phone call. He started the process in early 1972 when he telephoned to thank me for my review of his *Ghalib: Life and Letters*.[1] No one has ever done that since, although I have had the odd grateful letter; it was an act of generosity from a senior to a very junior scholar which was typical of him. In the late 1980s Ralph wrote a charming letter of thanks for my contribution to his festschrift.[2] Then contact became more regular as he arranged for me the business of paying for my copy of the *Annual of Urdu Studies*. Just before his death we had a heartening exchange of letters in which he revealed his great interest in the future of the study of Muslim South Asia in the UK. But there were other reasons for feeling that one knew Ralph so well. The first were the tapes which accompanied his *Essential Urdu* (1974). Anyone who used them to try to learn Urdu, as I did, had Ralph's voice constantly ringing in one's ears. The second was the work. Scholars rarely come upon their subjects by mistake. Ralph, working with Khurshidul Islam, was the great expounder of Urdu love poetry in English. This was evidently done by a man who understood the forms this 'madness' might take, and when it came to verse knew, as Mir said, that 'poetry is a task for men whose hearts have been seared by the fire of love and pierced by the wounds of grief.'[3] Moreover, Ralph was a memorable presenter of Urdu literature because it was his delight to engage with the humanity of the Urdu writer and enable us to share in it.

I began postgraduate research on India in autumn 1966 and by mid-1967 was coming to focus on the UP in general and its Muslim world in particular. There was no money available for learning Urdu but, beyond that, I was actively discouraged from doing so – an attitude of 'imperial' Britain which Ralph discussed at his 'Day' in 2007, and to which he refers in the authors' introduction to *Three Mughal Poets*.[4] This meant I was hungry for books which would take me beyond the Anglophone world of Muslim India (a very small world) to that of Urdu and the range of reference and sensibility that came with it. I was particularly concerned to have a stronger sense of what it meant to be human in the north Indian world of the nineteenth and early twentieth centuries. The publication of *Three Mughal Poets* in 1968 and *Ghalib* in the following year suddenly made this possible as never before.

It has taken some time, and indeed the help of a growing interest in the eighteenth century, to develop a proper appreciation of *Three Mughal Poets*, but the impact on me of *Ghalib* was immediate. The man, his great love affair, his household, his friends, his work as a poet, his endless search for patronage, and his passion for mangoes and for alcohol are brought wonderfully to life with skilful use of his correspondence as well as his poetry. So too, moreover, was the clash of the mid-nineteenth century between a somewhat brash, transforming industrial civilisation, and the high, courtly culture of the fading Mughal world. Ralph and Khurshidul Islam offer a vision through Ghalib's eyes, which has no match, of the horrors of the destruction of Delhi in the British suppression of the Mutiny Uprising and of the extraordinary changes confronting Muslim north India from the 1840s through to Ghalib's death in 1869. No other work enables one to engage so fully with what it meant to live at this time, and with the meaning of British rule. For this reason, I often return to it but also use it much in teaching; it is a good way of introducing students to the harder edges of imperial conquest.

My first meeting with Ralph at that weekend workshop hosted

by Peter Reeves had two outcomes. One was derived from the topic Ralph discussed formally at the workshop, Ashraf 'Ali Thanawi's *Bihishti Zewar*. It was the first time that I had heard of it. Ralph swiftly outlined its popularity – the most widely published book in Muslim India after the Qur'an – and whetted my appetite for it. I soon had my own copy, rather poorly translated into English. But it required Barbara Metcalf's *Islamic Revival in British India: Deoband 1860–1900* (Princeton: Princeton University Press, 1982), and her subsequent translation of part of *Bihishti Zewar*,[5] for me to understand the full weight of the text as a handbook for the formation of the 'Protestant' Deobandi mindset; and indeed, of the new Muslim emphasis on action on earth to achieve salvation which was to be the feature of reform across the Muslim world. Because Ralph had introduced me to *Bihishti Zewar* I was well prepared for Barbara's work and have found *Bihishti Zewar* most useful in research and teaching ever since.

The second outcome of the meeting was that Ralph introduced me to the work of the Progressive Writers and, either then or later, gave me a copy of an unpublished paper he had written on them. This lay fallow for five years. But in the autumn of 1978 a young Muslim came to see me who, now that General Ziya' al-Haqq was in power, had found Pakistan becoming rather hot for him. He was a communist who came with a sheaf of somewhat dense Marxist writings, and wanted to do postgraduate research. After much discussion it became clear that a thesis on the Progressive Writers might be the way forward. I gave him Ralph's paper. He went to see Ralph and received much encouragement and it was not long before he had produced a thesis on the subject which was subsequently published.[6] He is now a full professor in the University of London with, amongst other things, a major study of the Muslim communities of the UK to his name.[7]

In the 1970s Ralph and Khurshidul Islam published one of the more important articles to appear in *Modern Asian Studies*, 'The Satirical Verse of Akbar Ilahabadi'.[8] This was the first time that substantial quantities of verse from this sardonic commentator had been translated into English. He wrote on the impact of British rule on Sayyid Ahmad Khan, on the shallow and hypocritical behaviour of 'brown' sahibs, and on the dangers of what was good in the Muslim civilization of India being sacrificed in a headlong rush to embrace an English modernity. It was just too late, unfortunately, for his mixture of biting satire and perceptive comment to be included in my *Separatism among Indian Muslims*, which was also published in that year.[9] The article brought to life the world of humour in cartoon and verse of *Awadh Punch*, where Akbar published most of his output. But it also brought a new richness and nuance to my understanding of Muslim responses to change in the late nineteenth and early twentieth century. Akbar could be sceptical of what Sayyid Ahmad Khan was doing while still admiring the man; he could recognize the need for change while deploring what might be lost in the process. As with *Bihishti Zewar* I have found this presentation of Akbar of enormous value in thinking about the period and in persuading students to engage with it. On a more personal note, it meant much to me that these lines by Akbar were inscribed on the maqbara over the grave of Mawlana 'Abdul Bari of Lucknow's Farangi Mahall family of 'ulama', which would occupy much of my energies in the years from 1976:

> Oh heavens let the winds of passion blow
> Oh set the springs of action free,
> Let us work, let us strive,
> Let every shaykh like 'Abdul Bari be.[10]

What was most valuable for me about Ralph and Khurshidul Islam's translations was that they enabled me to sense the ways in which Indian Muslims saw their world being transformed – indeed saw a great civilisational change taking place – and how they felt about it, often with despair. This translation from Akbar below has always made the point most powerfully for me:

The minstrel, and the music, and the melody have all changed.
Our very sleep has changed; the tale we used to hear is no longer told.
Spring comes with new adornments; the nightingales in the garden sing a different song.
Nature's every effect has undergone a revolution.
Another kind of rain falls from the sky; another kind of grain grows in the fields.[11]

Such is the value of Akbar's literary output to the historian, regardless of its value for Urdu literature, that I am sorry that four decades after Ralph in this article urged the importance of a major study of Akbar, and indicated that materials to support such a study were plentiful, nothing to my knowledge has been done, in English at least.

The next work of Ralph's to make an impact on me was his *Anthology of Urdu Poetry* (1999) which was first published in 1995 as *Hidden in the Lute*, and I am afraid truly hidden from view. I reviewed it in the *Times Literary Supplement* in January 2001.[12] It is a particularly well-chosen collection, combining some of Sayyid Ahmad Khan's writing with that of his critic, Akbar Ilahabadi, evocative and affectionate memoirs of poets, a few of Ghalib's letters, an excerpt from Ruswa's *Umrao Jan Ada*, several short stories by Progressive Writers, and delightful examples of the popular literature that might be picked up at a bus or railway station bookstall – stories of Akbar and his sidekick Birbal, Mulla Dopiaza and Shaykh Chilli. The centrepiece, however, was the fifty pages he devoted to love poetry, to the ghazals of Mir and Ghalib. It is an outstanding exposition of this poetic form, its context, its elements of wordplay, multiple connotations and contrasts, its strict unity of form, well-defined single metre throughout, and the pleasures to be derived from the shape and sound of couplets not necessarily connected by a unifying theme. Ralph loved rhythmic music; his family tells us he was always singing. It was not surprising that he was in love with meaningful music made with words.

It was not surprising, too, that he did his finest work on the Urdu poetry of love. 'Loving is fundamental to being human', he declares in his autobiography, 'in one sense it scarcely matters who you love, or how much opportunity you have to express it; what matters is to love.'[13]

One of the expressions of Ralph's love was through service to his fellow humankind. This made him a communist from his teenage years because it was thus that he felt best able to serve – nothing was known of the horrors of Stalin's Soviet Union at the time. As an officer of the British Indian army building military roads into Burma, he spent his time trying to convert his sepoys to the cause. As a teacher on the staff of SOAS for thirty years and more he worked openly for the Communist Party. Then, in the 1980s, he found perhaps a more effective outlet for his desire to serve. He had come to realise that there was a real need for his skills both amongst the Urdu-speaking communities which were rapidly forming in Britain and amongst those in the host population who were trying to serve them. In 1985 he retired early from SOAS so that he could devote himself to this purpose full time. He had already produced an improved version of his Urdu course, *A New Course in Urdu and Spoken Hindi* (3 parts, 1980–82). Now, through his teaching activity in the community, through his campaigning for Urdu teaching in schools, and especially through his pupils he was able to create a space in British society for the language he loved. This work he continued to his last months in 2008. It is a humbling act of service and one which will always remain with me as an example of how to make one's scholarly knowledge socially useful.

In 2001 Ralph published the first volume of his autobiography, *Findings Keepings*, which covers his life up to 1946. Speaking at its launch forced me to pay greater attention to it than I might have done, and led to me immediately sharing it with my wife who, only vicariously associated with Muslim South Asia, was so impressed that she wrote a letter of appreciation. This volume has that openness about love, and in particular sexual relationships, which was pioneered in the UK by Bertrand Russell. Several strands run through the book. The first is Ralph's love of song, already alluded to, Yorkshire songs, London songs, school songs, army songs, lewd songs. His head was full of the music of song as well as of language. The second, unsurprisingly for someone growing up in the lower middle classes in twentieth-century Britain, was his consciousness of class, which in India he found transformed into racism by his British officer colleagues. The third was his engagement with communism, which had the enormously important effect that it drove him to learn Urdu so that he could proselytise amongst his soldiers. The final strand is love, which he sees as tying all his life together and which by example makes his particular mark on me. He declares towards the end of this book:

> There have been three main strands of my life – the commitment to the fundamental values which made me a communist, the study of Urdu, and an awareness of love as the fundamental feature of true humanity . . . to me the three strands have always been inextricably intertwined, each informing the other, and it is that interaction which has affected the way I have worked for Urdu, enabling me to understand things in Urdu literature and about the lives of Urdu speakers that would hardly have been possible otherwise. This in turn has had an effect on both my personal relationships and my understanding of what it means to be a communist. And it has been through my personal experiences as much as through the pressure of world events that my concept of how to live as a communist has changed.[14]

Notes

1. Francis Robinson, review of *Ghalib: 1797–1869: Volume I, Life and Letters*, trans. and ed. Ralph Russell and Khurshidul Islam (London: Allen & Unwin, 1969), *Modern Asian Studies*, 6, 1, January 1972, pp. 113–15.
2. Francis Robinson, '*Al-Nizamiyya;* A Group of Lucknow Intellectuals in the Early Twentieth Century', in C. Shackle, ed., *Urdu and Muslim*

South Asia: Studies in Honour of Ralph Russell (New Delhi: Oxford University Press, 1989).
3. Ralph Russell, *An Anthology of Urdu Poetry* (London: Carcanet, 1999), p. 157.
4. Ralph Russell and Khurshidul Islam, *Three Mughal Poets: Mir, Sauda, Mir Hasan* (London: Allen & Unwin, 1969), pp. xv–xxii.
5. Barbara D. Metcalf, *Perfecting Women: Maulana Ashraf 'Ali Thanawi's Behishti Zewar: A Partial Translation with Commentary* (Berkeley: University of California Press, 1990).
6. Khizar Humayun Ansari, *The Emergence of Socialist Thought among North Indian Muslims (1917–1947)* (Lahore, 1990).
7. H. Ansari, *The Infidel Within: Muslims in Britain since 1800* (London: Hurst, 2004).
8. Ralph Russell and Khurshidul Islam, 'The Satirical Verse of Akbar Ilahabadi (1846–1921)', *Modern Asian Studies*, 8, 1, January 1974, pp. 1–58.
9. Francis Robinson, *Separatism among Indian Muslims: The Politics of the United Provinces' Muslims 1860–1923* (Cambridge: Cambridge University Press, 1974).
10. 'Abd al-Bari and the Events of January 1926', in Francis Robinson, *The 'Ulama of Farangi Mahall and Islamic Culture in South Asia* (Delhi: Permanent Black, 2001), pp. 145–76.
11. Russell and Islam, 'Akbar Ilahabadi', p. 9.
12. See 'A Pit Full of Honey', in Francis Robinson, *Islam, South Asia and the West* (Delhi: Oxford University Press, 2007), pp. 247–50.
13. Ralph Russell, *Findings, Keepings: Life, Communism and Everything: An Autobiography, Part I, 1918–1946* (London: Three Essays Collective, 2001), p. 372.
14. Russell, *Findings*, p. 333.

13

Love on the Roof[1]

IRAN IS ONE OF THE world's storehouses of great literature. Its impact has been felt wherever Persian has been spoken, from the early Ottoman Empire and Central Asia through northern India to Bengal and Hyderabad. Arguably, it has also been felt in the West from medieval courtly romance through to the great Victorian renderings such as Arnold's *Sohrab and Rustam* to Fitzgerald's *Rubaiyat of Omar Khayyam*. Modern statesmen could do worse than turn to it to be reminded, both of Iranians' vision of their place in the world as carried in their literary heritage, and of the valuing of humanity which this heritage sustains.

These books are new translations of masterpieces. Of the two *Wis and Ramin* is much less well known in the West. Nevertheless, it is, as Dick Davis rightly tells us, 'one of the most extraordinary and fascinating love narratives produced anywhere in the medieval world, Islamic or Christian.' It was composed for the Seljuk governor of Isfahan *c.* 1050 by Fakhr al-Din Gorgani of whose other work only scraps remain. Gorgani reworked a story from the Parthian period 247 BCE–224 CE when Zoroastrianism was dominant. He was part of a movement of poets who reached back to the pre-Islamic period, when Iran held unquestioned sway over West Asia and its kings could truly style themselves King of Kings. Firdawsi's *Shahnameh*, completed in 1010, is the classic example of this genre.

This poem of complex plot begins with Shahru, Queen of Mahabad (now Hamadan in west Iran), refusing to marry King Mobad of Marw (in contemporary Turkmenistan), but promising him that if she bears a daughter she will give her to Mobad as a wife. She duly gives birth to a daughter, Wis, who is brought up by a nurse in the company of Mobad's younger brother, Ramin. When Wis is ready to marry, Shahru forgets her promise and marries Wis to her elder brother, Wiru. Mobad's people come to claim Wis, her father is killed in the subsequent fighting, and Shahru is persuaded to hand her over to Mobad. Most unwillingly Wis is carried off to Marw but succeeds in protecting herself from Mobad's attentions by persuading her nurse to use a charm which renders him impotent. By this time Ramin has already fallen in love with Wis. Through the nurse's intervention Wis is eventually persuaded to forget Wiru and turn to Ramin.

Wis and Ramin become lovers. The couple try all manner of ploys to be together: Ramin feigns illness to stay at Marw rather than campaigning with Mobad; Wis, seeing Mobad dead drunk in bed, asks the nurse to replace her at his side so that she can enjoy a tryst on the palace roof. More and more elaborate measures are taken to keep them apart, and each time love finds a way through locked doors and over high walls.

Then Gorgani gives the tale a new twist: the lovers are persuaded to part, Wis persuaded to perform her duty honestly to Mobad and Ramin to rule Gurab in western Iran. Before they part Wis and Ramin swear eternal love. But hardly has Ramin entered Gurab than he falls in love with, and marries, a noblewoman, Gol.

The news of Ramin's faithlessness sends Wis into despair. She sends a remarkable letter of love and yearning to Ramin, and the subsequent exchanges lead to Ramin rejecting Gol and returning to Marw. There follows a great set-piece interchange between the two lovers with Ramin kept for days in the snow while Wis speaks from a palace window, as with 'poison gathered in each bitter word' she pours out her rage at his desertion. Throughout this dramatic climax the listener is left wondering 'will they, won't they'. Eventually they do come together and:

Took shelter in a hunting lodge, where they
Washed their sorrows and fears away.

. . .

And though their hearts were hurt, their kisses brought
The love and pardon for which each had sought.

The poem ends with Ramin seizing Marw and its treasure, and Mobad being removed from the scene, killed hunting wild boar. Thus, the way becomes clear for Ramin and Wis to ascend the throne of Marw, and to be happy ever after.

The first striking point is that there appears to be no attempt to gloss over matters which might offend Islamic sensibilities, as for instance the *Shahnameh* does. The incestuous marriage practices of Iranian kings, which bear comparison with those of Egyptian Pharoahs, are accepted without comment. This goes, moreover, even for Ramin, who is not only Mobad's brother but also his son. In addition, wine is the constant companion of the lovers' amorous engagements, while drinking to the point of drunkenness is the custom of Mobad's court. This may tell us something about the Seljuk world at Isfahan.

Enjoyment of wine is just part of an unabashed enjoyment of sensual pleasures. Smell plays a key role in signalling attraction and the delights of love. It is Wis's scent which first draws Ramin to her. It is this which lets Ramin know that she is in the garden where he is hidden. It is this borne on the letter of love and yearning which makes Ramin realise that he cannot live without Wis:

But no not musk and roses filled the air,
The heady scent of Wis herself was there

. . .

Why should I turn away from your sweet hair?
Where could I find the musk that I find there?

The urgent need to satisfy erotic desire is candidly expressed.

After Wis had made the nurse share her drunken husband's bed, she fled:

> Up to the roof, on fire to see her friend,
> Where, with a kiss, she made his sorrows end.
> She tore away the fox and squirrel fur
> That might have sheltered and protected her,
> Baring her silver bosom to the rain.

Much of the poem speaks from the woman's point of view. Listen to the nurse, a figure not dissimilar in role to that of the nurse in Shakespeare's *Romeo and Juliet*, explaining the delights of love to Wis:

> God made us so that nothing's lovelier than
> What we as women feel when with a man,
> And you don't know how vehemently sweet
> The pleasure is when men and women meet;
> If you make love just once, I know that then
> You won't hold back from doing so again.

The poem's most strongly drawn character, whose voice is most frequently heard, is the high-spirited and determined Wis. She berates her mother for her promise to Mobad; she pours scorn upon Mobad's age to his emissary; she talks back at the man himself with pride and defiance. To Ramin she speaks wondrous words of love:

> Choose me, and no one else, within your heart
> As I choose you, and may we never part:
> Rejoice in me as I rejoice in you,
> Remember all our love, as I shall do.

As the poem progresses Wis's voice becomes more prominent and her feelings more complex right down to the dramatic denouement in the snow.

Moving through the verses is a constant reflection on the trials of love. So, at the beginning the nurse warns Ramin against travelling this path:

> If you persist and bind yourself to Wis
> You will never know another moment's peace.

Wis's letter of love and yearning is one long disquisition on the theme:

> How evil love has proved to be! In truth
> It's robbed me of my heart, and soul and youth.

While Ramin is constantly moaning about the pain of love down the denouement:

> Oh, I deserve to suffer and be sad,
> Why did I leave the happy life I had?

Wis and Ramin is played out in a courtly world of power and wealth. While the action of the plot takes place between Marw and Mahabad, we are reminded several times that the sway of Mobad's rule, and later than of Ramin, reached from Kairouan to China's shore. Of course, allowance must be made for hyperbole here, as it must also be in the descriptions of gold, silver, jewels, musk, ambergris, and the fine clothes 'from Shustar, China and the West' in which, for instance, Wis dresses Ramin as he sets out for Gurab. Nevertheless, this is a world which grows fat on the commerce of the Silk Route.

The poem was designed for oral performance. Indeed, one can imagine it being performed over several evenings at the Seljuk court. There are the rhetorical tricks of repetition: Wis's hair is musky, her breasts, jasmine-scented, the nurse, wily, and so on . . . Gorgani is a fine storyteller. On the one hand he feeds the imagination with vivid images:

> The firmament was like a canopy
> Studded with jewels, vast in its majesty,
> Secure and barely moving, strongly tied
> With heavenly guy ropes to the mountainside.

On the other hand, he keeps his listeners hungry for more. He does so, moreover, in spite of the great set-pieces, placed at intervals through the poem, like arias in an opera, which expose the inner lives of the characters, and stretch emotions to the limit.

As *Vis and Ramin* is such a remarkable poem, why is it not better known? In Iran it was a considerable influence on Nizami, the country's greatest romantic poet who lived in the following century. But after this the environment became steadily less receptive to a work which celebrated the carnal pleasures of the flesh and viewed with sympathy a woman who followed the dictates of her heart, preferring instead to focus romance on the soul's love for God.

In the West the poem had considerable influence in the Middle Ages, but at one remove. The excellent introduction to the work makes a convincing case for it being the origin of *Tristan and Isolde* transmitted to the crusading Franks through the Seljuk court in Damascus. Some extracts from the poem were translated into German in 1869, and the first full translation was in French in 1959. The first English translation was George Morrison's prose version of 1972. This translation by the poet Dick Davis, widely regarded as our finest translator of Persian poetry, is in heroic couplets, the closest English metrical form to Gorgani's. This wonderful work should win Gorgani the Western audience he richly deserves.

Gulistan is one of the world's most widely known books. Composed by Shaykh Sa'di, the thirteenth-century scholar-poet of Shiraz, it quickly became one of the first books studied by schoolchildren wherever Persian was used. It is the source of as many everyday maxims as Shakespeare in English. It was one of the first works of Oriental literature to reach the West, being translated into French in 1634, German in 1636 and English in 1774. This translation by the Harvard scholar, Wheeler Thackston, is accompanied by the Persian text plus excellent appendices on proper names, bibliography and Persian and Arabic vocabulary.

After his prologue, Sa'di divided the *Gulistan* into eight chapters 'like the number of heavens', each containing up to forty or so exemplary stories. In themes ranging from the 'conduct of kings' and the 'superiority of contentment' to 'love and youth' and 'feebleness and old age', Sa'di offers wisdom which speaks to the heart of the human condition. It is often supported with memorable aphorisms, as in this on the folly of old men taking young wives: 'if an old man cannot rise without using a staff, when will his staff rise?'

Sa'di's stories reflect an Iranian world, like that of Gorgani's, with connections from China and Ceylon through to Damascus and Egypt. He engages with humans of all types, and in the process shows his dislike of hypocrisy, the value of generosity, his sense of humour, the importance of justice, and the great importance of being humane. The following lines from *Gulistan* grace the entrance to the Hall of Nations of the UN building in New York:

> Human beings are members of a whole,
> In creation of one essence and soul.
> If one member is afflicted with pain,
> Other members uneasy will remain.
> If you have no sympathy for human pain,
> The name of human you cannot retain.

Note

1. Fakhraddin Gorgani, trans. and intro. Dick Davis, *Vis & Ramin* (Washington, DC: Mage Publishers, 2008), xlvii+517pp.; Shaykh Mushrifuddin Sa'di of Shiraz, trans. Wheeler M. Thackston, *The Gulistan (Rose Garden) of Sa'di*, bilingual English and Persian edition with vocabulary (Bethesda, Maryland: Ibex, 2008), ii+253pp.

14

Hunting the Tiger[1]

THE RELATIONSHIP BETWEEN language, religion and nationalist politics in South Asia has meant that Sufi literature in Hindawi, old Hindi, has not had the attention it deserves. For the Pakistani, or the Urdu-speaker more generally, Hindawi might not seem to be the appropriate vehicle for Sufi messages. For the Hindu nationalist of India there is the problem that the first major narrative genre in old Hindi, the forerunner of what is the official national language, is Islamic.

The Magic Doe, the *Mirigawati* of the Indian Sufi master, Shaykh Qutban Suhrawardi, was composed in 1503 as an introduction to mystical practice for disciples. Suhrawardi was attached to the court-in-exile of Sultan Husayn Shah Sharqi of Jawnpur in what is now eastern Uttar Pradesh. The Sharqi court was one of several regional courts in which literature and the arts flourished after the break up of the Delhi Sultanate in the fifteenth century. A particular feature of these courts was the expression of Islamic culture through Indic motifs. One cultural form, the Hindawi Sufi romance, was an important part of the storyteller's repertoire. Such romances were designed to be recited in public in courtly assemblies or in private amongst groups of Sufi disciples. For the Sufi novice there was clear direction as to the path he should travel. For the courtier in search of entertainment there was lush language, rich metaphor, and many a memorable couplet. For instance, on the exultation of love found:

> What doubt was there about this life? They had created
> a love to last through this world and the next.
> Uniting in bed, they played the game of *rasa* [aesthetic feeling],
> enjoying and eating nectar-sweet fruit.

Or alternatively on the Sufi way to be followed:

> If you walk steadily you'll gain the path, but only if you walk in truth.
> If you are true, truth will be your friend and the lions and tigers will
>   not eat you.

The story begins with a prince out hunting when he sees in the distance a glistening seven-coloured doe-woman Mirigawati, and follows her. Mirigawati has magical powers, being able to change shape, and appear and disappear. The prince falls in love, Mirigawati disappears into a lake, and the prince laments his lost love. The prince has several tantalising visions of Mirigawati but is unable to consummate his desire. Eventually he is told that he must seek her in her home, the City of Gold. Thus he sets out in the guise of a Hindu yogi, passing successfully through seven ordeals. On his journey he is forced into marriage with a princess, Rupmini. When he reaches the City of Gold Mirigawati summons him to her. He drops his yogic disguise and the two achieve what we should understand as mystical union although it is most carnally described:

> ' Take your pleasure, lead me and I'll follow!'
> He embraced her, grasping her breasts with his hand,
> and tasting the *rasa*, the juice of lovemaking.
> He clasped her close, crushing her breasts, and drank deep with his
>   lips.
> The maiden moaned and laughed proudly, then enfolded him with
>   her lips.

Meanwhile Rupmini sends him a message, a song describing her misery through twelve months of separation, very much a set-piece. The prince, full of remorse, goes with Mirigawati to find Rupmini. Of course the women get on badly. Eventually, they are made to embrace:

On their faces there was laughter but not liking.
The pain of being a co-wife never leaves one's chest.

All is resolved by the prince going out hunting for a tiger, the symbol of desire. He kills the tiger but dies in the process. The two women commit sati on his funeral pyre.

Some of the Sufi dimensions of the story are evident: the journey in search of love; the seven ordeals or stages along the way; the tension between earthly and heavenly love (Rupmini and Mirigawati); the final conquest of desire and the annihilation of self, the Sufi concept of fana. Indic elements are also evident: the prince as a yogi; the Sanskritic concept of rasa, the juice or savour of love, a jungle of tigers and also elephants; and women who commit sati. We are also reminded of elements in the story shared across the Islamic world system which linked South Asia with the Mediterranean. In one of his ordeals the prince/yogi found himself trapped in a cave by a cannibal herdsman, a predicament from which he only escapes by blinding the herdsman and escaping in a sheepskin – shades of Sinbad the Sailor and Homer's *Odyssey*.

We are very fortunate to have this remarkable work in a sparkling verse translation whose brio effortlessly carries the reader forward. All is well supported by a rich introduction. This is the work, and I must say the work of love, of a brilliant young scholar of the University of Pennsylvania, Aditya Behl, who died in 2009 aged 42. His teacher, Wendy Doniger of the University of Chicago, has ensured that it has been published. It should undermine the ignorance which has surrounded Hindawi literature and, most importantly, bring it to a wider audience.

Note

1. Review of Aditya Behl, trans., Wendy Doniger, ed., *The Magic Doe, Qutban Suhravardi's 'Mirigawati'* (New York: Oxford University Press, 2012), p. 221.

15

The Garden of the Eight Paradises[1]

ZAHIR AL-DIN MUHAMMAD BABUR (1483–1530) is a notable figure of the sixteenth-century world, in part because he founded the Indo-Afghan state which evolved into the Mughal empire but in part, too, because he left an autobiography – still too little known – which reveals him to be highly cultivated, sophisticated, artistic and deeply humane. Such is his iconic status today that he is reviled by India's Hindu nationalists, who sent shockwaves through the subcontinent when in 1992 they tore down his mosque at Ayodhya (UP) which it was claimed had been built on the ruins of a Vaishnavite temple dedicated to Rama. On the other hand, he is celebrated in the newly minted state of Uzbekistan, where Timur and his descendants are amongst the building blocks of nationhood and in whose easternmost city of Andijan, Babur's birthplace, it is he who symbolises past greatness.

Babur's autobiography, which was originally written in Chaghatay Turki, was translated into Persian at the behest of his grandson Akbar. It was brought to the attention of the Anglophone world by the early-nineteenth-century translation of William Erskine and John Leyden and the early-twentieth-century one of Annette Beveridge, a distinguished fellow of the Royal Asiatic Society. It has also been translated into Russian, French, Uzbek and Japanese. This has helped to stimulate many biographies of Babur and a growing quantity of research on the Central Asian, Afghan and north Indian worlds of his time. Particularly important in recent scholarship on Babur has been Eiji Mano's collated edition of the extant Chaghatay manuscripts of the autobiography, published in 1995,[2] and Bilal Yucel's collation of the numerous extant manuscripts of Babur's verse, largely in Chaghatay Turki, which led to the publication of the first complete edition of Babur's verse in Latin script, also in 1995.[3] Using these building blocks Stephen Dale has now written the first critical biography of Babur, offering, as he says, 'a skeptical reading of the *Vaqa'i'* and Babur's poetry in an attempt to understand his life, reconstruct his world and ultimately explain his climactic conquest.' Dale's method is to alternate thematic and narrative chapters. So, the first chapter deals with autobiography in the Islamic tradition, Babur's autobiography in particular, the nature of Babur's spare Turki prose, and the issues of artistic intent and 'truthfulness' the work raises. The second takes us through Babur's early struggle to recapture his patrimony of Samarqand from the Shaybanid Uzbeks to the point in 1504 when he had established a new base in Kabul. The third chapter explores Babur's 'cultural personality': the Timurid inheritance of urban living; of Perso-Islamic culture and respect for scholarship, not least in astronomy in which his forebear Ulugh Beg excelled; the world of language in which Turki and Persian mixed fruitfully; the world of Islam, Persian wisdom literature and the idea of 'Turk' as a racial and linguistic identity; and the significance of what Dale terms the 'Timurid Symposium', echoing the Hellenic form, an aristocratic gathering in which men ate, drank, recited poetry, listened to music and, more often than not, did so in a garden. Babur describes many such occasions. Chapter four deals with Babur's stay in Kabul from 1504, his work in establishing his own state through taxing agriculture and trade, his visit to Sultan Husayn Bayqara's Herat in its last months as a home to Timurid high culture, and his precarious existence as he confronted year by year the pressures of Shaybanid Uzbek power to the north. Chapter five, a chapter full of exciting scholarship, examines Babur's 600 or so extant poems in the context of his autobiography. We are reminded, quite properly, that poetry was a cultural skill on which Turco-Mongol aristocrats placed the highest value, and then Dale sets out to demonstrate how Babur's oeuvre enables us 'to study the literary evolution of a pre-modern poet and to feel the artistic tensions between the personal and the poetical, between life and art'. Chapter six tells the story of Babur's conquest of Hindustan from his first move against the Afghan stronghold of Bajawr northeast of Kabul in January 1519 through his victory over the Afghan forces of Ibrahim Lodi at Panipat in April 1526 to the seal which he set on his conquest by the defeat of Rana Sanga and his Rajputs at the battle of Kanwah in March 1527. Chapter seven analyses Babur's response to Hindustan: his gazetteer of flora and fauna, which reveals the systematizing and classifying nature of his mind; his discussion of the weather, landscape and customs of Hindustan, of which there was little favourable to be said; his analysis of the built environment, in which just nothing matched the standards of Herat and Samarqand; and then places Babur's views in the context of those of earlier Muslim visitors to Hindustan, al-Biruni and Amir Khusraw. The final chapter takes us through the last three years of Babur's life: the capture of Rana Sanga's fortress of Chandiri in early 1528; Babur's formal celebration of the establishment of his empire in autumn 1528; his commencement of a road system linking Kabul to Agra and the lands further East, the forerunner of the Grand Trunk Road; his depression at being stuck in India, away from the people and customary sites of Turco-Mongol sociability: 'Since I have neither friends nor districts, I have not one moment of repose. It was my choice to come here, yet I am not able to go away'; his last campaign against the Lodi Afghans around Allahabad and Ghazipur; and then the strange circumstances of his death on 2 December 1530. His son Humayun was dangerously ill. Akbar prayed that Humayun's illness should be transferred to him. It was, and he died. An epilogue considers the fate of the empire Babur founded, and his lives in the politics of twentieth- and twenty-first-century India and Uzbekistan.

This is an outstanding piece of research such as can be accomplished only by a scholar at the height of his powers. Dale explains and contextualises Babur's world as no one has done before. He brings this vibrant individual so much to life that we come to feel we know him as few others from his time. He does so, moreover, in a book which combines deep scholarship with real accessibility. The outcome is that the late-Timurid world is brought to a new level of understanding in a book which should support many a university course in the field and which richly deserves a paperback edition.

There is one small quibble. Dale is concerned to produce a realistic understanding of the impact of Babur's use of matchlockmen and his pioneering introduction of field artillery in India. He is probably right, therefore, to emphasise the decisive role of the Mongol cavalry, archery and swordwork in achieving the victory at Panipat. Dale again emphasises the role of the Mongol cavalry at the victory of Kanwah in the following year, but chooses to ignore the decisive role of gunpowder as recorded in the victory notice of Shaykh Zayn included in the autobiography: 'From the center of our dear eldest son, Muhammad Humayun, Mustafa Rumi brought forward the caissons, and with matchlocks and mortars broke not only the ranks of the infidel army but their hearts as well.'[4]

There is also quite an important point to be added. Dale notes that it is only after the battle of Kanwah that Babur refers to himself as a ghazi (heroic warrior for the faith) in his poetry and in the titles on his seal and coins. This gives a context for the composition of the autobiography in these years. Ali Anooshahr has noticed, as a result of intertextual analysis, the impact of at least two works relating ghazi activities on Babur's autobiography. The first is Utbi's *Yamini*, a popular history of the reign of Mahmud of Ghazni written in the early eleventh century; the second is *Gazavat-i Sultan Murad ibn Mehmed Khan* (the Holy Wars of Sultan Murad the Son of Mehmed Khan I), which was written by an unknown companion of the Ottoman Sultan Murad II and describes amongst other things the important battle of Varna (1444). Anooshahr suggests that Babur saw his life through a literary prism and that there is a constant interplay between what he has read of his ghazi predecessors and what he does. There is certainly no doubt that he has the great Muslim invaders of India firmly in mind. 'From the time of the apostle till this date only three padishahs gained dominion over and ruled the real Hindustan', he writes, 'the first was Sultan Mahmud Ghazi, who, with his sons, occupied the throne of Hindustan for a long time. The second was Sultan Shihab al-Din Ghuri and his slaves and followers, who ruled this Kingdom for many years. I am the third.'[5] On the other hand, the interplay between the autobiography and the other ghazi texts may tell us more about the art which went into its final composition, which was at the end of Babur's life.

Of especial merit is Dale's analysis of Babur's poetry in the context of his life. It has always been a merit of the autobiography that it enabled us to engage directly with this remarkable man as an individual, and Dale's analysis of his poetry takes us a step forward in engaging with the individual. Understanding well the formulas which dictate the shape of ghazals and ruba'iyat, he shows how engagement with his verse can sharpen our appreciation of Babur's feelings at real events. For instance, the famous moment when as an adolescent he fell in love with a boy he saw in the bazaar, a powerful memory in his emotional life:

> Whenever I observe my love I am badly disconcerted,
> My friends look at me and I look away.

Then, there is the ruba'i with which he closes the description of the battle of Kanwah in the autobiography, which can be read as a cry of relief at his success:

> I am become a desert wanderer for Islam.
> Having joined battle with infidels and Hindus.
> I readied myself to become a martyr,
> God be thanked I am a ghazi.

To conclude there is the depression, which runs through one of his last poems to be found in the *Rampur Diwan*, and which was probably written in 1528 at a time when his health was beginning to fail:

> Finally neither friends nor companions will be faithful.
> Neither summer or winter or companions will remain.
> A hundred pities that precious life passes away
> O, alas, that this celebrated time is futile.

One final point that Dale is concerned to make reminds us that it was a point which E.M. Forster made when he reviewed Annette Beveridge's translation of the autobiography in 1921; it is that Babur's late Timurid world bears many comparisons with the contemporaneous Italy of the Renaissance – for Samarqand read Florence, for Babur read, well just about, Lorenzo de Medici:

> And this is only one of many parallels between Italy and Central Asia which strike anyone familiar with both the Florentine, Sienese and Timurid worlds in the late fifteenth century. These include the cultivation and refinement of aesthetic sensibility amidst a brutal life of constant political and social violence, and the open, unashamed egotism of individuals.

There is little to choose, Dale tells us, between the formation of human types in these societies, apparently so far apart in space and current perceptions. The message is that the walls of the orientalist ghetto, to which Babur has been consigned, need to be broken down and the Florentine and late-Timurid worlds studied side by side. This accomplished book helps make possible this desirable development.

Notes

1. Review of Stephen F. Dale, *The Garden of the Eight Paradises: Babur and the Culture of Empire in Central Asia, Afghanistan and India (1483–1530)* (Leiden: Brill, 2004), xiii+520pp.+15 plates.

The Garden of the Eight Paradises 345

2. Eiji Mano, ed., *Babur-Nama (Vaqayi')* (Kyoto: Syodaka, 1995).
3. Bilal Yucel, *Babur Divani* (Ankara: Ataturk Kultur Markezi, 1995).
4. Wheeler M. Thackston, trans., ed., and annot., *The Baburnama: Memoirs of Babur, Prince and Emperor* (New York: Modern Library, 1996), p. 384.
5. Thackston, *Baburnama*, p. 329.

16

Uses for Grass[1]

'But what happiness to have known Babur!' wrote E.M. Forster in reviewing Annette Beveridge's translation of the *Babur Nama* in 1921. 'He had all that one seeks in a friend. His energy and ambition were touched with sensitiveness; he could act, feel, observe, and remember; though not critical of his senses, he was aware of their workings, thus fulfilling the whole nature of man.'

And what a man Babur was! Thirteenth in line of descent from Genghis Khan through his maternal grandfather, Yunus Khan of Tashkent, Great Khan of the Mongols, and fifth in line of descent from Tamerlaine through his paternal grandfather, Abu Sa'id of Herat, he was powerfully aware of his glittering ancestors and of the traditions of conquest they represented. Throughout his life he strove to emulate them.

Babur found himself catapulted into the competition for power in Transoxiana, in part with his own relatives, but increasingly with the Uzbek Turks, after his father died in 1494, when he was but twelve. Babur aimed to recapture Tamerlaine's capital of Samarqand which 'for nearly 140 years . . . had been in our family'. In his first ten years of campaigning he besieged it three times and conquered it twice. But in this period he was little more than a 'political vagabond' as he described it, subject to the fluid alliances of clan factionalism. At one moment he might be master of a great city; at another fighting for his life with a few followers. Crucial advisers at this time were his mother and grandmother.

From 1504, after Babur captured Kabul and turned it into a permanent base, his position began to change. He soon found himself fighting Afghans whom he noted surrendered by going 'before their foe with grass between their teeth, that is to say "I am your cow".' By 1507 he had strengthened his kingdom in the south by the conquest of the rich trading city of Qandahar. Most of his energies, however, were devoted to fighting the Uzbeks to the north and west. This involved the conquest of Herat and of Bukhara, for a time, and in 1511 his third conquest of Samarqand. But in the upshot the Uzbeks were able to bring greater power to bear in the lands of Transoxiana. In 1512 he was forced out of Samarqand for the last time, and had little further success in the region.

Failure in his family's traditional power centre meant that Babur increasingly looked east towards Hindustan, which Tamerlaine had invaded with conspicuous success in 1398. For years he was held back by the opposition of his officers, but by 1519 he succeeded in engaging them in the first of five probing raids into the region. Then in 1523 he received a formal invitation to invade from the governor of the Punjab; there was growing opposition to the Afghan Lodi regime which ruled much of north India. Babur prepared for the invasion by training his men thoroughly and by acquiring the latest gunpowder technology.

The future of India was decided in two great battles. On 20 April 1526 on the plain of Panipat, north of Delhi, Babur's army of 12,000 men faced Ibrahim Lodi's 100,000 supported by 1,000 elephants. He strengthened his position by using the town of Panipat to guard his right flank and a system of ditches to the left; across the centre of the battlefield he had seven hundred carts tied together in the 'Anatolian manner', matchlockmen being placed behind the carts and cannon in front. In the event Babur used his Mongol cavalry on the wings to drive the Afghan forces into the funnel he had created in front of his centre, where they were pounded into submission by arrows and gunfire. In the second battle, in

March 1527 at Kanwah, west of Agra, Babur used the same tactics to defeat an army of 200,000 fielded by a coalition of Rajputs and Afghans. There is debate as to the role of gunpowder in these victories. Babur, however, thought it crucial at Kanwah: 'From the centre', he wrote, 'Mustafa Rumi brought forward the caissons and with matchlocks and mortars broke not only the ranks of the infidel army but their hearts as well.'

Babur was one of four warriors of Turkic-speaking stock who, in a period of less than a century, founded a major state in the heart of the Eurasian region reaching from the Balkans to Bengal. The others were Mehmet II, the Conqueror (1432–81), who took Constantinople in 1453 and founded the Ottoman empire; Shah Isma'il Safawi (1487–1524), who founded the Safawid empire on the Iranian plateau in the early sixteenth century; and Shaybani Khan (1451–1510), who in the same period drove Babur out of Transoxiana and established Uzbek power in Samarqand. When Babur died in 1530, he had laid the basis of the Mughal empire which was to last until 1858 and which to the end of the seventeenth century was the greatest of these states in wealth and power. While remaining religiously inclusive for much of its existence this empire nevertheless continued to sustain the Muslim political frame established by the Delhi Sultans, which led to the subcontinent becoming home to one-third of the world's Muslims, a fact of major geopolitical significance.

Such is Babur's iconic status today that he is reviled by India's Hindu nationalists, who sent shockwaves through the subcontinent when in 1992 they tore down his mosque at Ayodhya in Uttar Pradesh, which they claimed had been built on the ruins of a Vaishnavite temple dedicated to Rama. On the other hand, he is celebrated in the newly minted state of Uzbekistan, where Tamerlaine and his descendants are amongst the building blocks of nationhood, and in whose easternmost city of Andijan, Babur's birthplace, it is he who symbolises past greatness.

Babur is also rightly famed for his autobiography, the *Babur Nama*. Throughout his life he kept a journal which in his last years he worked into autobiographical form. There is a charming moment when on 25 May 1528 he records a sudden burst of monsoon wind and rain bringing down the porch of his tent before he could gather up the sections of his book on which he was working:

> God preserved me! No harm befell me! Sections of the book were drenched under water . . . We laid them down in the folds of a woollen throne carpet, put it on the throne and piled blankets on it.

He was producing a considerable work: 600 pages in the latest printed text in Turki, even though sections covering fifteen years of his life (1508–19, 1520–5) have been lost.

The autobiography reveals that sensitive, observant, cultivated, highly intelligent Turco-Mongol warrior prince whom Forster would have liked to have befriended. He tells us when he weeps, which is as a young man quite often: 'I found such adversity hard to bear', he declares after losing Samarqand as a teenager, 'I could not help crying a good deal.' He tells us of his first discovery of love, of unreasoning passion: 'In those days I discovered in myself a strange inclination – no, a mad infatuation – for a boy in the camp's bazaar, his name Baburi . . .' He found himself speechless and overcome with confusion whenever he met the boy:

> In that maelstrom of desire and passion, and under the stress of youthful folly, I used to wander, bareheaded and barefoot, through streets and lanes, orchards and vineyards. I showed civility neither to friends nor to strangers, took no care of myself or others.

Babur was a sharp judge of character and ability. The autobiography is full of vignettes of men and women, artists, poets, rulers and retainers. 'Hasan Yaqoub was a small-minded but good-tempered and active man', he wrote of one of his father's followers. 'He was brave, a good archer and polo player, and leapt well at leap-frog competitions . . . But he lacked sense, was narrow-minded and somewhat quarrelsome.'

Close observation of nature runs all the way through Babur's work, whether he is commenting on the quality of the melons produced in this or that district or on the thirty-three different varieties of tulip to be found in the mountains around Kabul. He laid out several gardens and, for instance, in his much-loved Garden of Fidelity outside Kabul observed the performance of different plants. Moreover, he could be awed by nature's magnificence:

> Within two miles of the Ab-e Istada Lake we saw a wonderful sight. Something red like the rose of the dawn kept appearing and vanishing between the sky and the water. On getting close we learned this was caused by flocks of geese, not 10,000 or 20,000 in a flock, but countless.

A systematising mind also worked with Babur's talent for observation. The autobiography contains three surveys or gazetteers – of his Central Asian home province of Fergana, of Kabul, and of Hindustan. The last tells of his contempt for his conquest, as exemplified by the following which Forster tells us the British in India liked to repeat:

> Hindustan is a country of few charms. Its people have no good looks; of social intercourse, paying and receiving visits, there is none; of genius and capacity none; of manners none; in handicraft and work, there is no form or symmetry, method or quality. There are no good horses, no good dogs . . .

Any cultivated man of Babur's time would have pressed home his points with verse, and so did Babur. One of the many achievements of an outstanding recent study of Babur and his world by Stephen Dale, *The Garden of the Eight Paradises: Babur and the Culture of Empire in Central Asia, Afghanistan and India, 1483–1530* (Leiden: Brill, 2004), has been to relate the collected verse of Babur in Turki and Persian, which was published for the first time in the Latin script in 1995, to the autobiography. He shows us how a study of Babur's poetry enables us to be privy to those things he felt most deeply.

Babur, as we might expect, cared about the use of language. He required his son, Humayun, to write letters to him. Humayun, like many a young man of the pen, tried to impress with elaborate decorated prose. Babur replied with words echoed by George Orwell's 'Politics and the English Language':

> Though your letter can be read after much effort, it cannot be understood because of the obscure wording of yours . . . In future, write without elaboration. Use plain clear words. That will lessen your trouble and your reader's.

Once Babur's autobiography was merely enjoyed for its charm and plundered for what it could tell us about the late-Timurid world. But recently Dale has sensitised us to the artfulness in its construction and in the way in which he persuades us to take his point of view. Ali Anooshahr, moreover, in an imaginative intertextual reading has argued that it be considered ghazi (warrior for the faith) literature, noting the interplay in the text between Utbi's *Yamini*, a popular history of Mahmud of Ghazni, who invaded India in the early eleventh century, and the *Gazavat-i Sultan Murad*, the holy wars of the fifteenth-century Ottoman Sultan Murad II.

Furthermore, Babur's engagement with alcohol runs through the book like a theme through a sonata. There are the early intimations of the theme; his comments on the drinking habits of others and his early resistance to wine. It is developed when at last aged 29 discipline is surrendered to sensual appetite. The theme is further developed in many descriptions of drinking parties and of the stupid things said and done under the influence of drink. The theme is brought to its climax in the days before the fateful battle of Kanwah, when he publicly embraced the role of ghazi and renounced wine. The theme dies away with notes of regret:

> Through renouncing of wine bewildered am I;
> How to work know I not, so distracted am I;
> While others repent and vow to abstain,
> I have vowed to abstain, and repentant am I.

As a work of autobiography the *Babur Nama* stands alone in the pre-colonial Muslim world. Certainly, autobiography was part of the Islamic tradition and great men such as the scholar-mystic al-Ghazali (d. 1111) and the philosopher-statesman Ibn Khaldun (d. 1406) produced notable examples. But nothing matches Babur's work for its vital first-person narrative, its evocation of emotions we all share, its elements of self-dramatisation, indeed, its apparently 'modern' sensibility. As a work of world literature it has been rated a worthy companion of the confessions of St Augustine and Rousseau, and the memoirs of Gibbon. Dale quite rightly compares it with that other most revealing autobiography of the sixteenth century, *The Life of Benvenuto Cellini*, of the Renaissance sculptor and goldsmith. In doing so he goes on to make a further point that Forster also made, which is to note the similarities between the late-Timurid worlds of Samarqand and Herat and those of Renaissance Florence and Siena. In both, there flourished egotism and brutality alongside aesthetic sensitivity and high cultivation.

Babur wrote his autobiography in Chaghatay Turki, the language of most of his poetry and of the Turco-Mongol elite which surrounded him. By the end of the sixteenth century, however, few in the Mughal world knew Turki and it was translated into Persian and illustrated in the Mughal workshops, being one of several great books proclaiming the glorious history of the dynasty. It was first brought to the attention of the Anglophone world by a translation of the Persian text by William Erskine and John Leyden in the early nineteenth century, and then once more by Annette Beveridge's translation of the Turki text in the early twentieth century. The most recent translation into English is the fine edition of the distinguished Harvard scholar, Wheeler M. Thackston (New York: Oxford University Press, 1996), who notes that Beveridge's translation reads 'like a student's effort'.

This makes it a pity that Dilip Hiro has chosen the Beveridge text as the basis of his edition. Following Penguin's current policy of dumbing down great works for popular consumption, Beveridge's original 300,000 words have been cut down to 100,000. There are some helpful maps, notes and appendices, but the introduction is innocent of any knowledge of Dale's important work and there is no bibliography. With luck Hiro's edition will draw a new audience to the remarkable Babur. But for the real thing the reader will have to go elsewhere.

Note

1. Review of Zahir al-Din Babur, *Journal of Emperor Babur*, translated by Annette Susannah Beveridge, abridged and edited by Dilip Hiro (New Delhi: Penguin Books India, 2006), p. 424.

17

The Muslim Commander Bond[1]

'THESE DAYS MAWLANA GHALIB . . . is in clover,' wrote the great Urdu poet to a friend in 1861 . . . 'A volume of the *Tale of Amir Hamza* has come – about 600 pages of it . . . and there are seventeen bottles of good wine in the pantry. So, I read all day and drink all night.'

Ghalib, who was also tutor to the last Mughal emperor, is referring to the first edition of his namesake, Ghalib Lakhnawi's, *The Adventures of Amir Hamza* (Calcutta, 1855). A second edition edited by 'Abd Allah Bilgrami, which forms the basis of Musharraf Farooqi's translation, was published by the famed Newal Kishawr Press of Lucknow in 1871. Later, between 1883 and 1917, a monster edition of forty-six volumes each of 1,000 pages was published.

Ghalib is referring as well to that remarkable moment in the movement from oral to print culture in South Asia, and also in the Muslim world when the art of oral storytelling, cultivated as a prime form of human entertainment for thousands of years, came increasingly to be smothered by new media: first print, in particular in the form of the novel; then film and now, dare one say, by the television soap.

We tend to forget, although our children are never slow to remind us, the high rank of oral storytelling in human pleasure. In the Muslim world the storyteller was to be found everywhere: in the bazaars, in the coffee shops, around the camp fire, at court and in the nobleman's retinue. Today you might just get the genuine article in Marrakesh's Djemaa el-Fna. *Amir Hamza* is one of the great storytelling frameworks, open to elaboration according to the skill of the storyteller. As Hamid Dabashi tells us in his excellent introduction: 'it speaks of the moral imagination of peoples and worlds extended all the way from North Africa to Central Asia, from South Asia to China.' It is extant in Arabic, Persian, Balinese, Georgian, Malay, Turkish and a number of South Asian languages; it also forms an important part of the repertoire of the Javanese wayang shadow puppet tradition. *Amir Hamza* is one of those works of world literature which both stores collective memory and helps subsequently to shape it. It is on a par with the *Iliad* and the *Odyssey* of the European classical tradition, the *Ramayana* and *Mahabharata* of the Hindu world, *Beowulf* for the Anglo-Saxons, *Kalevala* for the Finns, and the *Arabian Nights*.

Amir Hamza tells the story of Hamza, paternal uncle of the Prophet Muhammad, an Arab who serves the Iranian emperor Nawshirwan as a military commander, and in doing so falls in love with the emperor's daughter, Mihr Nigar. Amongst the connecting threads of the story are Hamza's warlike deeds in lands from Egypt to India; the persistent enmity of Bakhtak, Nawshirwan's vizier; the comradeship of Amar Ayyar, trickster and wit, Aadi Hamza, foster brother and gluttonous eater, and Muqbil, faultless archer; the watchful counsel of Buzurjmihr, a merlin-like figure; the timely help of Khidr, the legendary Islamic figure; and the love of Hamza and Mihr Nigar. In this context Hamza defeats many enemies, converts many of the defeated to the True Faith, loves many women (whilst always honouring Mihr Nigar), enjoys much ribaldry and gets the better of the demons and fairies of the enchanted world. The action is played out against the central backdrop of Sassanian Iran with its court at Ctesiphon: the whole work, Dabashi tells us, is aware of and pays homage to Firdawsi's *Shahnameh*. At the same time it is linked to the rise of Islam through Hamza, who defends Mecca at the Prophet's behest, and meets his end.

This story has always been more popular in India than in Iran. There is a case for dating its reception in India from the time of the first Muslim invasions from the Persian-speaking world under Mahmud of Ghazni in the eleventh century. It certainly spread through the subcontinent wherever Persian was spoken. *Amir Hamza* was the special favourite of the great Mughal emperor, Akbar, who loved both to hear it told, and to tell it himself in the harem. Indeed, so much did he love it that it was the subject of his largest painting commission of 1,400 pictures on cotton backed with paper to be shown as the story was related – an early film show. It is tempting to suggest that Akbar, the great military commander, identified with Commander (Amir means 'commander') Hamza. In our own world Hamza's equivalent is perhaps Commander Bond, who plays in a similar fixed arena of women, treachery, violence, dangerous enemies, and fantasy.

What kind of world does *Amir Hamza* reveal? At one level it opens up that of the storyteller's art. There are the tricks of rhetoric, repetition, and suspense, laced with graphic action, humanity, death and denouement. For the listener, there are moments to cry out in fear, to tell Hamza not to go down that road, to laugh, to weep. At times we are caught up in a world of magical realism, where 'sense-stealing enchantment' is in play and one suspects the storyteller may have adopted a new style, rhythmic and hypnotic, as he brought to life a Tolkienesque world of demons, fairies and wizards. One could see that, if this was not killed off in the early twentieth century by the rise of the novel, it was certainly going to die at the hand of Islamic reform.

At another level *Amir Hamza* would have shaped a special geography in the minds of its listeners, with Iran at the centre, surrounded by China, India, Ceylon, Arabia and Egypt. It is a world in which much alcohol is drunk by men and women. It is one in which one of the finest set-pieces, for which there must have been many requests for repeats, involves Hamza and his school friends in hilarious action baiting their mulla teacher. There are many technical details which bring it up-to-date for the listener. The vizier, Buzurjmihr in seventh-century Ctesiphon, consults 'Indian,

European, Roman, Dutch and Gaelic clocks'. The warriors, amongst whom Hamza moves, at times use spy glasses and fire pistols, carbines and cannon.

It is a testament to the quality of Farooqi's rendering of the text into English that he both conveys a sense of the art of the 'sweet-lipped historians' and 'nimble scribes of fancy' and at the same time produces a real page-turner. Translator and publisher are to be congratulated on providing a new path into the popular culture of the pre-modern Muslim world and a whole new source of pleasure.

Note

1. Ghalib Lakhnavi and Abdullah Bilgrami, trans. Musharraf Ali Farooqi, intro. Hamid Dabashi, *The Adventures of Amir Hamza* (New York: Modern Library, 2007), p. 948.

18

Aromatherapy

IN THE PRE-MODERN MUSLIM world, from Spain to India, the garden was a central feature of life. Often it was a site of religious symbolism as in the great tomb gardens of India. But almost invariably it was a place of pleasure, a place for poetry and picnics, for male and female sociability. So, gardens were fashioned to delight the senses: trees were planted to create vistas; flowers were placed to delight the eye; water was managed to please both eye and ear; scented plants were positioned to perfume the air both by day and by night. 'Scent is the food of the soul,' declared a tradition of the Prophet Muhammad, 'and the soul is the vehicle of the faculties of man.'

In the pioneering *Scent in the Islamic Garden*, Ali Akbar Husain who teaches at the Indus Valley School of Art and Architecture in Karachi focuses in particular on the use of scent in the culture of the great cities of the early modern Deccan – Bijapur, Golconda and Hyderabad. His book falls into two sections. The first sets the scene: the geology of the Deccan; Hyderabad as the capital city of the Qutb Shahi dynasty, planned by an Iranian at exactly the same time as Shah Abbas was making his magnificent additions to Isfahan; the many gardens which depended on man-made water storage as compared with the wells and canals of northern India, and which reflected a willingness to draw on local plants as compared to the Mughal preference for those from Iran and Central Asia. He rounds off this section by treating us to an overview of the growth of horticultural knowledge in the Muslim world from the great compendium *Kitab al-Filaha*, written by Ibn al-Anwar in Sevile in 1180, down to the gardening manual, *Risala-e Baghbani*, written in Golconda in 1762.

The second section focuses on scent. Husain reminds us that aromatics have an important part to play in the Galenic system of medicine, which the Muslim polymath Ibn Sina (Avicenna, d. 1037 CE) brought to a peak in the Muslim world in his *Qanun*. To this day it underpins the so-called Unani system which is still followed in Iran and South Asia. Fragrance had an important part to play in producing that harmony of bodily humours on which good health was thought to depend. But fragrance was used more generally to furnish a space and to establish a mood. A comprehensive account of perfumery in seventeenth-century Bijapur, written for Sultan Ibrahim Adil Shah II, tells amongst other things of the nine ways of perfuming the royal bedroom with individual bouquets, each with a distinctive purpose and each having its own base notes and top notes. Among those purposes was the creation of an erotic mood.

Finally, in a *piece de resistance* Husain turns to Persian and Urdu poetry written in Bijapur and Golconda to illustrate the central place which gardens played in these early modern Muslim worlds both as context and as metaphor. He declares:

> The gardens in Deccan *masnavis* highlight the progress of Love; the power and splendour of a kingdom; the birth of a prince or a crowning; a victory in battle or its hope; a station in a journey; and the advent of a time of year. Deccan *masnavis* provide glimpses of a Garden of Union and a Garden of Separation; a Garden of the Book and a Garden of Revelation; a Garden of the Dervish and a Garden of Kamadeva; a Garden of the Battlefield, and a Garden of the Martyrs . . .

In all these gardens fragrance is present. It drips from trees like dew, musk and ambergris perfume a prince's pool, and in Love's flower gardens the moon throws open the caskets of the flowers scattering their colours and their fragrance on birds, bees and moths.

The book is well illustrated by plans and colour photographs of the remains of Deccani buildings and gardens. It is rounded off by eleven appendices. Six list the considerable number of flowers and trees which appear in the texts the author has consulted. One describes each of the scented plants mentioned. A final four translate descriptions of gardens from his poetic texts. An introduction by William Dalrymple provides the reader a sense of historical and cultural context.

The outcome is not a work of perfection. There is a tension which runs through the book between the focus on scent and the focus on gardens more generally. The composition, moreover, bears some of the marks of the Ph.D. from which it probably originated. This said, it is an important book which richly deserves its handsome second edition. Through the study of gardens it illuminates the way in which the Deccan Sultanates produced a synthesis of Persian inspiration and Indian essence, which was palpably different from that achieved by the Mughals. It underlines how under-researched the Deccan Muslim world remains as compared with that of the Mughals, and how much there is to be gained from paying attention to it. But most important, by dint of imagination and considerable scholarship, Husain has opened up new subject. It is a considerable achievement.

Note

1. Ali Akbar Husain, *Scent in the Islamic Garden: A Study of Literary Sources in Persian and Urdu* (Karachi: Oxford University Press, 2012).

19

Love of Mahal

BRITAIN, NOW THAT its Indian empire is disappearing into the mists of time, seems to be forgetting the history of the Mughals who ruled most of India but for a few years from 1526 to 1707. The subject is taught in few university undergraduate courses. In recent years little fresh research has appeared from British universities. This is a pity. The Mughal empire at its height was the greatest of the early modern Muslim gunpowder empires, ruling 100 million people as compared with the 22 million of the Ottoman empire and the 6.5 million of the Safawid empire. Indeed, it was surpassed only by China's Ming empire.

The wealth of the Mughal court made it a huge source of patronage, such as no European court could rival, and thus a destination for ambitious and gifted Arabs, Persians, Turks, and even the odd European. The men and women who ruled the empire (yes, there were two women who controlled the royal seal from the harem, and others who participated in government) were remarkable both for their gifts and for their personalities. There are great themes to capture the attention of the budding historian: from how to maintain central power in a vast agrarian region, and how to maximise the tax return to the state while also stimulating the peasant to produce more, through to the role of religion in a multi-faith empire, the changing cultural representations of power, and the strong feelings generated within the royal family, expressed in love, loyalty, and ruthless killing.

Shah Jahan, the son of the emperor Jahangir by a Hindu Rajput wife, lived from 1592 to 1666 and ruled as emperor from 1628 to 1658. He had been a favourite of his grandfather, Akbar, and had kept vigil by the old emperor's bedside as he lay dying. As a young man he was a successful soldier, being awarded the title Shah Jahan 'King of the World' by his father in 1617 on his return from successful campaigning in the Deccan. He continued to be personally involved in warfare up to his failed attempt in the mid-1640s to recapture the family patrimony in Samarqand. He loved music, singing in a light baritone and playing the violin. He was a connoisseur of jewels, studding his Peacock Throne with the most precious of them and deploying semi-precious stones in his signature white marble buildings. He is famous for his love of his second wife, Mumtaz Mahal, 'Most Exquisite of the Palace', who bore him fifteen children in eighteen years and died bearing her last child. His grief, the adventurer Manucci tells us, turned his black beard white in the space of a few days.

If he had any passion which rivalled that for Mumtaz, it was for architecture. From his teenage years he commissioned new buildings and altered old ones, developing the high Mughal style. His most notable achievements were Shahjahanabad, now known as Old Delhi, a completely new capital built for the effective display of royal power, and of course the Taj Mahal, his exquisite tribute to Mumtaz Mahal, rightly described by many as the eighth wonder of the world. It is a building which impresses even the most cynical of visitors. Shah Jahan spent his last eight years gazing at the Taj from his imprisonment in Agra Fort. Having seized power himself by ordering the murder of two brothers and at least six other relatives, he discovered that his sons were not slow to follow his example. 'How do you still regard the memory of Khusrau and Shahriyar', Awrangzib the victor asked him, 'whom you did to death before your accession and who had threatened no injury to you?'

Fergus Nicoll sets out to tell the history of the rise and fall of

Shah Jahan, combining scholarship with accessibility. His work is supported by wide reading in the primary and secondary literature; there are footnotes aplenty. Scholarly appendices explain complex issues such as dating (at least five different calendars are involved) and chronograms, the art of producing a verse about an event the value of the letters of which (each letter of the Persian alphabet has a numerical value) equals the date of the event. There are thirty-two colour illustrations, while the quality of the paper used enables long quotations to be printed in terracotta. Nicoll's style readily grabs the attention. The only problem for the scholar is that one does not know at which point his use of imaginative licence ends and facts supported by evidence begin.

Nicoll gives particular emphasis to three great succession struggles; those to succeed Akbar, Jahangir, and Shah Jahan. The Mughals did not practice primogeniture, so succession was a dog eat dog affair. Rulers did try and indicate who their successors should be. But it was a dangerous business; if one son became too powerful there was a chance that he might overthrow his father, a fact which made Jahangir keep Shah Jahan in uncertainty, damaging their relations. Whatever happened, as the emperor began to age, or suffer a temporary illness in the case of Shah Jahan, the princes would prepare for the showdown. They knew that only one of them would survive the outcome. Nicoll narrates these struggles with great verve and with alertness to the play of court factions.

Particular emphasis, too, is given to the role of women. Following Ruby Lal, who has demonstrated the centrality of women to the Mughal project in the sixteenth century, Nicoll sets out the important roles played in the politics of the era by Mumtaz Mahal and in particular Nur Jahan, the wife of Jahangir. Shah Jahan might have been married to Nur Jahan's niece Mumtaz Mahal but this did not prevent her from making his life miserable. Towards the end of Jahangir's reign Nur Jahan manipulated court politics to try to take the succession away from Shah Jahan in favour of Jahangir's son, Shahriyar, whom she had got married to her daughter by her first husband. Her aim, of course, was less that her daughter should be queen than that she should continue to be the power behind the throne.

Following Ebba Koch, whose masterly study of the Taj was published in 2006, and whose personal assistance Nicoll graciously acknowledges, proper attention is given to this building's design and construction. Shah Jahan was involved in every aspect of the project, which drew on the skills of craftsmen not just from India but from across the Islamic world to the Ottoman empire. An appendix lists which suras of the Qur'an can be found on particular parts of the structure. We are reminded that the Taj was just part of a much larger complex of buildings, including a bazaar and a caravanserai, and that it had a counterpoint across the River Jumna in the Moonlight Garden or Mehtab Bagh, excavated in the 1990s, in which the marble tomb was to be enjoyed at night.

One further point stressed by Nicoll is the extent of the correspondence between the Mughals and the Safawid rulers in Iran. They had common interests in keeping open the long-distance trade routes from north India through Iran to West Asia; the strategic city of Qandahar, which controlled the southern overland route, changed hands several times. Contestants in Mughal succession struggles usually sought Safawid support. On doing so in the early 1620s, Shah Jahan got short shrift from Shah Abbas I: 'God', he said, has 'enjoined sons to obey their parents; the prince should seek to do his father's will, thus removing his father's ground for complaint against him.' Shah Jahan may not have known that a few years earlier Shah Abbas had had his rebellious eldest son killed and two others blinded.

Some matters are surprisingly overlooked. After the death of Mumtaz Mahal, Shah Jahan threw himself into venery, which involved the wives of nobles, so the beggars might cry out as they passed: 'O breakfast of Shah Jahan! Remember us!' or 'O luncheon of Shah Jahan! Succour us!' The reason for his illness in 1657, which sparked the succession struggle leading to his overthrow, was the impact of aphrodisiacs taken to revive his flagging powers. Moreover, in that struggle it is worth noting the emperor's further misery in finding his able daughters on opposing sides. Jahanara going with Shah Jahan and his designated successor, Dara Shikoh and Rawshanara going with Awrangzib, and forming part of the group which condemned Dara to death for apostasy.

There are points where the scholarship is not entirely secure: Allahabad was never the capital of the Mughal subah of Bihar, being the capital of its own subah; Chishti Sufis are not usually linked by blood, as Nicoll suggests, but by spiritual descent; Balkh is not a mountainous kingdom but in the plains of northern Afghanistan; and 'Islamism' or 'political Islam' is a term of art in contemporary political science which is not properly applied to Shah Jahan's moves in an orthodox direction.

Nicoll makes several claims to establish new facts of which the strongest is his explanation for the five-year gap between Shah Jahan's engagement to Mumtaz Mahal, and his eventual marriage, in terms of her family falling out of favour because of her uncle's involvement in a succession plot. But his real claim to novelty is in providing the first book-length study of this remarkable emperor since Saksena,[4] and doing so in a manner which deserves to bring a new following to Mughal history.

Notes

1. Fergus Nicoll, *Shah Jahan: The Rise and Fall of the Mughal Emperor* (London: Haus, 2008).
2. Ruby Lal, *Domesticity and Power in the Early Mughal World* (Cambridge: Cambridge University Press, 2005).
3. Ebba Koch, *The Complete Taj Mahal* (London: Thames & Hudson, 2006).
4. B.P. Saksena, *History of Shah Jahan of Dihli* (Allahabad: Indian Press, 1932).

20

Cosmopolis of a Shared Worldview[1]

A FEATURE OF SCHOLARSHIP on Muslims and Islam in South Asia until recently was that it tended not to explore their connections beyond the subcontinent. The British as historians, though not as rulers, established this tendency. After Partition, Indian Muslims for very good political reasons chose not to draw attention to their historical links with the wider Muslim world. Recently this has all changed. Several books on the Mughals, in particular Moin Azfar's *The Millennial Sovereign: Sacred Kingship and Sainthood in Islam*[2] has demonstrated that it is not possible to understand Mughal kingship without becoming aware of its Timurid background. The same goes for much else of the Mughal period from the role of women at court through to Islamic scholarship. Nile Green in his *Bombay Islam: The Religious Economy of the West Indian Ocean, 1840–1915* has demonstrated that to understand Islam as practised in nineteenth- and twentieth-century Bombay it is not nearly enough to take into account its hinterlands in northern India and Hyderabad.[3] One must also take into account the great networks of trade, princely and Sufi connections linking the Indian Ocean worlds of South and East Africa, the Hadhramawt and Iran to the great seaport.

Seema Alavi is concerned to show how in the nineteenth century networks of primarily Indian Muslims grew in the spaces which lay between the British and Ottoman empires, and also to a lesser extent the Russian empire. Important underpinnings of these networks were the improved communications provided by the British Empire but also largely similar positions on Islamic reform, that is, being against worship at saints' shrines and for a personal engagement with scripture. Sufi connections were also there, in particular those of the reforming elements of the Naqshbandiyya, so too, frequently, were those of trade. Particularly important in fashioning a world of connected sensibility was print, only seriously adopted in the Ottoman and Indian Muslim worlds in the early nineteenth century. Printed books, and increasingly newspapers, helped to fashion a shared world of ideas and feelings. Thus, the Muslim world of India was linked with Mecca, Cairo, Istanbul and further afield. Alavi terms this world of personal connections and often a shared worldview a Muslim cosmopolis.

Alavi begins with an excellent chapter on the Muslim reformers in the context of the transition to British rule. She argues that the central processes of reform – the reduction of emphasis on the role of the Sufi pir, the greatly increased emphasis on scripture and the personal responsibility of the individual in engaging with it, were part of a larger process of Mughal crisis. In this, a whole world of Indo-Persian understandings of life and knowledge began to give way, in religion in particular, before an 'Arabic scripture-based tradition'. This set going a discourse which still continues in South Asia today, as it does through the rest of the Muslim world. The reformers who preached their message throughout South Asia were involved in a wide range of trading activities, including the arms trade, tribal politics and the Mutiny Uprising of 1857.

Alavi then focuses on five figures whose careers exemplify the working of her Muslim cosmopolis. The first is Sayyid Fadl (1824–1901) whose father had come from the Hadhramawt and established a major position of religious leadership in Malabar. Fadl, a religious reformer, was implicated in the Moplah jihads against the British presence and deported to the Hadhramawt in 1852. By

1876 he had become, with Ottoman support, the ruler of Dhofar. He had a network of connections that stretched from Acheh in Sumatra to North Africa. He cultivated good relations with both the British and the Ottomans, at times playing a broking role, and in 1880 was given the honorary title of 'wazeer' by the Sultan. In the same year the British resident in Istanbul reported that Fadl's influence in Turkey was huge.

A close associate of Fadl in the Ottoman Empire was Mawlana Rahmat Allah Kayranawi (1818–92). Rahmat Allah first came to notice in 1854 when at Agra he played the leading role in debating with the Christian missionary, Dr Pfander, on the authenticity of the Bible and the Qura'n. In 1857 he was a notable leader in the uprising and with a price on his head was forced to flee to Mecca. There, with the financial assistance of a Bengali lady, he established the Madrasa Sawlatiyya, which became a major focus for Indians of a reforming bent. He came to receive substantial honours and resources from Abd al-Hamid II, who asked that Rahmat Allah's brother should stay in Istanbul and be director of the Hamidiyah Library. At an earlier Sultan's request Rahmat Allah wrote the *Izhar al-Haqq*, the record of his debates with Dr Pfander, which was to have a substantial influence on Muslim critiques of Christianity. But, his madrasa was his first love; Alavi tells us that it was the inspiration for Deoband.

One teacher at Rahmat Allah's Madrasa Sawlatiyya was Hajji Imdad Allah (1817–99). Involved in the Mutiny Uprising at Thana Bhawan, he too was forced to flee to Mecca with a price on his head. In Mecca he wrote several books; much of his correspondence reflects his anxieties about publication. He taught many Indian students and gave spiritual guidance to Muslims in India by letter. Alavi regards Imdad Allah's best-known work, the *Ziya' al-Qulub*, as a classic example of cosmopolitanism, although in this case it was a cosmopolitanism of the mind rather than of life. He shows the Sufi to be mediating 'not only between the individual and God but between the local and the universal by setting standardized universal forms of devotion'. His cosmopolitanism was one of achieving consensus and harmony in the Muslim community

Alavi's fourth exemplar is Nawab Siddiq Hasan Khan of Bhopal (1832–90), a reformer and one of the founders of the Ahl-i Hadith movement. After arriving penniless in Bhopal he rose through the state administration and then capped his good fortune by becoming the consort of Shah Jahan, the Begum of Bhopal, who awarded him a jagir worth the immense sum of Rs 75,000 per annum. He used these advantages to write some eighty books promoting his reforming ideas. These were published simultaneously in Arabic, Persian and Urdu and from India, Istanbul, Cairo, Mecca and Medina. Imperial postal systems as well as networks of Indian merchants and agents helped to distribute his work across the region. They even reached the world of the Sudanese Mahdi and the Sanusiyya of the Sahara. While the British regarded him as a fanatical Muslim and a seditious subject, the Nawab regarded himself as a loyal citizen of the British Empire who happened to have a remarkable intellectual presence across the Central Islamic lands. He aimed to use this to help fashion 'a progressive social body – a civilizational frame that would function as a formidable force alongside the Western global imperium'.

The final exemplar is Mawlwi Jafar Thanesri (1838–1905). In 1863 he was arrested for trying to smuggle funds to the anti-British mujahidin on the Northwest Frontier and deported to the penal colony on the Andaman Islands. There he was integrated into the colonial administration and came to work closely with the deputy commissioner. Unlike the other exemplars, Thanesri did not travel outside the subcontinent. His writings, however, both from the Andaman Islands and from the mainland reveal a man whose vision of his land, his mulk, was formed by the British administrative and legal framework, the sarkar amaldari, while at the same time he had an Islamic identity with the capacity to range more widely, if not explicitly, within the Muslim cosmopolis. He had, as Alavi declares, 'an Islamic identity that was culled from within the networks of colonial rule even as it remained firmly rooted in the spiritual and moral frame of Islam.'

Alavi rounds off her book with what at first sight seems a strange excursus – the plotting of Dalip Singh, son of the former Sikh ruler Ranjit Singh, with the Russians to invade and recreate a kingdom in India. Her point, however, is to demonstrate how Dalip Singh used the networks of the Muslim cosmopolis in making his plans.

In this book, which is the product of considerable research both in the colonial archive and in the voluminous writings of her exemplary figures, Alavi has developed a strong case for the existence of her Muslim cosmopolis. We note its interdependence with the great empires of the time. We also note how some of its key figures, while not enamoured of British power, had great respect for British rule of law. We note, too, the common theme of a search in religious terms, though not necessarily based on the Turkish caliphate, for greater Muslim unity. Alavi makes the important point that the transnational Muslim sensibility represented by her cosmopolis is one which modern rulers, particularly in the West, would be wise to take more into account.

There are some odd statements. For instance: there was not a Viceroy called D. Grey in 1916 (p. 326); I do not think that Muhammad ibn 'Abd al-Wahhab can be described as anti-British (p. 362) – how much did he know of them? Moreover, I really do not think the reformists 'reinvented the Arabic-scripture-driven tawhid doctrine to suit their market-driven interests' (p. 84). Surprisingly, for a monograph published by a major university press there is no system of transliteration so Shahwaliulla is usually represented thus while another scholar with the same name is transliterated with the more usual Shah Waliullah. 'Abd al-Hayy Lucknawi is represented in three different ways. And perhaps rather prissily I got tired of ships 'carting' people across the oceans. But these should be regarded as mere quibbles to set alongside a great achievement. Seema Alavi has opened up a cosmopolis for others to study further. In the process she has cemented her position in the first rank of historians of South Asia.

Notes

1. Seema Alavi, *Muslim Cosmopolitanism in the Age of Empire* (Cambridge, MA: Harvard University Press, 2015).
2. Moin Azfar, *The Millennial Sovereign: Sacred Kingship and Sovereignty in Islam* (New York: Columbia University Press, 2012).
3. Nile Green, *Bombay Islam: The Religious Economy of the Western Indian Ocean 1840–1915* (New York: Cambridge University Press, 2011).

21

In Reverse[1]

'It is not pleasant being Arab these days', declared Samir Kassir, a Lebanese intellectual and supporter of Rafiq Hariri, after the prime minister was assassinated in Beirut on 14 February 2005. Just over three months later, as if to make the point, Kassir was blown up in his Alfa Romeo. Rogan tells this story early on in his excellent book, setting its tone in two ways: it is about the Arabs in recent centuries when they had lost control of their history; it is also a story told not, for the most part, out of the archives of Western governments but by Arab voices – Rogan believes that Westerners might view Arab history differently if they saw it through Arab eyes.

Thus, Rogan's history begins not as some notable histories of the past (for instance, those of Hitti, Lewis and Hourani) with the birth of the Prophet Muhammad and the five centuries of glory which followed, the time when in Hitti's words 'around the name of the Arabs gleams that halo which belongs to world-conquerors', but with the Ottoman conquest of Mamluk Egypt, and subsequently the rest of the Arab world, from 1517.

Ottoman rule did not change much, and therefore did not bring home the full meaning of the loss of power. The Ottomans ruled, as most empires do, in collaboration with local elites, and it is arguable that the process changed the empire more than it did Arab lives. The ambitions of some notables could come to clash with those of the empire, as did those of the Saudis of central Arabia, and their religiously puritan Wahhabi allies, who in 1802 drove northwards into Iraq, sacking the Sh'ia shrine city of Karbala, and then in 1806 did yet further damage to Ottoman legitimacy by annexing the holy cities of Mecca and Medina. Arab life under Ottoman rule in the pre-industrial era was not that harsh.

All this changed as the West began to engage with the Arab world in the nineteenth century. North Africa bore the brunt initially. The starting point was Napoleon's invasion of Egypt in 1798 where for three years the French spoke the language of Enlightenment ideals to a bemused local population, until they were chased away by the British. But the beginning of a truly bitter engagement began when in 1830 the French invaded Algeria, seeking satisfaction after its Dey had hit their consul with a fly whisk. The war of conquest lasted seventeen years, left over 100,000 Algerian civilians dead, and was accompanied by a major programme of French colonisation.

Growing awareness of European power led to programmes of self-strengthening. The most impressive was that led by Muhammad 'Ali and his descendants in Egypt. Muhammad 'Ali, an Ottoman officer, rose to power in the disturbed conditions following Napoleon's departure from Egypt. He began a process of technological and industrial innovation, and most importantly developed a peasant army after the French model, which was able both to suppress the Wahhabis in Arabia and win victories over Ottoman armies as far north as Anatolia. His successors tried to develop the economy further by making concessions to Western business, of which the Suez Canal, built by a French company, was the greatest. The problem was that the costs of self-strengthening made these Arab regimes bankrupt, placing them in the hands of European bankers. The last thirty years before World War One saw the European powers partitioning the Arab lands of North Africa amongst themselves, the French adding Tunisia (1881) and Morocco (1912) to Algeria, the Italians taking Libya (1912), and the British Egypt (1882), where the Suez Canal had become a vital imperial lifeline.

Events, during and immediately after World War One, suggested that Arab fortunes might be about to change. British and Arab forces united to drive out the Ottomans. In 1918 the British and French announced their support for the creation of national governments in Arab lands through a process of 'self-determination'. This was in the context, moreover, of President Wilson's fourteen points, of which the twelfth assured the Arabs of 'an absolutely unmolested opportunity of autonomous development'. There were high hopes of a brave new Arab future. Then, the French and the British, following their secret wartime Sykes–Picot agreement, decided that their imperial interests were more important than Arab freedom. In 1920 French colonial troops, many of them North African Arabs, drove the Arab nationalists out of Damascus, and so after they had been dressed up with the decency of mandates Syria and the Lebanon were added to the French possessions in North Africa. In the same year the British used 100,000 of their colonial troops to squash a national uprising in Iraq. This Arab land as a mandate, along with Transjordan and Palestine, was added to the British Empire. 'The Arabs', Rogan reminds us, 'were never reconciled to this fundamental injustice.' It is a recurring theme in the speeches of Osama bin Laden.

Arab experience of the European empire between the World Wars only gave them further reasons for bitterness. In 1925, for instance, the French in trying to impose their will on Damascus shelled the city for three days, killing 1,500 people and destroying many of the city's finest houses. The British found themselves in a totally hopeless situation in Palestine, where they had undertaken in their mandate to support the development of a Jewish homeland without interfering with the rights of the Palestinians. Eventually the contradictions of this arrangement led to the Arab revolt of 1937–9, which the British suppressed so ruthlessly that 10 per cent of the adult males were either killed, wounded, imprisoned or exiled.

The Nazi genocide of the Jews in Europe gave an extra push to the Zionist cause and the emergence of Israel out of the mandate in Palestine, a process known to the Arabs as al-Nakba, the disaster. In 1947 the Palestinians numbered 1.2 m as opposed to 600,000 Jews; they owned 94 per cent of the land. It was not surprising that they rejected the UN partition resolution which gave them only half of their country. There followed a war between the Palestinians and the Jews, which saw about 300,000 Palestinians driven, one way or another, from their homes. The British left in 1948, and after the war between the surrounding Arab states and the Zionists, Israel was established with 78 per cent of the original mandate territory and 750,000 Palestinian refugees. The defeat immediately sparked coups, assassinations and a revolution in the four Arab states surrounding Israel. It also meant the end of serious British influence in the region. The legacy was an enduring Arab sense of injustice.

The background of the Palestine disaster and the long history of Arab impotence helps to explain the fervour which met the Egyptian revolution of 1952 and the subsequent rise of Nasser as the hero of the Arab world. His defiance of the British, culminating in his successful resistance to what the Arabs call the 'Tripartite Aggression' but the British call the 'Suez Crisis', cemented his position. Nasser's prominence came to a peak when the United Arab Republic was formed in 1958 from the union of Egypt and Syria, which sent shockwaves through Arab capitals. 'For one brief heady moment', Rogan tells us, 'it looked as though the Arab world might break the cycle of foreign domination that had marked the Ottoman, imperial and Cold War eras to enjoy an age of true independence.'

But, as so often in modern Arab affairs, it was a false dawn. In 1961 the United Arab Republic broke up. Nasser had been warned by a former Syrian president that Syrians were difficult to govern: 'fifty percent . . . consider themselves leaders, twenty-five percent prophets, and ten percent imagine they are God'. And so it proved. As during the 1960s Arab states took sides in the Cold War, dreams of Arab unity faded.

Arab troubles continued. In 1962 Algerian independence was won from France but only at the cost of one million Algerian lives. Then there was the disaster, termed by Nasser al-Naksa, 'the reversal': the comprehensive defeat of Syria, Jordan and Egypt by Israel in the Six Day War of 1967. Control of the West Bank, the last significant piece of former mandate Palestine, which might form a Palestinian state, was lost to Israel. The Palestinians now realised that they could no longer rely on Arab rulers to promote their interests. They must take their fate into their own hands. This era of Arab hope was brought to an end by the death of Nasser in 1970, which produced an extraordinary outpouring of grief, in which Arabs certainly wept for 'The Lion', but also for themselves.

The 1970s saw two new players make a major entrance on the Arab scene. The first was oil. By this time the Arab states were the dominant producers in the world. This was a mixed blessing. On the one hand, oil wealth made them vulnerable and distorted development, but on the other hand it gave them, if they operated in unison, a weapon. The power of this weapon was demonstrated in the Yom Kippur War of 1973, when Arab action to quadruple the price of oil to put pressure on Western governments to try to end the war while Egypt still had military gains. Not all Arabs regarded Anwar Sadat of Egypt's military campaign as a success, but more had been achieved than ever before by Arab arms against Israel; the Egyptians recaptured the east bank of the Canal and the Syrians a piece of the Golan Heights.

The second new player was Islam. Arabs had been preparing for its political role from the foundation of the Muslim Brotherhood (Islamists) in the 1920s. The decline of Arab nationalism created the vacuum into which it was able to insert itself. The Iranian revolution of 1978–9, in which Islamic forces helped to topple an American-backed autocrat, sent a powerful signal. This was followed in November 1979 by the capture of the Great Mosque in Mecca by Islamist forces which threatened the Saudi state; in October 1981 by the assassination of President Anwar Sadat by a splinter group of the Muslim Brotherhood; and in 1981–2 by a brutal war between the Muslim Brotherhood and the government of Hafiz al-Asad in Syria. The Israeli invasion of the Lebanon in 1982 to drive out the PLO created the conditions for the emergence of the Shi'a Islamist party, Hizb Allah, a much more determined enemy.

Through the 1980s the Afghan jihad against the Russians – in which many Arabs participated – exercised a considerable influence, with many jihadis returning determined to fashion an ideal Islamic order in their countries. December 1987 saw the beginning of the first Palestinian Intifada against Israel, in which over one year 626 Palestinians were killed, 37,000 injured and 35,000 imprisoned. In this context, Hamas, the Islamic Resistance Movement, emerged out of the Muslim Brotherhood and quickly showed itself to be better organised and less corrupt than the secular PLO. By now Islamist values were coming to be expressed in Arab public space, which had once been strikingly secular, as young men wore beards and young women headscarves.

The end of the Cold War created a new context for Arab lives: but not a better one. The US was now the hegemonic power in Arab lands. Arabs quickly discovered what this meant when Saddam Husayn's occupation of Kuwait in 1990 was met by an assault on Iraq by the USA and its allies which left thousands of civilians dead. Arab states were evenly divided over the action, but for most ordinary Arabs it was another example of heartless Western imperialism. Their views were not changed by the Anglo-American invasion of Iraq of 2003, which was undertaken for specious reasons and which by 2009, according to the Iraqi government, had led to 150,000 civilian deaths.

US hegemony also meant that its client, Israel, seemed to have a freer hand to bring misery to its Arab neighbours. In 1996, in the context of Hizb Allah attacks on Israeli positions in southern Lebanon and missile attacks on northern Israel, Israel launched its Grapes of Wrath operation, which left 400,000 Lebanese displaced and much infrastructure destroyed. In 2006 Israel, irritated by a Hizb Allah raid across its northern frontier, attacked again and destroyed much of South Beirut and left one million Lebanese displaced. In January 2009, after a six-month ceasefire had led to no relaxation of Israel's control over Gaza's frontier, Hamas began to fire rockets. Israel responded with a two-week assault on this densely populated enclave, targeting UN agencies, hospitals, schools and residential areas. An estimated $1.4bn of damage was inflicted, 1,300 Palestinians were killed and 5,100 wounded. There were thirteen Israeli dead and eight wounded.

Let us repeat Samir Kassir's words: 'It is not pleasant being Arab these days.' By their actions, moreover, the West and its clients have shown themselves largely indifferent to Arab suffering. It is hardly surprising that Arabs, and Muslims elsewhere in the world, danced in the streets at the news of the 9/11 assault on the USA. As little has changed since 2001, it is to be expected that, if there were a similar assault, the Arab response would be similar.

Rogan has written an authoritative and wide-ranging history. The text is easy to read with useful summaries at the end of each chapter. Moreover, distinctive Arab voices make themselves heard, whether it be a Damascus barber commenting on the weakening of Ottoman authority, an Egyptian scholar noting the injustice of the British response to the Dinshaway incident, or the courageous resistance of Fatiha Bouhired and her twenty-two-year-old niece, Djamila, in the battle of Algiers.

Furthermore, in a context where partisanship is the norm, Rogan is even-handed. Yes, we are told about the unprovoked attack by Jewish forces on the Arab village of Dayr Yasin on 9 April 1948, which left 250 villagers dead. But this is immediately balanced by an account of a Palestinian attack on a Jewish medical convoy in Jerusalem in which 76 Jews were killed. Rogan is meticulous in giving the numbers of Arabs killed and wounded by Western and Israeli action in Arab lands. But he also makes clear the brutal ways of the Arabs with each other: Hafiz al-Asad's levelling of the city of Hama as he tried to suppress the Muslim

Brotherhood, Saddam Husayn's ruthless action against the Shi'as who rose against him after the first Gulf War, and the between 100,000 and 200,000 killed in the fifteen years of Lebanon's Civil War.

There is a school of thought which argues that if Arabs have had a miserable time in recent centuries, it is largely their fault. There may be some truth in this. But Rogan makes it clear that the West has much to answer for. He also makes it clear that Arab societies, as opposed to their rulers, are increasingly finding the answer to their problems in political Islam. 'In a free and fair election in the Arab world today,' he declares, 'I believe the Islamists would win hands down.'

Note

1. Review of Eugene Rogan, *The Arabs: A History* (London: Allen Lane, 2009).

22

Women, Leadership, and Mosques

Changes in Contemporary Islamic Authority[1]

TWO OF THE MOST important issues in the modern Islamic world are: first, religious authority and its maintenance at a time when change takes place with increasing rapidity, and second, conventional understandings of the position of women and their conflict with new interpretations drawn from religious reform, the requirements of the modern economy, the needs of the modern state, and globally supported positions on human rights. *Women, Leadership, and Mosques*, which had its origins in a conference, hosted by Hilary Kalmbach and Masooda Bano in 2009 at Oxford, embraces both of these big issues, but does so by focusing very specifically on women's religious authority. In the pre-modern era, in some Sufi contexts and in the transmission of knowledge, in particular Hadith, some women had authority. This book, however, concentrates on a contemporary phenomenon, the growing presence of women in madrasas and mosques, their growing involvement in religious learning, in religious interpretation, and even in giving religious leadership to men.

Hilary Kalmbach introduces the book with an excellent discussion of the theoretical issues involved in Islamic authority, making it clear that in Islamic terms we are in new territory:

> In the twentieth and twenty-first centuries female Islamic leadership has dramatically expanded . . . in part because of structural changes in Islamic authority . . . as well as shifts in the roles and activities of women in many Islamic communities . . . women have been able to claim exoteric, scholarly religious authority based on at least some – and occasionally a significant amount of – formal learning, mixed with reputation, teaching experience, charisma, a pious image, commitment to religious and charitable causes, and family ties.

Masooda Bano rounds off the collection by drawing out some of the common themes in the book in a study of the Jami'ah Hafsah, a women's madrasa founded in Islamabad (Pakistan) in 1986, whose teachers and students engaged in armed protest against the state in 2007. She offers an extreme example of women's religious authority at work in the form of Umm-i Hassan, a leading preacher at the madrasa, and shows how she and her followers were radicalised by moves on the part of the Pakistani state to demolish their madrasa, how they emerged in part at least as a result of the wish of Deobandi 'ulama' and were embedded within a broader Islamist network; and finally, how deeds were arguably more important than a capacity to interpret religious texts in consolidating religious authority. Umm-i Hassan lost both her son and her husband in the government's assault on her madrasa and the Red Mosque next door to it.

Twenty substantial essays lie between the introduction and conclusion, half of these focusing on women's authority in Muslim-majority societies, and the other half on women's authority in minority ones. They range from Morocco, Turkey and Iran through to China, Sweden and the USA. They are divided into three sections, representing the three major questions the book sets out to answer. The first question involves the creation of space for the exercise of women's religious authority, and the relative roles of male invitation, state intervention and women's initiative in making this possible. We are shown how male invitation in the context of state oppression of Muslims in sixteenth- and seventeenth-century China led to the foundation of the women's only mosques which are a feature of the contemporary Hui community. On the other hand, we are shown how the Moroccan state, in recent years, keen to counter the impact of Islamic revivalists, has deliberately created space for female leadership in the country's mosques. In Turkey the state has operated on a broader scale through its Directorate of Religious Affairs, which employs over 350 highly educated women, creating circumstances in which they produce fatawa and give sermons to men as well as women. In Saudi Arabia the role of the state has had the opposite effect. The state's desire to exclude women from most religious spaces has led over the past two decades to women carving out for themselves a parallel religious universe, both virtual as well as real.

The second question the book seeks to answer is how women have used the opportunities which they, state, and society have created to consolidate their positions as religious authorities. We see how women might circumvent the limitations of established religious spaces or official religious posts to create new opportunities, as in the case of Nalia Ziganshina of Kazan who used her position on the Tatarstan Islamic Spiritual Board both to run the Union of Muslim Women and to support the unofficial civil society association, the Social Organization of Muslim Women. So too we see how women have come to take the lead, particularly in Europe, where the needs of female students might contrast sharply with the teachings of male teachers trained abroad. Thus, for instance, a Swiss Muslim women's association distanced itself from male control by establishing itself as a legally independent association. A further striking example of the consolidation of a space for women's religious authority is the way in which the image of Fatimah al-Zahra has come to be manipulated in Iran. Traditionally, Fatimah was always a 'reserved obedient and domestic' figure but in contemporary Iran she is a 'proactive self-confident figure'. The key agent of this redefinition was the Iranian Islamist thinker, 'Ali Shari'ati, who died in 1977. The outcome has been a considerable development of this model and the emergence of major women Shi'i scholars.

The third section explores the impact of female religious authority on Muslim women. Some use their authority to reinterpret texts, to reorganise gendered space and to argue for new roles for Muslim women. We are shown, for instance, how two Egyptian women preachers pass on Islamic teachings which can empower women against either family attempts to control their lives or the demands of custom. We are shown, too, the impact of feminist readings of the Qur'an by Asma Barlas and Amina Wadud and the impact of the preaching and leadership of the latter both in the USA and South Africa. Muslim women, however, do not just adopt positions moving in a feminist direction; they are just as likely to use their authority to support traditional understandings of gender roles and orthodox senses of piety. An examination of the positions amongst Indonesian women's religious leadership clearly sets out this division.

Hilary Kalmbach and Masooda Bano, who are post-doctoral research fellows at Oxford, are to be congratulated on producing an outstanding book. Indeed, it is one of those rare books which opens up a whole new subject; it is a landmark in the field. The issue of women's religious scholarship is presented to us in rich and wide-ranging scholarship. The articles are invariably respectful of historical and social context; nuance tends to be embraced rather than ignored. Moreover, the whole work is extremely well-planned, so as to make its main arguments readily accessible. Much work must have gone into its editing. The outcome is essential reading for all those interested both in issues of authority in the contemporary Muslim world and in the new spaces opening up for Muslim women.

Note

1. Masooda Bano and Hilary Kalmbach, eds, *Women, Leadership, and Mosques: Changes in Contemporary Islamic Authority* (Leiden and Boston, MA: Brill, 2012), xvii+581pp.

Index

'Abduh, Muhammad, 50
'Ali, Mawlana 'Abd al- of Farangi Mahall, 160
'Ali, Mir Sayyid (painter), 261
'Ali, Muhammad (ruler of Egypt), 264, 373
'Ali, Mumtaz, 219
'ālim, xv
'Arabi, Ibn, 39, 42, 63, 64, 89, 97, 135, 207, 210, 242, 250
'Askari, Abu Hilal al-, 91
'Asqalani, Ibn Hajar al-, 118
'Azam, Abd Allah, 53
'Aziz, Hakim 'Abd al-, 196
'Azizi hakims, 194, 195
Abbas, Shah (Safawid ruler), 235, 236, 358
Abdali, Ahmad (Afghan invader), 259
Acheh, 18, 25, 44, 107–8, 269, 368
Act, Waqf Validation of 1913, Shari'a Application of 1936, Child Marriage Restraint of 1929, Dissolution of Muslim Marriages of 1939, 188
adab (the literary arts), 88, 91–2, 105
adab, xv
Afghani, Jamal al-Din al-, 42, 50
Africanus, Leo, 106
Afshar, Nadir Shah, 236

Ahl al-Qur'an, 6, 135, 165, 206
Ahl-i Hadith, 19, 135, 165, 182, 206
Ahmad, Ghulam of Qadian, 165, 207
Ahmad, Muhammad al-Mahdi, 47–8
Ahmad, Nadhir, 196, 219, 284
Ahmad, Sayyid of Rae Bareli, 45, 212
Ahmadiyya, 6, 6, 137, 149, 309, 313
Akbar (Mughal emperor), 11, 16, 64, 68, 105, 134, 143, 214, 234–5, 241, 259, 262, 263–4, 339, 341, 356, 362–3; Amir Hamza and, 356; Iranians and, 237; Persian and, 239
*Akhbārī*s, xv, 247
Alam, Arshad, 9
Alavi, Seema, 18, 193, 269, 366, 367, 370
Ali, Ameer, 221; the Prophet and, 184
Ali, Mawlana Mahomed, 218; his *Comrade*, 269, 272
Aligarh movement, 281, 282
All-India Muslim League, 13
Allah, Hajji Imdad, 19, 245, 368–9
Allah, Hajji Shari'at, 45
Allah, Hizb, 53, 66, 155, 377–8
Allah, Mulla Hasan Nasr 155

385

386 Index

Allah, Munshi Zaka, 284
Allah, Nawab Salim, 282, 290
Allah, Shah Kalim, 245
Allah, Shah Wali, 42, 43, 64, 75, 134, 164, 182, 205, 206, 250
Almagest, 70
Amin, Idi, 307
Amin, Mir Muhammad (of Nayshapur), 261
And-Argh-Muhammad of Timbuktu, 106
Andric, Ivo (Bosnian writer), 305
Anooshahr, Ali, 342–3, 351
Ansari, Dr M.A., 292, 295
Aqit of Timbuktu, 106
Arabia, 43, 44
Archbold, William, 293
Arcot, Nawabs of, 263
Ardabili, 'Abd al-'Aziz, 261
Arendt, Hannah, 79, 226
Asma'u of Sokoto, 118, 119
astrology, 8, 61, 70–1
astronomy, 8, 61, 69
Ataturk, *see* Mustafa Kemal
Attar, Shaykh Hasan al-, 263–4
Attewell, Guy, 196
authority, 9–10; assault on, 211–14; colonial model and, 191; crisis in the Islamic world, 152–79; literary leaders and, 196–8; print and, 33; religious leaders and, 181–93; rulers and, 198–200; strategies in Muslim South Asia, 180–203; Unani hakims and, 193–6; women's religious authority, 20, 380–3
Awadh, 234; Nawabs of, 263; a Shi'a state 246–7; 'Shiraz of India', 245, 263

Awrangzib (Mughal emperor), 106, 11, 236, 241, 259, 362, 365
Ayub, Gohar, 13
Azad, Abul Kalam, 207; his *al-Hilal*, 269
Azad, Muhammad Husayn, 196, 198, 250, 286
Azra, Azyumardi, 65, 135

Baba, Ahmad, 107
Babur, Zahir al-Din Muhammad (Mughal emperor), 15–16, 119, 234, 235, 259; as ghazi, 342–3; biography by Stephen Dale, 339–45; E.M. Forster and, 344, 346; mosque of, at Ayodhya, 348; Uzbekistan and, 348; verse of, 340–1, 343–4
Badauni, 'Abd al-Qadir, 261
Baghdadi, Mawlana Khalid, 45, 264
Bahr al-'Ulum Farangi Mahalli, 65, 246, 291
Bakri, Mustafa al-, 4, 43, 47
Balban (Delhi sultan), 158
Balfour Declaration, 266
Bangash, Yaqoob, 4
Banna, al-Hasan, 4, 51, 55, 148
Bano, Masooda, 20, 380, 381, 383
Bano, Shah 188
Barani, Ziya' al-Din (historian), 258
Bari, Mawlana 'Abd al- of Farangi Mahall, 164, 187, 268, 323
Barlas, Asma, 383
Battuta, Ibn, 63, 261, 301
Bazargan, Mehdi, 55, 171
Bedil, 'Abd al-Qadir, 263
Beg, Mirza Ghiyas, 237

Beg, Ulugh (Il-Khanid ruler), 101, 104, 235
Beg, Ya'qub, 46
Begg, Moazzam, 173
Begum, Gulbadan, 119
Behl, Aditya, 15, 338
Bell, Daniel, 226
Bellah, Robert, 226
Berkey, Jonathan, 94, 101
Beveridge, Annette, 339, 344, 352
Bhopal, Begums of, 263
Bhutto, Benazir, 56
Bhutto, Zulfiqar 'Ali, 309
Bigi, Jar Allah, 50
Bilal, Fakhar, 5
Bilgrami, Ghulam 'Ali Azad, 245, 281
Bilgrami, Sayyid Husayn, 281, 283, 294
Billah, Khwaja Baqi, 261
Binbas, Evrim, 64
Bobbio, Tommaso, 4
Boyle, Robert, 62
Bukhari, al-, 88
Bukhari, Murad al-, 264
Bulliet, Richard, 73
Bulqini, family of Damascus, 119
Butlan, Ibn, 88
Butler, Harcourt, 293

Caliphate, *see* Khilafat
Caliphate of Man, 41, 192
Carrell, Alexis, 167
Cellini, Benvenuto, 235
Charlton-Stevens, Uther, 4
Churchill, Winston, 267
Chelebi, Ewliya, 302
Chishti, Nizam al-Din, 233
Choudhury, Nawab 'Ali, 282
Ciller, Tansu, 56

coffee, 71, 73–4
Cohn, Bernard, 198
commodities, 71–5
Copernicus, 70, 71
cosmopolitanism, 3, 14, 18–19, 20, 300, 366–71; before the nation-state, 301–3; Hindu nationalism and, 308; Pakistan and, 308
cotton, 71, 72–3; Iranians and, 73
Curzon (Viceroy of India), 266–7, 294, 306

Dale, Stephen, 16, 235, 340, 351
Dalrymple, William, 360
Damad, Mir Baqir, 105, 241
Dār al-iftā, xv, 18, 208
Dār al-'Ulūm, xv
Dars-i Nizami, 106, 245
Davis, Dick, 15, 334
Dawwani, Jalal al-din, 104, 105, 241
Dayr Yasin (Arab village in Palestine), 378
Delhi Sultanate, 233, 257–9, 336
Deoband madrasa, 45, 135, 136–7, 164–5, 185–6, 191, 206, 207, 208; as a 'brand' 186; expansion into Iran, 138–9; hadith in, 184; influence of, 66; the past and, 214; women's madrasas and, 216
Deobandis, 3, 77, 182; and titles of Shams al-'Ulama' 190
Dershane, 145
Dharmapala, Angarika, 78
dīn, xv
Din, Mulla Nizam al-, 106, 241
Din, Taqi al-, 105
Dipanegara, 44

388 Index

Doniger, Wendy, 15, 338
Dudoignon, Stephan, 138
Durr, Shajar al-, 56

education, 20, 40, 85–130; impact of, 170; of children, 110–12; popular, 114–16; spiritual, 108–10; of slaves, 112–14; and women, 116–19
Eid un-Nabī, xv
Eisenstadt, S.N., 10, 210
Ephrat, Diana, 94
Epitectus, 317
Erbakan, Necmettin, 52
Erdogan, Tayyib, 143, 147, 265
Euben, Roxanne, 79, 226
European Reformation, 78

Fadl, Abul, 235, 260
Fadl, Khaled, Abou el-, 174
Fadl, Sayyid, 18, 269, 367–8
Fakhri of Herat, 119
Fanon, Frantz, 167
Farabi, al-, 89
Faraidi (Movement), 45
Farangi Mahall, 6, 8, 106, 121, 164, 181, 241, 263; awards of Shams al-'Ulama' and, 191; *Dars-i Nizami* and, 106, 245; *mawlid* ceremonies and, 183
Farangi Mahalli, Bahr al'Ulum, 93
Farid, Baba of Pak Pattan, 65; Chishti-Sabiris of, 191
Faris, Ibn, 99
Farooqi, Musharraf, 16
Faruqi, Munis, 18
firmān, xv
Fodio, 'Uthman dan, 48–9, 118

Gandhi, Indira, 70
Gandhi, Mahatma, 72, 271, 272, 273
Gasprinski, Isma'il Bey, 50
Gellner, Ernest, 225
Ghalib (poet), 249, 284, 322, 354
Ghani, 'Abd al- of Nablus, 42
Ghawth, Muhammad, 261
Ghazali, al-, 39, 70, 87, 89, 99, 110, 111, 155, 218–19, 286, 352
Gilani, Shaykh Muhammad 'Ali 'Hazin', 244, 247, 261
globalisation, 3, 14, 20, 300; definition of, 310; the modern state and, 309–14
Ghannushi, Rashid al-, 55, 171
Gilgamesh, epic of, 68
Gorgani, Fakhr al-Din, 15; *Vis and Ramin* and, 329–35
Graham, Bill, 211
Green, Nile, 302, 366
Gruzinski, Serge, 71
Gul, 'Abd Allah, 265
Gulen, Fethullah, 66, 145–4, 149, 313

ḥadīth, xv, 40, 75, 116, 118, 134, 212; new emphasis on, 183
ḥajj, xv
Hajj, Ibn al-, 115
ḥajjī, xv
ḥakīm, xv
Hali, Altaf Husayn, 196, 197, 219, 221, 250, 253, 283, 284, 289; *Musaddas* of, 284–6, 296; *Shikwa* of, 284–5
Hamas, 377, 378

Hamid, 'Abd al- II (Ottoman sultan), 368
Hamidullah, Muhammad, 221
Hamza, Abu, 173
Hamza, Amir, 16–17, 68, 112; Dastan-i, 262, 354–7
Haqq, 'Abd al-, 42
Haqq, General Ziya'al-, 52, 138, 167, 199, 222, 309, 323
Haqq, Mazhar al-, 290
Hardy, Peter, 188
Hare, Lancelot, 293
Hasan, Muhammad 'Abd Allah of British Somaliland, 48
Hasan, Nawab Mahdi 'Ali Muhsin al-Mulk, 281–2, 284
Hasan, Sultan al-Nasir al-, 102
Hashmi, Farhat, 141
hawza, xvi, 66
Hill, Christopher, 320
Hilton, Rodney, 320
Hindawi, 239, 336
Hindu, Ibn, 99
Hindu Sangh Parivar, 313
Hiro, Dilip, 16
Hishi, al-, 97
Hobsbawm, Eric, 320
Hodgson, Marshall, 60, 78, 121, 135, 154
Hua-long, Ma, 46
Huda, al-, 141
Hulegu (Il-Khanid ruler), 101
Humayun (Mughal emperor), 236, 259, 261, 341, 350–1
Huntington, Samuel, 61
Hurrem, consort of Sulayman the Magnificent, 118
Husain, Ali, Akbar, 358
Husain, Ed (author of *The Islamist*), 172, 173

Husayn, Saddam, 149, 377, 379
Husayn, Sharif of Mecca, 268, 271, 272

Idris, Ahmad bin, 47
Idrisiyya, 4, 48
ijāza, xvi, 63–4, 95–6, 99–100, 102, 105, 10, 115, 116, 118, 157, 166, 182, 188, 196, 212, 262
Ilahabadi, Akbar (poet), 134, 163, 213–14, 286, 323–5
'ilm, xvi, 85, 120–1
Ikhlasiyya (Herat), 101
Iltutmish (Delhi sultan), 260
Ilyas, Muhammad, 76, 140, 209–10, 218
Imam Hatip schools, 144, 147
Imam, Sayyid 'Ali, 290, 291
Imarat-i-Shari'a organisation, 139–40, 189
inshā, xvi, 244
Iqbal, Muhammad, 12, 31, 37, 41, 42, 50, 55, 56, 76, 7, 162, 184, 210–11, 263, 268, 286–7, 296, 303; the Caliphate of Man and, 168, 206, 210, 216, 218, 276; Pakistan and, 253; Persian language and, 252–3; Persian influence and, 252
Iran: Hindu service classes and, 244; Shi'a satrapies and, 246–7; Indian languages and, 248–50; immigrants, 238; influence on South Asia, 233–56; *ma'qulat* subjects and, 241–3; Persian language and, 239–41, 243–5; poets and the Mughals, 237; Sufism and, 242–3

Islamic Conference Organisation, 57, 66
Islamic modernism, 7, 49, 174
Islamic reform, 2, 10, 11, 20, 43, 77, 134–5, 136–7; from below 77–8, 131–51; human will and, 214–17; modernities and, 204–32; reification of Islam and, 221–2; religious belief and, 220–2; secularisation and, 222–4; transformation of the self and, 217–20
Islamic State in Syria (ISIS), 2
Islamic world: human conscience and, 192–3; Islamic revival in 7, 39–53; rebuilt from below, 8–9; western dominance in, 6, 9
Islamisation, 65
Islamist movements, 2, 32, 51–3
Isma'il, Muhammad, *see* Shahid
Isma'il, Shah (Safawid ruler), 236, 348
Isma'ilis, 313
Isnad paradigm, 211
Ispahanis (leading business family of Iranian origin), 239
Israel, 29–30, 38; assaults on Gaza, 275, 378

Jahan, Shah (Mughal emperor), 17–18, 16, 235, 361–5; Mumtaz Mahal and, 17, 238, 362
Jahan, Nur (Jahangir's favourite consort), 237–8, 363–4
Jahanara, 365
Jahangir (Mughal emperor), 18, 64, 235, 236, 362
jāhilīyya, xvi
Jakhanke of Senegambia, 106

Jama'a, 'Izz al-din ibn, 97
Jamal Miyan, of Farangi Mahall, 6
Jama'ati Islam, 2, 32, 66, 77, 141, 142, 167, 206
Jami, 'Abd al-Rahman, 119
Jami'at al-'Ulama'-yi Hind, 187; personal law and, 220–1
Janissaries, 113–14
Jawzi, Ibn al-, 116
jihād, xvii, 2, 44
Jinnah, M.A., 199
Jones, Justin, 6, 186, 187, 190
Jurjani, Sayyid Sharif al-, 92, 97, 104, 242, 261
Juwayni, Muhammad, 101

Kalmbach, Hilary, 20, 380, 383
Kamil, al-Malik al-, 92
Kandhlawi, Muhammad Zakariyya, 210
Kassir, Samir, 372, 378
Ka'ti, Mahmud, 107
Kayasth, xvi
Kayranawi, Mawlana Rahmat Allah, 19, 269, 368
Kemal, Mustafa, 26, 27, 50, 55, 133, 142, 154
Kemal, Namik, 50
khadi, 72
Khaldun, Ibn, 86, 88–9, 93, 94–6, 111–12, 156–8, 352
Khaled, Amr, 171
Khalid, Mawlana of Baghdad, 143
Khalīfa, xvi, 110
Khalwati Sufis, 42
Khan, Afzal (brother of Nur Jahan), 237
Khan, Aga, I & III, 238–9
Khan, Zafar 'Ali (of *Zamindar*), 269

Khan, Ahmad Rida (of Bareilly), 137, 183; 'ulama' in the tradition of, 164, 181
Khan, Amna, 5
Khan, Ayub, 13
Khan, Hakim Ajmal, 194, 195, 290
Khan, Genghis, 234–5
Khan, Mawlwi Sami Allah, 284
Khan, Muhammad Zafar Allah, 309
Khan, Sayyid Ahmad, 50, 76, 165, 167, 182, 183, 206, 209, 215, 218, 249, 282; the Prophet and, 183–4; memory of power and, 282–3, 288–9
Khan, Shaybani (Uzbek ruler), 348
Khan, Siddiq Hasan (Nawab of Bhopal), 19, 269, 369
Khatri, xvi
Khidr, Khwaja, 68
Khilāfat, xvi, 26, 57, 133, 154 213, 260; Allah, 192; movement, 271
Khilji, Ala al-Din (Delhi sultan), 258
Khumayni, Ayat Allah, 37–8, 52, 155, 169, 171, 206, 253
khums, xvi
Khusraw, Amir, 233, 258
Khwandamir, 101
Khwarizmi, 88, 99
Kiernan, Victor, 320
Kinra, Rajeev, 18
Koch, Ebba, 364
kufr, xvi
Kunta of Mauritania, 106
Kurani, Ibrahim al-, 43, 64, 108, 134

Kurdi, Mahmud al-, 47
Kuttab, 112

Laden, Osama bin, 29, 38, 53, 67, 169–70, 171, 173, 313, 374
Lal, Ruby, 18, 363
Lampedusa, Giuseppe di, 162
Latif, 'Abd al-, 86, 96–7, 99
LaTouche, James, 294
lay folk, rise of as transmitters, 54–5, 16, 171; Islamic scholarship and, 160
Lawrence, Bruce, 226
Lawrence, Walter, 294
Lewis, Bernard, 131
Lodi, Ibrahim (Delhi sultan), 259
Lucknow Pact, 295
Luther, Martin, 42

Macaulay's Minute on Education, 161, 198
Mackinder, Halford, 62
MacIntyre, Alasdair, 226
Madani, Husayn Ahmad, 37, 185, 189, 216
Madjid, Nurcholish, 174
madrasa, xvi, 8, 40, 100–3, 133; Bangladesh and, 139; India and, 139–40; Indonesia and, 147–8; Iranian influence and, 241–2; Mughal Empire and 105–6; Ottoman Empire and, 104–5; Pakistan and, 13, 189; sectarianism and, 189–90; *waqf* and, 102–3; women's, 381
Madrasa, Calcutta, 244
Madrasa Nizamiyya, 101
Madrasa Sawlatiyya, 19, 269, 368
Maghili, Muhammad al-, 92, 93

Mahal, Mumtaz (favourite consort of Shah Jahan), 17, 238, 362
Mahesar, Shuja 5
Mahdiyya, Sudanese, 47–8
Mahmud, Dr Syed, 218
Majlis Mu'id al-Islam, 187
Makdisi, George, 91, 93, 100, 102
maktūbat, xvii, 64; Sirhindi's, 143, 144, 264, 265
malfūzat, xvii
Mal, Raja Todar, 239, 240
Mamluks, 112–13
Mansur, Imam, 46
ma'qūlāt, xvii, 242
Marghinani, Burhan al-Din, 261
Marjani, Shihab al-Din, 50
marsiyā, xvii
Mashriqi, 'Inayat Allah, 207
maslak, xvii
Massignon, Louis, 167
mathnawī, xvii
Mawdudi, Mawlana, 12–13, 32, 41, 51, 52, 55, 56, 79, 141, 148, 167, 182, 188, 206, 210, 214, 215, 218, 226–7, 276; Islam as a system, 222
mawlānā, xvii
mawlawī, xvii
mawlid, xvii
Mehmet II (Ottoman sultan), 348
Metcalf, Barbara, 10, 183–5, 189, 190–1, 195, 196, 210
Mingxin, Ma, 43, 64
Minto, Lord (viceroy), 280, 294
Mirigawati, 68
Mitra, Sudipto, 5
Mizjaji family of Yemen, 43, 64

modern state, 7, 31, 35–6; cosmopolitanism and, 303–9; globalisation and, 311; human rights and, 315; humanitarian intervention and, 316–17; nation-state and, 300; problems of citizenship and, 305–9
modernities, modernisation, 2, 10, 79, 204–31
Mohurram, xvii; celebrations 246
Moin, Azfar, 366
Montagu, Edwin, 265, 271
Morgan, Daniel, 5
Morison, Theodore, 294
Morley, Lord (Secretary of State for India), 294
Morsi, Muhammad, 148
Mughals, as patrons, 234–8
Muhaddith, 'Abd al-Haqq, 182
muḥalla, xvii
Muhammad, Ghulam Sufi of South Africa
Muhammad, Prophet, 16, 26, 39, 40, 73, 152, 153–4, 183, 197; Ameer Ali and, 184; Iqbal and, 184; life of, 76; lives of, 183; *mawlid* ceremonies and, 115; Pakistan and Bangladesh and, 199; Perfect Man to perfect person, 219; Sayyid Ahmad Khan and, 183–4
Muhammadiyya, 44, 77, 147–8
mujaddid, xvii, 214
Mujahid women's madrasa in Kerala, 216–17
mujāhidīn, xvii
mujtahid, xvii
Mulk, Nizam-al (Saljuq vizier), 101

Mulk, Nawab Wiqar al-, 289
mullā, xvii
multiculturalism, 3, 14, 21, 300, 314–17
Munajjima, Bija, 119
Murshidabad, a Shi'a state, 247
Musaddas of Altaf Husayn Hali, 36, 59 n.7, 162
mushā'ira, xviii
Musharraf, Pervez, 12, 13
Muslim Brotherhood, 2, 51, 52, 66, 77, 148, 149, 313, 376–9
Muslim League sessions, 289, 290, 291
Muslim Memorial, of 1896, 280; of 1906, 280–1
Muslim 'political importance', 281, 282, 289, 291–3, 295, 296
Mutahhari, Ayat Allah, 41
Mutahsib, 111

Nabulusi, Shaykh 'Abd al-Ghani, 264
Nadim, Ibn al-, 88
Nadlatul 'ulama, 148
Nadwat al-'Ulama', 187, 191
Nadwi, Sayyid Abul Hasan 'Ali, 188, 206
Naim, C.M., 196
Nanawtwi, Muhammad Qasim, and the Prophet, 184
Naqshband, Shah Ghulam 'Ali, 264
Naqshbandi Sufis, 42, 43, 45, 46–7, 64–5, 110, 261, 313, 367; Mujaddidi phase, 264; in Turkey, 143–7
Nasafi, 'Abd Allah, 261
Nashi, Abhu'l-'Abbas al-, 91
Nasirabadi, Sayyid Dildar 'Ali, 247

Nasiri Sufis of the northern Sahara, 106
Nasr, Sayyid Vali Reza, 190
Nasution, Harun, 55
Na't, xviii
Nawa'i, Mir 'Ali Shir (Il-Khanid vizier), 101
Needham, Joseph, 320
Nehru, Jawaharlal, 275–6
Neuhaus, Richard, 226
Nicoll, Fergus, 362–5
Nomani, Manzoor, 221
Noreen, Sumaira, 4
Nurcular, 144–5
Nursi, Badi'al-Zaman, 40, 46, 65, 66, 144, 170–1, 264
Nisa, Zib al-, 119
Nizām-i Mustāfā, xviii
Nizari Isma'ilis, 65

oil, 71, 74–5
Oman, Sultan Qaboos of, 12
One Thousand and One Nights, 69
OPEC (Organisation of Oil-exporting Countries), 33
opium, 71, 74
oral transmission (of knowledge), 94–6
Osella, Filippo and Caroline, 10, 227
Ottomans, 25–6
Ozal, Turgut, 143, 145, 146

Padri movement, 44
Pahlawi, Rida Shah, 27, 50, 55
Pakistan, 50
Pamuk, Orhan, and *huzun*, 162
Partition of British India, 27
Pasha, Anwar (Enver), 268
pesantren, xviii, 40, 108

Pfandar, Dr, 368
pīr, xviii
Porkundil, Ismail Mathari, 5
Powell, Enoch, 307
power, memory of, 21
Principia of Newton, 121
print, 160; impact of, 32–3, 40–1, 54, 142, 166, 168, 212–13
'Protestant Turn': Buddhism and, 78; Hinduism and, 78–9; Islam and, 135, 166–7, 211, 225; religious piety and, 8, 10, 61, 75–9
Ptolemy of Alexandria, 70
Puri, Nikhil, 4

qāḍī, xviii, 87, 132
Qadiri Sufis, 110, 26, 313
Qa'ida, al-, 2, 29, 53, 58, 74
Qaradawi, Yusuf, 171
Qasmi, Ali Usman, 5–6
Qur'ān, xviii, 35, 40, 47, 75, 88, 93, 94–5, 115, 117, 134, 145, 152, 164, 182, 208, 212; study of grammar and, 90; transmission of, 156–7
Qutb, Sayyid, 32, 38, 41, 55, 79, 167, 226–7, 276

Radiyya, Sultana, 56
Rahim, Shah 'Abd al-, 250
Rahim, Sir 'Abd al-, 290
Rahman, Fazlur, 174
Rahman, Mujibur, 199
Rahman, Ziya'al-, 139, 199
Ra'uf, 'Abd al- of Singkel, 43, 64, 108
Rashid, Harun al- , 89
Rawshanara, 365
Razi, Fakhr al-din, 99

Reagan, Nancy, 70
Risale-yi Nur of Nursi, 145
Robb, Megan, 4, 6
Rogan, Eugene, 19–20, 372–9
Rosenthal, Franz, 85
Roy, Olivier, 173
Rukh, Shah (Il-Khanid ruler), 92, 235
rulers, British: Mughal symbols of authority and, 198–9; Indo-Saracenic architecture and, 199; Islamic symbols and, 199; Western symbols and, 199
Rushd, Ibn, 89
Russell, Ralph, 14–15, 320–8; autobiography, 321; true humanity and, 327; Urdu love poetry and, 325–6; Urdu teaching and, 326

sabhā, xviii
Sabk-i Hindi, 263
Sadat, Anwar, 52, 376
Safawids (rulers of Iran), 235; and Mughal politics, 235–6
Sakhawi, al-, 97, 119
Salih, Muhammad ibn, 4
Salzmann, Ariel, 303
Samad, 'Abd al- (painter), 261
Samman, Shaykh Muhammad, 43, 47
Sammaniyya, 47
Sanusi, Muhammad 'Ali al-, 48
Sarshar, Ratan Nath, 269
Sartre, Jean Paul, 167
Sa'ud, 'Abd al-'Aziz, 271
Sa'udi: family, 43; kingdom, 43
Seymour, Kirsten, 5
Shackle, Christopher, 69
Shafi, Muhammad, 293

Index

Shah, Bulhe, 248
Shah, Firuz (Delhi sultan), 259
Shah, Ibrahim Adil II of Bijapur, 359
Shah Jahan, *see* Jahan
Shah, Muhammad (Mughal emperor), 259
Shah, Nadir (Iranian invader), 259
Shah, Warith, 248
Shahid, Shah Isma'il, 185
Shahid, Tahrat, 4
Shahnama of Muhammad Juki, 235
Shahnameh of Firdawsi, 329, 331
shahr-i āshob, xviii
Sharar, 'Abd al-Halim, 244–5, 269, 286
Shahrour, Mahamed, 171
sharī'a, xviii, 51, 188
Shari'ati, 'Ali, 31–2, 37, 41, 76, 167, 253, 276; image of Fatima al-Zahra and, 382–3
Sharqi, Sultan Husayn Shah of Jawnpur, 336
Shaykhist movement, 247
Shi'a, 11, 155–6; *mujtahid*s, 181; of Lucknow, 186–7
Shibli Nu'mani, 187, 188, 194, 207, 245, 285–6
Shikoh, Dara, 365
Shinqit of Mauritania, 106–7
Shirazi, Fadl Allah, 105, 240, 241, 261
Shirazi, Ghiyath al-Din Mansur, 105
Shirazi, Mirza Jan, 105
Shirazi, Sadr al-Din, 105–6, 241
Shirazi, Shaykh Sa'di, 334; his *Gulistan*, 334–5
shijra, xviii, 109, 262
shirk, xviii

Sihalwi, Qutb al-Din, 106, 241, 245
Sijzi, Mu'in al-Din, 261
Sikand, Yoginder, 216
silsila, xviii
Sina, Ibn, 89, 99, 359
Sindhi, Muhammad Hayat al-, 43
Singh, Dalip (son of Ranjit Singh, Sikh ruler), 370
Singh Sabha, 78
sīra, xviii
sirat movement, 183
Sirhindi, Shaykh Ahmad, 42, 45, 64, 134, 143, 251, 264
Sistani, Grand Ayat Allah, 'Ali, 155
Smith, Cantwell, 183, 216, 219
Smith, Dunlop, 293
South Asia: Gulf area of strategic concern and, 275; impact on West Asia, 263; Islamic knowledge from Iran and, 260–1; Israel and, 275; Persian and Arab influence and, 258, 267–8; Persian language and, 260–1; post-Partition security threat, 273–4; West Asia and security and, 258, 258–9; Western influence and, 258
St Augustine, 70
Stark, Ulrike, 137
storytellers, storytelling, 7, 16–17, 60, 67–9, 115–16, 354–5; assaults against, 135, 166–7, 207, 251–2, 268; master–disciple connections, 63; *Mirigawati* and mystical practices, 336–8; *Ṣūfī*, xviii, 7, 43, 48, 54, 65, 132, 154–5
Sufi orders, 1, 9, 54
sugar, 71, 73

Suharto, General, 148
Suhrawardi, Shaykh Qutban, 336
Suhrawardi, Shihab al-Din Abu Hafs al-, 109
Sukarnoputri, Megawati, 56
Sulayman the Magnificent, 105
Suleymancis, offshoot of the Naqshbandiyya-Khalidiyya, 143–4
Sunna, xviii
sūra, xviii
Suyuti, Ibn, 92, 100, 107, 108, 116, 118, 158, 212
Syed, G.M., 291
Sykes-Picot agreement, 374

Taal, Hajji 'Umar, 47
Tabatabai, Ghulam Husayn, 240
Tablighi Jama'at, 40, 45, 56, 66, 140–1, 206, 208–9, 313
tadhkirah, xviii, 212
Taftazani, Sa'ad al-Din, 92, 104, 242, 261
Tahmasp, Shah (Safawid ruler), 236, 259
tajdid, xix
Taj Mahal, 238, 362
Taliban, 29, 45, 55, 74
Tanzimat, xix, 264
taqlid, xix, 208
Tariqa-yi Muhammad, 40, 45
taṣawwuf, xix; Sufism and, 89
tawḥīd, xix, 207
Taylor, Charles, 76, 79, 217, 226
Taymiyya, Ibn, 42, 134, 211, 261
ta'zia khāna, xix
Texin, Ma, 47
Thackston, Wheeler, 16, 334, 352
Thanawi, Ashraf 'Ali, 135–6, 189, 215; his *Bihishti Zewar*, 209, 215, 217–18, 221, 323
Thanesri, Mawlwi Jafar, 19, 369–70
Tibb, xix; indigenisation of, 194–5; as Islamic medicine, 194; Unani and, 194
Tignol, Eve, 5, 13
Tijani, Ahmad al-, 47
Tijaniyya, 47
Timbuktu, 107
Timur/Tamerlaine (conqueror), 92, 235, 259, 347
tobacco, 71, 74
Troeltsch, Ernst, 225
Thompson, E.P., 320
Tughluq, Ghazi al-Din (Delhi sultan), 258
Tughluq, Muhammad bin (Delhi ultan), 260, 261
Tukhiyya, Zaynat al-, 11
Tunahan, Shaykh Sulayman Hilmi, 143
Turabi, Hasan al-, 55, 171
Turkey, 8
Tusi, Nasir al-Din, 104

Uddin, Layli, 4
'ulamā', xix, 7, 8, 31, 43, 54, 55, 154, 181, 188, 251; constitutional progress and, 188–9; organisations as brands, 186, 193; pupil–teacher connections and, 63; strategies of authority and, 181–93
'ulūm-i 'aqlīyya, xix, 88, 104
'ulūm-i naqlīyya, xix, 88
'Umar (second caliph), 286
Ūnāni, xix, 9–10; authority and, 193–6; hakims and 181; scent and, 359; see also *Tibb*

Urdu, 14–15; rise of 248–50
USA, 28–9
Uṣūlīs, xix, 247
Uthmani, Zafar Ahmad, 184–5

Vahiduddin, Syed, 220
Vermana, Neha, 5
Vis/Wis and Ramin, 15, 68, 82, 329–35

Wadud, Amina, 174, 383
waḥdat al-shuhūd, xix
waḥdat al-wujūd, xix, 39
Wahhab, Muhammad Ibn al-, 43, 75, 134, 205
Waisi, Baha al-Din, 46
Wangara of Northern Ghana, 106
Warner, William Lee, 294
Weber, Max: Islamic reform and, 222–5
Wenxiu, Du, 46
West Asia: British Indian security and, 265–7; British South Asian power and, 270–1; Congress and, 272; French threat and, 265–6; Gandhi and, 272; Indian press and, 269; Muslim League and, 272; Persian Gulf and, 266; Russian threat and, 266; South Asian scholarship and, 263–4
West, Martin, 69
Western dominance, 20, 23–59, 131–5; bullying in the Islamic world and, 169; Islamisation and, 65; Muslim spread and, 65
women 7, 20, 21, 55–6, 219; feminist readings of the Qur'an and, 383; Islamic reform and, 215, 216–17; learning and, 116–19; patriarchal authority and, 174; reading groups and, 171; religious authority and, 380–3; feminist readings of the Qur'an and, 383
Wolfe, Robert, 314
World Muslim League, 57, 66
Wren, Christopher, 62

Zabdi, Muhammad Murtada al-, 43, 64, 107
Zaman, Muhammad, Qasim, 184, 189
Zarnuji, al-, 85–6
Zia, Khaleda, 56
Zindapir, Hazrat Shah of Pakistan, 65
Zionist movement, 306–7, 374–5

www.ingramcontent.com/pod-product-compliance
Lightning Source LLC
Chambersburg PA
CBHW020119240426

43673CB00038B/535